Sharing Risk

Sharing Risk

THE PATH TO ECONOMIC
WELL-BEING FOR ALL

Patricia A. McCoy

UNIVERSITY OF CALIFORNIA PRESS

University of California Press
Oakland, California

Library of Congress Cataloging-in-Publication Data

Names: McCoy, Patricia A., author.
Title: Sharing risk : the path to economic well-being for all / Patricia A.
McCoy.
Description: Oakland, California : University of California Press, [2025] |
Includes bibliographical references and index.
Identifiers: LCCN 2024048551 (print) | LCCN 2024048552 (ebook) |
ISBN 9780520390140 (cloth) | ISBN 9780520390157 (epub)
Subjects: LCSH: Financial security—United States—21st century. |
Risk—United States—21st century. | Households—Economic aspects—
United States.
Classification: LCC HG181 .M365 2025 (print) | LCC HG181 (ebook) |
DDC 362.5/820973—dc23/eng/20250118
LC record available at https://lccn.loc.gov/2024048551
LC ebook record available at https://lccn.loc.gov/2024048552

Manufactured in the United States of America

GPSR Authorized Representative: Easy Access System Europe,
Mustamäe tee 50, 10621 Tallinn, Estonia, gpsr.requests@easproject.com

34 33 32 31 30 29 28 27 26 25
10 9 8 7 6 5 4 3 2 1

To Barney and Bill

Contents

Figures

Preface

I really don't think politicians know what it's like to not
know where they're going to get their next meal from,
how they're going to pay their next bill.

"Tony," in Reston (2022)

In summer 2024, headlines proclaimed amazement that so many people
thought the economy was bad, according to the polls.[1] How could they
think that, with inflation down, stock prices up, and unemployment so
low? Plainly, the press hinted, those people had amnesia or were just plain
wrong.

But those press skeptics had no idea of the lived reality of many of the
people who answered those polls. If the individuals polled were representative of the US population, finances were a constant worry for many of
them and probably more than we know. They may have faced money woes
on numerous fronts, from meager pay, low savings, and high inflation
to debt collectors and medical bills. In an unrelenting time loop, those
problems may have played out over and over, forcing many to rob Peter
to pay Paul. For a substantial number, their prospects for getting ahead
were dim.

Today, the US system puts heavy economic risks on individual families
that they are not equipped to bear. But there are better ways of managing those risks and relieving ordinary households of those pressures. On
and off, the nation has used *risk sharing* to pool people's risks and spread
those risks over the entire population. Risk sharing can cover everyone's

exposure to risks, at lower total cost. We see risk sharing in a variety of contexts, from Social Security and unemployment insurance to health coverage. While many of those systems are outdated, they provide pillars for a robust, modern system of risk sharing that could boost financial security for everyone. In this book I examine what it would take, using risk sharing, to assure economic well-being for all.

I have been mulling over these issues for decades and have come full circle with this book. My parents, both academics on tight salaries in a small Kansas state university town, were rich in learning but financially pressed. The Great Depression had left them financially cautious about job security and strongly averse to debt. Through hard work and thrift, they managed to build a modest nest egg and paid for my college education from the proceeds of my grandmother's small dress store, sold after her death.

Not long after college, I first came face to face with the hurdles facing the poor while serving at Legal Services in a remote rural corner of Kansas. There, almost all of our clients under age sixty-five held jobs, yet their wages were so low that they officially qualified as poor. Meanwhile, my home visits to shut-in elderly clients opened my eyes to the sacrifices they made to survive.

In subsequent years I began exploring other themes affecting the economic well-being of families. In law school I immersed myself in labor and employment law, both as a journal editor and while studying with David Feller, Jan Vetter, and Herma Hill Kay. In practice I represented employees and senior citizens pro bono, with the generous support of my law firm and particularly Marc Gary, Joseph Sellers, and Adrian Steel. Meanwhile, friends, colleagues, family members, and others contacted me from time to time about their own financial issues. Our conversations illuminated the depth of their frustrations and the vexing nature of some of their predicaments.

Later, as an academic, I spent years writing on home mortgage foreclosures with my colleague Kathleen Engel, after tripping across some of the earliest subprime mortgage abuses in Cleveland. Based on that body of research, the founder of the Consumer Financial Protection Bureau, Elizabeth Warren, appointed me as the bureau's first mortgage markets regulator, in late 2010. That appointment plunged me into the clean-up of the 2008 subprime mortgage crisis, and I had many fruitful conversations with my colleagues at the bureau, including Raj Date, Peter Carroll, Kelly Cochran, Ren Essene, Patrice Ficklin, and Ethan Bernstein, to develop solutions. Michael Barr's insights on the challenges of foreclosure prevention also informed my thinking, as did those of Eric Belsky and Christopher Herbert.

My time at the bureau exposed me to additional problems of concern in this book. Most important were student loans, and in this area I benefited deeply from the insights of Rohit Chopra, Seth Frotman and Dalié Jiménez. Gail Hillebrand and I had long discussions (which continue) about financial literacy and savings strategies. Corey Stone, David Silberman, and Holly Petraeus were fonts of knowledge respectively about credit scoring, credit card debt, and the financial issues of service members. Elizabeth Vale kept me grounded by ensuring that I regularly talked with small-town representatives, especially from the South and Midwest. Meanwhile, Richard Cordray personified the best qualities of leadership, as did Rohit Chopra, and I was privileged to work with them both.

In a book as wide-ranging as this, the writer stands on the shoulders of giants, and I am no exception. Jacob Hacker's work *The Great Risk Shift* narrated the erosion of social safety nets in the United States. Abbye Atkinson's scholarship on credit as social provision contextualized consumer debt within the larger issue of waning social supports for households. Peter Diamond's trenchant ideas on reforming Social Security, Kathryn Edin's and Kaaryn Gustafson's innovative work on the real-life experiences of benefits recipients, and Mark Rank's analysis of financial risk over the life cycle deeply informed this book as well.

I owe a special intellectual debt to Senator Elizabeth Warren. Her groundbreaking scholarship documented the toll of crushing medical bills and the financial insecurity engulfing the middle class. Senator Warren championed our work on subprime mortgages when naysayers to our findings abounded, and I always will be grateful for her support. Meanwhile, I applaud her for continuing to fight for the economic well-being of ordinary families as senator.

Other advocates, policymakers, and academics contributed additional insights to this project. They include Anthony Pennington-Cross, Raphael Bostic, Lisa Donner, Kathleen Engel, Keith Ernst, Jonathan Glater, Laurie

Goodman, Marty Gruenberg, Andrea Levere, Adam Levitin, Deanne Loo-
nin, Jonathan Miller, Elizabeth Renuart, Stephen Shay, Dave Sieminski,
Rory van Loo, and Susan Wachter. Most of all, Erik Gerding spent endless
hours with me developing the ideas in this book. His contributions shaped
every chapter. To others I have inadvertently missed, my thanks as well.

In a separate vein, my thinking on risk sharing was deeply shaped by
the ten-plus years I spent as a member (and later director) of the Insurance Law Center at the University of Connecticut School of Law. Tom
Baker was my close colleague there, and I cannot overstate the importance of his writings. More recent work by James Kwak similarly informed
my work. John Cogan Jr. and my beloved friend John Day opened my eyes
to problems with health-care affordability. Jeremy Paul, my former dean
at Connecticut, and Travis Pantin helped me brainstorm about the book.
Above all, Peter Siegelman was a valued interlocutor, pushing me to refine
ideas and articulate answers to the hard questions that he posed.

In addition to my former colleagues in Connecticut, other readers
urged me on and contributed generously of their time to review drafts.
They include Abbye Atkinson, Ray Boshara, Christine Desan, Gail Hillebrand, Darrick Hamilton, Richard Kaplan, Brendan Maher, Kathryn
Moore, Dana Muir, Maria O'Brien, James Repetti, Natalya Shnitser, Norm
Stein, and several anonymous reviewers. My longtime colleague Brian
Atchinson gave me added insights into the workings of health insurance, for which I am grateful. Similarly, I thank the participants of the
13th Annual Employee Benefits & Social Insurance Conference, the Boston College Legal Scholarship Workshop, the Boston University Law Review Symposium, the Consumer Law Scholars Conference at UC Berkeley,
the Insurance Law Center Workshop, the Law & Society Annual Conference, the University of Connecticut Law Faculty Workshop, the American
Dream Symposium at Washburn Law School, the Money as a Democratic Medium 2.0 conference at Harvard Law School, and the Wharton
FinReg Conference for their close reading and insights. My students in
my consumer financial protection seminar added valuable perspectives.
Jonathan Glater, Ted Mermin, and Ben Hiebert at UC Berkeley's Center
for Consumer Law and Economic Justice cheered on this project, and it
heartened me to have their support. Howell Jackson briefed me on the
important savings initiatives of Commonwealth. Hiba Hafiz introduced

me to new works on monopsony and labor market structure, while Bijal Shah shared her observations on the evolving administrative state. Karen Breda and Yan Hong referred me to countless new research sources over the years, which I never would have found without them. Hilary Allen and Ray Madoff traded writing experiences with me as we all labored on books. Meanwhile, Arthur Wilmarth Jr., my dear friend and colleague, regularly alerted me to new analyses and findings.

Closer to home, this book would not have been possible without the support of Boston College Law School. The Liberty Mutual Professorship Fund furnished me with continuing summer funding, which I appreciated tremendously. The Rappaport Center for Law and Public Policy underwrote a research conference I organized on student loans, with the enthusiastic backing of Elisabeth Medvedow. Joseph Vitale located critical funding for the production phase of this book. Christopher Fitzgerald, with the invaluable support of Scott Sheltra, lent me his eyes and his elegant gift for words during the copyediting process. And my heartfelt thanks to David Quigley, our university provost, and my law school deans Odette Lienau, Vincent Rougeau, Diane Ring, Katie Young, and Paulo Barrozo, who provided me with invaluable support, both moral and material.

These acknowledgments would not be complete without recognizing the seminal contributions of my editor at the University of California Press, Maura Roessner. Maura is the most remarkable editor I have worked with, bar none. She is a superb editor in the traditional sense. But more than that, Maura is so deeply read in the field that she introduced me to other scholars and their work. She suggested new lines of thought that led in surprising and fruitful directions. At the same time, Maura ably shepherded the book throughout the editorial process.

Sharon Langworthy also deserves my warmest thanks for her invaluable work as my copy editor. She combined a sharp eye and meticulous hand with an exquisite sense of language, for which I will be ever grateful. Jessica Moll, as my production editor, was the talented impresario of all matters involving production, including many crucial details of which I am undoubtedly unaware. Thanks as well to Sam Warren for his fast and expert advice on publication matters big and small, Teresa Iafolla for her able marketing support, Jon Dertien for his contributions to the copyediting process, Neal Swain for arranging the audio version of the book, and Katryce Lassle for their important copywriting work. And my sincere gratitude to everyone else at the University of California Press who got this book over the finish line.

Finally, no project like this can take flight without the encouragement and patience of loved ones. My dear friends Lawrence Deyton, Harriet Duleep, Jeff Levi, Kunal Parker, and Sophie Smyth not only lent support but imparted useful advice based on their own extensive work as researchers and scholars. Other friends' unflagging interest in this book project amazed and buoyed me over the years. They include Bob and Ellen Alperin; Erika Crandall; Candace Jones and Jeff Barrell; Janice Pieroni and Jim Polianites; Susan White Haag and Mark Haag; other friends in Boston, Washington, and Maine; and my remarkable circle of old high school friends, whose get-togethers Dave May orchestrated on monthly Zoom calls. Throughout the writing process, Max was my constant and beloved companion. Finally, my deepest thanks to my brothers, Barney McCoy and Bill McCoy, who have been with me (almost) from the start and enlightened me as no one else could about the issues discussed in this book.

PART I The Bottom 50 Percent

1 The Cash-Strapped American Worker

Imagine you had $0 left after paying your debts. Buying a home would be hopeless. Paying for college, a pipe dream. You probably would have trouble covering medical expenses, let alone emergency repairs to your car. One surprise cost could knock you over. You would expect to work until you dropped.

That is not a fable; tragically, it's the reality for too many Americans. In fact, in 2022 in Chicago, the median Black family had a net worth of $0. The word *median* means that half of those families had a net worth of $0 *or less*. In comparison, the median White family in Chicago had net wealth of $210,000 that year.[1]

The huge racial wealth gap in Chicago is shocking. But this is not just a story about Chicago or the financial gulf between Whites and Blacks. It is well known that across the United States, a wealth gap divides the vast majority of families from the rich, regardless of color or race.[2] But even more alarming, staggering numbers of families are struggling with subpar income. The problem has gotten so bad that *more than half* of US households subsist on less than a living income.[3] In America, tens of millions of people earn an honest wage and still end up short.

Those families—the bottom 50 percent—are the subjects of this book. For them, the country has been moving in the wrong direction. Wealth and income disparities have widened since 1989 and embroiled the country in political and racial unrest.[4] A growing sense of "us" versus "them" has jeopardized our democracy and called into question the legitimacy of US political institutions. If there was any doubt, the insurrection at the US Capitol on January 6, 2021, and the 2024 presidential election results laid it to rest.

It wasn't always this way. Several decades ago, parents could send their children to public universities for rock-bottom tuition.[5] Retirees with traditional pensions didn't worry about running out of money, because they could look forward to monthly pension checks until death.[6] Unionized jobs offered health insurance, and health care cost less than today.[7] Jobs were more secure and paychecks stretched further.[8] And social supports for the poor were stronger.[9]

Of course, the past had its own disturbing problems. Structural racism denied economic and educational opportunities to people of color, numerous retirees lacked reliable pension plans, and individual health insurance had yawning coverage gaps.[10] Still, in other respects, social safety nets were stronger half a century ago than today.

What changed? For one thing, states phased out their generous subsidies to higher education, forcing public universities to hike tuition.[11] Consider my alma mater, the University of California (Berkeley), where in-state undergraduate tuition was free in 1968. Two years later, the university started charging tuition, and by 2024, Berkeley's in-state tuition and fees had skyrocketed to $20,572 a year.[12]

In another important change, employers converted their retirement benefits from defined-benefit plans offering traditional pensions to defined-contribution plans such as 401(k)s to offload the risk of market declines onto employees.[13] Now, traditional pensions at private companies have all but vanished, and it's up to individual workers to save enough, invest skillfully, and survive trading busts.

This switch coincided with a historic plunge in private-sector unionized jobs, generous blue-collar fringe benefits, and job security.[14] For an increasing number of workers, a living wage and a pension became a thing of the past as manufacturing jobs fled and the United States shifted to a service-sector economy.[15] These twentieth-century labor market problems accelerated in the twenty-first century with the transition to the "gig economy."

Just as the US economy experienced mass deindustrialization, Congress and the states rolled back welfare benefits and tied those benefits to work requirements.[16] Individual households were left holding the bag, laboring under new and mounting financial burdens that they often could not afford.

As governments and employers shrugged off financial risks onto ordinary people's shoulders, another pernicious development was underway. Increasingly, policymakers and society expected workers to pay for important personal goals by taking out loans. Do you want to send your kids to college? Take out student loans. Is your paycheck too small, or were your hours cut? Get a credit card cash advance. Did you get hit with large surprise medical bills? Time for a second mortgage on your house (if you're lucky enough to own one). Will you run out of money before you die? Get a reverse mortgage (that is, *if* you own a home).

In the process during the past fifty years, our society has increasingly moved to a lonely place where families are left to make it on their own, with few social safety nets to speak of. Too many families stagger under heavy debt as a result. In 2022, for instance, half of all households had debts totaling 29 percent of their assets or more. That same year, 8.5 million households spent over 40 percent of their incomes on debt payments, which economists consider a sign of financial distress.[17] That debt, and the interest payments needed to service it, made it even harder for ordinary families to accumulate small amounts of savings, let alone meaningful wealth.[18] The result is a system of debt peonage that makes it harder and harder for families to achieve financial security.

Following the 2008 financial crisis, Congress and Democratic administrations put tremendous effort into making consumer loans safer. That work was imperative and needs expanding. However, we cannot let the important work on consumer financial protection lull us into complacency about the bigger problem, which is our nation's overreliance on consumer loans.

As leading authority Professor Abbye Atkinson eloquently argued, the "notion that credit is a valid form of social provision for low-income

Americans . . . is deeply flawed."[19] We cannot talk about income and wealth inequality in this country without questioning why people should have to borrow money to make ends meet and achieve important financial goals. It is unrealistic and destructive to expect lower- and middle-income families to bear such large risks to their economic well-being. Doing so has consigned almost half of Americans to lives of financial insecurity, compounded racial discrimination, left the United States with a poorly trained workforce, and undermined American democracy.

This book reframes the traditional, narrow focus on protection from crushing debt to raise a more fundamental question. How can we, as a society, assure financial security for everyone, regardless of their station in life? What role should society play in redressing wealth and income gaps and providing safety nets? In short, what will it take to ensure economic well-being for all?

Here, it's worth stopping to ask what *economic well-being* means. For many, economic well-being connotes freedom from financial worry.[20] Others equate it with being able to survive financial hardship or having enough money to afford both needs and wants.

All of these definitions contain a germ of truth. Financial security is obviously essential to economic well-being. In the short term, financial security means being able to pay bills on time; in the long run, it means being able to cover unexpected expenses and withstand economic shocks. People who are financially secure control their finances and do not worry about making ends meet.

Financial freedom is another aspect of economic well-being. In the present, people with financial freedom can choose how best to use their money to enjoy life and splurge from time to time. In the future, financial freedom enables people to strive for and achieve their longer-term goals.

While these characteristics capture important aspects of economic well-being, they fall short in some respects. First, these definitions focus narrowly on the income and wealth available to individual households while ignoring the broader social context that shapes and limits the finances of most families.[21] A family's ability to earn, save, or flourish financially is affected by a constellation of outside forces, including laws, policies, markets, and economic cycles. While these phenomena affect everyone, they can devastate those who are struggling economically, including disproportionately people of color. A complete picture of economic well-being needs to take into account these outside forces and families' ability to control them.

Second, many definitions of economic well-being fail to acknowledge the enormous amounts of money that households need to achieve important long-term goals.[22] Many families hope to send their children to college. A secure retirement is another hoped-for goal. Achieving these goals, however, requires large cash outlays. If families are forced to finance their long-term goals out of personal resources alone, those goals will be out of reach for many in the bottom half or plunge them heavily into debt. It is no wonder that households' debt levels, compared to their disposable income, have mounted over the past thirty years.[23]

For these reasons, this book defines economic well-being as *having access to sufficient financial resources* to pay current bills in full, withstand financial shocks, have financial freedom, and achieve long-term financial goals. By emphasizing "*access* to sufficient financial resources," this formulation represents a departure from numerous other definitions of economic well-being. Contrary to other definitions, this meaning of economic well-being does not expect people who lack a living wage to "live within their means." Instead, it aspires to enough financial resources for every household to ensure financial security and have an enjoyable standard of living.

That leads to my next point. This definition of economic well-being does not require people to already have the resources they expect to tap. On the most basic level, of course, the financial resources available to each person will include his or her income and wealth. Other available resources may come from social support networks such as family members, charitable organizations, or churches. Beyond that, this book contends that when necessary, families should be able to tap pooled resources such as social insurance. This is not a new idea: most retirees receive Social Security, and jobless employees can apply for unemployment insurance. Both programs are risk-sharing arrangements that take risks that individual families otherwise would bear, pool money from millions of people to cover those risks, and spread the risks across workers. This book asks, should we extend risk sharing to other risks that fall on families today?

Society's decision about whether to pool and spread financial risks can make or break economic well-being, particularly for families in the bottom half. Defining economic well-being to require needed social support raises the question: When does it make more sense for an institution or institutions to bear financial risk instead of placing it on individuals?

It also raises the question: How many resources are we talking about? The answer is, enough resources to meet important long-term goals. Right now, society expects many to sacrifice some of those goals or go into debt to achieve them. Those sacrifices—whether they involve the lack of a college degree, a cash-strapped retirement, or something else—are destructive because they undermine financial security while deepening structural inequities. Accordingly, having enough resources to achieve important long-term goals is crucial to economic well-being.[24]

As this suggests, what we need is an *overarching approach* to economic well-being that integrates achieving personal financial goals over the life cycle. This integrated approach has four main features.

First, this integrated approach recognizes that economic well-being and wealth are not the same. For the ordinary family, wealth is necessary but not sufficient to provide financial security: sufficient income and social safety nets are necessary too.

Second, this integrated approach rejects the view that families hit by economic shocks should take out debt. There are times when borrowing is appropriate, such as when buying a home. But expecting people to borrow money to make it through the month or to pay for medical bills is a sign of deeper societal ills that individuals should not be expected to cure alone.

Third, an integrated approach recognizes that wealth and income are not randomly distributed. On the contrary, the haves and the have-nots are increasingly segregated by race. Consider data from 2022. The median family wealth for Blacks was only 15 percent of that for Whites, and over 17 percent of Black families lived in poverty, twice the rate of Asian American and White families.[25] With each succeeding generation, Blacks have lagged as the income gap persisted.[26] This growing gulf has entrenched historic injustices and blocked upward mobility for Blacks and other victims of discrimination.

Finally, an integrated approach to economic well-being addresses each major financial goal of a typical family. These five goals, which I call "milestones," include *making ends meet, buying a home, having quality health care, financing college,* and *paying for retirement.* Not every family will strive toward all five milestones, but three of them are essential, and many families aspire to four or all five. Fulfillment of these milestones will assure that families have enough to live on, enjoy good health, can achieve upward mobility, and are better positioned to give back to society.

The first and most basic milestone is *making ends meet.* This means having enough income and savings to cover household bills as they come due. Everyone has recurring expenses for housing, food, clothing, utilities, transportation, and more. Everyone also faces unexpected expenses from time to time. These can be for car and home repairs, school expenses, moving, care for relatives, and other things. People need an adequate and secure income, plus some modicum of savings, to pay for these needs.

For many families, *buying a home* is a second milestone. This necessitates a down payment and sufficient income and creditworthiness to qualify for a home mortgage. After making the purchase, homeowners need enough money to cover property taxes, insurance, and maintenance, on top of mortgage payments. As this suggests, it is not enough to *buy* a home; it is just as important to *retain* it. An integrated approach emphasizes homeownership that is sustainable.

Quality health care is the third important milestone. This requires affording health coverage plus the cost of uninsured medical expenses. Currently, the US system puts the onus on families for some of those costs and defrays the rest through private or social insurance. The health cost burden on many families remains excessive, and more progress is needed to increase good, affordable health care for millions of Americans.

Paying for college education is another key milestone for many families. In the class of 2021, over half of seniors at four-year nonprofit institutions graduated with student loans.[27] An integrated approach rejects this reliance on student loans and explores other ways to finance college.

The last major milestone is *paying for retirement.* This includes living expenses plus medical expenses, including insurance premiums, out-of-pocket health costs, home health assistance, and other long-term health care. Today, Social Security, Supplemental Security Income, and Medicare provide the main social safety nets for old age. Any other retirement income usually has to come from an employer-based plan and personal savings. Yet over forty million "American workers are not participating in retirement plans at work" because their employers do not offer retirement plans.[28] For workers with retirement accounts, the median balance was only $87,000 in 2022.[29] These troubling numbers emphasize the need for an integrated approach to retirement security gaps.

I argue that society can and should do more to assure economic well-being. The book unfolds in three parts. Part I has set the stage by describing economic well-being. Part II discusses the degree of household financial instability and how policies shifting financial risk onto individuals and miring them in debt fueled that instability. This part argues that personal savings strategies are not enough to reverse course and that in important instances, it makes more sense for society to pool and spread the financial risks affecting the lower half of workers than to make them shoulder those risks alone. Part III discusses the five milestones of ordinary families and the best ways to achieve those goals. Depending on the milestone, these interventions could range from living wage legislation to risk-sharing mechanisms such as social insurance. The book concludes by arguing that expanded risk-sharing arrangements can put economic well-being within reach for all.

PART II From Shifting to Sharing Risk

2 Counting the Ways

HOW FAMILIES ARE FINANCIALLY FRAGILE

Tarah was no stranger to financial stress. A single mom in upstate New York, in 2021 she worked two jobs to support her son: one as a medical secretary and one as an in-store grocery shopper. Tarah worked weekdays plus weekends and nights. Even moonlighting, she was behind on her heating bills. Almost half of her spending went to medical bills, and new ones kept popping up. She was swimming in debt, and creditors were pressing her for payment.[1]

Tarah's story was not unusual. She was a typical middle-class American in lots of ways. She had a white-collar job and a retirement account. But Tarah's story was typical in another way as well. For despite working around the clock, she couldn't get ahead. Even with two jobs, she couldn't make ends meet. In that respect, Tarah was like half of Americans.

The sheer number of economically distressed Americans is jarring. In the United States, we pride ourselves on being the world's most advanced economy. We like to believe that people can get ahead. In reality, though, the American dream is showing cracks. For one out of every two Americans, economic insecurity is a daily fact of life.

In this chapter, I focus on families' financial situation in 2019, the year before the COVID-19 pandemic descended. The close of 2019 marked the longest economic expansion in US history.[2] Unemployment had dropped to its lowest rate in fifty years, and median income had reached its highest point since 1967.[3]

Still, half of US families struggled to pay their basic expenses in 2019. The financial strain on families had ripple effects of all types, from the ability to provide food and shelter to proper medical care, the opportunity for a college education for their children, a secure retirement, and more.

HALF OF AMERICANS LACK A LIVING INCOME

Do US families make enough to live on? Poverty statistics give an initial glimpse into the answer. In 2019, thirty-eight million people (11.7%) were poor, according to the US Census Bureau's supplemental poverty measure.[4] Contrary to the stereotype, over two-thirds of poor people that year (twenty-six million) identified themselves as White. Still, Blacks and Hispanics had higher poverty rates of 18 to 19 percent, compared to 8.2 percent for non-Hispanic Whites.[5]

Gauging the number of poor, though, is just the tip of the iceberg. Like Tarah, many other people are above the poverty line but cannot cover their basic daily needs. We can start to grasp that problem by ascertaining what a family in the exact middle income-wise earned in 2019. That year, the median household—in other words, the household right in the middle—earned $68,703.[6] Half of households earned less. And many in the bottom half earned a lot less. In 2019, more than one out of three adults (37%) reported annual family incomes of under $40,000, and one out of four adults reported incomes of less than $25,000.[7] There were also troubling income disparities by ethnicity and race. The median Black family earned 40 percent less ($45,438), and the median Hispanic family earned 26 percent less ($56,113), than the median White family ($76,057) in 2019.[8]

So how many working families had a living income? The answer: less than half. MIT researchers define a living wage as "an approximate income needed to meet a family's basic needs [that] would enable the working poor to achieve financial independence while maintaining housing and food security."[9] For 2019, they estimated a living wage for a family of four at $16.54 an hour or $68,808 a year.[10] This was just over the median US income ($68,703) that year.[11] By 2021, in virtually every US county, the median wage was less than a living wage.[12] By 2022 a living wage for a family of four had skyrocketed to $104,078 annually or $25.02 an hour, well above the median income that year of around $70,000.[13] The upshot: over half of working households across the United States did not make a living wage.

Here, it is important to stress that a living income is not enough to live in comfort. Instead, a living wage only covers bare-bones necessities such as food, housing, clothing, personal care items, transportation, childcare, health care, and taxes. It does not allow for amenities such as entertainment, eating out, gifts, vacations, or holidays, let alone cable television, streaming subscriptions, high speed internet, or expenses for school. Similarly, a living income budgets no money for savings. Instead, it is a subsistence wage, just enough to "get by."[14]

To reiterate, nearly one out of two Americans lacks enough income to even meet their basic needs.[15] Throughout this book, I refer to this group as the "bottom half" or the "bottom 50 percent." The bottom 50 percent naturally includes people defined as "poor" because their income is below either the federal poverty level (FPL) or the supplemental poverty measure.[16] It also includes the "near-poor," people who are not technically poor but live on less than 200 percent of the federal poverty level.[17] But the bottom 50 percent reaches further, right up into the middle class.[18] It included almost seventy-seven million people in 2019 who were not officially poor or near-poor, but still struggled to pay for the necessities of life.[19] Many of them lived in nearly constant want.

TENS OF MILLIONS OF FAMILIES HAVE BARELY ANY MONEY IN THE BANK

In an ideal world, families would have sufficient savings to tide them over to the next paycheck. In reality, the cash reserves of tens of millions of families are paltry.

In 2019, if we ranked households according to income, most people in the bottom 20 percent (about twenty-six million households) had checking and savings accounts but no other financial assets.[20] For those with bank accounts, the median balance was only $940. Precious few (only one out of ten) had retirement accounts, and the median balance was small ($15,000). Instead, people in the bottom fifth mostly put any meager savings they had in bank accounts. The numbers were only marginally better for the next 20 percent up.[21]

There were also large racial and ethnic disparities in family savings, regardless of income. In 2019 White families had $8,100 on average in liquid bank accounts and prepaid card accounts. In contrast, Black families only had $1,500 and Hispanic families $2,000 on average in those same accounts.[22]

Long story short, large swaths of households had worryingly little cash reserves in 2019. Not surprisingly, people in that spot had trouble paying bills. In 2019 almost three people out of ten could not pay all their monthly bills in full or doubted they could do so if a $400 surprise expense cropped up. The percentages were worse for Black and Hispanic households with no college degree.[23]

This dearth of personal savings, coupled with insufficient income, put vast numbers of families in financial straits. According to the Federal Reserve, over one-third of American adults were at high risk of material hardship in 2019.[24] This played out in terms of poor medical care and housing insecurity. Over seven million families in 2019 anticipated being late on one or more rental, mortgage, or utility bills, at the risk of eviction or a cutoff of water or electricity.[25] Twenty-six million people lacked health insurance in 2019, while large numbers skipped needed medical care due to the cost.[26] These households had to juggle bills to make it to the next paycheck.

HOUSEHOLDS WHO CANNOT MAKE ENDS MEET TURN TO DEBT OR PUBLIC BENEFITS

Over the past few decades, financial pressures pushed a substantial number of households into unmanageable debt. According to three leading economists, as "US income inequality began a marked increase in the 1980s, the richest one percent of households increased their savings while the bottom ninety percent fell into debt." Between the 1980s and 2007, the amount of household debt the bottom 90 percent owed grew by forty percentage points.[27]

While home mortgages comprised the lion's share, student debt, auto debt, and medical debt also surged.[28] Over three-fourths of US households (over one hundred million) carry medical debt, while over forty-three million borrowers owe student debt.[29] The frequency of elderly debtors also has ballooned, with each older generation being more in debt than the generation before it.[30]

In a sign of financial stress, it is common for people to borrow instead of paying for unexpected bills in cash. When people were asked in 2019 how they would pay for a surprise $400 cost, over one-fourth said that they would sell something or borrow the funds.[31] People with sparse savings are under particular pressure to borrow when hit with unexpected expenses.

In turn, over-indebtedness puts a significant number of households in credit distress. In a 2018 survey, almost one out of five reported that a debt collector had contacted them in the past year.[32] Similarly, in 2019 one out of every eight households was late on debt payments.[33] People with medical debt were under especially heavy financial stress. In 2019, 57 percent of patients with outstanding medical bills could not cover their other monthly bills or would have had difficulty if a surprise $400 bill materialized.[34]

Other families with insufficient income ended up resorting to social safety nets. In 2019, one out of fourteen adults received unemployment insurance or cash government assistance targeted by income. One out of seven adults received noncash support such as food stamps.[35]

And that was during a relatively strong economy. The following year, the pandemic sparked mass layoffs. By April 2020, just weeks after COVID-19 struck, US unemployment spiked at 14.8 percent (leaving almost twenty million people jobless) before subsiding to 6.7 percent (9.5 million people) by year's end.[36] By July of that year, almost one-fourth of US adults were receiving unemployment benefits, food stamps, or donated food.[37]

Bottom line, the income shortfalls afflicting half of Americans exert a heavy financial toll. Some families go deeply into debt and others fall into poverty, with or without public assistance. Other struggling families are not officially poor but still cannot make ends meet. And there is a good chance they will experience poverty at some point during their lifetimes. The financial status of US families is so shaky, in fact, that almost 60 percent will dip below the poverty line between ages twenty and seventy-five for at least one year of their lives.[38] At some point, 65 percent of Americans between the ages of twenty and sixty-five will receive Medicaid, food stamps, or some other type of income-targeted government aid.[39] Most people's stints of poverty are short.[40] Still, the number of Americans who will experience poverty at least once in their lives is profoundly disquieting and a sign of deeper structural problems in the American labor market.

LOW PAY BLOCKS PATHS TO ECONOMIC OPPORTUNITY

We've seen so far that half of American families do not have enough money to cover their basic needs. For these families, college and homeownership are important avenues to economic mobility and financial security. A secure retirement is another important financial goal. Yet for too many Americans, amassing large savings for these longer-term goals is out of the question. This dearth of financial resources affects not only their ability to pay bills, but their ability to advance in life.

College is a prime example. There are reams of evidence that a college degree is critical to people's economic mobility and future wage growth. People who complete their bachelor's degrees earn substantially higher median pay than people who do not.[41] However, lower-income households must rely on student loans more heavily than better-paid families to send their children to college.[42] This dependence on student loans also hurts college graduation rates, with Black and Latino children being less likely to graduate due to debt aversion or unmanageable debt.[43] For students from poorer families who do incur student debt, millions struggle later to repay their loans.[44]

Homeownership is another well-trodden path to economic mobility and increased wealth. But lack of savings and poor credit block access to homeownership for many Americans. In 2019 the median first-time homebuyer made a 6 percent down payment and had an above-average credit score of 725.[45] That 6 percent down payment required a first-time homebuyer purchasing the median home in 2019 to pony up $12,900 in cash—and that didn't include closing costs.[46] Low credit scores often pose another barrier to homeownership, accounting for 28 percent of home mortgage denials for first-time buyers in 2019.[47] Soaring home prices increased these barriers after the pandemic.[48] In the process, too many unsuccessful homebuyers become locked into a cycle in which they cannot amass wealth.

These factors contributed to large homeownership gaps by income and race. At the end of 2019, only 44 percent of Black households owned homes, compared to 74 percent of non-Hispanic Whites.[49] That nearly thirty-point gap was larger than the homeownership gap for Blacks before the Fair Housing Act of 1968 was passed.[50] Lower-income families of all races were also less likely to own homes. In 2019 households making less than $50,000 a year accounted for 38 percent of all households but owned less than 20 percent of all owner-occupied homes with mortgages.[51]

Another window of financial vulnerability opens with old age. Poorer workers are more likely to end up poor when they become old. Social Security payments only replace 42 to 77 percent of the average career earnings of low- and moderate-income workers, with the lowest earners receiving the highest replacement rates.[52] To bridge this gap, our system expects retirees to supplement their Social Security checks with private pensions and personal savings. However, ever-fewer retirees have defined-benefit plans offering traditional pensions. Instead, the overwhelming majority of retirement plan participants only have defined-contribution plans, in which market risk falls on them.[53]

There's an even bigger problem, which is that tens of millions of employees have no workplace retirement plans at all. Companies do not have to offer retirement plans, and many of them do not. Consequently, over one-fourth of civilian workers—at least forty-three million—lacked access to those plans as of March 2023 and, for the worst-paid 25 percent, the percentage was more than half.[54] Due in part to this coverage gap, up to one-fourth of Social Security recipients age sixty-five and up depend on their Social Security checks for at least 90 percent of their income.[55] One-third of elderly households run out of money or are in debt after paying their basic expenses every month.[56]

In sum, tens of millions of families find themselves in financial distress. Half of households lack a living income, and many have a dearth of savings. Paying for expenses often is a struggle, and many are forced into debt. Ordinary lifetime goals such as homeownership, college, or a secure retirement are often unattainable. As the next chapter discusses, this plight is through no fault of their own.

3 Power Play

THE FIFTY-YEAR ASSAULT ON WORKERS'
ECONOMIC SECURITY

There is a vicious blame game today, censuring people for not having enough money. But in most cases, people's cash-flow problems are not their fault. Rather, powerful political and private interests off-loaded financial risk and dumped it onto workers over the past half century.[1] This occurred on multiple fronts: by depressing wages, slashing unemployment insurance and welfare, discontinuing traditional pensions, and eliminating state subsidies for college education. Together, these actions amounted to one big power play that decimated the ability of ordinary families to make it through the month and achieve milestones such as college and a comfortable retirement. Economically, governments and employers slammed workers, then abandoned them to sink or swim.

It didn't used to be like this. Fifty years ago, on balance, paychecks stretched further, jobs were more secure, and social safety nets were stronger. Back in the 1970s, well-paid manufacturing jobs were common, union protections were strong, and laid-off workers could expect to be recalled. Unemployment benefits covered more workers and replaced more of their income. Single mothers could qualify for welfare without having to work. Private pensions were more secure for those who had them. And states heavily subsidized tuition at public universities and colleges.

This chapter chronicles how institutions unloaded financial risk onto workers over the past half century. This history imparts two lessons. First, the economic insecurity afflicting workers is recent and not written in stone. Second, in past decades the United States routinely used risk-sharing mechanisms to relieve ordinary families of excessive financial risk. Those same or improved mechanisms could be used today to alleviate households' financial distress.

STAGNANT WAGES AND GROWING JOB INSECURITY

We saw in chapter 2 that half of US families make less than a living income. This state of affairs has gotten worse over the past five decades. Since 1979, in fact, hourly wages have stagnated or declined for everyone (after adjusting for inflation) except the top 5 percent of workers in terms of pay. At the same time, the buying power of paychecks for the lowest-paid workers has shrunk.[2] To add insult to injury, worker productivity has grown 4.4 times faster than pay since 1979.[3] This combination of depressed wages and productivity growth means that investors essentially hijacked a slice of the national income that used to go to workers.[4]

A top reason for this stagnant pay has been the tectonic change in labor markets over the past half century.[5] Decisions by US corporations to close domestic plants and ship well-paid manufacturing jobs abroad helped set this change in motion.[6] The downward trajectory started in June 1979, when manufacturing jobs hit a 19.5 million high.[7] After that, domestic factory employment took a dive. By January 2020 the United States had lost nearly one out of three manufacturing jobs, dropping to 12.8 million positions right before the onset of the global pandemic.[8]

This slump in factory positions occurred in lockstep with the loss of unionized jobs. Union positions dropped by two-thirds after 1945, mostly in the private sector.[9] This decline was so steep that by 2020, fewer than 7 percent of private-sector workers enjoyed union protection.[10] The disappearance of bargaining units stemmed from multiple factors, including employer opposition to unionization, deregulation facilitating the entry of new, nonunion competitors, weakened labor laws, and plant closures.[11] The lost union jobs had paid more on average and offered pension protections and group health benefits.[12] As union representation plunged, workers lost crucial bargaining power.[13]

Companies also resorted to anticompetitive tactics to weaken workers' bargaining positions. Some industries only have one or a few employers, which can use their market power to keep wages down. In other industries, companies (both big and small) can introduce "frictions" to induce jobseekers to accept and stay in jobs at lower wages instead of searching for work at higher pay. These frictions include concealing the wages that employers pay, requiring workers who quit to repay their training costs, making them sign noncompete agreements that limit their job options if they resign, and misclassifying employees as independent contractors.[14]

As well-paid jobs took a hit, service sector jobs rushed into the breach.[15] Increasingly, blue collar workers became hostage to the service sector's low pay. One major study reported, for instance, that the "frequency of very large declines in hours worked . . . increased, on net, between the early 1970s and early 2000s and . . . jumped considerably higher in recent years." Similar declines appeared in households' real earnings per hour.[16]

To get a sense of the size of these changes, consider workers in the leisure and hospitality industry. Between 1979 and 2019, their average hourly pay hovered around 60 percent of the average hourly wage for factory workers. They also received fewer hours of work, only about two-thirds of the hours on average worked by manufacturing workers between 1979 and 2019. This combination of lower hourly wages and weekly hours pushed the average weekly pay of leisure and hospitality workers down to only *38 percent* of the weekly pay of manufacturing workers.[17] With service sector pay so low, the loss of manufacturing jobs dealt workers a grave blow. The federal minimum wage, which has been stuck at $7.25 an hour since 2009, did nothing to cushion the sharp fall-off in pay.[18]

As manufacturing jobs vanished, so did steady work. Retail and food workers increasingly only got part-time schedules with erratic hours.[19] The rise of the gig economy was a further jolt to full-time work. By 2019 almost one-third of US workers were gig workers. As independent contractors, gig workers cannot unionize and enjoy fewer protections and benefits than employees. Partly due to their weak bargaining position, most gig workers only work part-time.[20]

The growing refusal of employers to offer full-time work has consigned many workers to incomes that fluctuate month to month. This can happen when jobs are seasonal, when pay consists of tips and commissions, when employers do not guarantee hours, when workers are self-employed or work gig, or when employers deduct hours missed due to sickness or childcare from pay. One study found that the average lower-income household experienced income swings of 25 percent or more for at least five months a year. Some months, families made more, but other months, money was "very tight."[21] These income swings destabilize many families financially and make it hard for them to cover monthly bills. Households with unstable incomes also are less likely to have rainy day funds than those with steady pay.[22]

The decline in job security had the further harmful consequence of longer spells of unemployment. Temporary layoffs are a thing of the past, replaced by prolonged stints of joblessness following permanent layoffs.[23] Additionally, the United States increasingly has experienced recessions with "jobless recoveries," in which gross domestic product recovers before hiring. With each successive recession, this lag in reemployment has gotten worse, with almost 40 percent of jobless workers enduring long-term unemployment after the 2008 financial crisis.[24]

In short, for the past fifty years, US workers have been at the mercy of larger forces that successively eroded their pay. Employers flexed their economic might during that period to close plants, ship manufacturing jobs abroad, evade union protections, cut hours, and depress wages. Together, the loss of higher-paid jobs, the rise in irregular hours, longer stints of unemployment, the decline in unionization, the surge in gig work, and anticompetitive practices by employers trapped millions of workers into lower pay. Meanwhile, the social safety nets that buffered workers from the vicissitudes of the labor market were receding as well.

THE VANISHING SOCIAL SAFETY NET

The free market economy in the United States has always presupposed a high degree of labor mobility among employers and workers. Workers are free to leave their jobs, while private-sector employers have extraordinary latitude to terminate workers. To be sure, today's laws against employment discrimination and whistleblower retaliation place some limited constraints on employers' freedom to fire. In theory, union protections against termination impose added constraints, but those protections evaporated with the decline in collective bargaining. Otherwise, US companies have broad freedom to dismiss their workers. Today, the risk of job loss is so pervasive that two-thirds of Americans will experience unemployment by the time they reach age sixty.[25]

This job insecurity spawns the need for social safety nets for workers hit by job loss. Historically, the United States has offered support to replace the income of jobless workers. Over the last half century, however, this safety net has shrunk while job insecurity has grown. Other important social safety supports in the areas of pension benefits, college subsidies, and public assistance also have been curtailed.

Unemployment Insurance

Unemployment insurance (UI) is the program that is supposed to provide a basic safety net when employers terminate workers. UI is ridden with holes, however, and is badly showing its age. As a result, UI benefits are paltry for workers who get them, and over two-thirds of jobless workers do not qualify for them at all.

Unemployment insurance has two purposes: to replace income for workers who lose their jobs and to stabilize the economy during downturns by boosting consumer spending.[26] The regular UI program is called "basic UI" and is run by the states with federal oversight. Basic UI is a public-private insurance program in which the states pay UI benefits and employers finance those benefits through taxes. A second UI program provides longer unemployment benefits when economic conditions deteriorate. When this Extended Benefits (EB) program is in effect, jobless workers may qualify for thirteen to twenty more weeks of UI benefits, depending on the state.[27]

For the most part, Congress entrusted the states with running basic UI, so each state determines who qualifies for benefits in that state. The eligibility test for basic UI has both "monetary" and "nonmonetary" requirements.

The monetary test requires applicants to prove that they earned "enough money" to qualify, which most states define as earnings over some threshold amount during the first four of the last five complete calendar quarters before applying for UI.[28] In addition, applicants must meet

several nonmonetary requirements. First, most states only grant UI benefits to workers who are fired or forced by compelling circumstances to quit
their jobs. Employees who voluntarily quit are usually ineligible. Second, a
worker must have been an "employee" for someone else, not self-employed
or an independent contractor. This means that people who work gig or
through corporate outsourcing normally do not receive basic UI. Third,
temporary agency workers also are disqualified from basic UI. Finally,
most states require terminated workers to show that they are prepared to
take a job and are looking for full-time work.[29]

These eligibility rules disqualify important categories of jobless workers
from UI. Numerous low-paid, part-time workers who lose their jobs do
not earn "enough" to meet the monetary test. Adults who had to leave
work to care for children or elderly relatives also cannot qualify in many
states. The same is true for workers who were forced to leave because
their employers cut their pay or hours or assigned them unpredictable
job schedules that made meeting their other responsibilities impossible.
Meanwhile, the basic UI program excludes workers whom employers mis-
classify as independent contractors.[30]

As a result of these exclusions, fewer than three in ten jobless workers
in 2019 received basic UI. This approval rate was even worse for Black,
Hispanic, Asian, female, and disabled workers who lost their jobs, because
these groups, compared to White men, are overrepresented among people
who do not meet the UI eligibility criteria.[31]

For the lucky unemployed workers who qualify for basic UI, their benefits are not enough to live on.[32] In 2019, for instance, UI payments only
averaged $371 a week (just 38% of lost wages). This is a national aver-
age, moreover, and many states paid less.[33] Moreover, benefits are tied
to wages, so lower-paid workers receive lower weekly benefits than their
better-paid counterparts.[34] It is also rare for states to top off UI benefits
with allowances for dependents.[35]

The temporary nature of UI further limits how much basic UI benefits are paid. The typical state pays up to twenty-six weeks of benefits,
but some states only pay twelve.[36] In addition, recipients with a history of
part-time work, including caregivers and the infirm, are dropped from UI
rolls in many states unless they are actively searching for full-time work.[37]
All told, basic UI is a stingy program that expects jobless workers to have
a savings cushion to survive on, when many do not.[38]

When Congress enacted unemployment insurance in 1935, it designed UI for labor market conditions that were a far cry from those today. The New Deal UI program placed priority on assisting laid-off manufacturing workers who usually were called back once their factories reopened. Congress assumed that job loss was temporary and that employers would rehire laid-off workers once their inventories ran low. It expected jobless workers to have savings or union stipends to help them weather unemployment.[39] At the same time, to permit racial exclusion and thus win passage, Congress cynically delegated authority for eligibility standards and benefits to the states.[40]

As this suggests, UI benefits were never generous in the best of times. More recently, however, states have competed to lure businesses to their jurisdictions (and retain employers) by curtailing UI eligibility and shortening benefits periods. This pattern has reared its head whenever workers needed UI benefits most—during recessions—as states looked for ways to replenish their depleted UI trust funds without raising taxes on employers.[41] Because employers pay the premiums for basic UI, they use their lobbying might to push for rollbacks. At the same time, companies increasingly escaped UI taxation by recharacterizing their workers as independent contractors and closing plants.[42] As a result, the share of jobless workers who received UI benefits fell from an already low 36 percent in 2007 to 28 percent in 2019. States also slashed the maximum length of basic UI benefits to reduce the amounts they paid out.[43] These shorter benefit periods reduce the total lost wages that are replaced and trap workers in future low-paid work by pressuring them to accept poorly compensated job offers.

In sum, states colluded with employers to shift more of the financial risk from job insecurity off their balance sheets and onto workers. The vast majority of terminated workers no longer qualify for UI, and those who do receive a pittance.

Backlash against Welfare

Unemployment insurance, meanwhile, usually does not support adults who have to leave the workforce for reasons unrelated to work, such as caregiving responsibilities. Welfare benefits, if available, would provide many of these adults with a needed source of support.

Welfare, though, is one more example of where the government increasingly abandoned lower-income adults to fend for themselves. Over the past decades, welfare has contracted and become more punitive.

The original federal welfare program, Aid to Families with Dependent Children (AFDC), enacted in 1935, provided cash benefits to destitute single mothers. AFDC was premised on the belief that mothers should stay at home to care for their children. As a result, AFDC, as originally conceived, did not require recipients to work.[44]

Before the 1960s, AFDC largely was reserved for poor White women because numerous welfare agencies used stratagems to disqualify Black and Hispanic mothers from benefits. Subsequently, however, after welfare finally opened up to minority women, this development ignited a racially charged debate over cash relief and personal responsibility. The controversy exploded after President Ronald Reagan made racist comments denigrating "welfare queens."[45]

The "welfare queen" debate fueled growing public pressure to condition welfare on work. As hostility to welfare mounted, President Bill Clinton acceded to calls to cut benefits by signing the Personal Responsibility and Work Opportunity Reconciliation Act in 1996. The legislation replaced AFDC with a new program called Temporary Assistance to Needy Families (TANF), which required beneficiaries to work at least thirty hours a week and placed a five-year lifetime cap on benefits. The program was administered with one goal—to reduce welfare rolls—and discouraged poor people from applying in multiple, degrading ways. TANF remains in effect today, with minor modifications.

With TANF's enactment, welfare rolls plummeted but poverty persisted.[46] By 2019 only about 916,000 families were on TANF, just a drop in the bucket in a nation of 328 million.[47] With numbers so low, welfare has been reduced to conservatives' bogeyman, the program they love to hate but that almost no longer exists. Poverty lived on, though, with thirty-eight million people being poor in 2019 according to the supplemental poverty measure.[48] Almost none of them received TANF benefits.

Pension Cutbacks

Pensions are another crucial area in which institutions purged financial risk from their books and thrust it onto individuals. Fifty years ago, the most common type of pension was the traditional *defined-benefit* (DB) pension, which was offered through the workplace.[49] In a DB plan, an employer or a union agrees to pay a fixed monthly pension to eligible retirees until their death. The beauty of a DB pension is that workers can count on receiving steady pension income for life, no matter how poorly markets perform. As a result, employees bear little of the financial risks of DB plans, which instead are borne by the employers or unions that sponsor those plans.[50]

More recently, however, *defined-contribution* (DC) plans have steadily supplanted DB plans, at least in the private sector. DC plans took off after Congress approved pretax employee contributions to 401(k) plans in 1978.[51] In DC plans, employers offer individual retirement savings accounts that are funded by the employees, the employers, or both. Typically, employees invest their contributions in mutual funds or private annuities and can take their account balances when they leave their positions.[52]

In most respects, DC plans are riskier for workers than DB plans. To grasp why, consider the seven main risks of retirement planning: longevity risk, cumulation risk, market risk, security risk, inflation risk, solvency risk, and mobility risk. DB plans are safer than DC plans for six out of seven of those risks.

The first risk, *longevity risk*, refers to the danger of outliving one's money.[53] DB plans lift this uncertainty by requiring employers or unions to make monthly pension payments for life. In DC plans, in contrast, the longevity risk falls on retirees, because they can run out of savings before death.[54]

The second danger is *cumulation risk*, which entails investing too little for retirement. DB plans relieve workers of cumulation risk by making employers or unions responsible for sufficient contributions to those plans.[55] In contrast, workers bear cumulation risk in DC plans. That risk, moreover, is large and real. In 2022, for example, the median worker's retirement account contained just $87,000, nowhere near enough to fund a lengthy retirement.[56] Needless to say, the inability of so many American households to earn a living wage contributes heavily to these savings difficulties and to cumulation risk.

Market risk is an added hazard when planning for retirement. This is the danger that participants could lose their principal when markets slump. DB plans shield workers from market risk because plan sponsors have to pay the promised benefits, regardless of how poorly the underlying portfolios perform. Workers in DC plans, conversely, bear market risk themselves. Their balances can and do decline when markets fall. Witness the 2008 financial crisis, when the sharp drop in markets inflicted severe losses on many 401(k) participants.[57]

Security risk—the risk that someone will steal a person's life savings—is another frightening concern for retirees. Elderly people are particular targets for theft, especially when they have substantial savings or are susceptible to cons due to cognitive decline. DB plans only pose a limited danger of misappropriation, but the risk of theft is troublingly real for DC plans.

Inflation risk is the fifth risk to a secure retirement. The average US retirement lasts seventeen years, which raises the question of whether retirement incomes will keep up with inflation.[58] DB plans help defray the impact of inflation in one and sometimes two ways: by seeking investment returns that outpace inflation and, on rare occasions, by providing annual cost-of-living adjustments (as Social Security does).[59] In contrast, the onus is on workers to beat inflation themselves in DC plans.

Solvency risk, the sixth risk, is the chance that a plan could go broke through theft or mismanagement. In the private sector, the Employee Retirement Income Security Act of 1974 (ERISA) heavily regulates the solvency of DB plans.[60] On top of that, if the worst happens and a private-sector DB plan fails, the Pension Benefit Guaranty Corporation (PBGC) guarantees basic pension benefits, up to set dollar limits, to the plan's participants.[61] In contrast, DC plans are not regulated for solvency and do not have PBGC protection.

Finally, *mobility risk* is an added risk to workers from pension plans. DB plans pose the hazard that employees who leave their jobs—whether voluntarily or due to firing—will forfeit their pensions or receive a smaller benefit due to their abbreviated time on the job. In contrast, DC plans are portable and workers who have vested retain their balances when they leave their positions.[62]

To summarize, DC plans only beat DB plans when it comes to mobility risk. In every other way, DB plans provide superior protection to employees because the other six risks fall on employers or unions, not workers. As a consequence, DB plans offer substantially more security and higher average retirement incomes than DC plans.[63]

Unfortunately, DB pensions have gone the way of the dinosaur, at least in the private sector.[64] Over the past fifty years, employers have replaced

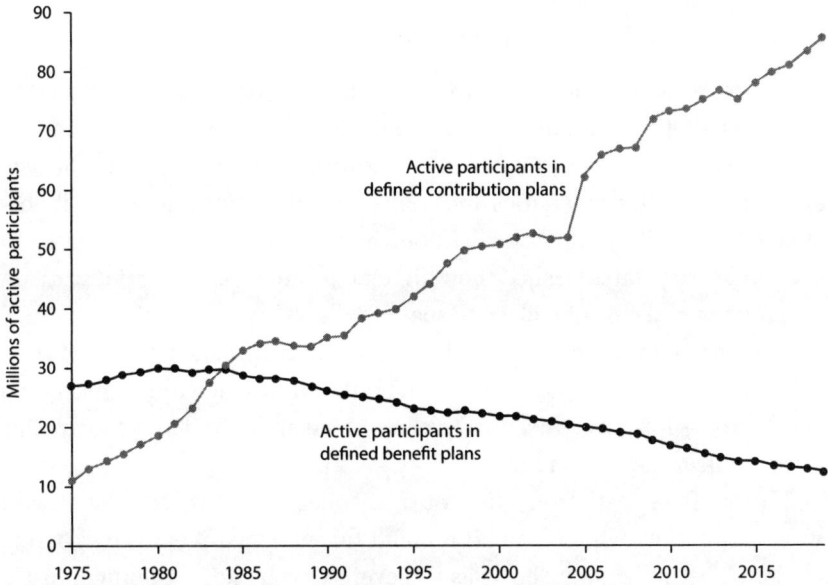

Figure 1. Active participants in private-sector pension plans, 1975–2019. *Source:* Congressional Research Service (2021a).

DB plans with DC plans (see figure 1).[65] By 2019, private-sector DB plans only covered 12.6 million active participants; private-sector DC plans, in contrast, covered 85.5 million.[66]

As private pensions gravitated toward the DC model and away from DB plans, employers and unions shifted substantial risk onto individual workers. Now the responsibility is on workers to save enough for a secure retirement. To boot, every worker has to acquire enough investment expertise to manage successfully the market risk and inflation risk in their retirement accounts.

This assumes, moreover, that workers even have access to workplace pension plans. But tens of millions do not, leaving many to survive mostly on Social Security in retirement.[67] With Social Security benefits so low and the Social Security Old-Age and Survivors Insurance Trust Fund projected to deplete its reserves in 2033 unless Congress intervenes, workers who lack retirement plans face poverty in old age.[68]

Rollbacks in Higher Education Subsidies

Studies repeatedly have shown that for most, a bachelor's degree leads to higher lifetime earnings and greater financial security.[69] Throughout the 1980s, college degrees were relatively affordable because states heavily subsidized public universities and colleges.[70] Those subsidies made it possible to get a college education without going heavily into debt. Starting in 1989, however, states slashed their higher education spending per student, causing the real cost of college to soar.[71]

Since then, public colleges and universities have made up for lost state subsidies by sharply raising tuition.[72] Those tuition increases outstripped wage growth for lower-income families. Meanwhile, student scholarships did not offset the tuition hikes.[73]

This shift in costs from the states to college students coincided with wage stagnation, which made it difficult for many parents to cover rising tuition. The budget squeeze was so severe that by 2017, the median US family by income would have had to spend 23 percent of its yearly wages to pay for one year at a public university.[74]

Under these circumstances, something had to give. Soaring tuitions discouraged some students from attending college, especially lower-income youth and students of color.[75] In the meantime, many students who did attend college had to pay for it by taking out more debt. In 2019–2020, for example, the average new bachelor's degree graduate with student debt owed $35,530, compared to $30,940 in 1999–2000.[76] While these balances may appear manageable, that appearance is deceiving because student loan defaults are mostly concentrated among graduates with lower balances.[77]

Bottom line, as states shifted the cost of public higher education onto households ill-equipped to pay for it, heavy student debt became the price. For many borrowers, that debt increased their risk of financial distress.

AS SAFETY NETS FRAYED,
FAMILIES TOOK ON MORE DEBT

This history reveals how employers and government progressively dismantled social safety nets relied on by households. As those safety nets frayed, many households were forced to respond by increasingly resorting to debt.[78] Two indicators shed light on this trend. The first takes household debt and compares it to gross domestic product. Between 1946 and 2009, this indicator rose sixfold and remained elevated after that.[79] The second indicator gauges how much households spend on debt payments every month. Starting in 1950, this indicator also marched upward and reached unsustainable heights by 2007, culminating in the 2008 financial crisis.[80]

While debt-to-income ratios eased subsequently, the decline after 2007 was not a sign that all was well.[81] Rather, according to the Federal Reserve, it "implie[d] that households either defaulted on their loans or reduced consumption expenditures in order to slow the accrual of new debt or to pay down existing debt."[82]

This debt load on families is a direct result of the contraction in risk-sharing arrangements. Major institutions—both companies and the government—used to pool and spread financial risks that fall on individuals today. Today's shift to the individualistic allocation of risk has exacerbated income and wealth inequalities and left tens of millions of households in financial distress. But thrusting unmanageable financial risks onto individuals, instead of pooling and spreading those risks, does not have to be a given. It is time to question the individualistic approach and to revisit when financial risks now shouldered by families should be shared.

4 The Broken Savings Discourse

Over the past fifty years, the financial risks for ordinary families have ballooned to unmanageable proportions. Yet the frequent policy response is to inveigh households to "just save more." Policymakers exhort people to build emergency savings, salt away money for college, save for a down payment, and sock away a million dollars (or more) for retirement. These savings demands are positively daunting.

This savings drumbeat often also comes with a moral expectation that people are responsible for their own financial self-sufficiency. The implication is that households cannot count on social safety nets and must weather any emergencies through personal savings. Meanwhile, people who lack savings are pegged as personally irresponsible.

Of course, there are good reasons to encourage savings. Savings can tide people over when costs rise or incomes fall. Nest eggs can also help people invest in college education, a small business, or a home.[1]

All the same, is it realistic to expect people to save large sums when half of families live paycheck to paycheck and have little discretionary income to save?[2] Hard, cold data tell us it is not. Many millions are not remotely close to hitting the savings targets that advisers recommend.

Experts advise people to save 15 to 20 percent of their income for re-tirement plus another three to six months' worth of expenses in emer-gency funds in case they lose their jobs.[3] Yet 46 percent of US families lacked enough emergency funds to cover three months' worth of ex-penses in 2023.[4] Many of those families were not poor; they included "most married families with children and even many high income fam-ilies."[5] That same year, 42 percent of households lacked enough savings to cover a $1,000 expense.[6] They were "highly vulnerable to income or expense shocks" due to thin cash reserves.[7] Meanwhile, over two-thirds of households in the bottom 40 percent by pay lacked retirement ac-counts in 2022.[8]

Suffice it to say, policymakers' insistence on savings over social safety nets has failed for the tens of millions of families who lack even emergency funds. The fact that large proportions of people have sparse savings is a distress signal that families face significant barriers to building nest eggs. Some even question whether cash-strapped families *should* save more, in-stead of paying down their debt.[9]

The personal responsibility narrative asserts that people who act re-sponsibly will exercise self-control and put money away. But it's a little-acknowledged fact that most people do not save much money on their own. Instead, people who manage to save usually are enrolled in formal savings plans that are sponsored by employers.[10] These plans are con-sciously designed to help people save.

By and large, however, these formal savings plans have a hitch: not everyone has access to them. There are plenty of formal plans for higher-income families. But many poorly paid workers work for employers who do not offer savings plans. Others have access to plans but do not reap the same financial benefits from those plans as do better-paid coworkers. Even worse, welfare laws actively penalize applicants with savings by dis-qualifying them for benefits in many states.

In short, lower-income workers face a different and inferior savings en-vironment than people who make more. The system mostly helps affluent employees get richer; it does little to help blue-collar workers save. Essen-tially, the edict to "save more" is empty rhetoric when it comes to people who are lower paid.

THE FEDERAL BIAS TOWARD HELPING
AFFLUENT PEOPLE SAVE

The bias toward helping better-off households save rears its head in at least two ways. For one thing, federal policy favors long-term investments and health savings over the short-term savings that lower-income families usually need most. That is because the Internal Revenue Code offers large tax subsidies for retirement accounts, college savings, health expenses, and homeownership, but almost never for emergency funds. In addition, many long-term investments enjoy preferential tax rates, because long-term capital gains are taxed at a lower rate than interest on savings accounts, which is taxed at higher, ordinary rates.[11]

Federal Tax Subsidies for Retirement Savings

The federal preference for long-term investments first shows up in retirement plans, both in and outside the workplace. At work, employees with 401(k) or similar plans can exclude their payroll contributions to those plans from income. Federal income taxes are not due on those plans until withdrawal, when the principal and gains are both taxed at ordinary rates.[12] The contribution limit in 2024 was a handsome $23,000, and employees age fifty and up could contribute an extra $7,500, for a total of $30,500.[13]

Outside of work, many earners can deduct contributions to traditional Individual Retirement Accounts (IRAs) from taxable income and do not owe federal income tax on the principal and gains until withdrawal.[14] IRAs, unlike workplace plans, are available to everyone. However, the annual contribution limits for IRAs are significantly lower than for 401(k)s and other workplace plans. For 2024, annual IRA contributions were capped at $7,000, with an added $1,000 "catch-up" contribution (totaling $8,000) for individuals age fifty and up.[15] To encourage more people to save, Congress also gave lower-income taxpayers a nonrefundable federal tax credit of up to $1,000 for contributions to workplace retirement or IRA accounts through 2025.[16] This "saver's credit" did not make much of a dent in the retirement savings rate of lower-income households, however, because those households often did not incur a federal income tax liability that would benefit from the credit.[17] Instead, the bulk of federal subsidies for retirement savings goes to upper-income earners, as this chapter discusses.

Further Tax Subsidies for College Savings Plans

College savings also receive preferential treatment under the Internal Revenue Code. For 2024, each parent could contribute up to $18,000 a year per child for college in 529 savings plans without triggering the federal gift tax.[18] Gains in 529 plans accrue untaxed, and withdrawals also go untaxed so long as they are used to pay for postsecondary education.[19] Despite these benefits, later we will see that lower-income families rarely use college savings plans.

Tax Shelters for Health Savings Plans

Similarly, the Internal Revenue Code provides three types of tax-favored plans to encourage saving for medical expenses.[20] Few lower-income families participate in these plans, however.

The first type is health savings accounts (HSAs), which people with high-deductible health insurance can use to pay for medical expenses.[21] Contributions to HSAs are excluded from income, the gains grow untaxed, and funds can be withdrawn to pay for eligible medical expenses without owing tax. For 2024, individuals could contribute up to $4,150 annually to an HSA ($8,300 for a family), and those over age fifty-five could contribute another $1,000.[22] Taxpayers can open HSAs on their own, and there are no income caps for contributions to HSAs.[23]

Flexible savings arrangements (FSAs) are the second type of tax-sheltered health savings plans. These are salary reduction agreements offered by employers to reimburse employees for certain medical costs. Worker contributions to FSAs are exempt from income and employment taxes and were capped at $3,200 per employee for 2024. Employers can also provide a match.[24]

Finally, some employers offer health reimbursement arrangements (HRAs) to reimburse their employees for qualified medical expenses. Unlike HSAs and FSAs, only employers, not employees, may contribute to

HRAs. Reimbursements are free from federal income and employment taxes.[25]

Tax Benefits from Homeownership

In addition to tax benefits for retirement, college, and health savings plans, Congress confers substantial tax subsidies to people who own homes. These tax benefits are off-limits to many lower-income families because homeownership is more common among better-off households.[26]

Under federal tax law, homeowners can deduct their mortgage interest payments and property taxes on their primary residences from their federal income taxes, subject to caps.[27] In addition, homeowners who have lived in their principal residences for at least two out of the past five years may exclude any capital gain on sale up to $250,000 ($500,000 for joint filers).[28]

Weak Federal Support for Emergency Savings

Federal law pumps large tax subsidies into homeownership and retirement, college, and health savings. But it provides scant support for the emergency savings that lower-income families most need.[29] Traditionally, the closest that the federal government has come to supporting short-term reserves for lower-income taxpayers has been indirectly, through the Earned Income Tax Credit (EITC). However, the EITC is relatively small dollarwise for taxpayers without children and is not available to people with no earned income.[30]

In 2022 Congress did take small steps in the SECURE 2.0 Act to create tax-favored emergency savings vehicles. First, employers offering retirement accounts may now auto-enroll their employees in emergency fund accounts that sit side by side with their workplace retirement accounts.[31] And second, Congress authorized employees to withdraw up to $1,000 for emergencies penalty free from their retirement accounts.[32] Both provisions depend on access to workplace retirement plans, however, which is far less common for lower-paid workers.

Bottom line, there are no universally available tax subsidies for emergency savings. This is highly troubling given the importance of rainy day funds to lower-income households. Further, this imbalance deepens

wealth disparities because most tax subsidies for saving flow to the affluent, who can then save even more.[33]

MOST FEDERAL TAX SUBSIDIES FOR LONG-TERM
SAVINGS GO TO THE AFFLUENT

The favorable tax treatment of savings plans and homes is worth much
more to upper-income taxpayers than to lower-income households.[34] This
shortchanges less well-paid workers because people in higher tax brackets receive bigger subsidies than those in lower brackets for investing the
same amount of money in a tax-sheltered plan or home.

Consider, for instance, a well-paid employee in the top 37 percent tax
bracket. He will save $3,700 in federal taxes if he puts $10,000 into his
401(k) plan. A lower-paid worker in the 12 percent bracket will only save
$1,200 in taxes for making the same $10,000 contribution to her 401(k).
What this means is that Uncle Sam is subsidizing the exact same $10,000
contribution for the first person by $3,700 but for the second person by
only $1,200. On top of that, the subsidies only kick in for savers who pay
income taxes. Normally, at least 40 percent of all families do not owe federal income taxes in a given year, and so those families receive no subsidies for investing.[35] This bias in favor of the wealthy also pervades college
savings plans, because lower-income families are unlikely to incur gift tax
liability under any circumstance.

When it comes to homeownership, there are added reasons that tax
subsidies do little for lower-income families.[36] For starters, the majority of
people at the bottom of the income spectrum rent, not own.[37] People who
rent are disadvantaged taxwise compared to homeowners, because they
cannot deduct any part of their housing payments or their interest payments on nonmortgage debt such as credit cards.[38]

Even when lower-income taxpayers do own homes, almost none gain
any tax benefit from mortgage interest or property tax payments because
they claim the standard deduction instead of itemizing.[39] Furthermore,
higher-bracket taxpayers usually generate bigger deductions than item-
izers in lower brackets because they typically pay higher mortgage interest
and property taxes.

When all these effects are combined, tax-sheltered savings programs "are enormously regressive" and "the poor benefit very little."[40] In 2017, for instance, less than 1 percent of the federal tax subsidies for retirement savings flowed to the poorest fifth of taxpayers. In contrast, the richest fifth of taxpayers collected 62 percent of those subsidies that year.[41] And the largesse to the wealthy does not stop there. Affluent people similarly reap the biggest benefits from federal tax subsidies for homeownership and health and college savings plans.[42]

As a result, federal tax policy turns its back on the poorest families, who deserve the strongest rewards for saving. To compound this inequity, many lower-paid workers are shut out of the most generous retirement and health savings plans, which are formal plans offered at work.

OBSTACLES TO ACCESS TO TAX-SHELTERED SAVINGS PLANS

Not everyone qualifies for savings plans at work. Instead, employers have a choice of whether to offer formal savings plans to their employees. In many instances ERISA requires employers to offer lower-income employees the same tax-advantaged pension plans (called "qualified plans") they offer to high-income employees.[43] But ERISA also allows employers to offer pension plans to no one. In addition, ERISA does not apply to many less tax-favored savings plans (referred to as "nonqualified plans"). This allows employers to discriminate in favor of high-income employees by offering them several types of nonqualified plans while offering nothing to lower-income employees.

As a result, about 30 percent of private-sector employees work for firms with no retirement plans.[44] Companies that do offer those plans are more likely to employ white-collar professionals and other higher-paid workers. In contrast, firms that predominantly employ lower-paid workers are much less willing to offer retirement plans. In 2023, in fact, less than half of private-sector workers in the bottom fourth by pay had access to a workplace retirement plan, compared to nine out of ten in the top 25 percent.[45] The best-paid workers almost always have retirement plans at work, while many blue-collar workers do not.

Flexible spending accounts and health reimbursement accounts also have unequal access. Employers are not required to provide them. Further, FSAs and HRAs are not available to self-employed workers, retirees, or disabled people because those accounts can only be offered through employers.[46] These dynamics block many lower-income households, unlike their better-paid counterparts, from access to FSA and HRA plans. As a result, the top 10 percent of earners were more than five times more likely to have access to FSAs in 2021 than the bottom 10 percent.[47]

In short, millions of lower-income families are denied access to the most generous tax-preferred savings plans, which are sponsored by employers. While these families have access to other savings options outside of the workplace, the participation rates and amounts saved are low.

DIY SAVINGS FALL SHORT

We just saw that higher-income people usually have access to workplace savings plans with generous tax subsidies. Because these plans are only offered at the discretion of employers, poorer households often lack access to them.

In theory, lower-income workers could get around this problem by opening savings accounts outside of work. We can think of these accounts as "do-it-yourself" (DIY) accounts because, unlike workplace plans, individuals have to research these accounts and how to open them. Some DIY accounts are tax subsidized, such as HSAs, IRAs, and 529 savings plans. Others, such as plain vanilla savings accounts at banks, are not. Regardless of their tax treatment, the take-up rate of DIY savings accounts by lower-income households is disappointingly low.

Take HSAs. In 2021, only 11 percent of the lowest-paid workers used HSAs, compared to 59 percent of earners in the top 10 percent.[48] Similarly, people who use 529 plans for college savings are almost exclusively higher income.[49] The same lopsided pattern appears with IRAs for retirement. Even though everyone is eligible to save through an IRA, virtually no lower-income families contribute to them. This was glaringly apparent in 2018, when the number of people in the bottom 40 percent of earners who reported investing in an IRA was statistically *zero*. That same year, about 18 percent of people in the top 20 percent invested in IRAs.[50]

As this shows, while lower-income families have opportunities in theory to save for retirement and college (and sometimes medical expenses too) outside of work, few do. A similar pattern appears with bank accounts.

People assume that everyone can and does open bank accounts with equal ease, but the reality is different. In 2021, almost one-fifth of US households making less than $15,000 a year lacked bank accounts, and the same was true for 9 percent of households making $15,000 to $30,000 a year. That compared to only 2 percent of people making $50,000 or more annually.[51] While there are sundry reasons for this disparity—ranging from prohibitive minimum balance requirements and costly fees to distrust of banks—the gap in bank account ownership by income is one more sign that unbanked customers face institutional obstacles to saving.[52]

In sum, the track record of DIY savings vehicles is dismal for lower-income households. But the savings dearth of lower-income families is not for lack of interest. Many do aspire to save. Researchers have found, for instance, that many poor households squirrel away small, one-time receipts of cash and spend the balances over the next few months on needed expenses.[53] Analysts also reported that the poorest participants in pilot savings plans known as Individual Development Accounts (IDAs) saved "a higher proportion of their income" than participants who earned more.[54] This paralleled a finding that almost one-third of people making under $25,000 a year in 2018 spent less than their income, an encouraging sign that some had the capacity to save.[55]

This paradox—between lower-income households' interest and their difficulty in saving—suggests that the savings system is the problem, not the households themselves, and that obstacles to saving need to be removed. One obstacle consists of inferior institutional arrangements that make it harder for many lower-income workers to save. Another obstacle consists of outright penalties for savings by poor people, in the form of asset caps for public benefits. These limits perversely *discourage* the poorest families from scraping together even modest emergency funds that could help them withstand financial crises by disqualifying them for benefits, as I now discuss.

ASSET CAPS IN PUBLIC BENEFIT PROGRAMS

Asset caps for income-targeted support pose one of the worst hurdles to the ability of lower-income households to save. Many public assistance programs impose asset limits for applicants to qualify and for recipients to remain eligible. These programs include TANF, the Supplemental Nutrition Assistance Program (SNAP), and the Low Income Home Energy Assistance Program (LIHEAP). These asset limits can cause low-income households who anticipate needing public assistance down the road to refrain from saving to preserve eligibility.

A Thumbnail Sketch of Asset Limits in Public Assistance Programs

Asset limits in income-targeted programs have been around for years and rest on moral assumptions about the need to restrict public support to the "truly needy." Over time, however, asset caps have come into question for destabilizing poor households financially. In 2017, for instance, households who received cash support had 97 percent less wealth (with a median net worth of $1,835) than other households ($74,530).[56] This left families on public relief with barely any financial cushion for emergencies.

The federal government and many states responded to these concerns by relaxing asset caps to a limited extent.[57] Today, asset caps vary widely depending on the program and the state. By 2022, more than two-thirds of states had relaxed their asset caps for SNAP and LIHEAP.[58] Meanwhile, in the Affordable Care Act, Congress removed asset caps for the Medical Assistance (Medicaid) program in all fifty states (except for Medicaid nursing home benefits).

TANF, however, retains strict asset limits. In 2014, twenty-six states had asset caps for TANF of $2,500 or less, twelve had caps of $3,000 to $9,000, and eight had no asset caps for TANF.[59] In 2022, these numbers remained largely unchanged.[60] While some states exempt home equity and more often one or more vehicles from their asset caps for TANF, asset limits commonly apply to bank accounts; matched savings accounts; and retirement, education, and health savings accounts.[61]

Asset Limits Do More Harm Than Good

Asset caps have come under increased fire because they do not have their intended effect. Relaxing or removing asset caps does not induce more households to go on public relief. According to Pew Charitable Trusts, the seven states that scrapped their asset limits for TANF between 2000 and 2014 saw no statistically significant uptick in their TANF participation rates.[62] Similarly, there was no significant increase in SNAP participants in the thirty-four states that repealed their asset caps for food assistance over that same period.[63]

Asset limits also raise concerns about the costs associated with program churn (where households cycle in and out of relief programs). Recipients on public assistance must continue to observe those caps to remain eligible for benefits. But those who receive a one-time payment such as an EITC or student scholarship check may exceed the asset caps and lose their eligibility. Generally, those one-time funds are quickly exhausted, after which a recipient may reapply, often within a month of disqualification. Meanwhile, each time a household goes off and on assistance, the state spends money to recertify eligibility.[64]

Pew Charitable Trusts found that relaxing asset limits reduced administrative costs in TANF, possibly by lowering costs related to churn.[65] In another study, economists reported that reducing or abolishing asset limits for SNAP lowered the chance that households would cycle on and off of SNAP, while not increasing the total time recipients were on those benefits.[66]

Another open question is whether more generous asset caps (or none at all) make poorer people more likely to save, knowing that their savings will not disqualify them for future benefits if they need them. While the evidence is mixed, one leading study found that raising or eliminating asset limits for SNAP increased the chance that a low-income household had a bank account with $500 or more.[67]

In sum, asset limits do not benefit the states by reducing relief rolls or costs. At the same time, there is evidence that asset caps discourage poor families from saving. It is hypocritical to expect families who live close to the edge to save when state and federal laws penalize them harshly for doing so in times of need.

POOR PEOPLE DO NOT HAVE THE SAME ACCESS AS RICHER PEOPLE TO INSTITUTIONAL SUPPORT TO HELP THEM SAVE

So far, this chapter has explored why the "save more" admonition has failed for lower-income families. A common thread runs through most of those reasons: employees with retirement and health savings plans at work are much more successful at saving than lower-paid workers who lack those benefits. Partly, employees with workplace plans are better paid on average and presumably have more discretionary income to save. But another force is at work. Specifically, employees with workplace savings plans enjoy a double advantage—regardless of income—because those plans are better designed than DIY savings plans to help people save. Most workplace plans set up employees for success to a degree that DIY plans do not. The design features of those plans—not willpower or pay—are largely what make it possible for participants in these plans to save.[68]

Take the lucky employees who have 401(k) or similar retirement plans at work. Unlike with DIY plans, these employees do not have to sort through available retirement plans, providers, or thousands of investment options. Instead, their employers do the heavy lifting. The employers or their vendors research the relevant plans and laws, recruit plan administrators, and select the investment menus (ideally with the best low-fee index funds). Meanwhile, when new employees start their jobs, human resources offices walk them through their retirement savings options and help them complete the paperwork to start investing. The same is true for workplaces offering medical savings plans. In essence, workplace savings plans reduce inertia through the HR version of one-stop shopping.

This handholding continues after hiring. Many companies with savings plans continue to coach employees on the value of those plans throughout their tenure. Coaching can take the form of workshops, one-on-one counseling, and text or email reminders to workers to start saving or increase their savings rates. Many employers also offer retirement planning to older workers approaching retirement.

In addition, federal law allows and sometimes requires employers to add extra features that have been proven to help employees save. For instance, in 2022 Congress required most employers with retirement savings plans to auto-enroll all new, eligible hires in those plans unless they wish to opt out.[69] Research has shown that auto-enrollment dramatically boosts employee participation in retirement savings plans. One landmark study of three companies reported that participation rates for workers on the job six months jumped from a range of 26 to 42 percent before those companies instituted auto-enrollment to a range of 86 to 96 percent afterward.[70] Remarkably, less than 1 percent of employees who were automatically enrolled dropped out over the succeeding twelve months.[71]

In contrast, IRAs have markedly lower participation rates, in part because they do not offer auto-enrollment. On a similarly discouraging note, automatic enrollment of employees into emergency savings accounts faces legal hurdles and so has not been launched in the United States.[72]

Some employers offer employees a match to encourage them to save. When a match is on the table, the employer will pitch in money for every dollar that the employee contributes to a 401(k), up to the maximum match (which is 3.5% of salary at the median employer).[73] Half of companies with 401(k) plans do offer matches.[74] These matches have been shown to increase workers' 401(k) participation rates.[75] In contrast, IRAs and most other DIY accounts lack this powerful inducement because they do not offer matches.

Other bells and whistles in workplace plans help workers increase the amounts they save. Some plans, for instance, allow workers to instruct their companies to raise their annual contribution rate (e.g., by an extra $1,000 or 1 percent with each passing year). These and other auto-escalation features have been successful in boosting employees' savings.[76]

Finally, white-collar employers usually offer direct deposit of paychecks to their staff, which nudges those employees to open and maintain bank accounts. Lower-paid workers, however, are less likely to enjoy direct deposit arrangements at work.[77] Whenever that is the case, unbanked workers lack an important inducement to have bank accounts.

In short, lower-income people often lack the institutional support that helps better-off employees save. For employees fortunate enough to have access to them, these savings aids and subsidies make a difference in prompting them to save. Other people—who are generally poorer—fall outside this support system. Instead, they are relegated to the DIY world that is littered with roadblocks to saving.[78]

MORE EFFECTIVE SAVINGS PLANS FOR LOWER-INCOME HOUSEHOLDS HAVE NOT COME TO SCALE

In general, as we have seen, families who are less well-off are shut out of support systems to help them save. Despite that, there *have* been occasional savings innovations for lower-income households. These programs have not reached scale, however, and so they benefit relatively few people.

One promising development consists of low-fee or no-fee savings accounts at banks. Researchers have found that "[s]ubsidizing the costs of opening and maintaining bank accounts . . . increase[s] the take-up of formal savings accounts and, in some cases, savings balances."[79] Large banks have been reluctant to offer subsidized savings accounts to lower-income customers, however, with only 25 of the 101 largest banks offering them on attractive terms in 2020.[80]

Another interesting initiative involves IDAs, which are matched savings programs for low-income participants that are offered on a pilot basis in many states.[81] IDAs have been successful in helping people save. However, by 2008 "no IDA program ha[d] yet reached the scale of serving millions of people," and the first Trump administration later axed funding for the program.[82] The cost involved in matching savings likely has been a hurdle to the large-scale adoption of IDAs.

A third innovation consists of prize-linked savings accounts (PLS), which are targeted at ordinary households. In these programs, participants who regularly deposit money into savings accounts receive the right to enter lottery contests. Some participants win a prize, while the rest still have the money they saved, plus interest. PLS accounts have been slow to get off the ground, however, due in part to anti-gambling laws that prohibit banks and credit unions from offering those accounts in many states.[83]

Finally, Congress created tax-advantaged ABLE accounts in 2014 to allow disabled people to save money (up to $18,000 annually in 2024) without losing eligibility for Supplemental Security Income cash benefits.

However, the take-up rate is low, with only 1 percent of eligible people having ABLE accounts in 2021.[84]

FINANCIAL LITERACY IS NOT A PANACEA

Some financial experts also insist that people would save more if they had financial education. It is not clear, however, that financial knowledge alone results in more saving. On the contrary, successful savings programs frequently are centered on providing dollars through deposits or matching funds. But simply delivering the knowledge that savings are helpful does not overcome the real economic barriers people face in saving. Further, the cost of literacy programs may exceed their benefit.[85] In sum, financial education is not going to solve the lack of savings in so many families.

The call to save more has obvious appeal. People are on better footing financially the more they can save. As a result, thoughtfully designed policies to encourage discretionary savings have their place. I propose such a policy for emergency savings in chapter 6.

It is a different matter, however, to thrust heavy financial risks onto ordinary people and then insist, after they are left holding the bag, that they save enough money to absorb those risks alone. The personal responsibility ethos that underlies this policy is hypocritical, given the enormous offloading of risk from corporations and governments onto individuals in the past fifty years. Even more importantly, the paucity of savings by so many Americans confirms that the admonition to save more is fundamentally flawed, especially for lower-income families.

This chapter has identified multiple reasons why savings alone have failed to improve economic well-being for the bottom half of Americans. There are scant federal tax subsidies for the emergency savings that these families most need. In contrast, the federal government bestows lavish tax subsidies on homeownership and retirement, college, and health savings accounts. Most of those subsidies flow to richer taxpayers, and people in the lowest tax brackets receive little to no tax incentives to enroll in those plans. In addition, the most generous retirement and health savings plans, which white-collar employees demand, are off-limits to most reduced-wage workers because their employers rarely offer them. The DIY savings options that *are* available to lower-income households lack the same institutional support that workplace savings plans offer and that have made a major difference in helping people save. Finally, asset limits for public assistance actively penalize many poorer families for saving. Together, these policies make it significantly more difficult for lower-income families to amass savings.

Bottom line, the campaign to "save more" has failed to improve the economic security of lower-income families. Further, there is an even bigger problem with policymakers' fixation on savings. That fixation ignores the fact that it is more effective to pool many financial risks across groups than to drop those risks on individuals' shoulders. That is why most people have health insurance, for example, instead of saving up for all their medical bills themselves. In the next chapter, I explore when it makes sense to use risk sharing to lift financial risks off individuals and spread those risks more broadly.

5 The Importance of Sharing Risk

> Everybody is vulnerable to a sudden reduction in income,
> regardless of his or her station in life. Society needs some
> mechanism to guard against the risk when it is most likely
> to occur.
>
> Stanford D. Ross in *Family Weekly*, June 24, 1979,
> quoted in Varian (1980)

Over the past fifty years, society's commitment to economic well-being backslid, shunting large financial risks onto individuals that government and employers used to bear. By no means was that inevitable. In the past, the United States repeatedly has harnessed institutions to lift unmanageable risks off of individuals and spread them across society.[1] Some of those institutions, such as unemployment insurance, have broken down. Others, such as Social Security, remain a mainstay. In this chapter, I argue that it is time to revive America's risk-sharing tradition and expand it to relieve the excessive financial risks on ordinary households.

AN INTRODUCTION TO RISK AND RISK SHARING

Risk sharing, essentially, is an arrangement for mutual self-protection. In it, people pool sums of money to spread some risk across the pool. Individuals who contribute qualify for compensation by the pool if they later are hit by that risk and incur a loss.[2]

Before we unpack the concept of risk sharing, first we need to define the term *risk*. At a purely intuitive level, risk refers to the idea that the future could result in "more than one outcome."[3] Economists use the word *risk* in two ways, and both pertain here. In its narrow sense, risk refers to a possible future loss whose likelihood and magnitude are *knowable* because statisticians can estimate them. For instance, the federal government calculated that the chance of dying in a car accident in 2020 was 1 in 8,527.[4] This calculation describes a risk in its narrow sense because the risk was knowable. In other words, the government was able to pin down the likelihood of death due to a car crash (1 in 8,527) and the severity if a fatal car crash occurred (which, by definition, was a death).

Some risks, however, do not lend themselves to quantification. Statisticians may not be able to gauge the chance of a loss at a given point in time. Or if a loss occurs, they may not be able to predict its size. The economist Frank Knight termed this situation *uncertainty*, and economists also use the word *risk* in this broader sense.[5] The chance of a future financial crisis and the risk of loss from climate change are both uncertain risks. As this chapter discusses, this distinction between uncertain risks and knowable risks affects the ability of private insurers to insure a risk.

Turning now to risk sharing, virtually everyone faces financial risks, ranging from the chance of job loss to catastrophic medical costs. Risk sharing takes a risk that someone otherwise would absorb alone—say, losses due to a fire—and spreads the cost of that risk across a bigger pool of people, each of whom originally contributed funds to help cover the losses. In the best circumstances, the risk never comes to pass, and no one suffers a loss. If the worst happens, though, and the risk materializes, the injured person will no longer bear the loss alone. Instead, the pool will defray most or all of the loss. In the process, risk sharing improves social welfare by protecting members from financial losses while affording them peace of mind.[6]

Risk sharing raises intriguing questions. Why would someone join a risk-sharing scheme? Who is likely to sign up, and who is not? These questions commonly arise in the private insurance setting.

THE ROLE OF PRIVATE INSURANCE IN SHARING RISK

When people think of risk sharing, private insurance usually comes to mind. There are good reasons for that. The purpose of insurance is to relieve individuals and businesses from potentially crushing financial risks by spreading those risks across a pool. That begs the question, however, of why people would spend their hard-earned money to join a pool in the first place.

In a perfectly rational world, people would not care whether they paid insurance premiums or gambled on a possible future loss, so long as their expected wealth turned out the same.[7] For instance, say that the chance of getting into an automobile accident in any one year is 6 percent. A rational woman would not care if she paid 6 percent of the expected cost of a car accident in auto insurance premiums every year or simply waited to see if a collision occurred. In either case, her wealth would be the same. We would call this rational woman *risk-neutral*.

But indifference to risk does not sound especially practical or comforting. Most of us lack the knowledge or skill to know whether our expected wealth would be the same. More to the point, many people live so close to the edge that they could not afford a devastating loss, even if the likelihood was small.

Understandably, then, most individuals are *risk-averse*. They are nervous that disaster will wipe them out financially, even if the probability is slight. People who are risk-averse do not like unpredictability and will pay a modest sum to eliminate it. They would rather pay a small amount up front to avoid a larger but unknown future loss.[8]

Risk aversion is what makes risk sharing possible. People contribute to a kitty to cover future losses of some of the people in the pool, because no one in the pool knows exactly who will suffer a loss in the coming period. If someone knew for sure that she would not experience a particular loss, she would not participate. In contrast, uncertainty about the future makes people willing to contribute money to a pool to defray the risk of a loss.

But for risk sharing to take place, there has to be someone on the other side who is risk neutral: in other words, someone who must be willing to accept the risk that risk-averse people want to off-load, in return for a premium payment. That is the insurer.

Query, though: Why aren't insurers risk-averse too? In other words, why are insurers willing to assume other people's risks and reimburse them if they suffer an insured loss? This is why: insurers are willing to take on our risks when statistics make it profitable. Insurers cannot predict exactly who will suffer a loss. But often, by using statistics, they can predict the chance that some people in a large group of individuals will be harmed and the likely size of their losses. So insurers even out the probability that any one of us will suffer harm by insuring people as a group.

This ability to estimate losses accurately allows insurers to offer insurance at attractive prices. Once again, let's assume that the chance that a random driver will have a car accident in a given year is 6 percent. Spreading the losses from six thousand auto accidents over one hundred thousand people significantly lowers the premiums that each person pays, while covering any losses and providing peace of mind. In this way, insurance improves the welfare of everyone in the pool.[9]

Private insurance is the most familiar form of risk sharing, and examples abound. People buy insurance to insure their homes and cars. They buy insurance to pay their medical bills. They even buy policies to insure their lives.

Still, private insurance has its limits. A risk has to satisfy certain requirements for private insurance to be profitable. As a result, there are major risks—such as unemployment or medical care for the elderly—that flunk these requirements and that private insurers refuse to cover. These coverage gaps have given rise to other forms of risk sharing that are better suited to handle the uncertainty posed by those risks.

THE LIMITS OF PRIVATE INSURANCE

As we have seen, insurance is *actuarial* because it depends on the ability to forecast two numbers: the likelihood of a loss and the expected size of that loss if it occurs.[10] An insurer needs to pin down these two statistics to set the premiums to cover its costs and turn a profit. Because insurers are in business to make a profit, they will not insure a risk unless they can project its probability and the size of the expected loss. That means that uncertain risks are uninsurable, at least by private insurers.[11]

Wildfires due to climate change are one example of an uncertain risk. As climate change has surged and wildfires have exploded in scale, insurers have lost confidence in their ability to predict future wildfire trends. As a result, property insurers are threatening to exit the market for wildfire risk in states such as California.

Insurers have difficulty covering wildfires for a second reason, which is that wildfires pose correlated risk.[12] If a wildfire consumes one person's home, the home next door is likely to burn down too. Wildfires pose a correlated risk because they spread easily, exposing neighbors to fire losses as well.

Correlated risks make it hard to charge affordable premiums because they can trigger widespread, simultaneous losses to much of the pool. As the percentage of policyholders expected to sustain losses rises, premiums also must rise. If premiums increase to unaffordable levels, demand for the coverage may dry up. To avoid this scenario, private insurers try to limit their coverage to independent risks, where the chance that one person will experience an accident does not increase the chance that the same type of accident will befall someone else.[13]

Correlated risks are not confined to natural disasters. They also can include major financial risks affecting economic well-being. A recession, for instance, can trigger a chain reaction of unemployment as depressed sales cause employers to slash jobs, which further depresses sales as the buying power of jobless workers dries up. There is no private market for unemployment insurance during recessions because mass unemployment is a correlated risk.[14]

Insurers also may decline to cover a risk due to moral hazard concerns.[15] Moral hazard refers to decisions by policyholders to take more risks or fewer precautions *because* they are insured.[16] Arson—when an owner torches his property to collect on the insurance—is a classic illustration of moral hazard.

Insurers have a slew of techniques, from copays and deductibles to risk-based pricing, to discourage moral hazard.[17] Still, if policyholders retain too much control over whether an insured risk materializes, private insurers may refuse to insure the risk.[18]

Adverse selection is another issue that may prompt insurers to refuse coverage.[19] Adverse selection can arise when customers have confidential knowledge about their risks to which insurers are not privy.[20] Someone shopping for health insurance might privately know, for instance, that he will need a hip replacement operation, while insurers do not. Adverse selection occurs if he and other hip repair candidates rush to enroll in health insurance and drive up the size of the average claim.

If insurers cannot distinguish healthy customers from sick ones in advance, they may raise premiums to cover the risk of higher claims. Low-risk customers who find the premiums too costly may opt out of insurance. A vicious cycle could then ensue as rising claims force insurers to hike premiums, driving more safe customers away. Meanwhile, competitors will have incentives to cut their premiums to lure those safe customers away.[21]

Real-world examples of this adverse selection "death spiral" are rare. Nevertheless, there are historical examples of gaps in private coverage due to adverse selection. In the years leading up to Medicare's 1965 enactment, private insurers were reluctant to offer individual health policies to the elderly "because they comprised a high-risk group."[22] The problem became so pronounced that over half of older adults had no health insurance.[23] More recently, insurers curtailed or denied individual health coverage to almost half of those with preexisting conditions before the Affordable Care Act (ACA) was passed.[24]

So far, this discussion has focused on gaps in the supply of private insurance. But the insurance market also can break down due to lack of demand.[25] For instance, there may be insufficient demand for insurance if consumers underestimate the chance of a loss. Young adults who skip health insurance because they think they will live forever (the so-called Young Invincibles) are a well-known example of this phenomenon.[26]

People also may forgo private insurance because they expect the government to compensate them for losses.[27] In other circumstances, people may go uninsured due to the cost.[28] Sometimes the only available insurance coverage is overpriced (because carriers offering that insurance charge customers more than their expected losses). At other times, coverage may be fairly priced yet unaffordable (as residents are discovering with flood insurance in coastal zones).[29]

In short, while we like to think of private insurance as the quintessential form of risk sharing, some risks lack private coverage. Repeatedly throughout the years, society has responded by developing other risk-sharing mechanisms that are equipped to overcome the obstacles to private insurance. The next section turns to one of the leading alternative mechanisms for sharing risk, social insurance.

THE SPECIAL ROLE OF SOCIAL INSURANCE
IN POOLING AND SPREADING RISK

Many years ago, the economist and Nobel Prize winner Kenneth Arrow wrote that in the United States, when private insurance has coverage gaps, there is a long tradition of "nonmarket social institutions . . . attempting to bridge" those gaps.[30] Social insurance is a leading example.

Social insurance offers coverage that the traditional private market does not supply. In most cases, social insurance has government involvement, which can take several forms. The government may be the sole provider (as with Social Security and Original Medicare). Alternatively, the government may organize the market for the insurance, but outsource its delivery to private-sector insurers (as for individual marketplace policies under the ACA). In a third, hybrid model, the private sector provides the first line of insurance, but the government provides a financial backstop. This can take the form of loss sharing (in which the government covers part of the claims) or the creation of special government insurance plans filling in part of the market (such as state residual auto insurance plans for high-risk drivers).[31]

Social insurance plays a unique role in pooling and spreading risk because it draws on special powers to solve some of the limitations on private insurance.[32] One limitation involves uncertain risks, in which insurers have difficulty estimating the probability of occurrence and the size of expected losses.[33] Often for these risks, statistical forecasts become fuzzier as the time horizon grows longer. That makes private insurers reluctant to underwrite those risks, because overly optimistic projections could result in catastrophic losses and capsize the insurers. These risks include many that are central to households' financial security, including the risk of a recession, the risk of poor health, and the risk of outliving one's money.[34] Accordingly, social insurance has a special role to play in ensuring economic well-being.

Of course, there is no reason to think that the government is any better positioned than the private sector to forecast risks accurately. But the government has two advantages with respect to uncertain risks that private insurers lack. First, the government has the powers to tax and to borrow and so is better equipped to defray the financial toll from underestimated losses.[35] Second, the federal government has sovereign immunity, so it cannot be forced into receivership.[36] This stands in contrast to private insurers, who, if they go broke, likely would end up in receivership and have to renege on their commitments to policyholders.[37] This difference allows customers who fear that private carriers might be forced to close their doors to trust the federal government to stay in business. The federal government's immunity from forced insolvency is one reason Social Security has a level of public trust to which private annuities only can aspire.

To be sure, Congress could curtail social insurance programs prospectively. But doing so would risk high political costs. For one thing, most social insurance programs have such broad coverage that much of the population is personally invested in the programs' continuation. For another, when individuals have paid into the system—often for decades—they naturally believe that they have earned their benefits. Both dynamics make programs such as Social Security and Medicare difficult to cut.

Governments have powers to address insufficient demand for insurance as well. One of the most potent, and controversial, powers is the power to compel citizens to enroll in social insurance plans. Only the government—not private insurers—can make insurance mandatory. The federal government effectively requires broad swaths of workers to participate in Social Security and Medicare by assessing them payroll taxes to finance both programs. Another more recent and explosive example is the original health insurance mandate imposed by Congress in the ACA.[38]

Compulsory insurance combats adverse selection and its mirror image problem, a lack of demand by low-risk customers. It does so by requiring everyone—including low-risk individuals—to join a social insurance pool.[39] Universal participation ensures a larger pool and helps the program cover its costs. It also improves social welfare by ensuring that people who don't think they need coverage now will have it later if they need it.[40]

Compulsory participation can raise other issues, however, by requiring some participants to pay premiums that they cannot afford. To address this issue, social insurance programs often subsidize the premiums that some policyholders pay. Sometimes this is achieved by requiring some participants to pay more than other participants who cannot afford as much. In other cases (such as Medicare Part B), the government subsidizes the pool from general tax revenues.[41]

Adverse selection can result in another serious problem that econo-mists discuss less often.[42] Private carriers may respond to perceived ad-verse selection by denying high-risk customers coverage or refusing to renew their policies. Social insurance can deal with this problem through "community rating" provisions. These provisions restrict the ability to re-ject people for coverage or deny coverage of specific risks.[43] A good ex-ample is the ACA, which grants eligibility to almost everyone under age sixty-five and insures important health risks that private carriers had de-clined in the past.[44] In these ways, social insurance makes use of unique governmental powers to overcome obstacles that generate gaps in private insurance coverage.

RISK SHARING AND SOCIAL INSURANCE

Up to this point, I have called on policymakers to rely more heavily on risk sharing to insure against large financial risks that individuals now bear. Some critics argue, however, that social insurance is not actually risk sharing, but redistribution in disguise. For instance, the community rat-ing provisions in the ACA could be deemed redistributive because they prohibit charging older, sicker policyholders their full risk-adjusted cost.[45] Based on these redistributive aspects, some critics disparage social insur-ance as a cousin to welfare.

These critics are mistaken on several scores. For one thing, redistrib-utive elements can (and often do) flow just as much to the rich as to the poor.[46] More importantly, social insurance uses many of the same tech-niques to pool and spread risk as private insurance. Both rely heavily on contributions by participants to cover losses. Eligibility for payouts fre-quently depends on a record of sufficient prior contributions to the pool. Everyone is familiar with that model in Social Security, in which workers pay payroll taxes into the fund and qualify for old-age benefits after ten years of contributions.

Social insurance further resembles private insurance because it uses an actuarial model to bring in sufficient cash—in terms of contributions plus earnings on investments—to cover claims payouts and overhead. Difficul-ties in forecasting uncertain risks and losses mean that social insurance cannot always adhere to an actuarial model as strictly as private insurance. Nevertheless, social insurance programs take actuarial projections seriously and use those projections to balance their books whenever possible.[47]

Finally, and also like private insurance, social insurance normally only covers potential future events, not risks that already materialized.[48] Both private and social insurance spread the risk of future events across people who bear that risk.[49] The difference is that social insurance often defines the people who face a particular risk according to a substantially longer time frame than private insurance, which typically only looks forward one year at a time.[50] As James Kwak has stressed, this difference—the short policy period that private insurers typically use versus the lifelong time horizon that social insurance sometimes employs—is key to understanding why what looks like redistribution in social insurance actually is risk pooling and spreading.

This risk sharing protects a group of people against a risk *that has not yet materialized.* In contrast, redistribution shifts funds from people who have not experienced a loss to people who have. Redistribution looks backward because the loss being compensated already has occurred. Risk sharing, in contrast, is prospective. In risk-sharing arrangements, the risk being insured is strictly limited to future events, and so by definition, none of the members of the pool has yet sustained a loss at the beginning of the policy period. Bottom line, redistribution compensates losses that have already happened, while risk sharing insures against future losses.

How one draws this distinction can depend on the time frame. We don't think of Social Security as primarily redistributive, for example. But imagine that the policy period for Social Security started on New Year's Day each year and lasted one year. The Social Security Administration would know who would reach full retirement age during the coming year, starting on January 1. Most of those people would start collecting Social Security and thus would start drawing on the pool. Meanwhile, younger people would be paying into the Social Security system to pay for their old-age benefits. Using a one-year snapshot makes Social Security look redistributive because workers subsidize retirees for a risk (reaching retirement age) that is certain to materialize.[51]

But snapshots in time can be misleading. Imagine instead defining the "policy period" of social insurance, not as one year starting every

January 1, but as the length of each person's life, starting at birth. When we redefine the policy period this way, the redistributive impression fades away. That is because, at the moment of our births, virtually all of the risks that will confront us over our lifetimes are, by definition, *unknown*. Our work history, our earnings trajectory, our health, our wealth, and our lifespan at that point are nothing more than question marks and will only reveal themselves with time. At birth, none of us knows who will suffer losses and how severe that harm could be. Some infants may be at higher risk for poor health or low earnings than others, but almost no one is immune from these risks over a lifetime.

The cradle-to-grave nature of social insurance means that social insurance covers the unknown risks facing us at birth. As such, social insurance *is* risk sharing in its classic sense, as Kwak argued, because "it spreads the risk of uncertain future events across the people who face that risk."[52] This form of insurance still may retain a redistributive element in its pricing.[53] Nevertheless, when we describe social insurance programs as social safety nets, what we are really saying is that social insurance is there to guard against the chance that some bad event will strike, not over one year, but over one's lifetime. This is a risk that every newborn faces.

Seen from the perspective of each person at their birth, social insurance thus is a central part of the venerable American tradition of risk-sharing arrangements. Risk sharing, moreover, is not just limited to private and social insurance. It also is a feature of income-targeted programs, as I now discuss.

INCOME-TARGETED PROGRAMS SIMILARLY POOL AND SPREAD RISK

Welfare and other income-targeted programs are at the top of the list of complaints about redistribution. These programs appear redistributive because they transfer money in real time from higher-income taxpayers to people who qualify as poor.

But like social insurance, income-targeted programs pool and spread risk. They do so by managing the risk that people's incomes will drop below the level required for basic living needs. As the acclaimed economist

Hal Varian pointed out in the quotation at the start of this chapter, everyone faces this risk, starting at birth and continuing throughout their lives. When seen from this lifelong perspective, income-targeted benefits similarly pool and spread risk.[54]

Some might contest this, arguing that poverty is handed down from generation to generation, and so is wealth. According to this thinking, some never will face poverty during their lifetimes because their parents are wealthy. Others are born into poverty and will remain poor all their lives.

These are just assertions, however, and we can test them by examining the evidence. A large proportion of US adults *do* experience significant drops in income from time to time, confirming Varian's observation that "everybody is vulnerable to a sudden reduction in income, regardless of his or her station in life."[55] About one-third of households made less in 2005 than they did in 1996.[56] These so-called negative income shocks have gotten worse over the past fifty years and doubled between 1969 and 2004.[57] While income fluctuations are nothing new, since 1980, "large downward movements in earnings (what could be thought of as disaster shocks)" have outnumbered large increases in income.[58] Income volatility—and the chance of loss of income—has gotten worse for all demographic groups and ages in the United States over past decades.[59] The greatest volatility is seen among earners at the top and bottom of the income spectrum.[60]

Moreover, these negative income shocks are much bigger than previously assumed. The economist Fatih Guvenen reports, for example, that "extremely large shocks are experienced far more often than a bell curve would have us believe."[61] By his estimates, the chance that a worker will suffer an 80 percent drop in income "is eight to 12 times higher in the data than under normality."[62] According to Hacker and Jacobs, "around 15% of workers experience a drop in their earnings of 50% or greater every year."[63]

Here, a caveat is necessary. Some pay cuts are the result of people's voluntary decisions to reduce their income (by cutting back work hours, for instance, to enjoy more leisure time). Many negative income shocks, however, are due to outside forces over which people lack control.[64] For instance, households suffer large income drops more frequently during recessions.[65] Similarly, declines in real hourly pay are likely to be involuntary because workers are generally reluctant to cut their hourly rates.[66]

Other external events also can depress income. As people age, for instance, their incomes generally fall, starting in their fifties or sixties and continuing beyond.[67] Divorce also ups the chance of a drop in income.[68]

To get some sense of the risk of lost income due to external forces, it is worth asking how many people will experience poverty in their lives. Almost no one chooses to be poor. Yet almost 60 percent of American households ages twenty through seventy-five experience poverty for at least one year in their lives.[69] And while they are poor, their level of financial strain "is troubling."[70]

At the same time, poverty is not permanent for most. From 2013 through 2016, for instance, only a tiny fraction—2.8 percent—of the US population lived in poverty all forty-eight months.[71] Another study that examined poverty starting in 2007 found that only one out of twenty people was continuously poor "for all 11 years through 2018."[72] Instead, there is substantial upward mobility out of poverty, with people on the lowest income rung experiencing the biggest percentage increases in income compared to people making more.[73] Still, negative income shocks caused many of them to become poor in the first place, and rising unemployment is a top reason people go on welfare.[74]

All told, large percentages of people experience an involuntary loss in income sometime during their working years.[75] Despite that, virtually everyone pays income and/or payroll taxes during their lives. For example, 91 percent of households studied over a ten-year span paid those taxes for all or part of that period. When retirees were excluded, that percentage rose to 96 percent of households ages twenty through sixty-two.[76] The authors of that study concluded that the average person paid $142,534 in federal income taxes while receiving $7,290 in cash government benefits over the period studied, meaning that the average person paid in $135,244 more than they took out in benefits.[77]

For these reasons, income-targeted programs act as risk-sharing mechanisms. Virtually everyone pays income or payroll taxes during their careers. Meanwhile, the government sponsors public assistance programs to guard against the risk of involuntary loss of income that most people face at some point in their lives. People pay up-front taxes in exchange for knowing that income-targeted programs are there to support them if they become impoverished.[78] In that respect, income-targeted programs resemble other risk-sharing schemes.

To conclude, risk sharing is strongly preferable to forcing households to bear large financial risks alone. Risk sharing takes risks that could devastate family finances and disperses them throughout a pool that is better equipped financially to bear them. In the process, risk sharing improves welfare in a number of ways. It reduces risk for every member of the pool while alleviating financial anxiety. It frees up money in household budgets for other financial goals that increase economic well-being. And it positions everyone in the pool to flourish economically and lead more productive and rewarding lives.

THE LONG AMERICAN TRADITION OF POOLING AND SPREADING RISK

We saw in chapter 3 that social safety nets have frayed, leaving households to fend for themselves. Submerged within that story is a more hopeful narrative, however. When we go back in time, we find that the United States has a long history of risk-sharing systems that are designed to protect families from economic ruin. These systems range from private insurance to social insurance and income-targeted support.

While some of these risk-sharing arrangements have dwindled, others remain firm, and newer ones have come to the fore. These arrangements provide the scaffolding for a more robust system of risk sharing that could improve economic well-being for tens of millions of struggling families.

The genesis of these arrangements dates back to the late nineteenth century, when the United States shifted from an agrarian economy to industrialization and growing numbers of laborers migrated to cities to work in factories. A turning point came shortly after 1870, when the majority of adult laborers had left agriculture.[79] Previously, when so much economic activity had centered on farms, families had been more self-sufficient because they produced their own food and other necessities. Farm communities also had a long tradition of rallying to support neighbors when disaster struck, whether from injury, death, or otherwise.

With the rise of industrialization and specialization, however, factory workers relinquished their old support systems and self-sufficiency for near-total dependence on wages. Unemployment, which had been uncommon on farms, suddenly became a terrifying prospect for industrial workers. Factory workers were at the mercy of forces including firings, workplace accidents, poor health, disability, and old age. If they became unable to work, workers often were "totally without resources, unable to fall back on home production or on the mixture of part-time employment and self-employment which might be found in rural society."[80]

Industrialization and the ensuing vulnerability to wage loss generated pressure for the adoption of risk-sharing mechanisms for laborers. One of the earliest developments was the introduction of industrial life insurance in the late nineteenth century. Private insurance companies marketed exorbitantly priced policies to workers as nest eggs for surviving family members in the event of their deaths.[81] Workers shelled out even more for other private insurance that only covered one type of risk—for instance, a workplace accident or firing. In many cases, the insurers who supplied those policies were precarious financially and had inadequate reserves to cover claims.

In view of the shaky nature and meager payouts of these early workers' policies, progressive reformers pushed for more comprehensive workers' coverage by the government. Their earliest victory was the passage of workers' compensation by most states by 1920.[82] Workers' compensation pays employees who are injured or killed at work for lost wages and medical bills, without requiring them to prove that their employers were negligent. In exchange for immunity from tort judgments for workplace injuries, the government compelled employers to pay premiums to finance workers' compensation.[83] In this fashion, workers' compensation spreads risk by taking a cost that previously had fallen almost exclusively on injured laborers and dispersing it across employers.[84] Today, workers' compensation is a well-established plank of the US system of worker protections.

The Great Depression ushered in the next three major advances in risk-sharing mechanisms for workers: unemployment insurance, Social Security old-age pensions, and welfare benefits, all of which Congress enacted in the Social Security Act of 1935.[85] Two of the poor relief programs instituted by the 1935 Act—Old Age Assistance and Aid to the Blind—were targeted at elderly and blind persons who did not qualify for Social Security or were otherwise too poor to maintain a basic standard of living. Later, in 1972, Congress replaced both programs with the Supplemental

Security Income (SSI) program. The 1972 legislation also authorized SSI benefits to the poor who were permanently and totally disabled.[86]

A companion provision of the Social Security Act authorized support for needy children in households without fathers. That program became AFDC and continued until 1996, when Congress replaced it and cut benefits in TANF.[87]

In the wake of the Great Depression, meanwhile, health coverage mostly remained the province of the private sector. During World War II, employers began offering private health insurance more often to their workers. Despite the uptick in private health insurance during World War II, large gaps in medical coverage remained. Among them were spotty health coverage for the aged, whom insurers considered a "bad risk" due to their declining health.[88] In addition, some younger and middle-aged people who did qualify for private health insurance could not afford the premiums.

Congress addressed both problems in 1965 with the passage of Medicare and Medicaid. Medicare provides federal health insurance for all age sixty-five and up, without regard to income. Medicaid, meanwhile, provides health benefits to indigent persons of all ages.[89] Medicare spreads the risk of illness through payroll contributions paid by employers and workers, while Medicaid finances the spreading of health risks for the poor through tax revenues.

With expanded health coverage in place, Congress circled back to the topic of income supports for workers. To encourage more people to work, Congress enacted a new tax credit in 1975 to boost the pay of low-income workers.[90] The credit, which eventually became known as the EITC, had broad bipartisan support.[91] Today, the EITC is "the largest permanent federal needs-tested antipoverty program that provides cash assistance."[92]

In 1997 Congress mandated a second federal tax credit for workers, known as the Child Tax Credit, with both parties' support.[93] The CTC reduces the federal income tax liability of most parents for every eligible child, while spreading the risk of childcare costs across the federal tax base.[94]

The most well-known risk-sharing initiative in recent years, of course, is the expansion of health insurance in the ACA in 2010. Although Medicare and Medicaid vastly improved health care for the elderly and the poor, the rest of the population faced yawning gaps in health coverage.[95] The ACA sought to close those gaps through improved risk sharing. The act created new health exchanges that expanded the size of insured pools in the individual market. This enabled a given patient's health bills to be spread across a much larger population. In addition, the ACA's original mandate swept many healthy younger adults who previously were uninsured into insured pools.

In short, the United States has a long history of risk sharing to protect individual households from economic hardship. Some of these arrangements are offered by the private sector, while others are sponsored by the government. Some of those programs, such as private and social insurance, are overtly contributory in nature, while other government programs are means-tested and shift risk intertemporally from taxpayers during flush periods in their lives to future periods when they might need government support.

There are two important takeaways from these programs, whatever their form. The existence of these programs stands as a testament to the long American tradition of risk sharing. At the same time, some of the most important risk-sharing arrangements are showing their age.

Given the heavy financial burdens on tens of millions of Americans, there is an urgent need to institute new forms of risk sharing that are better suited to today's labor conditions. The juxtaposition of the older, New Deal–era programs with their newer risk-sharing counterparts raises important questions in that respect. How can risk-sharing programs be better designed to protect families against poverty without getting mired in the blame game against the poor? How can obsolescent programs be redesigned to address the realities of today's work landscape? Should we continue to provide key risk-sharing supports for employees through the workplace, or should those systems be transferred to the government? Finally, how can we marshal public support for spreading other financial risks that workers continue to face? In the remainder of the book, I explore these questions in five areas that are vital to economic well-being: making ends meet, buying a home, adequate health coverage, paying for college, and a secure retirement.

PART III

The Road to Economic
Well-Being

6 Making Ends Meet

When Luis turned twenty-three and became a single dad, he took a job at McDonald's at $7.25 an hour, which was the federal minimum wage. That didn't pay for a crib for his two-month-old infant, let alone diapers. One year in, he asked for a raise, but his boss said no. Three years later, he was promoted to manager, but only got a raise of $1 an hour. Luis finally decided, "I can't support my child on this," and got a second job while going to school and caring for his girl.[1]

Luis worked himself to the bone but still could not support his daughter or pay his bills. His constant worry—just making ends meet—is the most pressing objective of economic well-being. It is a top priority because it is crucial to securing the food, shelter, and clothes that come first in Maslow's hierarchy of needs.[2] Unless families can make it through the month, other milestones such as owning their homes, paying for college, and worry-free retirement will be out of reach. Consequently, making ends meet is the linchpin of the other milestones of economic well-being.

Making ends meet requires a living income. A living income is just enough to subsist on, no more. Yet half of American households are forced to live on less.[3] This problem is so widespread that it dwarfs the extent of poverty in size. It spans tens of millions of households who are not officially poor but are barely treading water. The fact that every other person struggles to make ends meet is the biggest obstacle to economic well-being in the United States.

In order to assure working families a living income, two problems must be addressed. The first is the lack of a sufficient regular income for low-paid workers. This will require boosting their earnings from work. The second problem is the lack of adequate social safety nets when workers lose their jobs. These two challenges—a living income while working and a safety net for unemployment—are the focus of this chapter.

ATTAINING A LIVING INCOME

To make ends meet, people need enough cash to pay for basic expenses as they come due. Almost everyone pays their bills out of income. As a matter of principle, everyone should be assured enough income to make it through the month without having to incur debt.

In the labor context, pay levels are the product of bargaining conditions over wages. Traditionally, private-sector pay has been set through negotiations between employers and workers. The widespread lack of a living wage reflects the power imbalance between labor and employers in wage negotiations. That imbalance has gotten worse over the past fifty years.

During the heyday of unionization, organized labor was able to exact substantial wage increases for union members due to the threat of mass strikes. After private-sector unionization withered away, however, blue-collar workers were left to negotiate their pay one-on-one, with little reliable information about prevailing wages. The demise of collective bargaining gave companies the upper hand in wage negotiations. That, combined with the loss of well-paid manufacturing jobs, the rise in unpredictable work schedules and part-time hours, and anticompetitive practices by employers, depressed pay for tens of millions of workers below a subsistence wage.[4]

Poorly paid workers bear the brunt of low wages on multiple fronts.[5] Their paychecks do not cover basic necessities, including housing, food, transportation, childcare, and health expenses. By 2021, this shortfall was so severe that a minimum-wage worker could not afford rental housing anywhere in the United States.[6] Additionally, many find saving difficult and struggle with debt.

The harm from subpar pay further burdens society at large. Millions of low-wage workers have to go on public support despite working full-time. Almost half of families with at least one low-wage worker (47%) were enrolled in at least one public safety net program between 2015 and 2019.[7] Among those families, most were enrolled in the Earned Income Tax Credit program (53%), followed by Medicaid (40%), and SNAP food assistance (26%).[8] More than two-thirds of wage-earning adults on Medicaid and SNAP in 2018 worked full-time.[9]

In the process, employers of low-wage workers force taxpayers to subsidize their workforces through social safety nets. Typically, these companies are not mom-and-pop employers, by the way.[10] McDonald's, Walmart, and Amazon dominated lists of employers with the largest number of workers on public benefits.[11] Meanwhile, state and federal taxpayers paid the price, at an average cost of $107 billion annually between 2015 and 2019.[12]

With workers' budgets at the breaking point, higher pay is of top importance. There are three main ways to achieve that. The first is passing minimum wage laws, which require employers to internalize more of the cost of their workforces. Universal basic income proposals are the second approach and would draw on tax revenues to provide households with an income floor. Finally, proposals have been advanced to expand current tax subsidies to working families through the EITC and the Child Tax Credit.

MINIMUM WAGE LAWS

Congress enacted the federal minimum wage in 1938.[13] Unlike other policies discussed in this book, minimum wage laws do not spread risk per se. Instead, those laws require corporations and other employers to foot their own payroll costs rather than forcing taxpayers to subsidize workers who are paid less than a subsistence wage.

Currently, the federal minimum wage stands at $7.25 an hour.[14] A full-time worker would earn $15,080 a year at that rate. That is barely more than the federal poverty line (FPL) of $14,580 in 2024 for one person and is seriously under the poverty line for a family of two or more.[15] Anyone paid at today's federal minimum wage could work full-time and still be poor. More than 60 percent of all employees have worked for the minimum wage at some point, so the low minimum wage has far-ranging effects.[16]

The federal rate governs unless a state (or a city) has adopted a higher minimum wage for local residents. Forty-five states have their own minimum wage laws. In 2022, thirty states plus the District of Columbia set their minimum wages higher than the federal floor. Twelve of those states mandated further increases to their rates by 2026 to $15.00 an hour.[17]

Despite the ubiquity of minimum wage laws, critics have argued for decades that employment will shrink if the minimum wage is raised.[18] This was such an article of faith that the *New York Times* trumpeted in 1987: "There's a virtual consensus among economists that the minimum wage is an idea whose time has passed." The headline read: "The Right Minimum Wage: $0.00."[19] But in an earth-shaking article in 1994, economists David Card and Alan Krueger toppled that received wisdom with new data showing that a law raising New Jersey's minimum wage did not reduce total fast-food employment in New Jersey and even may have had a small positive effect.[20] Card and Krueger kicked off a whole new line of research, which replicated their findings.[21] Years later, while reviewing that research, the economist Alan Manning proclaimed: "It is time to call a truce" and "acknowledge that no clear evidence of a negative effect [of minimum wage laws] on employment has been found."[22] That same year, Card won the Nobel Prize in Economics for his and Krueger's work. Poignantly, Krueger did not receive the Nobel, having tragically died two years earlier.

With their findings, Card and Krueger redefined the terms of the debate. Today, the central issue is the minimum wage's failure to assure subsistence pay.[23] MIT researchers estimated that for 2022, a family of four needed to earn $25.02 per hour, or $104,077.70 per year, pretax, to make a living income.[24] Even though a living income only covers the bare necessities and no frills, the $7.25 federal minimum wage pays less than one-third of that amount (with both parents working). Even in states where the minimum wage is scheduled to increase to $15.00 an hour, those rates are substantially lower than the 2022 living wage for a family of four.[25]

Most minimum wage laws have another flaw, which is that they do not keep up with inflation. Since 2009, the federal hourly rate of $7.25 has not increased a cent, the longest period in history without an increase.[26] Meanwhile, by 2019 the buying power of the federal minimum wage had shrunk nearly one-third from its 1968 peak.[27]

Coverage loopholes are another defect of our minimum wage laws. Federal law, for example, exempts employers from paying the $7.25 minimum wage to people with disabilities, teenage workers, and workers paid through tips, among others.[28]

Together, these flaws make the minimum wage laws obsolete. For starters, Congress should eliminate the current loopholes in the federal minimum wage. These exemptions consign people who are in desperate need of wage protection to poverty-level pay, especially waitpersons, teenage workers, and employees with disabilities. In this day and age, to assert that these groups do not deserve $7.25 an hour—let alone a living wage— is untenable.

For the general workforce too, US minimum wage laws are stuck on "low" and need to be raised to a subsistence wage. The question is how high. Under the principle of equal pay for equal work, the new federal minimum wage should not pay workers differently based on family size. Instead, it should be set at the living wage for a single full-time worker with no dependents. Because the living wage varies by locale, the legislation also should adjust the federal minimum wage for local cost conditions and phase in those increases over several years.[29]

Finally, a new national law should index the federal minimum wage automatically for future inflation. This cost-of-living adjustment would ensure that the minimum wage maintained its purchasing power, without the need for legislative reenactment.

In sum, raising the federal minimum wage to a living wage is badly overdue. But that is only a first step. The new minimum wage would only provide a living income to full-time single workers with no kids. Low-wage workers with dependents and unpaid caregivers would need added support to have a living income. How to deliver that support is the subject of vigorous debate, as the next sections explore.

UNIVERSAL BASIC INCOME

The nagging inability to achieve a living income through minimum wage laws has contributed to increased calls in many countries for enactment of a universal basic income (UBI). UBI, in its purest form, would pay a regular cash stipend to all individuals with no strings attached, regardless of employment status, income, disability status, having children, or age.[30]

For the most part, UBI remains aspirational. However, there have been local pilot projects of UBI in the United States and elsewhere in the world.[31] In part due to those pilot projects, proposals for UBI have become part of the mainstream debate.

Nevertheless, UBI has not gained permanent traction anywhere to date.[32] The biggest reservations involve fiscal concerns. The International Labour Office (ILO) has reported that "ensuring adequate benefit levels . . . comes at a substantial cost."[33] In the United States, a UBI that paid 100 percent of the federal poverty level to every adult and child would cost about 28 percent of gross domestic product.[34] Paying such a heavy cost would require eliminating current cash benefits programs, raising taxes, or both.[35] Even at lower payment levels, the Executive Board of Directors of the International Monetary Fund considers UBI infeasible due in large part to its cost.[36]

Proposals for UBI also raise concerns about who would win and who would lose from a full-throated UBI program. In its purest form, the wealthy would count themselves among the winners because UBI would pay the highest-income earners the same cash benefits as the poor. Meanwhile, the less well-off, who are most in need of income support, could end up being losers if UBI supplanted their current public benefits with lower cash support. The most aggressive libertarian versions of UBI would replace Social Security and targeted benefits such as welfare and SNAP with UBI payments below the poverty line.[37] This approach, if it were budget-neutral, would deepen poverty and inequality by cutting current benefits.[38] Meanwhile, the winners would include employers, who no longer would have to pay Social Security taxes. The result would be to shift even more financial risk onto low-paid workers, as the ILO has emphasized.[39]

ARE UNIVERSAL PROGRAMS NECESSARY
TO WIN POLITICAL SUPPORT?

One reason UBI offers universal entitlements is to secure political support for its enactment. That raises the question of whether such broad entitlements are advisable or necessary for other income support programs to gain passage.

Recent US experience shows that income-targeted programs *can* win passage if they are thoughtfully designed.[40] In particular, targeted programs that extend beyond the poor and into the middle class have a track record of approval and expansion. The well-received EITC, for instance, paid benefits for 2024 to married couples with two children earning up to $62,688.[41] That year, the CTC was even more generous, going to joint filers with modified adjusted gross incomes of up to $400,000 a year.[42]

These two tax credits flip the narrative about who deserves government support by presuming that workers are entitled to assistance unless they make *too much.* The EITC and CTC also have broad support because people view them as "earned," and recipients have to file income tax returns in order to get the credits.[43] In part for these reasons, the EITC and the CTC have proven so popular that Congress has expanded them fourteen times since 1984.[44] The Republican Party platform espoused by the second Trump administration advocated even further expansion of the CTC.[45]

In another case of successful targeted benefits, Congress expanded Medicaid eligibility to millions of near-poor households in the Affordable Care Act in 2010.[46] After the Supreme Court ruled that states did not have to offer "Medicaid Expansion," voters nevertheless voted to adopt it in seven conservative states.[47]

In the ACA, Congress also subsidized premiums for households who enrolled in the ACA's Marketplace health insurance coverage. Initially, anyone earning up to four times the FPL qualified for premium subsidies. Then, starting in 2021, Congress extended those subsidies to everyone enrolled in Marketplace coverage, regardless of income, and later extended those subsidies through 2025.[48]

Authors Theda Skocpol and Robert Greenstein have argued that benefits targeted by income are more likely to win passage if they are designed with specific features in mind.[49] Programs providing benefits to the middle class and not just the poor are more likely to garner support. At the same time, benefits can be phased out by income so that the most generous amounts go to those who earn the least.[50] Programs linked to income also are significantly cheaper than universal programs and less likely to generate opposition from fiscal hawks.

When it comes to cash support, programs serving working families or people whom society does not expect to work (such as older adults, the disabled, and children) have greater prospects of enactment than programs serving unemployed, nondisabled adults. Similarly, programs offering in-kind benefits, such as SNAP, typically attract more support than cash assistance. Still, cash support can win passage if it is delivered through the tax system (such as the EITC) or financed with payroll taxes on workers (as with Social Security).[51] In fact, the Internal Revenue Service relies on this logic when it urges people to claim the EITC, saying: "You earned it, 'now file, claim it and get it.'"[52]

In short, there are proven ways to deliver income support effectively without incurring the high cost or political controversy of UBI. The United States, in fact, already has the foundations of such a system in the form of the EITC and the CTC. An expanded EITC and CTC would go a long way toward helping low-wage families attain a living income.

A MORE EFFECTIVE TAX CREDIT SYSTEM FOR LOWER-INCOME WORKERS

For working families to enjoy economic well-being, the minimum wage must be increased. However, that alone will not assure everyone a living income, because paying workers according to their number of dependents would violate the principle of equal pay for equal work. Consequently, even if Congress adopted a minimum wage that was adequate for a childless worker, minimum-wage employees with dependents still would lack a living income without added support.

Congress took steps to address this problem when it enacted, and later expanded, the EITC and the CTC. Today, the EITC and CTC only go part of the way toward providing the added needed support for lower-income families. But they provide the foundation for an expanded, future program that actually could enable struggling families to achieve a living income.[53] They do so, moreover, at a significantly lower cost than UBI while avoiding wasteful UBI payments to affluent households that do not need them.

The Earned Income Tax Credit

The EITC supports lower-paid workers who file federal income tax returns by granting them a tax credit that offsets their tax liability dollar for dollar. If the credit exceeds someone's federal income tax liability, the EITC usually pays the balance as a tax refund. For instance, a lower-income taxpayer who receives an EITC of $3,000 but owes $2,000 in federal income taxes will receive a $1,000 refund.[54] Furthermore, eligible filers do not need to owe income taxes in order to receive a refund for the full tax credit.[55] The vast majority of EITC recipients do receive refunds.[56]

Remarkably, the EITC has grown to be the largest permanent federal cash support program targeted by income.[57] As just one indication of its importance, the twenty-seven million low-wage workers who received the EITC in 2019 dwarfed the slightly more than nine hundred thousand families on TANF welfare benefits that year.[58] The EITC has had remarkable success in encouraging work and stabilizing family incomes. It has lifted more children out of poverty than any other government program.[59] Meanwhile, it has led "to increases in employment for single parents with children," with little to no reduction in employment of married couples.[60]

The EITC has achieved this success by spreading the risk of inadequate income across federal taxpayers. According to the IRS, "about one-third of the EITC eligible population turns over each year."[61] This means that many of today's EITC recipients paid income taxes in the past to subsidize this tax credit. Other current EITC recipients will cycle into higher-wage jobs and pay future taxes to help finance the EITC. As a result, the EITC is a risk-sharing program in which our past or future selves pay taxes to avoid the risk of poverty wages today.

Despite the EITC's importance, Congress hamstrung the program in multiple ways that handicap its ability to serve people who need support.[62] First, the EITC pays the poorest filers less for every dollar they earn than better-paid workers. The EITC divides its recipients into three brackets according to income: bottom, middle, and top. For the bottom-income

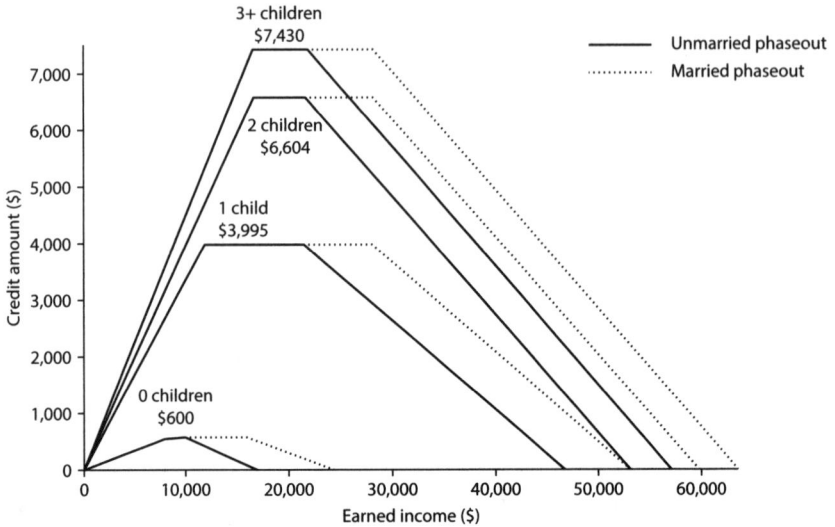

Figure 2. Amounts of the EITC by number of qualifying children, marital status, and income, 2023. *Source:* Congressional Research Service (2023).

group, the EITC is $0 for those making $1 a year and rises as a percentage of income for every additional dollar earned until reaching its top amount. It stays at that top amount for everyone in the middle-income group, after taking number of children and filing status into account. For the top-income group, the credit gradually phases out until it hits $0 (which was at $52,918 in 2023 for a single filer with two children).[63] (Figure 2 depicts the three brackets in tax year 2023.)

Presumably, Congress cut the EITC for the bottom bracket to induce the poorest filers to earn more. Doing so, however, unfairly penalized many workers for inadequate pay or hours, which generally are out of their control. In the process, Congress undermined the EITC's ability to lift the poorest workers out of poverty.

Second, the EITC generally is only available to workers with taxable income.[64] As a result, unpaid caregivers of dependents cannot collect the EITC unless they earn income from some separate source.[65]

Reforms to the EITC would fix these problems and improve working families' prospects of attaining a living income. Everyone in the bottom and middle brackets should receive the same size tax credit for every dollar earned, after adjusting for filing status and number of children. In addition, Congress should extend the EITC to people who make valuable contributions to society but who do not participate in the labor market. This mirrors the proposal by the late economist Anthony Atkinson for a "participation model" by defining certain types of valuable "social contributions" as work.[66]

The EITC should build on this approach. Most importantly, "work" should include contributions by unpaid caregivers for children or disabled or elderly adults. Without their sacrifices, economic productivity would suffer, and so would society's success in rearing children. Meanwhile, many older and incapacitated adults who currently receive care for free likely would become charges of the state without that care.[67] Congress further should expand the EITC to reward adults who enroll in job training or degree programs to improve their job prospects and pay.

To conclude, pairing the EITC with a higher minimum wage would provide a successful platform for assuring a living income. Doing so would build on the EITC's popularity and demonstrated success, while reducing child poverty and encouraging labor force participation.

The Child Tax Credit

In 1997 Congress instituted a companion program to the EITC, the CTC, again with broad bipartisan support.[68] The CTC provides eligible tax filers with a tax credit of up to $2,000 for every eligible child under age seventeen.[69]

As it did with the EITC, Congress saddled the CTC with restrictions that hamper its effectiveness. First, parents cannot claim the CTC unless they make at least $2,500 a year from employment.[70] As a result, stay-at-home parents cannot claim the CTC unless they report outside earned income.

Second, the CTC pays no or only partial benefits to children of low-wage workers, despite paying full benefits to children of better-paid workers, including many who are affluent. Today, as with the EITC, the value of the CTC to a particular family depends on the family's income. And like the EITC, the CTC divides tax filers into three brackets: bottom-income, middle-income, and higher-income. Tax filers in the bottom-income bracket do not receive the full CTC and could even receive zero. That is because families making less than $2,500 annually receive no credit at all. Once a family reports income of $2,500 a year, the CTC starts to phase in. By virtue of this phase-in, everyone in the bottom-income bracket who makes $2,500 or more qualifies for a partial CTC, but not the full CTC of $2,000 per child. This phase-in also ignores the number of children in the household. As a result, it is entirely possible for big families in the bottom-income group to receive only the same total CTC dollarwise as a family with just one child.[71]

In contrast, the CTC treats the middle-income bracket more generously. For married filers with two children, this middle group starts at couples earning almost $36,000 a year up to couples making a whopping $400,000 annually. Every filer in this middle bracket receives the full CTC of $2,000 for each eligible child. The CTC then phases out starting at incomes of $200,000 and $400,000 a year for single and married filers respectively.[72] Because the full credit goes to so many affluent earners, "most of the spending" on the CTC "goes to families far above the poverty line."[73]

The CTC treats lower-income families more harshly in another respect as well. If a family's CTC exceeds what it owes in federal income taxes, its refund is capped (at $1,700 per child for 2024).[74] In this sense, the CTC is only partly refundable, unlike the EITC, which is fully refundable. This partial refundability causes households in the bottom bracket and some poorer households in the middle bracket to receive only a partial CTC.[75] As a result of the phase-in and partial refundability, the Tax Policy Institute estimated that almost nineteen million children under age seventeen (28% of all children in that age range) would not receive a CTC or only would receive a partial one for tax year 2022.[76] That included over half of Black and Hispanic children, who lived in families who did not make enough to qualify for the full CTC.[77]

As this suggests, changes to the CTC would move millions of families with children closer to a living income. First, Congress should grant everyone in the bottom bracket the same full CTC per child as families in the middle bracket. Denying a full CTC to children from the poorest families penalizes them for their parents' low incomes, while favoring children from better-off families, who receive the full credit. In a related vein, granting the CTC to families with no earned income would provide desperately needed support to unpaid parents and other relatives who stay at home to care for children.[78]

Congress has enacted both reforms before and can do it again. In the American Rescue Plan Act of 2021 (ARPA), as part of a COVID-19 stimulus plan, Congress temporarily increased the CTC to grant every child a full credit (except children from high-earning families).[79] Congress also lifted the exclusion for families making less than $2,500, so that the full CTC went to children from families making zero earned income. This provision was only in effect for tax year 2021, however, and lapsed in tax year 2022.[80]

In addition, Congress should make the CTC fully refundable. Families who owed no taxes then would receive the full CTC as a refund. Again, there is precedent for this change. Congress made the CTC fully refundable in ARPA (but only for 2021).[81]

A third needed change is to lower the point at which the CTC starts phasing out below the current $200,000 for single parents and $400,000 for married couples. It is a waste to shower that type of largesse on affluent families, especially when children from the poorest families only receive a partial CTC or none. Furthermore, this measure is politically feasible. In ARPA, Congress managed to expand the CTC while lowering the phase-out thresholds for 2021 down to working families making up to $150,000 for a couple or $112,500 for a family with a single parent.[82] (The phase-out thresholds bounced back to $200,000 and $400,000 for tax year 2022.) As ARPA showed, it is politically possible to lower the phase-out levels and still get the needed votes.[83]

Fourth, Congress should redirect the money saved from phasing out the current CTC for high earners to increase the size of the CTC for children from families making less. Again, there is recent precedent for this approach. In ARPA, Congress used similar savings to increase the CTC temporarily to $3,000 a child for children between six and seventeen and $3,600 a child for children under six years old.[84] Congress should reinstate that increase for single parents making up to $112,500 a year and married parents making up to $150,000 a year.

The 2021 experience resulted in major improvements to the economic well-being of poorly paid families. In ARPA, Congress instructed the IRS to temporarily disburse half of the new, higher CTC amount in the form of advance payments. During the six-month period in late 2021 when families received those monthly payments, the payments drove down child poverty an astonishing 30 percent.[85] Of particular importance, those CTC advance payments caused a "significant reduction in the number of material hardships experienced by families with low incomes," particularly hunger and lack of funds for utility and medical bills.[86] Those advance payments moved the dial significantly closer to a living income for lower-income families by helping them pay for basic necessities. At the same time, census data showed that a larger percentage of parents worked *more* "because they could better afford child care and other work expenses."[87] These outcomes militate in favor of reinstating the 2021 changes to the CTC and making them permanent.

A UNIVERSAL SAVINGS PLAN

Another reason so many families have trouble making ends meet is that tens of millions have no emergency savings to speak of. Subpar wages are partly to blame, but so is the lack of any national policy to facilitate short-term savings. Even $250 to $749 in savings reduces the chance that a household will miss rent or utility payments, undergo eviction, or go on public assistance.[88] A national program for short-term savings accounts would provide financially stressed households with a vital buffer against surprise expenses.

What would an effective short-term national savings policy require? For starters, we would need to stop penalizing lower-income families for saving. That would require liberalizing asset caps on benefits.

In addition, the federal government should establish a no-fee, federally insured, interest-bearing savings account for every worker, along the lines of Jacob Hacker's proposal.[89] Employees would be enrolled automatically and make contributions through automatic payroll deductions. The minimum deductions would be small, but individuals could increase their contributions or opt out of participation altogether. On top of that, lower-income savers would qualify for a federal match to incentivize savings. Higher-paid taxpayers also would participate, but without a match.

Importantly, the accounts would come with no strings attached, allowing accountholders to tap their balances for personal needs, including emergencies.

This universal savings plan would put households on firmer financial footing in powerful ways. Every worker would have access to the plan, instead of at the option of employers. This would guarantee lower-income workers access to the same robust savings infrastructure that more affluent people use to save successfully. Auto-enrollment and the match, along with the no-fee and interest-bearing features, would boost savings. Federal deposit insurance would protect accountholders from losses due to bank failures. Together, these design features would give workers a realistic way to build emergency savings.[90]

Even with today's minimum wage laws, the EITC, and the CTC, half of families fall short of a living income. As the solution, I propose a trio of reforms: a higher federal minimum wage that is set at the living wage for a single, childless full-time worker; an expanded EITC and CTC to raise incomes of struggling families to the level needed to cover life's essentials; and universal savings accounts as an added shock absorber. Unlike a UBI, these reforms are politically feasible. Already a substantial number of states have raised the minimum wage. And Congress enacted a substantial, albeit temporary, expansion of the CTC in 2021. These developments show that attaining a living income for all is within reach: *if* Congress can summon the political will.

WHEN LIFE KNOCKS PEOPLE DOWN:
RISK-SHARING SYSTEMS TO BLUNT LOST INCOME

Minimum wage laws and the EITC and CTC serve people who are already working by boosting their pay from work.[91] Those laws and programs are ill-suited, however, when people lose their income source entirely.[92] As chapter 5 discussed, most people suffer negative income shocks such as job loss at one time or another. The COVID-19 pandemic drove home that the risk of negative income shocks is tragically real.[93] These income hits are another reason households cannot make ends meet.

When negative income shocks strike, it is not realistic to expect rank-and-file workers to amass sufficient savings to survive those emergencies alone. Even if workers had the means to save such large sums, it "would be an inefficient use of their resources, requiring setting aside tens of thousands of dollars in savings yearly to guard against events that may never occur and that may be difficult or impossible to anticipate."[94] More to the point, most families do not have the financial wherewithal to withstand such blows on their own.

This combination of a risk that virtually everyone faces with a disastrous potential loss is precisely the situation in which it makes sense for people to pool their contributions and reimburse members who suffer a loss. Risk sharing is ideal for this situation because it harnesses modest premium payments from a large number of workers (or their employers) to avoid the shared risk of a catastrophic loss of income. Unemployment insurance is just such a program.

Unemployment is one of the top two causes of negative income shocks, with sporadic work hours being the other.[95] Given unemployment's leading role, the rest of this chapter focuses on negative income shocks from job loss and irregular hours. Later, chapter 10 discusses the separate problem of negative income shocks arising from old age, disability, and the death of workers with dependents.[96]

As chapter 3 discussed, unemployment insurance is the main source of replacement income when people lose their jobs. The basic UI system—which is financed by the states through UI taxes assessed on employers—is designed for situations in which the reasons for termination are specific to a company or an industry and not the product of a wider recession. These situations are easier to insure because terminations hit people randomly and do not affect workers across the board.

Over time, however, the basic UI system has not kept pace with changes in the labor market and has become badly riddled with holes. Many of these holes consist of coverage exclusions, which have ballooned to the point that 72 percent of workers who lost their jobs in 2019 did not qualify for UI.[97] These exclusions have swallowed UI and crippled its effectiveness.

One such exclusion is the monetary test, which disqualifies workers who lost their jobs but made too little while working to meet the test.

As sporadic hours and part-time schedules have proliferated, this exclusion and its harmful effects have grown. A second exclusion, for employees who voluntarily resign, unfairly penalizes workers who leave due to irregular schedules or cuts in pay or hours. Meanwhile, the independent contractor exclusion has barred increasing numbers of workers from UI as the gig economy and other outsourcing arrangements have spread. And even when unemployed workers do qualify for UI, their benefits are a pittance.[98]

UI needs modernization if it is to provide a financial life buoy to workers who lose their jobs. Of top importance, Congress should make the federal government solely responsible for funding UI and setting UI's minimum standards.[99] Federal standards for UI eligibility, duration, and benefits would eliminate the current race to the bottom among the states to cut UI premiums in order to attract companies and jobs.[100]

Next, coverage needs to grow to address today's altered work landscape. The monetary test should be scrapped because it discriminates against the worst-paid workers, who often are both low-paid and seasonal or part-time. Instead, that "dollars" test should be replaced with an "hours-worked" test that bases UI eligibility on working a minimum number of hours during the base period.[101] Today, the state of Washington is the only state that uses an hours-worked approach.[102] The United States should follow Washington's lead and adopt this approach nationwide. Congress should also extend UI permanently to independent contractors and the self-employed, as it did temporarily in the Coronavirus Aid, Relief, and Economic Security (CARES) Act in 2020.[103]

UI should further cover workers who quit their jobs because their employers violated their legal rights, slashed their hours or pay, or assigned them unreasonable job schedules. Some states already grant UI benefits for resignations for "good cause."[104] That approach should be adopted nationally. This change would allow workers to escape poor working conditions and still qualify for UI.[105]

In addition, Congress should define "good cause" to include workers who resign for compelling family reasons nationwide.[106] In the American Recovery and Reinvestment Act of 2009 (ARRA), Congress took steps down this path by granting funds to states that permanently defined "good cause" for purposes of UI eligibility to include voluntary separations to take care of an ill or disabled family member and cases of documented domestic violence.[107] At least twenty-one states took Congress up on the offer and now include compelling family reasons in their definitions of "good cause."[108] Together, these measures would significantly reverse UI's shrinking coverage by extending eligibility to categories of jobless workers who historically have been shut out of unemployment benefits.[109]

Another needed reform would help part-time workers who are fired. Traditionally, UI has required recipients to be actively seeking full-time work in order to remain qualified. This requirement has excluded many part-time workers from continued coverage. In response, in ARRA, Congress provided incentive payments to states that allowed part-time workers to receive UI even if they only sought part-time work. In the roughly half of states that made this change, UI eligibility was expanded for younger and poorly paid workers and those with erratic work hours.[110] Congress should leverage that experience and adopt this reform nationwide.[111]

Finally, UI benefits need to be increased. All recipients, regardless of state, should be eligible for up to thirty weeks of basic UI benefits.[112] UI also should replace a larger percentage of lost income for workers in the lower half by pay and use automatic triggers to increase the replacement rate when unemployment rises.[113] Last, Congress should augment basic UI with an allowance of $35 per week per dependent nationwide, adjusted for inflation.[114]

The United States, with its proud history as the greatest industrial power in the world, still has not managed to produce enough full-time jobs at sufficient pay to ensure laborers and their families a living income. This chapter focuses on changes that are needed to make a living income a reality. The first of those proposals would peg the federal minimum wage at the level of a living wage for a single, childless, full-time worker. The second proposal would expand federal tax credits for families to bridge the gap between the minimum wage for single full-time workers and a living income. Third, I propose a national savings plan that would provide working families with emergency savings accounts. Finally, the United States needs to revamp UI to alleviate the job insecurity that so many workers face.

This chapter has focused on adequate income as the cornerstone of economic well-being. But income plays only one part. Having some modest wealth is important as well. One avenue for building wealth consists of the universal savings plan that this chapter proposes. Traditionally, another important avenue has been homeownership. In the next chapter I explore the American love affair with homeownership and what is necessary to make homeownership successful.

7 Owning a Home

When it comes to the economy, Republicans and Democrats famously clash over aid to the less well-off and the proper role of government in that regard. But both sides agree on one thing: that government *should* subsidize homeownership.

In 1995, for example, President Bill Clinton unveiled The National Homeownership Strategy, a hundred-point plan to achieve homeownership for eight million more households by 2000.[1] Seven years later, President George W. Bush visited the home of Darrin West, a Black policeman in Atlanta, where he called for increased minority homeownership.[2] Later that day, the president warmed to his theme, hailing the "economic security" that comes from owning a home. He called on Congress to "use money, taxpayers' money, to help a qualified low-income buyer make a downpayment."[3] President Bush signed the American Dream Downpayment Act into law the following year.[4]

The man the president called on that day, Officer West, had bought his townhouse with an adjustable-rate mortgage and $20,000 in down payment assistance. Later, however, when Officer West moved from Atlanta, he could not sell his home for what he owed. Instead, he gave the keys to the bank in 2007.[5] Far from attaining "economic security," Officer West became enmeshed in the events leading up to the financial crisis of 2008. In the aftermath, at least 10 percent of homes in his development went into foreclosure.[6]

His experience raises the question, is homeownership unequivocally good? Homeownership offers substantial rewards but comes with hefty risks. The federal government magnified those risks when it deregulated home mortgages before 2008. During those years, lenders slashed credit standards and issued high-risk mortgages to legions of unsuspecting borrowers.[7]

Eventually the house of cards collapsed and the 2008 crisis ensued, wreaking havoc on millions of homeowners. In the aftermath, at least five million households lost their homes to foreclosure.[8] Meanwhile, those foreclosures decimated neighboring property values, particularly in the hardest hit areas.[9]

The 2008 crisis set back Black and Hispanic homeownership rates for years. Before the crash, Black and Hispanic homeownership rates had hit highs of almost 50 percent. After 2008, Black homeownership slid to 40.6 percent (less than when the Fair Housing Act of 1968 was passed), and Hispanic homeownership fell to 44 percent, mostly due to foreclosures.[10]

Today, both rates have risen, but neither has recovered. At the end of 2022, the Black homeownership rate was 44.9 percent, almost thirty percentage points lower than the 74.5 percent rate for Whites. The Hispanic rate was not much better, at 48.5 percent.[11] Racial disparities in housing costs, mortgage rates, home appreciation, and mortgage defaults also persist.[12] These disparities manifest the toll of historic racism in property ownership.

When does homeownership improve economic well-being, when does homeownership harm it, and what is necessary to make homeownership successful? These are vital matters because there are large potential benefits to owning a home. Homeownership satisfies the basic need for shelter. It also affords intangible benefits, ranging from autonomy, privacy, and security to increased civic engagement and the emotional satisfaction of owning a home.[13]

Beyond that, homeownership is the single biggest source of wealth for lower- and middle-income households. Even after 2008, home equity remains the leading source of wealth for everyone except the affluent, including Black and Hispanic households.[14] Homeownership's importance as the engine of wealth for ordinary families explains its strong support on both sides of the aisle.

Here, it is worth asking *why* homeownership is the largest middle-class investment? In a stroke of genius, homeownership takes a necessary expenditure—housing—and transforms it into an investment. Most households have to pay for housing anyway, so mortgage payments act as forced savings. With each monthly payment, a homeowner accumulates home equity and wealth.[15] For these reasons, many find it easier to invest in a home than in other asset classes.

Other dynamics enhance the value of homeownership as an investment.[16] One, naturally, is home appreciation. Deductions for mortgage interest and local property taxes also generate tax write-offs for homeowners who itemize.

Another major benefit comes with financing. Most homeowners take out home mortgage loans to buy their homes. The smaller their down payments, the bigger their potential return on equity. Take a couple who purchases a home for $300,000 and sells it a few years later for $350,000. If they paid all cash for the house, their return on equity, in finance speak, would be their profit ($50,000) divided by what they paid ($300,000) or almost 17 percent. But if they only put $30,000 down and took out a mortgage for the rest, their return on equity would be $50,000 divided by $30,000, or 166 percent. This effect is called *leverage*, and it works like a gear: borrowing 90 percent of the purchase price allowed our couple to boost their return almost tenfold. That is the power of leverage.

At the same time, homeownership is no guarantee of wealth. When homeownership goes south, the fallout can be disastrous. Homeownership presents big risks precisely *because* most people finance their homes with loans. A home mortgage is most homeowners' single biggest obligation.[17] Moreover, a household's payments almost certainly will rise with property taxes, homeowners' insurance, and interest rates (for adjustable-rate mortgages).[18] Consequently, the credit risk associated with home mortgages is large and real. If the homeowner defaults, he or she faces foreclosure plus ruined credit for years.[19] On top of that, a foreclosed owner forfeits home equity plus any future chance to accumulate wealth from owning the home.[20]

Affording monthly mortgage payments is the key to avoiding default. Making consistent on-time payments is easier said than done, however. To do so, homeowners have to survive negative economic shocks for the entire length of their mortgages. Income shocks can come in many forms, with unemployment, divorce, illness, and death leading the list. Similarly, unanticipated costs such as car breakdowns, major home repairs, or medical expenses can capsize budgets and result in missed mortgage payments, especially for lower-income borrowers.[21]

On top of that, home values can fall. When home prices go down, borrowers who are having trouble paying their mortgages may not be able to sell their homes for enough to pay off their loans.[22] This is the problem of "underwater mortgages" that Officer West experienced. Small down payments increase the risk of going underwater.[23]

The consequences of going underwater can be dire. From mid-2006 to early 2012, the national slump in home prices reached catastrophic proportions.[24] By 2013, almost one-fourth of households who bought homes after 1999 no longer were homeowners.[25] While there were different reasons that those households returned to renting, the spike in foreclosures certainly played a part. Tragically, Black and Latino homeowners were even more prone to underwater mortgages and foreclosure.[26]

For all of these reasons, homeownership is a risky proposition. In any other circumstance, financial advisers would caution people against investing their entire nest egg in an illiquid and volatile asset. That same advice holds for homeownership. Yet too many homeowners are house poor because they put most of their cash into their homes. They have little left over to get through the month. And many of them lack emergency savings as well.[27]

One way to avoid defaults would be to help borrowers build emergency reserves. These reserves are proven to reduce the risk of default.[28] Perversely, though, federal policy does not support (and sometimes penalizes) the short-term savings that could finance emergency funds, even though it subsidizes renters heavily to become homeowners to begin with. These subsidies include the considerable tax benefits discussed in chapter 4 from owning a home. But public subsidies for homeownership do not stop there. The government's support ranges from downpayment assistance to affordable homeownership mandates and government-subsidized mortgage rates.[29] In addition, the federal government sponsors much of the housing finance system, which offers additional programs to usher working families into homeownership.[30]

To reiterate, the heavy official priority on homeownership stands in contrast to the government's low priority on short-term savings. As a result of this lopsided incentive structure, homeownership is the most rational wealth-building strategy for middle- and lower-income families, often to the exclusion of cash savings. The resulting lack of diversification hurts these families by leaving them vulnerable to economic shocks.

The official preoccupation with homeownership also detracts from households' need to attain other life goals. Low-income homeowners who pour their cash into mortgage payments and home maintenance have no other savings or wealth on average apart from their home equity.[31] They are hard-pressed to save for college, medical expenses, and old age. Some argue that these goals can be financed through debt, especially college (and retirement through reverse mortgages). However, going into debt to pay for those goals is freighted with risk. Families living paycheck to paycheck would be burdened by the added loan payments and ruin their credit if they could not repay.[32] Unless policymakers integrate homeownership with other financial goals, middle- and lower-income homeowners may overinvest in housing and underinvest in education, health, and retirement.[33]

Three strategies would make homeownership safer while integrating it with other financial goals. The first is to keep mortgage payments down. The second is to reduce additional sources of default risk in home mortgages. Finally, policymakers should coordinate their policies for all five economic milestones so that homeownership does not crowd out other goals, and other goals do not crowd out homeownership.

BUT FIRST, A CAVEAT

So far, I have criticized the official stress on homeownership for eclipsing other household goals. That emphasis is further problematic because it suggests that renters deserve less respect than homeowners.

That message is wrong and destructive. The decision to rent should not be freighted with social disapproval. Homeownership is not for everyone, nor should it be. Some people prefer to avoid the hassles that come with maintaining a home. Some people are too peripatetic, or their plans are too uncertain to commit to long-term ownership. Others may nix home-ownership due to the financial risks or trade-offs. There are many rational reasons for choosing renting over owning, and society should support either decision.

Some who do aspire to owning a home may not be in a position to buy one, at least not at the moment. Others in somewhat stronger financial condition may be able to squeak through the mortgage approval process, but still are at risk of missing mortgage payments if their finances later crumble. This points to another danger of advocating homeownership so heavily, which is pushing people in over their heads financially, as happened during the lead-up to 2008. While subsequent reforms addressed many of these problems, more steps can be taken to set up homeowners for success. Keeping monthly home payments down is at the top of the list.

MANAGEABLE MONTHLY PAYMENTS

Cost is one of the biggest barriers to buying a home. In many places, buyers are experiencing serious sticker shock as they shop for homes. But there are a number of techniques for keeping monthly payments in check during the home-buying process.

The first is finding a home at an affordable price. In some places, such as Cleveland, modestly priced homes are in healthy supply. But that is not the case in many parts of the country, where entry-level homes are scarce. Several reasons are at play. Zoning restrictions requiring detached single-family homes on large lots block the building of affordable condominiums and townhouses. Even when zoning laws permit multifamily housing, often there is a dearth of buildable lots, and the few that exist are expensive. Construction costs have risen due to supply chain problems that drove up the price of new homes. Meanwhile, all-cash buyers have pushed up home prices in many areas and outcompeted buyers who need mortgages. Tackling this short supply will require easing zoning restrictions, providing incentives to develop affordable units, and employing affordable housing covenants.

Buyers in expensive markets have several strategies for staying on budget when purchasing a home. One is buying a smaller, more affordable

condo or townhouse. Another is being flexible as to location. A good real-
tor can spot well-priced houses before they go on the market. Some buyers
purchase homes with two or three units and live in one while renting out
the others to generate cash. Fixer-uppers are another way to lower costs,
although the often-poor condition of those homes introduces added financial risks. Finally, obtaining prequalification or preapproval on a mortgage
can provide a reality check on how much homebuyers can afford while
making their offers more competitive.

Affordable payments also depend on getting the best possible price on
a mortgage. There is a standard repertory of tips for keeping down the
price. That includes shopping for the best interest rate, paying points in
some cases, improving one's credit history before applying for a loan, and
coming up with the largest downpayment possible.

For new or less sophisticated homebuyers, however, this advice can
be challenging to follow. The risk-based pricing system, in which lenders
charge higher prices to customers with weaker credit, is a serious impediment to comparison shopping. Lenders' pricing systems, which trade off
interest rates, downpayments, and points, confuse loan applicants searching for the lowest rates. Meanwhile, homebuyers' attempts to improve
their credit records can expose them to fraudulent credit-repair services.

In short, a host of competitive problems hampers consumers' ability to
get the best price on mortgage loans. This makes institutional support and
safeguards vital to ensuring fair pricing for consumers.

One such safeguard is free consumer education and counseling, which
the US Department of Housing and Urban Development and the Consumer Financial Protection Bureau (CFPB) together support.[34] No amount
of consumer education or counseling is enough alone, however, to overcome exploitative marketing of home mortgages. Aggressive lenders and
brokers excel at reeling in loan applicants before they can consult nonprofit
consumer counselors or government educational materials. On top of that,
the mortgage decision-making process is so complex that it is difficult for
consumers to know when they have made a good decision. Accordingly,
stronger safeguards are crucial to protecting consumers in the mortgage
shopping process.

Post-2008, Congress adopted a slew of legal measures to protect homebuyers in the Dodd-Frank Wall Street Reform and Consumer Protection

Act (Dodd-Frank).[35] One reform provides consumers with better federal mortgage disclosures that conspicuously flag risks that borrowers need to know.[36] Another requires lenders to present homebuyers with several pricing options, including the cheapest plain vanilla loan, the loan with the lowest interest rate, and the loan with the lowest fees—but only if homebuyers "express interest" in pertinent transactions.[37] This duty should apply automatically, regardless of whether a homeowner initiates a request. A third reform prevents mortgage brokers from boosting their compensation by steering unsuspecting borrowers into costlier loans.[38] Other federal rules regulate higher-priced mortgage loans more heavily than cheaper ones.[39] In some circumstances, federal law also requires homeownership counseling.[40]

These Dodd-Frank reforms significantly cleaned up the mortgage market. However, more needs to be done. The biggest challenge lies in providing reliable price quotes to consumers. Under our current system of risk-based pricing, comparison shopping is maddeningly cumbersome. In order to comparison shop effectively, consumers need to submit separate loan applications to individual lenders (possibly with an application fee for each) in order to generate loan estimates. These loan estimates provide the most reliable quotes because they are tailored to the applicant's credit profile and can only increase at closing under limited circumstances. Few consumers go to the length of submitting multiple mortgage applications to generate these quotes, however. Instead, the plurality of homebuyers only seriously looks at one lender, and few give a serious look at more than two.[41]

An online market with accurate, competitive price quotes would provide a better way of comparison shopping for home mortgages. Today, commercial platforms market themselves as offering this service. However, the price quotes they generate are unreliable and often false. For one thing, major mortgage lenders usually do not participate in these platforms. Further, the platforms lack solid information about the user's creditworthiness because they do not pull actual income information or credit scores. In the worst cases, platforms mislead shoppers by inflating rates, purporting to provide firm prices when they do not, or steering consumers to disreputable lenders or brokers.

A government-sponsored online market, like the one for health insurance policies under the Affordable Care Act, could address these problems.[42] The government could increase price competition by incentivizing all mortgage lenders to participate. In addition, with customers' consent, the market could pull their actual credit scores, as well as income figures from the IRS, to produce firm quotes that are properly adjusted for creditworthiness. A government market also would encourage more standardized mortgage terms and fees, which would facilitate comparison shopping. Meanwhile, neutral government sponsorship, instead of private platforms infected by commercial conflicts of interest, would guard against misrepresentation and abuse.

Strengthening oversight of lending discrimination also will lower mortgage prices. Studies consistently show that Black and Hispanic borrowers pay more for mortgage loans on average than comparable White borrowers.[43] This disparity persists despite two federal statutes—the Equal Credit Opportunity Act and Title VIII of the Fair Housing Act—banning discrimination in mortgage lending based on race, color, national origin, religion, sex, and other prohibited grounds.[44] Individuals who suspect they were subject to credit discrimination often cannot plead a successful complaint because they lack access to confidential, internal data documenting that they were treated worse than comparably qualified applicants. The shift toward artificial intelligence and algorithmic lending only complicates this problem.[45]

On the margin, ramped-up government enforcement of lending discrimination violations would provide added relief. But other, bolder measures could be taken to prevent discriminatory overcharges or inform borrowers when they occur. The online government market detailed earlier specifically would be designed to generate race-neutral price quotes. *Rewarding* lenders to provide borrowers with quotes through that market would limit their discretion to engage in discriminatory pricing. Meanwhile, the CFPB has taken initial steps to blunt discrimination from black-box algorithmic credit models by requiring lenders to provide loan applicants with specific and accurate written reasons for adverse credit actions.[46]

Finally, even a perfectly competitive market cannot fix the challenge of affording a home in an exorbitant market for homebuyers who, but for budget constraints, are otherwise well-qualified to buy. These are people with strong credit records but who lack a large enough down payment or income to qualify for mortgage loans at today's rates. For customers who are close to qualifying for credit but fall just short, financial support from a state housing finance agency can help secure a mortgage. These agencies, located in all fifty states, back mortgage loans to first-time homebuyers who meet income guidelines at subsidized, below-market rates.[47] Typically, these agencies also provide down payment assistance of up to 3 percent of the loan amount. These programs cannot help everyone, particularly customers with extremely low incomes or serious credit blemishes. But for promising candidates who make more but not enough to qualify for a mortgage on their own, a financial boost from one of these state programs can help them achieve homeownership.

To summarize, cost barriers are one of the biggest hurdles to acquiring a home and the wealth-building potential it provides. But these barriers are not always insuperable. Together, the reforms and strategies just discussed substantially can increase the number of households who can buy homes.

MAKING MORTGAGES SUSTAINABLE

Buying a home is a major life achievement. But it is not worth attaining at any cost. Later, if the homeowner defaults on the mortgage, it can wreck the household's finances for years. Accordingly, achieving homeownership is not enough; it also is important to make home mortgages sustainable. This includes steps to avoid default and to prevent unnecessary foreclosures if defaults do occur.

Reducing Default Risk

On the front end, manageable payments help reduce defaults.[48] The right-priced home will keep payments down, as the last section discussed. So will getting the best mortgage rate. On the back end, mortgage loans have risks that homeowners must manage over the life of their loans. Making mortgages *sustainable* will increase the chance that homeowners pay their mortgages on time, every time.

Some of the back-end risks relate to the type of mortgage loan itself. The basic question is this: Will the principal and interest payments stay flat, or will they rise over time? This is the issue of "payment shock." As the 2008 crisis demonstrated, mortgages come in different "products," and most of those products present the risk of payment shock. Fortunately, fixed-rate mortgages do not, because their principal and interest payments never go up (assuming that the loan is "fully amortizing" because it will pay off the principal by the end of the loan term).

Other types of home mortgage loans, however, *do* present payment shock. For instance, the interest rate on an adjustable-rate mortgage can climb over time and with it the monthly payments. Balloon-payment loans require payment of a large sum, often in the tens of thousands of dollars, when the loan comes due. Interest-only mortgages allow borrowers to skip principal payments for a time. But eventually, principal payments will come due, and then the monthly payments will jump. The most exotic mortgages—the so-called option payment mortgages or negative amortization loans—actually cause the principal to *grow* over time and with it, the monthly payments.

For homebuyers with tight budgets, a fixed-rate, fully amortizing mortgage is the safest mortgage product by far. Economists consistently have shown that fixed-rate mortgages have the lowest rates of default and foreclosure. Every other mortgage product increases the chance of missing mortgage payments and losing the home, compared to fixed-rate loans.[49] Accordingly, borrowers can boost their chance of successful homeownership with a fixed-rate, fully amortizing loan.

Sometimes homebuyers find adjustable-rate mortgages or other risky products tempting because the initial monthly payments may be lower than for fixed-rate mortgages. In rare cases, when buyers are sure they will move in a few years, adjustable-rate mortgages (at least the fully amortizing ones) may make economic sense. In most cases, however, the default risks of mortgage loans with payment shock far outweigh the advantages, because the monthly payments often do rise. To position themselves for success, homebuyers are best advised to go for fixed-rate mortgages, even if it means buying less-expensive homes.

The CFPB has advanced the ball by requiring lenders to disclose the payment shock, if any, for every loan for which a consumer applies. These disclosures not only tell people if their payments could rise, but also *how high* their payments could go during every single month of the loan.

Federal law also now prohibits lenders from granting mortgages to applicants who cannot repay. In Dodd-Frank, Congress barred lenders from extending mortgage credit without first making a reasonable determination, as of when the mortgage is granted, that the consumer can repay the loan.[50] The CFPB adopted strong regulations for giving this requirement bite.[51] Dodd-Frank further gave lenders strong incentive to make safer mortgages—known as "qualified mortgages"—by shielding qualified mortgages from legal liability.[52]

As a result, today home borrowers have much greater protection than they did pre-2008. Meanwhile, unsafe mortgages (read negative amortization loans, interest-only loans, and most balloon loans) have become a rarity because they are not eligible for the "qualified mortgage" safe harbor from lawsuits by injured borrowers. These reforms set up residential borrowers for greater success.

Still, after closing, life events can undermine homeowners' ability to make timely loan payments. These can range from unemployment or health problems to divorce or a breadwinner's death. Similarly, property damage from physical disasters or maintenance problems can make it difficult to keep up with mortgage payments.[53]

These vagaries underscore the importance of policies for stabilizing incomes to keeping distressed homeowners in their homes. Unemployment poses the biggest threat to stable homeownership.[54] When joblessness hits, unemployment insurance makes a big difference in retaining homeownership. Between 2008 and 2013, for example, unemployment benefits helped prevent roughly 1.3 million foreclosures.[55] Consequently, UI reforms don't just help people make ends meet. They also help homeowners stay in their homes.

The potential for future shocks tees up another issue, which is the topic of reserves. Many homebuyers have to decide how much savings to spend on a down payment versus retaining for a future emergency. Both choices reduce default risk. Homebuyers with larger down payments have more home equity, which reduces their chance of default if property values fall.[56] At the same time, homeowners with as little as $1,000 in savings are less likely to default on mortgages.[57] Since lower-income homebuyers usually have difficulty saving for a down payment, it may make sense to obtain down payment assistance and put the spare cash into an emergency fund.[58] A universal savings plan, as chapter 6 proposes, would beef up emergency reserves and help protect homeowners from foreclosure due to temporary cash-flow problems. In the process, this universal savings plan would pay added dividends—over and above making it through the month—by stabilizing homeownership and building wealth.

Foreclosure Prevention

So far, this discussion has focused on how to avoid missed payments. But when delinquencies do occur, more measures are needed to save the homes. Since 2008, officials have placed heavy emphasis on foreclosure prevention to keep delinquent borrowers in their homes. Foreclosure prevention has a mixed record of success, but when it works, distressed homeowners can hold onto their homes.[59]

Mortgage companies that process loan payments (known as servicers) do not—and usually cannot—file foreclosure proceedings just for one missed payment.[60] Rather, a homeowner usually does not go into default until payments are 120 days past due.[61] Once a homeowner is in default, however, things go downhill quickly, and the possibility of foreclosure becomes real.

To avoid the point of no return, servicers need to reach out proactively to newly delinquent borrowers. Research has shown that rapid outreach by servicers after the first missed mortgage payment improves homeowners' chance of resuming payments and retaining their homes.[62] For this reason, federal law requires servicers to initiate live contact with every delinquent borrower within thirty-six days of the first missed payment.[63]

Sometimes, after this outreach a borrower can rectify the situation immediately. Other borrowers with short-term cash-flow problems may be able to negotiate breathing room (in the form of temporary forbearance) to get back on track. Meanwhile, homeowners with longer-term financial difficulties may be able to reduce their monthly payments through loan modifications that cut the interest rate, the principal, or both. To be sure, some homeowners' financial difficulties are too far gone to qualify for loan modifications. But if the investor in a distressed mortgage loan would recover more from modifying the loan than from foreclosing on the home, a loan modification would be a win-win for everyone.[64]

The availability of loan modifications hinges on the discretion of individual guarantors, insurers, or investors.[65] Today, four federal entities—Fannie Mae, Freddie Mac, the Federal Housing Administration (FHA), and the Department of Veterans Affairs—are the largest residential mortgage guarantors and insurers, accounting for about two-thirds of first-lien mortgage originations in 2024.[66] All four entities have formal policies for granting loan modifications and similar relief to delinquent borrowers.[67]

Although loan modification policies are now in place, their implementation can be messy.[68] The CFPB significantly improved that situation by adopting and enforcing mortgage servicing rules. Today, mortgage servicers must provide delinquent borrowers with accurate information about their loan modification options and evaluate their loan modification applications properly.[69] Servicers normally are prohibited from initiating or proceeding to foreclosure if a timely loan modification application is pending.[70] This regulatory scheme—along with generous forbearance policies and foreclosure moratoria—kept foreclosures at historic lows during the COVID-19 pandemic.[71] Other needed changes, including servicer compensation reform and servicing systems with better automation, would further reduce erroneous denials of loan modifications.

To conclude, retaining homeownership is just as important as achieving it. But for homeownership to be sustainable, conscious decisions have to be made by homebuyers and policymakers alike. These decisions involve keeping payments down, choosing a traditional fixed-rate mortgage, ensuring that homebuyers have the ability to repay, improving UI and other safety nets for when income shocks strike, adopting a universal savings plan to help homeowners build savings, and maintaining robust foreclosure prevention programs. Some of these measures are in place, while others—especially UI expansion and a universal savings plan—are not. It is time for politicians in both parties to put their money where their mouths are and enact these measures to make homeownership more sustainable.

INTEGRATING HOMEOWNERSHIP WITH OTHER FINANCIAL GOALS

I opened this chapter arguing that the national preoccupation with homeownership presents hazards. One is the risk of default, which this chapter just explored. Another is the risk that homeownership could crowd out other financial goals. The United States has made progress on both scores, but more could be done to enable less well-off homeowners to attain other major milestones.

How do we make it easier for homeowners to juggle their mortgage obligations and other financial goals? When it comes to homeownership, the first imperative is to do no harm. Foreclosures jeopardize families' other life goals by triggering a downward spiral from which it is hard to recover. On the most basic level, seriously delinquent homeowners have greater difficulty putting food on the table.[72] Some distressed homeowners jeopardize their retirement security by raiding their 401(k) plans, with almost half of 401(k) hardship withdrawals being to avoid eviction or foreclosure.[73] Foreclosure also can put college out of reach, including by disqualifying parents from federal PLUS loans.[74] Consequently, the measures discussed earlier to make homeownership sustainable also are important to ensuring that foreclosure does not impede other financial milestones.

Smart mortgage strategies can help release cash for other milestones. One is keeping mortgage payments down in the ways just discussed. Meanwhile, fixed-rate mortgages allow homeowners to devote their pay raises to other goals, because principal and interest payments remain flat over the life of the loan. Homeowners can free up even more cash toward achieving other goals by refinancing their mortgages when interest rates drop. Finally, retirees who have paid off their homes can reduce their costs by living there mortgage-free.

The crowd-out effect of homeownership poses special concerns when it comes to health. In 2020, more than one out of five homeowners spent at least 30 percent of their income on housing.[75] This large cost burden pressures them to prioritize paying their mortgages over needed medical care, at risk to their health.[76] Similarly, homeowners experiencing foreclosure are more likely to skip prescribed medications due to cost.[77] Medical care is thus one more example of where integrating homeownership with other top goals—in this case, good health—is of the utmost importance, as the next chapter discusses.

8 Affording Health Care

In the early 1990s, when Heather Meyer was twelve, insurers denied health coverage to her and her dad because they were Type I diabetics. Without that coverage, sometimes they had to skip insulin shots due to the cost. But all that changed in 2010, when Congress required insurers to cover preexisting conditions in the Patient Protection and Affordable Care Act (ACA).[1] Once Heather had ACA coverage with subsidized premiums, she was able to get the regular insulin injections she needed. Her health stabilized, her career took off, and Heather later went on to win election to the Kansas legislature.[2]

As Heather's story illustrates, everything in life—working, going to school, enjoying retirement—depends on good health. People need to know that their health care is affordable and their health coverage is good.

Here, there is encouraging news. Health insurance is one of the biggest success stories of expanded US risk sharing in the past sixty years. After years of political wrangling, most US residents have *access* to health insurance today. Still, too many people struggle with the cost, often due to high premiums, deductibles, coinsurance, or copays.

Today, the United States is the only major industrialized country that does not guarantee *affordable* health care to its residents.[3] Numerous households have to settle for subpar medical care because health care is so expensive. In the process, the United States has ended up with the costliest health-care system yet the worst health outcomes among leading high-income countries.[4] Meanwhile, over one hundred million Americans are in debt to pay their medical bills. A disturbing number have gone bankrupt or lost their homes as a result.[5]

This chapter opens by tracing the US tradition of risk sharing for medical expenses. After a thumbnail sketch of the major types of health insurance, the chapter describes the successful road to greater health insurance access in the United States. Then comes the central topic: the overwhelming cost burden for health care that many households still carry. The chapter closes by examining what is needed to remove cost barriers to adequate health care.

THE AMERICAN HISTORY OF RISK SHARING FOR MEDICAL COSTS

So far, this book has examined how US risk-sharing mechanisms have contracted over time, exposing households to mounting financial risk. But health care is a shining exception. Since 1965, Congress has expanded health insurance on two major occasions.

US health coverage dates back to at least the 1930s, when private health insurance emerged. Later, during World War II, a growing number of employers offered health insurance, possibly to retain their workers after the federal government instituted wartime wage caps.[6]

Over time, however, private health insurance became unstable. In the 1950s and 1960s, private insurers increasingly denied individual policies to older adults or priced those policies prohibitively, citing adverse selection.[7] Later, as private-sector unions declined, numerous employers dropped employee health benefits, particularly for low-wage workers.[8] Meanwhile, in the individual market, private carriers increasingly excluded preexisting conditions, again on grounds of adverse selection.[9] Other times, insurers instituted steep rate hikes, pricing many customers out of individual health coverage.

As health insurance receded in segments of the market, Congress stepped up government's role in coverage. Medicare, enacted in 1965, provided health insurance for almost everyone age sixty-five and up. Medicaid, also passed in 1965, provided free or nearly free medical coverage to the poorest households. Then, almost half a century later, Congress passed the ACA, which expanded access to health coverage in numerous other ways. It did so, first, by increasing employers' incentives to offer coverage on the job. Second, the ACA revived individual coverage by offering most households under age sixty-five the choice to buy private policies on the newly formed Marketplace. Third, the ACA expanded the number of people who qualified for Medicaid.

In other important provisions, the ACA mandated quality coverage. Under the so-called individual mandate, most people must attest that they have "minimum essential coverage" every month.[10] This coverage includes a broad menu of ten "essential health benefits," including standard inpatient and outpatient care, plus preventive care, maternity coverage, substance abuse counseling, mental health treatment, and prescription drugs, which private carriers often had refused to reimburse before the ACA.[11] Medicare Part A hospital coverage, Medicaid, Marketplace plans, and eligible employer-based plans must all offer these essential health benefits.[12]

Consistently throughout these reforms, Congress rejected a "single-payer" system in which the government provides medical care directly to everyone at little or no cost. Instead, it opted for a hybrid public-private model using private health providers and for-profit health insurers. This model incorporates profit margins and higher private-sector spending, which drive up medical costs.[13]

THE FRAGMENTED US HEALTH INSURANCE SYSTEM

Health insurance is the main way people cover their medical expenses in the United States. Unlike other leading industrialized nations, this country does not guarantee health coverage to every resident. Instead, the US system provides several separate health insurance schemes, each covering a different segment of the public. Which program applies depends on a person's employment status, residence, income and age. Some people fall between the cracks, and others end up in expensive plans.

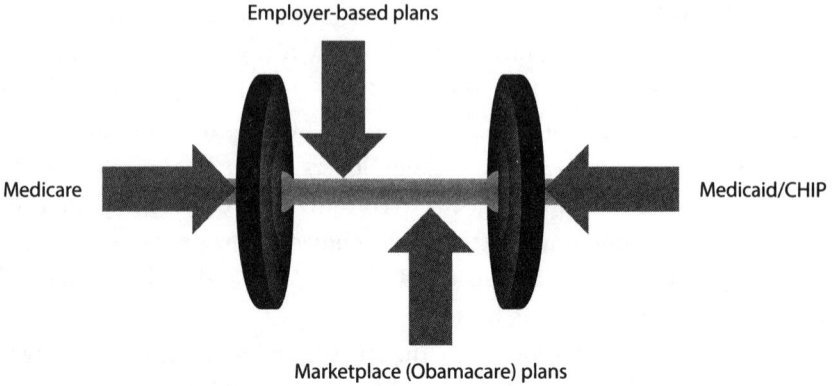

Figure 3. US health insurance system. *Source:* Author.

The easiest way to visualize the US health insurance system is as a barbell with government health insurance on both ends and private insurance in the middle (see figure 3).

On one end of the barbell is Medicare, which covers most US residents age sixty-five and up.[14] Medicare comes in two versions, both administered by the federal government. The first, Original Medicare, provides direct federal reimbursement to private health providers who agree to treat Medicare patients at government rates. The second is Medicare Advantage, in which beneficiaries enroll in private insurance plans. Medicare Advantage insures about half of all Medicare recipients, and Original Medicare covers the rest.[15]

On the other end of the barbell is Medicaid, which furnishes nearly free health insurance to eligible indigent households, including impoverished senior citizens and poor people with disabilities.[16] In addition, the federal government provides low-cost coverage to near-poor children and pregnant women through the Children's Health Insurance Program (CHIP).[17]

Private-sector insurance is in the middle of the barbell and serves the remaining working-age households, most of whom do not qualify for Medicaid. Here, there are two main options: employer-based plans and Marketplace plans. Under the ACA, large employers must offer health coverage or pay a tax penalty. Smaller employers may offer employer-based plans voluntarily.[18]

The other private option is the Marketplace, which the ACA unveiled and is the main source of individual policies today. Marketplace plans are available to most people who do not qualify for Medicare. This includes workers under age sixty-five, who can choose between employer-based plans (when those plans are offered) or Marketplace plans (also known as Obamacare).[19]

Most people experience the Marketplace as an online exchange where they can buy individual policies from private carriers. This exchange is organized, designed, and hosted by the state or federal government (depending on the state).[20] While this government sponsorship is the most obvious difference between the Marketplace and a truly private market, it is not the only difference. Private insurers who provide individual policies through the Marketplace also operate under strict federal rules requiring easy eligibility, improved coverage, and cost controls.

Despite the ACA's very real improvements to US health coverage, the country's health finance system remains a complicated mishmash of health insurance programs with vexing gaps. Even after the ACA's passage, some people do not meet the eligibility criteria of any plan. In addition, when people are forced to rotate off one plan (such as Medicaid after losing eligibility or an employer-based plan after leaving a job), they can end up uninsured.[21] These problems impede access to health coverage and medical care.[22]

ACCESS

When policymakers talk about "access" to health insurance, they are referring to the question of whether someone qualifies for high-quality health coverage at all. The United States has made major progress in expanding health coverage access since 1965. Medicare largely closed the gap for senior citizens. Medicaid and CHIP expanded coverage to the poor, and Medicaid increased that coverage with the passage of the ACA.[23] These advances cut the uninsured population almost in half, from 48.3 million (16% of the US population) in 2010 to an all-time low of 25.3 million (7.7%) in early 2023.[24]

It is a myth to think that these uninsured households get free medical care. Although federal law requires hospitals to treat everyone who seeks emergency room care for medical emergencies, regardless of whether they are insured, few hospitals provide that care for free.[25] Instead, federal tax law simply requires nonprofit hospitals to maintain financial assistance policies to retain their tax-exempt status.[26] Too often, those policies are poorly publicized, toothless, and honored in the breach.[27] More often, hospitals (for-profit and nonprofit alike) bill uninsured patients, including the poor and emergency room patients, for needed medical treatments, frequently at their highest prices.[28]

Consequently, health insurance is a must if households are to have good medical care at reasonable cost. To get quality coverage, first people have to be eligible for it. While eligibility is still not universal in the United States, it is broadly based, and most US residents qualify for coverage, with a few troubling exceptions.

Access for Older Adults and Younger People with Disabilities

Medicare is the main health insurance plan for people age sixty-five and up, plus younger people with disabilities or end-stage renal disease. All three groups can enroll in Medicare, regardless of their income, health status (for those age sixty-five and older), or preexisting conditions. Thanks to Medicare, senior citizens have the best health coverage rate of any group, with over 99 percent of people age sixty-five and older insured in 2022.[29]

Despite Medicare's broad scope, two subsets of the elderly and people with disabilities or end-stage renal disease lack Medicare access. One consists of immigrants without green cards and those with green cards who do not meet Medicare's five-year residency requirement. The other includes prison and jail inmates, who can qualify for hospitalization and outpatient coverage during incarceration but face high administrative hurdles to enrolling and staying enrolled.[30]

Otherwise, most senior citizens and people with disabilities qualify for Medicare. This—plus the fact that Social Security automatically enrolls many recipients in Medicare's inpatient and outpatient coverage—accounts for the remarkable Medicare participation rate among the elderly. The real issue for many Medicare beneficiaries is cost, not access.

Access for Those under Age Sixty-Five

For people under age sixty-five who lack disabilities, there are three main avenues for health coverage: employer-based plans, Medicaid and CHIP, and Marketplace plans. Each has eligibility criteria that applicants must meet in order to enroll.

EMPLOYER-BASED PLANS

Employer-based plans are the biggest source of health insurance today, covering almost 157 million people under age sixty-five in 2022.[31] That year, 95 percent of workplace plans offered family coverage too.[32] The tax treatment of workplace plans explains some of their popularity: employers can deduct their contributions toward premiums from their income and payroll taxes, and those same contributions are usually tax-exempt for employees.[33]

Employer-based plans provide group health insurance, either purchased from private carriers or funded through self-insurance. Despite the prevalence of employer-based plans, not every worker has access. For one thing, one's employer actually must offer health benefits. But only about half of employers do, with the availability hinging on the employer's size. Under the ACA, over 90 percent of large employers (those with fifty full-time employees or more) offer workplace health plans to avoid paying an IRS penalty.[34] In contrast, smaller employers face no tax penalty for not offering health plans. As a result, only 47 percent of smaller employers provided health benefits to their workers in 2022.[35]

People who work at firms without health coverage are shut out of the workplace option (unless their spouses have it). But working for a company with health coverage is no guarantee of access. The vast majority of employers offering health benefits exclude part-time and temporary workers from participating.[36] In 2022, 22 percent of workers did not qualify for health coverage offered by their employers as a consequence.[37] Exclusions for part-time and temporary workers hit low-wage workers particularly hard, because they are most affected by the trend toward part-time schedules.[38]

Meanwhile, employees who do have health benefits at work lose that coverage if they resign or are fired or laid off. This is a constant problem, but it reaches crisis proportions during recessions. Under the Consolidated Omnibus Budget Reconciliation Act (COBRA), former employees can keep their workplace benefits for up to eighteen (and sometimes thirty-six) months after termination, so long as they foot the cost of coverage themselves.[39] But COBRA coverage has serious drawbacks, both because it is temporary and usually is the most expensive health insurance option by far (with annual premiums ranging from $7,012 for single individuals to $20,599 for family coverage in 2019).[40] Accordingly, few ex-employees enroll in COBRA.[41]

For people who do not qualify for workplace health benefits—either because they do not work or they work somewhere where they lack benefits—their two principal remaining options are Medicaid/CHIP and Marketplace plans.[42] Medicaid and CHIP are reserved for the lowest-income households, while the Marketplace aspires to serve everyone else. But certain groups lack access to those programs, either legally or as a practical matter.

MEDICAID

For low-income residents who qualify, Medicaid is an extremely precious benefit because it covers health care at virtually no cost. Through a partnership funded jointly by the states and the federal government, the federal government sets minimum Medicaid eligibility standards, and the states are free to expand them.[43]

Until 2010, traditional Medicaid was the only type of Medicaid available. But in the ACA, Congress relaxed Medicaid's eligibility standards through what became known as Medicaid expansion.[44] Post-enactment, during the pitched political battles over the ACA, Medicaid expansion landed before the US Supreme Court, which ruled in the *Sebelius* case that the states did not have to participate in Medicaid expansion unless they opted into it.[45]

Despite that decision, more and more states signed up for Medicaid expansion over time, largely due to popular demand and permanent federal funding, which picks up 90 percent of expansion costs.[46] As of 2024, forty states plus the District of Columbia had opted into Medicaid expansion.[47] The ten remaining "opt-out" states—mostly in the South—only offer traditional Medicaid, with its stricter eligibility requirements. As the number of Medicaid expansion states grew, the number of uninsured shrank, with over seventy-two million people enrolled in Medicaid as of August 2024.[48]

Under traditional Medicaid, states must provide Medicaid benefits to certain "mandatory" groups, which reflect a narrow vision of who constitutes the "deserving" poor. Under those rules, eligibility is mostly limited to low-income children and pregnant women, plus Supplemental Security Income

(SSI) recipients who have disabilities or are over age sixty-five.[49] Other adults in opt-out states are usually banned from receiving Medicaid.[50] Traditional Medicaid even excludes most parents in opt-out states, unless they live in crushing poverty (typically with incomes well under the federal poverty line, FPL).[51] Incarcerated individuals also are ineligible for Medicaid.[52]

Traditional Medicaid disqualifies other people as well. Undocumented immigrants do not qualify, nor do most noncitizens who are in the United States for educational reasons, travel, or work. Even lawful permanent residents are barred from Medicaid participation for the first five years after they receive their green cards (unless their states have lifted that waiting period). Indigent refugees and immigrants granted asylum can qualify without waiting five years, however.[53] All told, in 2019 an estimated 4.3 million poor immigrants were ineligible for Medicaid.[54]

In the ACA, one way Congress sought to reduce the number of uninsured was by expanding Medicaid eligibility while ditching the notion of the "deserving poor." As a result, in expansion states, nearly everyone in households making less than 138 percent of the FPL now qualifies for Medicaid.[55] This expansion provided Medicaid to numerous parents and childless adults who had not qualified for traditional Medicaid before. Medicaid expansion remains off-limits to the same noncitizens just mentioned for traditional Medicaid, however.

Bottom line, tens of millions of residents now qualify for free or low-cost Medicaid coverage because they make so little. Nevertheless, a sizeable group falls between the cracks of Medicaid and Marketplace plans. This group consists of nearly two million indigent adults in opt-out states who do not qualify for Medicaid.[56] Perversely, these working-age, nondisabled adults fall into a twilight zone known as the "Medicaid gap" because they are shut out of Medicaid but make less than the FPL and so do not qualify for Marketplace subsidies.[57] As a result, many of these desperately poor people lack access as a practical matter to any health insurance. Almost all of them reside in the South, six out of ten are people of color, and another six out of ten work in low-wage jobs.[58]

MARKETPLACE PLANS

When Congress enacted the ACA, it envisioned the Marketplace as a new, improved version of individual health coverage that would serve virtually everyone who was not otherwise insured. A decade or so later, most of that promise of open access has been fulfilled.

The Marketplace makes it easy for most people under age sixty-five to qualify. Most US citizens are eligible for Marketplace coverage, apart from citizens living abroad, Medicare recipients, and prisoners. The Marketplace also accepts a much broader group of foreign residents than Medicaid, including most documented immigrants and other US visa holders who reside in the United States. Undocumented immigrants, however, are not eligible for Marketplace coverage.[59]

When Congress liberalized access to Marketplace plans, it outlawed many of the practices that had blocked people from qualifying for individual health insurance in the past. Now in Marketplace plans, insurers cannot deny coverage due to poor health or preexisting conditions.[60] Similarly, insurers cannot cancel Marketplace policies or refuse to renew them based on health, claims history, or preexisting conditions.[61] Together, these "guaranteed issue" provisions give people access to Marketplace plans regardless of their health. In addition, Congress banned lifetime dollar limits on benefits in Marketplace plans.[62]

With these improvements, the Marketplace greatly expanded access. But access is not the same as affordability. Marketplace policies are offered, for the most part, by for-profit insurers, and the price of admission is cost. While many Marketplace customers qualify for premium subsidies, certain groups do not and are discouraged from enrolling in Marketplace plans as a result. Meanwhile, only limited Marketplace subsidies are available to help defray deductibles, coinsurance, and copays, which makes out-of-pocket charges the biggest issue confronting Marketplace participants. These out-of-pocket costs deter struggling households—particularly lower-income and sicker households—from seeking needed medical care, to the detriment of their health.[63]

To recap, health insurance has vastly improved with the expansion of risk sharing in past decades. Minimum essential benefits requirements have improved the quality of health coverage. Broader eligibility has led to a significant drop in the uninsured.

More progress is needed, however. A stubbornly large number of people remain uninsured. Others with insurance have significant coverage gaps, including dental, vision, and hearing benefits. Finally, for people on tight incomes, the big issue is cost. For them, cost raises a barrier to getting insurance in the first place and to affording health care when they are insured. When cost stands in the way, it is equivalent to having no health insurance at all.

COST

While health insurance is widely available in the United States, that does not mean that health care is affordable. Premiums, deductibles, coinsurance, and copays swamp too many households, who either go "bare" or struggle to pay for coverage.

This problem is widespread. Almost half of US adults reported in 2022 that they could not pay a $500 medical bill out of pocket.[64] Despite this, the US health-care system is built on the cockeyed premise that most households can pay thousands of dollars every year in deductibles, coinsurance, and copays (and sometimes premiums as well). No wonder almost half of US adults surveyed in 2022—47 percent—reported that it was somewhat or very difficult to afford their health-care bills.[65] Meanwhile, four out of every ten adults were mired in medical debt.[66]

We can think about three categories of health-care costs, which each can pose a hurdle to needed medical care. The first category consists of unreimbursed medical bills. For patients who are uninsured, this usually amounts to all of their medical bills. For people with insurance, these are medical bills that are excluded from coverage and have no insurance at all.

The second category consists of health insurance premiums. Premiums must be paid to obtain and keep coverage, even if the policyholder has no medical bills in a given year. Prohibitive premiums can result in no coverage at all.

Finally, most health insurance customers who incur medical expenses face costs in the form of deductibles, coinsurance, and copays (together referred to as "cost sharing"). Deductibles are a fixed amount of medical bills (say, $5,000) that patients must pay themselves each year before insurance starts to cover the rest of their bills. After a patient meets the deductible and insurance payments begin, then coinsurance and copayments apply. Under coinsurance and copayments, insurance pays most of each bill, but the patient pays the rest (either a percentage [for coinsurance] or a flat dollar amount [for copays]). Typically, the more medical care someone receives, the higher the coinsurance and copays.

Typically, policymakers argue that deductibles, coinsurance, and copays counteract adverse selection by discouraging people from getting unnecessary medical care. The theory behind cost sharing is that patients who have to foot part of their medical bills will be "smarter" consumers because they will reject wasteful health treatments while getting the medical services they need. But this theory is seriously flawed. In reality, deductibles, coinsurance, and copays operate as overkill, by discouraging people on tight budgets from getting needed medical care, sometimes at serious harm to their health.[67] As we will see, cost sharing is doubly problematic because it drives many people into debt.

Insurance is supposed to provide protection from crushing costs. But for many, the reality is starkly different when it comes to health care. For virtually half of Americans, high health costs exert a heavy strain on them financially.

Medicare

Of all age groups, senior citizens are the hardest pressed to pay for health care. On average, they need more medical services and are in worse health.[68] Their median incomes are lower, at $3,120 a month for men and only $2,052 a month for women in 2022.[69] And many older people are no longer physically able to work. Consequently, health costs easily can capsize senior citizens' fixed incomes. With almost sixty million people age sixty-five and older in 2023, this problem affects tens of millions of older adults.[70]

Medicare charges its recipients premiums, deductibles, coinsurance, and copays. Its cost structure is mind-numbingly complicated, largely due to the fact that Medicare divides medical treatments into three parts: Parts A, B, and D.[71] Part A pays for inpatient stays in hospitals, skilled nursing home stays, some home health care, and hospice care. Part B covers doctors' visits, other outpatient services, preventive care, and other home health care. Part D is Medicare's outpatient prescription drug coverage, which patients receive through private plans under contract with Medicare.[72] Each part has its own premiums, deductibles, coinsurance, and copays, burdening Medicare recipients with layer upon layer of costs. The thing to keep in mind is how those costs can add up.

So how high are these costs? In 2016, the average person on Original Medicare paid $5,460 for Medicare premiums and cost sharing. Women and patients lacking supplemental coverage for cost-sharing expenses on average paid more. The cost burden was especially crushing for desperately poor seniors. In 2016, half of Original Medicare participants who lived on $10,000 or less a year spent 18 percent of their income or more on health costs, compared to the median Original Medicare recipient, who spent 12 percent.[73]

These costs have several drivers. The first consists of premiums. In 2025, Medicare premiums cost a minimum of $185 a month, but could soar hundreds of dollars higher each month, depending on the person and the plan.[74]

Cost sharing pushes senior citizens' out-of-pocket health spending even higher. The biggest issue here is whether those deductibles, coinsurance, and copays are capped. Original Medicare does not cap out-of-pocket expenses for hospital stays, skilled nursing care, or outpatient treatment.[75] Add to that, in 2025, Original Medicare Part A charged a $1,676 deductible for *each* inpatient hospital benefit period, with no annual cap in the event of repeat hospitalizations.[76] Accordingly, Original Medicare puts a crushing financial burden on elderly patients who need prolonged, costly medical care.

For a price, Original Medicare patients can buy private supplemental Medigap policies to help defray their deductibles, coinsurance, and copays.[77] But Medigap premiums can be pricey, ranging between $48 and $363 a month in 2023 in a typical state.[78] For senior citizens with incomes at or below 150 percent of the FPL, there are special federal supplemental coverage programs to pay their Medicare premiums and cost sharing.[79] But those programs are marred by low participation rates and limited eligibility, due to their low income limits, strict asset caps, and onerous application processes.[80] Anyone who makes even a penny over the income limit receives no relief. As a result, 5.6 million Original Medicare beneficiaries in 2018 had no supplemental coverage of any type. Almost two-thirds of them survived on $40,000 a year or less.[81] With no supplemental coverage, these people bore the full cost of their deductibles, coinsurance, and copays, which Original Medicare did not cap.[82]

In contrast, Medigap policies and Medicare Advantage plans must have annual out-of-pocket limits on deductibles, coinsurance, and copays, which vary according to the plan. For Original Medicare patients with Medigap coverage in 2024, those annual limits went as high as $7,060.[83] For Medicare Advantage plans that year, the annual cap for Parts A and B combined was $8,850.[84]

These exorbitant caps on annual out-of-pocket expenditures (not to mention the absence of caps for Original Medicare Parts A and B) make health costs arduous for many Medicare beneficiaries of limited means. Original Medicare participants who lack supplemental coverage report the greatest difficulty covering their health costs, followed by people on Medicare Advantage. Original Medicare recipients with supplemental coverage find the cost burden the easiest, but it is still not negligible.[85]

Marketplace Plans under the Affordable Care Act

Like Medicare, Marketplace plans charge premiums plus deductibles, coinsurance, and copays. The exception is for preventive care (including vaccinations, annual physicals, and in-network screenings), which the Marketplace covers with no deductible.[86]

To help consumers compare prices, the Marketplace assigns each plan to one of four groups. These groups are ranked from top to bottom in order of Platinum, Gold, Silver, and Bronze and offer different trade-offs between the cost of premiums and the maximum deductibles, coinsurance, and copays.[87] Bronze plans have the highest cost sharing but the lowest premiums; Platinum plans have the highest premiums but the lowest deductibles, coinsurance, and copays.[88]

The exact price of a Marketplace plan depends on the state where someone resides, plus a handful of factors unique to each consumer.[89] In the old individual health insurance market, private carriers engaged in aggressive "risk-based pricing," in which they varied the price depending on customers' personal risk profiles, including good or poor health. In the ACA, Congress curbed this practice and especially pricing based on health. Instead, Congress ordered Marketplace plans to use a modified form of "community rating," in which prices more closely reflect the risk posed by the larger pool of insureds. Under this system, insurers can only take two characteristics of Marketplace customers into account: any tobacco use and their age group (with older people paying more). Insurers also may charge individuals and families different rates.[90]

During the 2024 open enrollment period, the average unsubsidized premium for a Silver benchmark plan was $5,724 a year.[91] That same year, the average deductible was $5,241 for a Silver plan and $7,258 for a Bronze plan, with the maximum annual expenditure for deductibles, coinsurance, and copays capped at $9,450 for individuals and $18,900 for families.[92] When you add these numbers up, Marketplace policies were prohibitively expensive for most people unless they received subsidies.

MARKETPLACE SUBSIDIES

When Congress enacted the ACA, it was painfully aware that it could not diversify the Marketplace risk pool or substantially cut the number of uninsured unless it subsidized premiums and cost sharing. For those who pay full freight, Marketplace plans are expensive, but the ACA offers subsidies to tens of millions of enrollees to help defray their costs. There are two different subsidies, with different eligibility requirements: one for premiums and the other for deductibles, coinsurance, and copays.

Premium Subsidies

In the ACA, Congress authorized something called "premium tax credits" to help reduce the premiums on Marketplace plans.[93] These subsidies can be used to lower the premiums on Bronze, Silver, Gold, or Platinum plans (but not on catastrophic plans).[94] During the COVID-19 pandemic in 2021 and again in 2022, Congress enhanced these premium tax credits through 2025, which further reduced the uninsured rate by making the subsidies more generous.[95] Middle-income families benefited the most from these changes, while older people and residents in areas with higher premiums also stood to gain.[96]

The amount of the premium tax credit varies by income. At the bottom of the scale, households with incomes between 138 and 150 percent of the FPL can enroll in a benchmark Silver plan for a premium of $0 or almost $0.[97] Above that threshold, households contribute a percentage of their income toward the premium. This percentage starts at zero percent, then rises according to income, topping out at 8.5 percent of income for households enrolled in benchmark Silver plans with incomes just over 400 percent of the FPL.[98] (In 2025, 400% of the FPL was $60,240 for an individual and $124,800 for a family of four.)[99] Above the 400 percent level, premium subsidies gradually phase out.[100]

As a result, the vast majority of Marketplace policyholders receive subsidized premiums today. In the 2024 open enrollment period, that amounted to 90 percent of customers who enrolled.[101] The average 2024 monthly premium was $111 after subsidies were applied, and half of customers paid net monthly premiums of $10 or less.[102] These subsidies were sufficiently generous that most households could afford Marketplace premiums—*if* they qualified for the subsidies.[103] At the same time, people right above the poverty line struggle to pay even heavily subsidized premiums. The lowest-income consumers are significantly more likely to remain uninsured if their Marketplace premiums exceed $0, even by a few dollars a month.[104]

Of even greater concern, two million or so indigent adults in opt-out states are barred from receiving premium subsidies at all, regardless of how little they make.[105] Because these adults have the misfortune to fall into the so-called Medicaid gap under the ACA, they do not qualify for Medicaid expansion but must pay the full, costly premiums for Marketplace coverage, which is virtually impossible because they make less than the FPL.[106]

Subsidies for Deductibles, Coinsurance, and Copayments

On top of premium subsidies, Congress authorized a second, less generous set of subsidies to help cover deductibles, coinsurance, and copayments under Marketplace plans. These are called "cost-sharing reductions" (CSRs).

Cost-sharing reductions have much stricter income cutoffs than premium subsidies. CSRs are only available to households with incomes between 100 and 250 percent of the FPL. In 2025 those income limits stood at $37,650 for an individual and $78,000 for a family of four.[107] Meanwhile, households who do not qualify for premium subsidies are ineligible for CSRs.[108] Given these rules, far fewer households receive CSRs than premium subsidies.[109]

For households below the income cutoffs, the amount of CSRs varies on a sliding scale. Those with incomes at 201 to 250 percent of the FPL receive the lowest CSRs. The CSRs for this group are so paltry that an individual making 250 percent of the FPL in 2025 had an average out-of-pocket limit of $7,350, even with the CSRs.[110]

Customers with CSRs still have out-of-pocket health expenses, because CSRs *never* pay 100 percent of deductibles, coinsurance, and copays.[111] Meanwhile, the remaining 52 percent of Marketplace policyholders who did not qualify for CSRs had to pay the full cost of deductibles, coinsurance, and copays themselves. Those families were on the hook for up to $18,400 in cost-sharing charges in 2025.[112] These are frightening amounts of bills for the average middle-class household (not to mention those who lacked the cash to even pay a $500 medical bill). And to reiterate, *Marketplace coverage will not kick in until the annual deductible is met*, which averaged $5,241 for Silver and $7,258 for Bronze plans in 2024.[113]

The stingy amount of CSRs means that cost-sharing expenses impose a much heavier burden on Marketplace participants than premiums. This cost pressure is particularly brutal for lower-income Marketplace participants and those with high medical costs.[114] And the data bear that out. In 2022, fully 44 percent of people surveyed with individual-market or Marketplace coverage paid such high out-of-pocket costs that their policies were not affordable.[115] Steep cost-sharing expenses cause some families with tight finances to opt out of health coverage entirely or to put off needed medical care or basic essentials if they are insured.[116]

Employer-Based Plans

Just as Marketplace plans have problems with affordability, so do employer-based plans. Federal law does not tell employers how much, if anything, to contribute toward workplace plans. Furthermore, the deductibles on workplace plans are typically higher for lower-wage workers, compared to subsidized Marketplace plans.[117] Workers at organizations with health insurance are in a bind, however, because the ACA precludes most of them from subsidies if they want to buy Marketplace policies instead.

It is a well-known fact that the premiums for workplace coverage have been rising steadily. Employers have limited capacity to increase the percentage of premiums borne by workers, because doing that will hamper their ability to compete for labor. Accordingly, most employers cover the lion's share of the premiums for workplace policies.[118]

Employers have responded to rising premiums, however, in other ways. First, they pay lower wages in order to foot health-care premiums.[119] And second, they shift health costs onto workers in less visible ways.[120]

One way employers have passed costs on to workers is by raising the total dollar amount of premiums that employees must pay (even if the employer's percentage match remains the same). By 2021 the average employee contribution toward a family plan at work had risen to $5,969 a year, and it was even higher—$7,710—for employees at small firms.[121] As workers had to spend a growing cut of pay on health insurance premiums, they had less remaining for other basic needs.[122]

In addition, employers increasingly have replaced preferred provider organization (PPO) plans, which are popular with employees but expensive, with high-deductible health plans (HDHPs) with lower premiums but deductibles running in the thousands of dollars.[123] These high deductibles make it harder for workers to pay their medical bills and also deter them, especially those making under $75,000 a year, from seeking primary and preventive care, resulting in more avoidable emergency room visits.[124]

In workplace policies, moreover, deductibles have become the rule, not the exception. Meanwhile, the average size of those deductibles almost doubled, from $1,025 in 2010 for a single-coverage plan to $2,004 in 2021.[125]

These health costs hit lower-income workers the hardest. Most employers charge workers the same amounts for premiums and deductibles, regardless of their wage.[126] As a result, lower-paid workers have to spend a bigger slice of their pay on premiums and deductibles than better-paid workers. Those workers also spend more in total median dollars than better-paid employees on workplace plans, which reflects their reduced bargaining power over the terms and conditions of their employment.[127] In another troubling pattern, lower-paid workers are more likely to opt out of insurance at work. Their take-up rates are especially low in poorly paid service industries.[128] This reinforces concerns that low-wage workers are turning down coverage due to the cost.[129]

In sum, the cost of employer-based plans pushes health-care expenses past the limit for high numbers of workers. In 2022, 29 percent—almost one-third—of workers in employer-based plans reported making too little to afford their out-of-pocket costs under their policies.[130] If these workers qualified for subsidized Marketplace plans, they could save substantially. In 2025, for example, the federally mandated out-of-pocket maximum in private-sector workplace plans was $9,200 for individuals, three times the $3,050 out-of-pocket maximum for an individual Marketplace participant at the FPL.[131] But under the ACA's "firewall" provision, workers who are eligible for employer-based plans do not qualify for Marketplace subsidies unless their employers' plans flunk the ACA's standards for being "affordable," offering "minimum value," and meeting the caps on cost sharing.[132]

The Biden administration took two steps to address this problem. In 2022 it eliminated the "family glitch" that denied premium tax credits to family members of workers with access to "affordable" plans at work.[133] The following year the administration made it easier for workers with access to workplace coverage to qualify for Marketplace premium tax credits by reducing the level above which workplace plans are deemed "unaffordable" to 8.39 percent of household income.[134] These changes lower, but do not, eliminate the "firewall" that blocks workers who qualify for workplace coverage from subsidized Marketplace policies. Congress should go further and dismantle the firewall completely for poor and near-poor workers.

Medicaid

Medicaid clearly has the lowest cost burden on recipients compared to other major health plans. This is largely because the federal government restricts the states' ability to charge premiums and cost sharing for Medicaid.[135] Under those rules, states may not charge premiums to Medicaid participants with incomes under 150 percent of the FPL without a federal waiver. Federal rules also strictly cap cost sharing and exclude certain health services from cost sharing altogether. Finally, total premium and cost-sharing charges to Medicaid families may not exceed 5 percent of any household's income.[136]

As of early 2020, only a few states charged premiums for Medicaid. However, thirty-five states charged copays to adults on Medicaid, generally in the single-dollar digits.[137]

Not surprisingly given these federal limits, Medicaid participants have substantially lower out-of-pocket costs on average than Marketplace participants.[138] Despite their modest size, Medicaid's out-of-pocket charges still have undesirable effects. The poorest households live so close to the edge that even a few dollars in Medicaid premiums per month can deter them from enrolling in or keeping Medicaid coverage, and many end up uninsured. Similarly, even small copays of $1 to $5 discourage Medicaid participants from seeking essential health services and may encourage costlier emergency room visits.[139]

THE HARMFUL EFFECTS OF UNAFFORDABLE HEALTH COSTS

The sticker shock from health costs is not just a matter of money. Instead, high costs can set off a chain reaction, harming families in serious ways. Steep health costs torpedo family budgets, swamp untold numbers with medical debt, short-circuit other financial goals, force some into financial ruin, and worse, deter people from getting essential medical care, with adverse health consequences.

On the most basic level, spiraling health costs can wreck families' finances. Millions of people who struggle with medical bills end up paying for them with credit. This medical debt is so pervasive that *over one hundred million US residents*—41 percent of adults—carried it in 2022. Medical debt was especially prevalent among those living on less than $40,000 a year and Black and Hispanic adults.[140]

Harsh consequences await those who cannot pay their medical bills, ranging from ruined credit to foreclosure.[141] Unpaid medical bills are the biggest reason people end up in third-party collection.[142] And collection is not limited to debt collectors. Hospitals regularly sue patients to collect and push patients to enroll in medical credit cards in order to get paid.[143] Meanwhile, medical debt is a top reason people end up in bankruptcy.[144]

Costly medical bills have a further crowd-out effect by preventing many patients from reaching other financial milestones. Almost two-thirds of those with medical debt in 2022 cut their spending on necessities such as food and clothing. Almost half with medical debt depleted all or most of their savings—including retirement and college funds—to pay for medical bills. Twenty-eight percent of them deferred pursuing an education or buying a home for the same reason.[145]

The negative effects of high health costs do not stop there. Prohibitive medical expenses discourage large numbers of people from getting the medical care they need, at risk to their health. In 2022, 43 percent of people surveyed put off medical treatment and prescriptions against doctors' orders due to the cost. That percentage was even higher for uninsured adults, people with larger deductibles, those making less than $40,000 a year, and working-age adults.[146] Medical debt similarly hinders obtaining medical care.[147] Meanwhile, some unscrupulous health providers (including nonprofits with favored tax status) have denied care to patients because they owed medical bills.[148]

Inadequate coverage is another deterrent. In 2022, for example, adults were most likely to postpone dental services and vision services (including eyeglasses) due to cost concerns.[149] Many traditional health plans do not cover those services. And even plans with coverage typically offer measly dental and vision benefits.[150]

The harmful physical effects of unaffordable medical treatment are not hypothetical. The health repercussions of missed care can be grave, especially when serious diseases go undetected.[151] Perhaps for that reason, people with no or poor health coverage and high health costs have worse health on average than those with better coverage.[152] Insured adults are more likely to interrupt life-saving treatments and have higher death rates when their coinsurance and copays for prescriptions go up.[153] Medical debt also is associated with adverse health outcomes later in life.[154]

High health costs similarly have grave consequences for social inequality and the quality of overall US health care. Skyrocketing medical bills contribute to worse health outcomes for lower-income families and for Blacks, Hispanics, and Native Americans, compared to higher-income households and Whites.[155] These disparities have left America with two health-care systems: world-class care for people who can afford it and a broken system for those who cannot.[156] Soaring health costs for patients were a major factor why the US health-care system ranked last among eleven leading nations in 2021.[157]

Despite the real advances to date, US health coverage remains a work in progress. Most of the nation's residents (except prisoners and undocumented immigrants) qualify for some sort of health insurance. That alone is a signal achievement. While the future of health coverage became murkier with the election of the second Trump administration, the broad public support for improved coverage would make cutbacks politically perilous.

If anything, Congress should *expand*, not curtail, coverage. No one should have to forego daily necessities in order to pay for health care. No one should be driven into debt, bankruptcy, or foreclosure because they cannot pay medical bills. And no one should be forced to delay or forego needed medical care due to the cost.

On the issue of health coverage affordability, recent past events showed encouraging signs. Since 2021, Congress has twice passed legislation temporarily expanding the premium subsidies for Marketplace policies. These expanded premium subsidies spurred large numbers of uninsured households to sign up for Marketplace plans.[158] While the expanded subsidies are set to expire at the end of 2025, eliminating them would be a highly visible move that would invite political blowback.

Instead, it is time to build on the progress in recent years by making premiums and cost-sharing expenses affordable. In this discussion, I focus on the health insurance system in its current form. Necessarily, that approach does not address other pressing issues facing health reform, such as proposals for a single-payer plan or the best way to get high medical costs under control. Instead, I proceed from the fact that Congress *has* accomplished other major health reforms in recent years. These reforms provide a strong foundation on which to build.

Reducing the Uninsured

Although the ACA cut the uninsured rate virtually in half, a stubbornly large number of people—over twenty-seven million—remained uninsured in early 2024.[159] That number had risen as the temporary expansions in coverage and subsidies enacted during the COVID-19 pandemic expired.[160] Almost two-thirds of uninsured adults under age sixty-five cite the high cost of coverage as the reason they lack health insurance.[161] Consequently, improved affordability is the key to reducing their numbers.

The problem of the uninsured mostly involves children and working-age adults. Almost half of them are poor or near-poor, living on incomes at or under 200 percent of the FPL.[162] Today, the Marketplace offers the broadest access of any health insurance option for this group. Given the ease in qualifying for Marketplace policies, it makes sense to make the Marketplace the default health insurance option for everyone not on Medicare or Medicaid. But to make the Marketplace a *meaningful* default option, Marketplace plans must become more affordable. Five steps are needed to close the affordability gap.

The first is to extend Marketplace premium tax credits to poor adults in the Medicaid gap. According to researchers, this would be one of the most effective ways to reduce the uninsured.[163] It is unconscionable that higher-income adults receive these subsidies when some of the poorest adults do not.

Next, Congress should extend Marketplace premium subsidies to all workers making 138 percent of the FPL or less, regardless of whether they have access to "affordable" coverage at work.[164] Practically speaking, this would be necessary only for workers in opt-out states, because workers below 138 percent of the FPL in expansion states qualify for Medicaid.

Third, Congress needs to make the enhanced premium tax credits permanent. This would powerfully boost the number of insured, judging from the fact that the Marketplace gained about 3.6 million new enrollees in 2023. Congress's decision to extend the enhanced premium subsidies in the Inflation Reduction Act was the biggest reason for that gain.[165]

Fourth, the government should step up outreach to help people who lose their Medicaid, Medicare, or workplace eligibility locate replacement coverage.[166] Falling between the cracks of health plans is a solvable problem if people who lose their coverage can be placed in affordable Marketplace plans. A robust Marketplace Navigator program—which is the free program that helps households enroll in the Marketplace—would make a big difference in closing coverage gaps.

Finally, lower deductibles, coinsurance, and copays would persuade more uninsured households to enroll in health insurance.[167] Lower cost sharing similarly would benefit people who already have coverage, as the next section discusses.

Lower Out-of-Pocket Costs

Two disquieting statistics—the nearly half of US adults who lack the cash to pay a $500 medical bill and the one hundred million plus in medical debt—drive home the fact that large swaths of people who *do* have health insurance still cannot afford the medical care they need.[168] If these households are to enjoy good health and financial security, the nation must get out-of-pocket health expenses under control.

PREMIUMS

For most people, premiums are the gateway to health insurance. If they can pony up the premiums, they are covered; otherwise, they are not. A lot is at stake, because whether they seek medical care and enjoy good health depends on having insurance.

After Congress enhanced Marketplace premium tax credits in 2021, Marketplace premiums became affordable for most people who qualified. Accordingly, the Marketplace would provide a good template for affordable premiums if Congress made the enhanced premium tax credits permanent and extended them to people in the Medicaid gap and workers making less than 138 percent of the FPL in opt-out states. With those changes, the Marketplace would be the economical, quality, comprehensive health insurance option for many more people (except those on Medicare or Medicaid).[169]

Similar reforms to Medicare would be necessary to rein in health-care costs for older adults and people with disabilities. Unlike the Marketplace, Original Medicare expects most participants to pay multiple premiums for adequate coverage, including for Part B, Part D, and Medigap policies. This premium structure discourages enrollment in Part D outpatient prescription drug coverage and Medigap coverage for Original Medicare participants, as demonstrated by their discouraging take-up rates.[170] Close to fifteen million Original Medicare recipients were not enrolled in Part D in 2021. Two-thirds of them were poor or near-poor, with incomes under 150 percent of the FPL.[171] Similarly, in 2018, 5.6 million Original

Medicare participants with incomes less than $40,000 a year lacked any supplemental coverage, from Medigap or otherwise, for their cost-sharing expenses.[172] Their limited incomes strongly suggest that they could not afford Medigap premiums *or* cost sharing. Meanwhile, the federal supplemental coverage programs now in place have failed to alleviate the Medicare cost burden on the near-poor elderly population.

Recent proposals to address these problems focus on tying the amount of Part B and Part D premiums to income and repealing asset limits to extend cost relief to more low-income senior citizens.[173] While the details of these proposals vary, all of them would cut those premiums substantially for recipients with incomes below 200 or 400 percent of the FPL, depending on the proposal. The proposals generally would eliminate premiums for beneficiaries with incomes below 135 or 150 percent of the FPL, again depending on the proposal. Those with incomes of 400 percent of the FPL or greater would pay higher Part B and Part D premiums than they do today (up to a dollar cap on the premium), but the annual cost-of-living adjustment to their Social Security benefits would usually cover that increase. Pegging Medicare premiums to income would make it easier for lower-income Medicare recipients to afford their premiums, while defraying the cost by requiring recipients with incomes greater than 400 percent of the FPL to pay more.

DEDUCTIBLES, COINSURANCE, AND COPAYS

Today, the United States has no good model for making cost sharing affordable for seriously ill patients or near-poor families. Although the cost-sharing reductions in the Marketplace are calibrated by income, still too few families qualify for those CSRs. Furthermore, CSRs are too small dollarwise to shield lower-income families from potentially devastating medical costs.

Congress should address these problems with two sets of reforms. First, Congress should extend CSRs up to 400 percent of the FPL. Second, Congress should set CSRs high enough so that cost-sharing charges do not exceed households' actual ability to pay, after allowing for basic living expenses. A leading proposal would subsidize 95 percent of cost-sharing expenses for Marketplace participants with incomes of up to 200 percent of the FPL, 90 percent for those with incomes between 200 and 300 percent of the FPL, and 85 percent for those with incomes between 300 and 400 percent of the FPL.[174]

Along with these reforms, extending subsidized Marketplace coverage to workers earning less than 138 percent of the FPL would reduce the need to address cost-sharing issues with workplace policies. Making Marketplace policies affordable for those workers regardless of their benefits at work would substantially help solve the health-care affordability problem for people under age sixty-five.

Medicare cost sharing also is crying out for reform. In theory, the federal government covers Medicare cost sharing for recipients who are close to or below the FPL, but those programs have dismal take-up rates due to their low asset limits and bureaucratic red tape.[175] Instead, Medicare should have only one deductible for all medical care during the year, whether those services are inpatient, outpatient, or prescription drug in nature. In addition, Original Medicare should adopt a total annual cap on out-of-pocket patient expenditures. Finally, and most importantly, both Original Medicare and Medicare Advantage should adjust the deductible and the annual cap according to recipients' incomes, so that cash-strapped senior citizens can pay their other essential bills while affording medical treatment when they need it.[176]

To conclude, the United States has evolved to an uneasy place where more have health insurance but the high price of cost sharing makes their insurance unusable except for catastrophic expenses. The sticker price of insurance deters millions of other people from signing up for health coverage at all. For these households, the high price of health insurance bears no reality to their limited means or the numerous other demands on their budgets.

Families who struggle with health expenses have scant hope of economic well-being. Paring down those costs to a manageable level will give them a fighting chance to make it through the month, to buy a home, and to set aside some money to save. An additional, important goal—how to finance college for their children, on top of medical expenses—is the subject of the next chapter.

9 Paying for College

Today, a bachelor's degree is the price of admission to the middle class, and a costly one at that. In the twenty-first century, paying for college frequently means going into debt. Tens of millions of adults are saddled with student loan payments for years.[1] While society tells high school seniors that college is the path to success, it doesn't add that student loans can hold them back economically and result in financial distress.

Paying for college used to be different. Today's dependence on student loans did not take off until higher education expanded. Back in 1960, the nation was much less well educated, with less than 8 percent of US adults holding bachelor's degrees.[2] To improve that situation, the federal government launched a successful national campaign after World War II to increase the number of college graduates. By 2022, almost half of US adults had at least a certificate or technical degree, and 36 percent held a bachelor's degree.[3] This rise in college-educated adults held true for all races and ethnicities and propelled the innovation economy that is the hallmark of the United States.[4]

During the expansion of higher education, Congress liberalized financing in the Higher Education Act of 1965 to make college accessible to virtually anyone. That liberalization included the pivot to student debt, when, in 1965, federal student loans became broadly available.[5]

Today, about forty-three million adults owe federal student loans, while 30 percent of adults have had student loans at some point in their lives.[6] For a snapshot of student debt carried by new graduates of public and private nonprofit universities, consider the class of 2023. Exactly half of that year's graduating class owed student loans on the day they received their diplomas. At graduation, they owed $29,300 on average in student loans, up from $27,700 for the class of 2006 after adjusting for inflation.[7]

THE ASCENDENCE OF STUDENT DEBT

Sixty years ago, when the push to expand higher education took wing, tuition was affordable and government footed much more of the cost of higher education. As college financing shifted toward student loans in recent decades, college became costlier and riskier to students as a financial proposition.

Government supports higher education for students in three main ways. First, government can subsidize colleges and universities through appropriations designed to reduce the tuition charged to students. Second, government can provide cash grants to students to defray their tuition and living expenses. Third, government can lend funds to students to pay for college education.[8] All three funding streams operate today.

Over time, however, the mix of direct subsidies to universities, student grants, and student loans changed. Through the 1980s, states supported public higher education by heavily subsidizing college tuition.[9] Starting in 1989, however, the amount of state appropriations per college student dropped.[10] In the process, taxpayers and government dumped much of the responsibility for financing college onto individual students and their parents. This thrust heavy new educational costs onto numerous students and families for which they were unprepared. The magnitude of that cost shift, moreover, was enormous. Back in 1988, students only provided one-fourth of the financing for public universities and colleges, mostly through tuition payments; by 2018, they provided one-half.[11]

Meanwhile, public institutions made up for lost appropriations by jacking up tuition.[12] In prior decades, tuition at public universities had been a bargain due to generous state support. In 1979–1980, for example, the average published in-state tuition and fees at a public four-year university came to $2,444 a year—and that's in 2020 dollars.[13] Over the next four decades, tuition and fees grew fourfold, faster than the rate of inflation.[14] By 2020–2021, the published in-state tuition and fees at a public four-year university averaged $11,990.[15]

As the cost of college increased, tens of millions of students "amass[ed] more debt" to attend college.[16] Over thirty years, the total amount of federal student loans originated annually quadrupled, from $22 billion in 1991–1992 to $88 billion in 2020–2021, in inflation-adjusted dollars. This growth was so fast that student debt overtook auto loans in 2009 as the second largest type of outstanding consumer debt, topping $1.6 trillion in 2023.[17] Today, student borrowing remains "substantially above" the level where it was in the mid-1990s and comprises the majority of nonmortgage household debt.[18]

Rising college enrollment, soaring tuition, underfunded scholarship grants, and easy credit all coalesced to make student debt so prevalent.[19] In the process, the US higher education system morphed into one that charges high tuition and finances it with student loans.

ELIGIBILITY FOR STUDENT GRANTS AND LOANS

Student financial aid involves multiple providers, with federal student assistance being the biggest source by far.[20] Given the federal government's lead role, the following discussion focuses on federal student grants and loans.

Federal Student Grants

Today, Pell Grants form the largest federal scholarship program for undergraduates. Pell Grants are based on need and are only available to students from lower-income households. Pell Grants are not merit-based; instead, recipients only need to be high school graduates who have not yet received a bachelor's degree.[21]

For 2024–2025, Pell Grants ranged from $740 to $7,395 per student, with the majority of students receiving smaller grants, depending on their financial need, college expenses, and other factors.[22] Typically, the lower a household's income, the bigger the grant.[23]

As of last count, 30 percent of undergraduates received Pell Grants.[24] According to the latest available data (dating back to 2015–2016), 32 percent of White, 47 percent of Hispanic, and 58 percent of Black undergraduates were Pell Grant recipients.[25] More than half of all Pell Grant families survive on $20,000 or less annually, and 80 percent live on $40,000 or less.[26] Three-fourths of Pell Grant families have zero net assets, meaning they usually owe more than they own.[27]

Despite the financial strains on those households, the Pell Grant program has become stingier. Total federal expenditures on Pell Grants shrank by 42 percent between 2010–2011 and 2021–2022. Over that same period, the number of students awarded Pell Grants fell 35 percent, from 9.3 million to 6.1 million recipients, and the average size of a Pell Grant fell by about $500, after adjusting for inflation.[28]

What this means is that the buying power of Pell Grants has not kept up with costs.[29] Pell Grants do not come close to paying a full year's cost of college today. The maximum Pell Grant of $6,895 in 2022–2023 was less than one-fourth of the average estimated budget ($27,940) for in-state tuition and fees, room and board, transportation, and other personal expenses at a public four-year university.[30] Even taking grants from other sources into account, the average first-time, full-time, in-state student at a public university was short $19,250 of the money needed for school that year.[31]

Long story short, in order to stay in college, lower-income undergraduates usually have to bridge the gap in scholarship monies with other funds. In many cases, their choice comes down to three unsatisfactory options: drop out, work their way through school, or incur student loans. Many pick student debt as the path of least resistance, because the average financial aid package offers less in student grants and more in student loans.[32] As a result, "borrowing for college has become more prevalent over time," and students have put "increased reliance on loans to pay for college."[33]

Federal Student Loans

The US Department of Education is the largest student lender today, accounting for a whopping 93 percent of outstanding student debt in

2022.[34] Most new student loans are federal direct student loans under Title IV of the Higher Education Act of 1965.[35] In second quarter 2024, the forty-three million or so borrowers with outstanding student loans owed $37,860 on average per borrower.[36]

College students can qualify for one, and sometimes two, types of federal student loans: direct subsidized and direct unsubsidized. Both charge below-market interest rates set annually by the Department of Education, which are not adjusted for credit risk. For 2023–2024, the annual interest rates on loans to undergraduate and graduate students were 6.53 percent and 8.08 percent respectively.[37]

Only undergraduate students with financial need qualify for direct subsidized loans. The federal government does not start charging interest on those loans until the seventh month after the borrower leaves school. In contrast, the government charges interest on direct unsubsidized loans from the date the loan is made, including while students are in school. Students can receive direct unsubsidized loans regardless of need.[38]

Federal direct loans have dollar caps that are intended to protect student borrowers from incurring excessive debt. During the 2023–2024 school year, the total maximum that undergraduates could borrow in federal student loans was $31,000 for dependent and $57,500 for independent students.[39] For professional and graduate students, the total cap was significantly higher, at $138,500 (including undergraduate federal student loans).[40]

Federal student loans have relaxed eligibility criteria, which make it easy to qualify. Students must be enrolled at least half time in an institution of higher education or a postsecondary vocational school.[41] Otherwise, they do not need proof of income or creditworthiness.[42] Student loans are so easy to obtain that the overwhelming majority of student borrowers take out the maximum amount allowed.[43] This permits college students to rack up tens of thousands of dollars in student debt with no income or credit history.

After borrowers leave school, normally they have a six-month grace period before their loan payments begin. The standard repayment plan gives them ten years to repay. That ten-year schedule is often demanding because it requires fixed, fully amortized payments, irrespective of the borrower's income.[44] As a result many borrowers have difficulty making on-time loan payments under the standard repayment plan.

In response, the Department of Education launched various income-driven repayment (IDR) plans, starting in 1994, to assist borrowers who cannot manage the ten-year repayment schedule.[45] IDR plans limit minimum student loan payments to a percentage (usually 10 or 15%) of each participant's discretionary income, which usually makes IDR payments less—substantially less—than under the standard plan. In addition, IDR plans offer repayment schedules of twenty or twenty-five years plus loan forgiveness for any remaining balance at the end of that term. Increasing numbers of borrowers have signed up for IDR plans in recent years, going from 10 percent of borrowers in 2013 to 33 percent in 2022.[46]

Borrowers who skip student loan payments for more than 270 days face harsh consequences if their servicers designate their loans as in default. Their loan balances become due, and the government can withhold tax refunds and garnish their paychecks and federal benefits payments.[47] Student borrowers who default become ineligible for future student loans and may be barred from continuing to work in licensed occupations.[48] Their damaged credit jeopardizes their ability to obtain future loans and possibly jobs, auto insurance, rental housing, and utilities. Finally, borrowers cannot discharge student debt in bankruptcy except in cases of undue hardship, which can be difficult to prove.[49] The easy availability of student loans and the severe consequences of defaulting on those loans make it essential to ensure that students can pay for college without becoming overindebted.

TRADE-OFFS OF STUDENT LOANS

For years, too little attention has been paid to the risks of student loans. Proponents of student loans often point to the experience of the average student borrower, without drilling down into the experience of historically vulnerable groups. They tout studies finding that student borrowers enjoy higher average lifetime earnings than adults who do not attend college.[50] The implicit message is that student loans invariably are worth the cost.

But there are wide variations, good and bad, in the outcomes of different groups. For instance, there is troubling evidence that college-educated adults in the bottom half by income and borrowers of color—especially Blacks—are especially dependent on student loans to pay for college.

Lower-income and Black households whose children earn baccalaureate degrees are more likely than richer households to take out student loans.[51] Similarly, Black borrowers leave college with substantially higher average student loan balances than Asians, Hispanics, or Whites.[52]

These disparities emerged against the backdrop of the sharp rise in the prevalence of student debt over the past thirty years.[53] Whether this growth in student loans is good is the subject of debate.

In theory, student loans allow high school graduates who otherwise might not be able to afford college to attend and increase their lifetime earnings potential. It is well established, for instance, that the median college graduate who took out student debt has higher lifetime earnings than the median adult who only earned a high school diploma. Over a lifetime, this earnings difference amounts to almost $1,000,000 and "far exceeds" the student debt that someone typically owes at graduation.[54] And paradoxically, higher loan balances are linked to better outcomes in many cases. Students at four-year institutions who take out more student loans attend for more years, are more likely to complete their bachelor's degrees, and have higher annual earnings on average.[55] These outcomes lend credence to the argument that attending college is better than not going, even if it means incurring student debt.

Not everyone enjoys the same large wage premium from college education, however. College graduates from lower-income backgrounds enjoy less earnings growth than their wealthier classmates.[56] Similarly, Black debtors take longer on average to see earnings gains from higher student loan balances than White or Hispanic borrowers.[57] And for-profit schools have a woefully poor record of placing their students in better-paid careers.[58]

All this is to say that when undergraduates borrow money to finance college and those loans do not pay off, the resulting debt can undermine, not enhance, their economic well-being.[59] It is easy for inexperienced undergraduates to run up student loan balances well in excess of what they eventually will be able to repay. For this reason, statistics about the lifetime earnings of the *average* student debtor do not settle whether college is worth the cost for borrowers who do not match the average profile.[60]

The earnings trajectories of college alumni are a crap shoot in which some people lose out.[61] For example, take the 10 percent of working college graduates ages thirty-five to forty-four who made $20,000 a year or less in 2015. They may have drawn the short straw for various reasons. They may have attended for-profit schools or left college before completing. Some may have been sidelined by family responsibilities or illness. Others may have entered the job market during a recession or lacked sought-after job skills. Any of these circumstances can reduce the payoff from a college education.[62]

EFFECTS OF STUDENT DEBT ON ATTAINING PERSONAL FINANCIAL GOALS

The risks from student loans fall into three broad groups. First, student loans can devastate borrowers' finances if they miss payments. In addition, student debt may obstruct borrowers' ability to achieve important personal goals. For instance, student borrowers are less likely than their debt-free classmates to start new businesses or enter lower-paid public interest work.[63] Student debt also is associated with delays in marrying and having children.[64]

But third, student debt also hampers borrowers' ability to attain other vital milestones toward economic well-being. In each case—making ends meet, affording health care, buying a home, or paying for retirement—student loans create barriers.

Covering Basic Living Expenses

Numerous student borrowers have trouble paying their bills because their loan payments do not leave enough to live on. The credit scores of student borrowers provide a troubling window into this problem. In one recent study, the average standard repayment plan participant only had a credit score of 595.[65] Credit scores this low, which are deep in subprime territory, are the product of delinquent payments and a sign of the inability to pay bills when they come due.[66]

Similarly, borrowers on the ten-year standard plan are up to six times more likely to receive monthly cash infusions from family or friends than IDR plan participants.[67] Their heightened reliance on financial help indicates trouble meeting their monthly expenses.

Segments of student debtors report financial distress as well. For instance, one survey found that almost half of student debtors under age forty who lacked a bachelor's degree said they were not doing okay financially, compared to about 8 percent of college graduates who had repaid their loans or never took out student loans at all.[68] The high percentage of noncompleters in financial distress mirrors other findings that student borrowers who never finished college are less likely to pay their bills on time than people who graduated.[69]

Finally, student loans impede saving for emergencies. Over half of college graduates in student loan repayment said that college expenses prevented or delayed them from amassing emergency savings, compared to only 9 percent of those who graduated debt-free.[70] These signs of financial distress point toward the same conclusion: student loans make it harder to cover basic living expenses.

Effects on Health

Good health is a basic human need that student debt can jeopardize. College students with student loans are more likely to postpone mental, physical, or dental appointments in order to pay bills than students without loans. Undergraduates with student debt report worse physical and mental health and more major medical problems than their debt-free classmates.[71]

These adverse effects persist after college. College-educated adults with student loans are more likely to report that they cannot afford to seek hospital care, see doctors or dentists, or fill prescriptions than adults who attended college without student debt.[72] Borrowers who are delinquent on student loans or in collection are even more likely to delay health care, to report being in poor health, and to be late paying medical bills.[73] Overall, student loans can discourage borrowers from seeking needed medical treatment, with negative effects on their health.

Effects on Homeownership

Multiple studies have determined that student loans delay homeownership.[74] Young people delay buying a home by one year on average for every

$3,000 they owe in student loans.[75] In contrast, college graduates who finish debt-free buy homes earlier on average, and their homeownership rates exceed the rates of graduates with student loans through at least age thirty-two.[76] Up to 35 percent of the recent drop in the homeownership rate of young adults can be blamed on student loans.[77]

There are several reasons that student debt makes it harder for young adults to buy homes. Most of those involve obtaining a mortgage loan. First, student loans, on balance, depress the credit scores of borrowers. Data show that the higher the student loan balance, the greater the chance of a weak credit score.[78] In addition, monthly student loan payment obligations make it harder for borrowers to meet the debt-to-income ratio tests that mortgage lenders typically require in order to approve mortgages. Finally, monthly student loan bills hamper the ability to save for down payments.[79]

Effects on Retirement Savings

Student debt further hampers saving for retirement. By age thirty, college graduates with student debt only have half as much retirement savings as adults who graduated from college with no student loans. With their smaller balances, student borrowers lose out on the investment returns that they otherwise could have earned on their missed retirement contributions.[80]

For older age groups, the results are noisier. By age fifty-seven, there are only "tiny" differences in the retirement savings of student borrowers and other college alumni. But when the value of defined benefit pensions are added in, "non-borrowers have higher balances, on average."[81] Meanwhile, the time lag before student debtors amass retirement savings contributes to the wealth gap between student debtors and adults who did not incur student loans.

WEALTH

Historically, the typical college graduate accumulated more wealth than someone without a college degree. But this wealth premium from a college education dropped steadily for more recent generations, and for many it has disappeared. In fact, for college graduates born in the 1980s, "Whites are the only racial or ethnic group . . . for whom a bachelor's degree provides a family with a reliable wealth advantage" over people who never earned a college degree.[82]

Student loans help explain this vanishing wealth premium.[83] The typical person who took out student loans has markedly less wealth than classmates who left school free from student debt. In 2019, for instance, the net worth of the average adult was almost $750,000, three times the net worth ($240,800) of the average adult with student loans.[84] This wealth gap grows larger after age forty and persists over a lifetime.[85] Possibly due to this wealth lag, student borrowers plan to retire later than nonborrowers who went to college.[86]

This suggests that people who attend college debt-free have a head start in accumulating wealth by embarking on homeownership and building savings earlier.[87] The resulting wealth gap surfaces around the age of forty, when enough time has passed so that people in the debt-free group are starting to enjoy the compounding effects of their earlier investments. For too many borrowers, student loans turn college into a zero-sum game, in which the cost of repaying student debt comes at the expense of building wealth. This wealth gap is one more way in which student debt blocks many borrowers' ability to advance their economic well-being.

DAMAGED CREDITWORTHINESS

So far we have seen how student loans stall borrowers' progress on important steps, such as savings, homeownership, or health, to foster their well-being. But that is not the only adverse effect of student loans. Student debt also can decimate borrowers' finances. In particular, college-educated adults in the lower half by income and borrowers of color—especially Blacks—are likely to suffer financial harm from student loans.[88]

Of course, many student borrowers do pay off that debt.[89] But those who do demonstrate a paradoxical pattern. On average, people who take out more student loans are less likely to default on those loans than those who take out less—*if* they went to a public or private nonprofit school.[90] While this sounds counterintuitive, economists have found that many debtors with higher balances used their added student loans to invest in more education, which paid dividends through higher salaries and an increased ability to repay.[91] This return on investment supports the idea that student loans are "good debt."

Still, the flip side of this story is that borrowers with smaller balances are more likely to default. And the wage premium story does not hold for Black borrowers, who have higher student loan balances on average without a higher earnings potential.[92] Both observations point to a real and looming problem, which is the large number of student debtors who struggle after leaving school to repay their loans.

The extent of these repayment difficulties is mind-boggling. Delinquency and default rates for student loans spiked after the 2008 financial crisis. By 2012, the delinquency rate for student loans soared past the rate for mortgages, credit cards, and auto loans, and it remained stuck on high until COVID-19 hit in early 2020, long after those other types of consumer debt had recovered.[93]

Some of the most sobering default data come from year-end 2019, right before the federal government temporarily suspended federal student loan repayment obligations and interest charges due to the global pandemic. At the end of 2019, only about half (50.7%) of all federal student loan borrowers who were past the grace period were current on their student debt payments. The other half (fifteen million borrowers) were delinquent or in deferment, forbearance, or default.[94]

Defaults are not the only signs of financial distress from student loans. Student loan repayments also have slowed to a crawl. In 2021, for instance, during the COVID pause on repayments, two-thirds of all borrowers had federal direct student loan balances that were flat or increasing. Only about one out of four student borrowers paid down even a penny of their balances that year.[95] Nonpayment was especially common among the lowest-income borrowers.[96] Elevated default rates, plus the increased use of forbearance and deferment, and the rollout of a more generous income-driven repayment plan all contributed to slow repayments.[97]

These numbers mask other troubling trends. When we drill deeper into the default data, two different worlds emerge. First is the world of borrowers who successfully graduate from college and make enough to pay off their student loans. Then there is a second world, in which borrowers did not have the experiences and advantages that would set them up for repayment success. In this second world, certain groups of borrowers have alarming difficulty repaying their student loans.

Which groups have special difficulty making student loan repayments? Lower-income borrowers—and especially those from families making less than $50,000 a year—have particular trouble.[98] For example, two-thirds of borrowers who entered college in 2003–2004 and defaulted on their student loans over the ensuing twelve years were poor or near-poor, with family incomes under 200 percent of the federal poverty level.[99]

Many lower-income borrowers do not earn enough after college to shoulder student loans. As a rule of thumb, experts advise borrowers to spend no more than 8 to 10 percent of their gross income on student loan payments.[100] Yet this number—known as the student "debt-to-income ratio"—rose from 12 percent in 1989 to 32 percent on average in 2010 and kept climbing after that.[101] These rising debt-to-income ratios hit lowest-income borrowers the hardest, because they have to devote a much bigger bite of their paychecks to student loan payments compared to richer borrowers.[102] For the median borrower in the bottom 10 percent (earning $30,000 a year), that bite in 2022 was 30 percent, but for the median borrower in the top 10 percent (earning $182,000 a year), it was only 18 percent.[103] No wonder, then, that richer borrowers have greater success repaying their student loans.

Black and Hispanic borrowers also have greater average difficulty than Whites with repayment. These numbers have reached crisis proportions, especially for Black college-educated adults. In the 2003–2004 entering class, for instance, Black borrowers were three times more likely to default on their student loans (38%) than Whites (12%). The default rate for Hispanic borrowers was also higher, at 20 percent. Moreover, graduating from college did not improve these odds for Blacks as much as for Whites. In fact, the default rate for the average Black bachelor's degree recipient who started college in 2003–2004 was 21 percent, more than five times that of the average White graduate (4%). That 21 percent rate even exceeded the default rate for the average White adult who started but never completed college (18%).[104]

Borrowing outcomes are significantly worse for Black college-educated adults in another way. Normally we anticipate that debtors, after leaving school, will pay down their student loans over time. That turns out to be true for White and Asian bachelor's degree recipients and, to a lesser extent, for Hispanic graduates. In contrast, Black graduates start out owing the most in student loans on average when they first leave college and then their balances keep growing—substantially—for at least the first twelve years after starting college.[105] Twenty years out, the average Black student borrower still owes 95 percent of the original loan balance, while the average White borrower only owes 6 percent.[106] For too many Black borrowers, student loans become a debt trap that drives up their default risk and makes credit checks unnerving for things like jobs and homes.

Several things explain these troubling outcomes for Black borrowers. The average Black college graduate has lower earnings after graduation than the average White, fueled by wage discrimination.[107] Their depressed earnings, along with their higher average loan balances, require typical Black borrowers to spend a higher percentage of their incomes on student loans than Whites.[108] In addition, Black borrowers have less family wealth to fall back on if they have difficulty repaying.[109] They are less likely to complete college than White undergraduates, in part due to their financial constraints.[110] Finally, Blacks are more likely to attend for-profit schools than Whites.[111] As a result of these dynamics, student loans weigh down many college-educated Blacks without the same payoff in earnings and wealth that Whites enjoy from college education.[112]

The disastrous Black experience with for-profit schools shines a light on the dismal loan performance of for-profit schools generally. The default rates for borrowers who attended for-profit schools are off the charts.[113] To take just one statistic, in the 2003–2004 entering class, almost half— 46.5 percent—of students who went to for-profit schools defaulted within the first twelve years. That was almost four times the default rate for alumni of nonprofit colleges and universities. That 46.5 percent default rate, moreover, was *double* the rate for the 1995–1996 entering class, indicating rapid deterioration.[114]

Finally, borrowers who never finish college are at substantially higher risk of defaulting on their student loans than those who manage to graduate.[115] Once again, the experience of the 2003–2004 entering class is eyeopening. The twelve-year default rate of noncompleters in that class was 24 percent, four times the 5.6 percent default rate of the bachelor's degree recipients.[116] Almost half of the people who defaulted in that class never received their degrees.[117] That may help explain why borrowers with the lowest student loan balances have the highest default rates: their low balances are likely because they never completed college.[118] Noncompleters end up in the worst situation of all because lacking a degree condemns them to stagnant lifetime earnings, yet they are stuck repaying student loans.[119] Disproportionately, borrowers in this boat are Black, Hispanic, or from lower-income backgrounds.[120]

The United States has long prided itself on access to higher education for all. In reality, however, the system forces students from underprivileged backgrounds to pay for college with student loans, even though student debt is a destructive proposition for Black and Hispanic borrowers and students from lower-income households of any race.[121] These students get the statistical short end of the stick, with drastically higher odds of default and harsh consequences if they do default. If equal access to college is to be more than lip service, then society needs to find a better way of supporting disadvantaged students financially when seeking their degrees.

RETHINKING SOCIETY'S ROLE
IN FINANCING HIGHER EDUCATION

There are two rationales for requiring students to finance higher education so heavily through student loans. The first is that the benefits of student loans to individual borrowers outweigh the costs. And second is that college-educated adults capture all of higher education's benefits themselves, with no spillover benefit to society.

By now, we have seen that the first point—that the benefits of student loans outweigh the costs—does not hold for certain groups of borrowers. This rationale leans heavily on the proposition that "the earnings premium for a college degree has risen dramatically" since 1965.[122] But this income advantage is shrinking and "may have declined for" recent college graduates in "some demographic groups relative to older graduates."[123] Today, there is little or no income advantage for the average Black graduate, for many lower-income graduates regardless of race, for the average alumnus of a for-profit school, and for large numbers of debtors who took out student loans but did not finish college. For these groups, it is doubtful that student loans are worth the cost.

The wage premium rationale has another flaw, which is that it focuses on lifetime earnings, while blithely assuming that borrowers will have the cash flow to make student loan payments while paying their other bills. But today's low rate of student loan repayment drives home how stretched many borrowers are. When borrowers default—and excessive numbers do—the vaunted economic benefits of a college education are lost and the debtors are ruined financially.

The United States has long championed college as the path to social mobility.[124] That is empty rhetoric, however, if lower-income and Black and Hispanic students are forced to assume unmanageable debt loads as the price of enrolling in college. Society's insistence on student loans as the way for poorer students to pay for college undermines the hard work by those students to climb the socioeconomic ladder. Student debt makes it hard for those households to reach other financial goals to allow them to survive the economic risks thrust on them by society. And student debt magnifies the risk of default and its aftermath for the very students whom social mobility initiatives aim to help. A real commitment to social mobility will require society to make college available to disadvantaged students at low or no cost and free from student debt.

We should also spread more of the cost of higher education across tax-payers, instead of forcing disadvantaged students into student debt, because of the positive spillover effects to society. Higher education generates numerous important benefits to society—termed *positive externalities*—that society should foot. The average college-educated adult pays more taxes and generates more consumer spending over a lifetime than the average adult who never went to college.[125] People who go to college have lower health-care expenses because they have better health on average.[126] They also are less likely to go on public assistance.[127]

Higher education pays added dividends in terms of a more vibrant and sophisticated economy. One such payoff is greater labor productivity.[128] In addition, the deep US investment in four-year research universities offering graduate degrees has made it the world's leader in technological innovation.[129]

These benefits to society are the product of choices by individual high school students to go to college, however, and cannot be taken for granted. Every time young adults invest in college education, they generate positive externalities, to society's benefit. But high school students are unlikely to consider those social benefits when deciding whether to apply to college. Recently, there have been serious concerns that debt aversion discourages some bright high school students from going to college.[130] This has been documented especially among Hispanic high school students, who enroll in college at lower rates partly due to debt aversion.[131] And this phenomenon is growing. College enrollments have slumped and high school seniors increasingly are deciding that college is not worth the debt.[132] In the process, society loses the benefits it would reap if those seniors went to college. Those lost dividends provide strong reasons for moving away from student loans and toward greater public financing of higher education.

A NEW SYSTEM OF COLLEGE FINANCE

Since as far back as the 1950s, the United States has taken the stance that college education is a valuable social investment and justifies public support. In pursuit of that policy, the federal government has bankrolled colleges and universities with hundreds of billions of dollars in student grants and loans.[133] For most of the past three decades, however, the mix of that federal support increasingly has tilted away from student grants and more toward educational loans.[134] Time has shown that federal reliance on student loans as the financing mechanism of choice is flawed.

To be sure, Congress and the executive branch have not been completely blind to the harm from student loans. The response, however, has been to tinker around the edges while keeping the student loan system intact. Successive presidential administrations have sweetened IDR plans to stretch out distressed borrowers' payments while reducing defaults. The federal government offers deferment and forbearance to tide over troubled debtors temporarily. The Obama and Biden administrations also cracked down on for-profit schools.[135] President Biden's erstwhile plan to cancel student debt, while needed, did not address future student loans.[136] Instead, an unholy alliance of governments, universities, and taxpayers keeps expecting college students to incur tens of thousands of dollars in student debt to pay for their educations.

Bold reforms are needed to address the outstanding debt burden of current borrowers while ramping down the use of student loans going forward. Some of those reforms are retroactive in nature, while others are prospective.

The retroactive changes would address the unmanageable size of the current outstanding student loan balances for struggling borrowers. After the Supreme Court struck down the Biden debt cancellation plan due to lack of congressional approval, it became apparent that the student debt of most distressed borrowers would not be cancelled soon.[137] Instead, servicers offered most of them IDR plans that cut their payments and stretched those payments out over twenty years or more.[138]

Under this strategy, the federal government continues to demand its pound of flesh from distressed borrowers. While the default rate is lower under IDR plans, it still is troublingly high.[139] In addition, the promise of lower monthly payments and possible eventual forgiveness under IDR plans goes unfulfilled for over half of IDR participants, who fail to recertify their incomes annually due to bureaucratic hurdles.[140] These IDR dropouts lose their reduced payment schedules and probably the opportunity for eventual loan forgiveness.[141]

Even when IDR borrowers recertify their incomes and retain their lower payments, their longer repayment schedules are costly in three respects. First, those schedules prolong interest payments for double the time or more, costing borrowers thousands of extra dollars. Second, IDR borrowers have difficulty paying down principal, with one report finding that over three-fourths of IDR borrowers who started payments in 2012 "owed more than they had . . . borrowed" by 2017.[142] Finally, the long, drawn-out repayment schedules raise concern that IDR borrowers will postpone needed medical care, other essentials, and saving for the future.

The nation's broken student loan system allows young adults to amass student debt without regard for their economic well-being or ability to repay. Consequently, the aim of retroactive reform should be to improve the financial footing of borrowers who are over their heads in student debt. Targeted debt forgiveness is preferable to IDR plans because it is the best way to reduce default risk while giving distressed debtors the breathing room they need to tackle other financial goals. Student debt cancellation has the further benefit of boosting incomes and job mobility.[143]

Congress has the authority to decree debt forgiveness, and it should exercise that power. To hold the budgetary cost down, Congress should restrict student loan cancellation to borrowers from lower-income families, lower-balance debtors, and those who attended for-profit schools that failed to deliver on promises of gainful employment. Borrowers who do not make enough to cover their basic living expenses after servicing their student debt also should receive relief. These borrowers lost out in the wage premium lottery and need debt forgiveness.

Prospective relief also is crucial because debt forgiveness does not resolve how to pay for college going forward. Under the current loan system, too few promising high school seniors are starting and finishing college, resulting in lost positive spillover effects to society. Meanwhile, the harm from student loans to disadvantaged students has reached the breaking point.

Consequently, it is time to replace student loans with other forms of public support. The question is, what form should that support take: increased appropriations or student grants?

The appropriations approach has a number of drawbacks. Larger appropriations do not necessarily translate into lower tuition rates in states where public universities have their own authority to set tuition. Even when appropriations do reduce tuition, tuition appropriations are inefficient because they extend aid to affluent students who do not need it. Similarly, the state appropriations approach does not address the student debt problem at private colleges and universities because appropriations are limited to public institutions. Finally, lower tuition may lead to lower-quality education and reduced caps on the number of students admitted.[144]

In contrast, student grants are more efficient because they can target students with financial need. Needs-based grants help students who need cost relief the most and at a smaller cash outlay than tuition subsidies. Student grants also can apply to public and private institutions alike. Accordingly, student grants do the best job of channeling aid where it is needed, with a lower fiscal impact. The best way to accomplish this would be by expanding Pell Grant support.[145]

Back in 2004, former Federal Reserve Board chairman Alan Greenspan dismissed concerns about the rising family debt loads from subprime mortgages because "ever-wealthier households" had an "increased capacity . . . to service debt."[146] As the events of 2008 showed, Greenspan was wrong. Now it is time to realize that the nation made the same mistake with student loans. It relied on student debt to expand the ranks of the college-educated middle class, while assuming that their incomes and wealth inexorably would rise with no downward drag from student loans.

Instead, student loan burdens continue to mount for many households. The nation has ended up with a system in which half or more of student debtors do not pay down their loans, disadvantaged groups risk financial distress as the trade-off for going to college, and student borrowers struggle to reach other financial goals. If college finance is not revamped, it will jeopardize people's retirement security as well, as the next chapter discusses.

10 A Financially Secure Retirement

Shari Biagas loved her job as an information technology manager and planned to work as long as she could. But her employer gave her the pink slip after outsourcing her department. At the time, Shari did not anticipate retiring at sixty-two and assumed she "had at least a few more years to work." But after being laid off, she could not find another job, and health issues made working harder. Shari ended up taking early Social Security, even though her 401(k) account and savings could run dry in five years. Meanwhile, she had seven years remaining on her mortgage.[1]

In many ways, the last milestone of economic well-being—a financially secure retirement—resembles the first, which is making ends meet. The difference is that older people have greater difficulty supporting themselves if their work lives end due to forces beyond their control, as happened to Shari. Without some sort of pooled arrangement—such as Social Security or pensions—numerous retirees would end up destitute.[2]

In the United States, retirement security is supposed to be a "three-legged stool," with three sources of retirement income: Social Security, workplace retirement plans, and personal savings.[3] Unfortunately, the three-legged stool and the financial security it envisions have turned out to be a pipe dream for millions of older people.

Only one of the stool's three legs—Social Security—is truly universal. Almost 97 percent of the US population age sixty and above receives or will receive Social Security.[4] In October 2024, this included fifty-four million people on old-age benefits.[5] Consequently, most retirees can depend on Social Security income in old age. Far fewer enjoy income from pensions, however. That would be less of a problem if Social Security benefits were enough to live on. However, they are not.

HOW SOCIAL SECURITY WORKS

Social Security is thought of primarily as an old-age benefits program. But it also provides disability payments to younger impaired workers and survivors' benefits to the closest survivors of workers who die before retirement age.[6]

Social Security differs from numerous other government assistance programs because it is not means-tested. Instead, workers *earn* their entitlement to Social Security by paying payroll taxes on their wages. In 2024, employers and workers each paid taxes of 6.2 percent on earnings of up to $168,600 (while self-employed workers paid 12.4 percent).[7] Workers must pay payroll taxes for at least ten years of covered work to qualify for old-age benefits.[8] People who become disabled or die before retirement age, however, can qualify for disability or survivors' benefits based on fewer years of work.[9]

Social Security also differs from means-tested programs because each person's Social Security benefits are tied to his or her lifetime earnings and years of covered work. For 2024, Social Security paid newly eligible beneficiaries ninety cents on the dollar of a worker's average indexed monthly earnings of up to $1,174, thirty-two cents on the dollar for earnings between $1,174 and $7,078, and fifteen cents on the dollar for earnings above $7,078.[10] Under this formula, the longer you work and the more you make, the bigger your Social Security check.

Social Security's design—in which people must work to qualify and receive larger benefits the more they earn—has been the secret to the program's broad support. At the same time, Social Security has features to protect retirees from poverty.[11] The earned entitlement and anti-poverty features sometimes come into tension, as we will see later in this chapter.

Social Security gives workers flexibility about when to start receiving benefits, while rewarding them with larger benefits for each month they delay. Workers who wait until their full retirement age to claim receive their full Social Security benefit. Full retirement age is set at sixty-seven for people born in 1960 or later, but slightly younger for people born before 1960, depending on their birthdates. Alternatively, people can claim old-age benefits as early as age sixty-two, but only at reduced amounts. For instance, benefits claimed at age sixty-two are 30 percent lower than those claimed at full retirement age at sixty-seven. Meanwhile, people who wait to claim benefits past full retirement age, up to age seventy, receive 8 percent more in benefits for each year they delay past full retirement age.[12]

Once an individual's old-age benefits start, Social Security also pays an annual cost-of-living adjustment to help keep up with inflation. This is an especially valuable feature that most workplace pensions and private annuities lack.[13]

This cost-of-living adjustment plus the growth in average life expectancy and the retirement of the baby boomers have eroded Social Security's solvency. The federal government draws on three revenue streams to pay Social Security benefits. Those sources include payroll taxes paid by workers and employers, a small amount of revenue from income taxes that retirees pay on their Social Security benefits, and interest on bonds owned by the Old-Age and Survivors Insurance Trust Fund (Trust Fund).

Social Security is a pay-as-you-go system in that tax revenues cover benefits as they come due. When the tax revenues exceed the benefits paid, as they did for many years, the excess taxes accumulate in the Trust Fund.[14] Starting in 2010, however, tax revenues no longer covered the full benefits due every year, so the government started tapping the Trust Fund to pay for the balance. The Trust Fund is declining as a result and is due to run dry in 2033.[15] Unless Congress acts, Social Security will not be able to pay retirees their full promised benefits beginning in 2035.[16] At that point, current tax revenues will cover much of the promised benefits, but not all.

The prospect of benefits cuts puts lower-income workers at particular risk because their benefits are already low. Those low benefits flow from the fact that Social Security never was designed to serve as retirees' sole source of support. To illustrate, Social Security benefits only replaced 37 percent of the average career earnings of workers who retired at age sixty-five in 2022.[17] Compare that to the standard advice of financial planners, who recommend having enough retirement income to replace at least 70 percent of preretirement wages.[18] Low-income workers need an even higher replacement rate of 96 percent, according to Vanguard Research.[19] Given these numbers, most observers agree that Social Security benefits are "likely to fall short of maintaining the average standard of living experienced during working years."[20]

Social Security partly seeks to address this shortfall through its old-age benefits formula. That formula is *progressive* in the sense that Social Security pays more cents on the dollar for workers with the lowest lifetime earnings (up to ninety cents on the dollar) than for higher lifetime earners.[21] But the growing life expectancy gap between rich and poor has eroded this progressivity.

Over the last seventy years, the gains in average US life expectancy have been astonishing. In 1950, for example, the average American could expect to live sixty-eight years; by 2019, the average US lifespan had grown to almost seventy-nine years, before backsliding to seventy-six after the global pandemic.[22]

Those gains in average lifespans were mostly limited to the top half of earners, however. One landmark study found that at age forty, men in the top 1 percent by income could expect to live to 87.3 years, while men in the bottom 1 percent could only expect to live to 72.7 years, *14.6 years shorter* than for the top 1 percent.[23] This gulf in life expectancy affects "the entire bottom half of the population" by income, such that the bottom half only "experienced very small gains in life expectancy," unlike the top half.[24] The bottom 40 percent of women actually experienced a decline.[25] Furthermore, the gap in life expectancy has grown worse over time.[26]

This gap has left Social Security's supposed progressivity in tatters. Due to shorter expected lifespans, lower-income workers collect old-age benefits for fewer years on average and those who die before age sixty-two do not collect them at all.[27] Well-paid earners also receive bigger benefits in absolute dollars than those lower-paid. These dynamics produce a sizeable gap, with the highest earners collecting three times or more in total lifetime benefits than the lowest earners.[28] This gap has widened in lockstep with the gap in life expectancy and is projected to get even bigger over time.[29]

In short, with each passing year, lower-paid workers get a smaller and smaller share of lifetime Social Security benefits. Worse, their benefits are not enough to subsist on. This raises concerns because a large number of retirees live mainly on their Social Security checks.

THE EXTENT OF OLDER PEOPLE HEAVILY RELIANT ON SOCIAL SECURITY

Even though Social Security was never meant to provide retirees' main source of income, the reality is different for millions of beneficiaries. Between 40 and 50 percent of recipients age sixty-five and up (at least twenty million people) rely on Social Security for half or more of their income. Up to one-fourth of that age group depends on Social Security for at least 90 percent of their income.[30]

These numbers suggest that pensions provide scant retirement income for millions of retirees. The data bear that out.

PENSION PLANS: MISSING IN ACTION

While official policy touts the three-legged stool for a worry-free retirement, the United States comes nowhere close to achieving it. Retirees are supposed to have three sources of income, but almost no one does. In fact, only one out of fourteen older people today has income from all three sources.[31] For most people, the three-legged stool is a fiction.

If almost no one has all three types of retirement income, then how many retirees at least have income from a pension? According to one report, only about 45 percent of older people received retirement income from a defined-benefit (DB) or defined-contribution (DC) plan.[32] This group is overwhelmingly middle- or higher-income.[33] Another report examined the *amount* of income retirees received from DB or DC plans and again found that almost all of that income went to better-off households. In contrast, older people in the bottom 40 percent income-wise only got a "trivial" amount of income (less than 8% on average) from DB and DC plans.[34] Most of them lacked the extra income boost that DB or DC plans would provide. For them, a crucial leg was missing in the three-legged stool.

As a result, lower-income retirees face the risk of exhausting their meager reserves before death. The Employee Benefit Research Institute projected that 40 percent of US households headed by someone between ages thirty-five and sixty-four would run out of money in retirement.[35] In an even gloomier prediction, Vanguard Research concluded that *everyone* except those in the top 5 percent income bracket is at risk of falling short of spending needs in retirement.[36]

This is worrying, given Social Security's low benefits levels for the vast majority of lower-income retirees. For 2024, the Social Security Administration estimated that the median retiree received a Social Security benefit of $1,937 a month, with half receiving less.[37] Those paltry amounts raise concerns about financial hardship, which turn out to be warranted.

THE EXTENT OF FINANCIAL HARDSHIP AMONG OLDER PEOPLE

A troublingly large proportion of the nation's elders lack enough money to meet their basic needs. Even with Social Security, almost one-third of those age sixty-five and up are poor or near-poor, with incomes at or below 200 percent of the federal poverty line (FPL).[38] The proportions are even higher for older women, Blacks, and Hispanics.[39]

Many of those poor or near-poor retirees are on public assistance. In 2019, one out of every six people age sixty-five or older was on means-tested relief, such as cash benefits, food aid, rental subsidies, or Medicaid.[40] Although most were on Social Security, they were destitute enough to need public assistance too.

As for other older people who are not on public assistance, large numbers still lack enough income to pay for basic necessities. Researchers at the University of Massachusetts Boston developed The Elder Index to measure the budgetary needs of older adults who live independently without relying on means-tested benefits, gifts, or loans. The Elder Index only allows for the bare essentials, consisting of food, transportation, and shelter plus health care, clothing, a telephone, and personal hygiene and cleaning supplies. The Elder Index makes no allowance for vacations, dining out, savings, gifts, or entertainment.[41]

For 2022, The Elder Index calculated that older homeowners without a mortgage needed $23,880 to cover basic expenses if they lived alone or $36,300 for couples. Renters needed more, at $28,920 for older people living alone and $41,340 for couples. Older homeowners with mortgages required $36,300 if they lived alone or $48,720 for couples.[42]

So how many older adults could not afford basic necessities in 2022? That year, virtually half (48%) of older adults living alone—and 21 percent of older couples—had retirement incomes below the Elder Index. This amounted to twelve million older people who lacked a subsistence income in retirement.[43]

Many older people caught in this squeeze experience financial hardship because they have such high shelter costs. Experts consider people "cost-burdened" if their housing expenses eat up 30 percent of their income or more. In 2021, over eleven million adults age sixty-five and up spent more than 30 percent of their income on housing, and over half of them spent more than 50 percent. Many of them had to slash their food and health expenditures due to high housing costs.[44]

High medical costs also cause older people to forego other essentials.[45] One-fourth of people age sixty-five and over skimp on food, utilities, clothing, or medications to pay for health care.[46] Meanwhile, over half—56 percent—of older Americans who subsist solely on Social Security went without seeing a doctor or a dentist in the prior year.[47] This trend is especially worrisome in an aging population in declining health.

In another sign of financial strain, one-third of senior citizens have credit card or student debt and consider that debt a problem.[48] From 1989 to 2016, the percentage of older people with credit card debt grew from 30 to 41 percent. Over that same period, the share with student loans tripled from 3 to 10 percent.[49] Seniors' loan balances grew faster than their incomes and assets, leading to mounting debt stress.[50] In 2016, one-fourth of senior citizens in the lowest fifth by income spent over 40 percent of their income on debt payments. Economists consider that debt burden excessive.[51]

However we gauge the number of older people in financial straits, the level is high. Almost one-third are poor or near-poor. One out of six requires public assistance. Twelve million cannot afford basic living expenses. One-fourth are overindebted. This level of financial distress underscores the degree to which the US system for retirement security has failed.

THE HARSH REALITIES OF RETIREMENT INCOME TODAY

Whenever the financial straits of older people are up for debate, some analysts exhort them to find new sources of income. These proposals range from working longer to more DC accounts with bigger balances and even reverse mortgages. None of these proposals, however, will fundamentally improve the economic privation affecting millions of older residents.

Defined-Benefit Plans

One proposal for boosting future retirees' income—the traditional pension—is dead on arrival. Few consider the return of the DB pension likely. While a handful of contrarians argue that conditions are ripe to unfreeze old DB plans, DB plan participation continues to trend down.[52] In the meantime, private industry opposition, along with employees' demands for portable retirement benefits, continue to undermine support for reinstating DB plans.[53]

Consistently since 1980, DB pension benefits have accounted for only a pittance of the income of retirees in the bottom 40 percent by income.[54] That is one reason proposals to increase retirees' income center on expanding DC plans. Those calls ignore the fact, however, that DC plans do not work for most lower-income workers.

Defined-Contribution Plans

Today, the single biggest proposal for boosting retirement income involves extending DC plans to more low-wage workers. The fixation with DC plans, however, is based on a host of questionable assumptions. First, with over half of households making less than a living wage, it is questionable how many can fund an adequate retirement.[55] A recent report by Vanguard Research concluded that the savings ability of the bottom half of earners is so limited that they have virtually no prospect of saving enough for retirement.[56] The fact that the median retirement account balance for the bottom 40 percent of households in 2022 was under $20,000 magnifies those doubts.[57]

Further, workers who do have retirement accounts often erode their balances through early withdrawals. One study concluded that 40 percent of contributions to DC accounts were withdrawn prematurely.[58] Withdrawals are especially common among lower-income families who suffer layoffs or other income declines.[59] This is one more way in which the savings demands on lower-income households for competing goals such as emergency funds and retirement accounts are unrealistic.

DC plan proposals are based on additional assumptions that do not hold water. As chapter 4 discussed, the tax incentives in qualified DC plans are worth little to workers in lower tax brackets or who do not pay income taxes at all. Meanwhile, asset caps on many public assistance programs actively discourage retirement savings by the poor and near-poor.

Lack of worker access to DC plans also continues to be a problem, although there is some progress to report. At least eleven states have established state-run retirement plans for affected workers since 2017.[60] Nine more states have passed legislation to create those plans, and other states are considering similar legislation. The state-run plans give employers who lack their own DC plans a choice: either pay a fine or sign up their employees and forward the employees' payroll contributions to the state-run plans.[61] Typically, the state-run plans auto-enroll workers in Roth IRA accounts but provide them with the right to opt out.[62]

To be sure, this trend toward state-run plans represents an improvement if it helps some low-wage workers build retirement savings. The evidence on point, however, is mixed. At state-run plans in California and Illinois, workers have been opting out at rates of 36 to 39 percent, high compared to the opt-out rates for company 401(k) plans.[63] And 25 to 31 percent of the balances were withdrawn prematurely.[64] Strikingly, in the Oregon plan, over half of the eligible workers who remained enrolled had no funds in their retirement accounts.[65]

These results indicate that there probably are limits to what DC plans can achieve when targeted at low-wage workers.[66] Together, the high opt-out rates, the low percentage of workers who contribute while enrolled, and the high withdrawal rates suggest that numerous low-wage workers do not have much discretionary income to save for retirement.[67] To that point, workers in lower-paid industries who opted out of Oregon's plan were more likely to say that they couldn't "afford to save."[68]

Even if none of these issues were an impediment, low earners still would be ill-positioned to bear the risks of DC plans because they have so little financial cushion to begin with. For all of these reasons, any notion that DC plans will lift poorer workers into secure retirements does not square with reality.

Reverse Mortgages

In recent years, tapping retirees' home equity to generate income similarly has gained attention. The high homeownership rate of older adults is propelling this strategy, with four out of five people age sixty-five and up owning their homes in 2022.[69] Many amassed substantial equity after paying down their mortgages and experiencing home appreciation. Those nest eggs have fueled discussions about how to convert that equity into income for financially pressed seniors.

Today, the Federal Housing Administration's Home Equity Conversion Mortgage (HECM) program insures most reverse mortgages.[70] HECMs are limited to homeowners age sixty-two and up with substantial home equity and target the senior market.[71]

Currently, the volume of newly endorsed HECM loans is small (just twenty-six thousand loans in fiscal year 2024), but the number could rise as more baby boomers retire.[72] Reverse mortgages have features that make them tempting for financing retirement. Chief among them is the ability to extract cash with no monthly loan payments while staying in the home. Instead, repayment is postponed until the sale of the home, the borrower's death, or the borrower moving out permanently, whichever comes first.[73] In addition, homeowners with weaker credit histories can qualify for HECMs, so long as they can pay their homeowners' insurance, property taxes, and related carrying charges.

Due to these advantages, some financial advisers recommend that older homeowners who lack pension income and retirement savings live off the proceeds of a reverse mortgage while waiting to claim Social Security.[74]

This advice keys off the fact that retirees can increase their Social Security checks substantially for every month that they wait up to age seventy to claim benefits.[75] The Consumer Financial Protection Bureau has questioned this strategy, however, because the cost of a reverse mortgage normally exceeds the added lifetime benefits that the borrower would receive from delaying Social Security benefits.[76] That is largely because the loan balance keeps growing and the equity declines as interest, mortgage insurance premiums, and servicing fees for the reverse mortgage are added to the principal every month.[77] In an added risk, reverse mortgage borrowers could default and face eviction through foreclosure if they fail to pay their homeowners' insurance, any homeowners' association fees, or property taxes.[78]

Policymakers only seized on reverse mortgages as a solution for retirement security after traditional pensions faded away and the shortcomings of DC plans for lower-income workers became apparent. But the reverse mortgage option is one more misguided policy initiative that puts the onus on retirees who are broke to go into debt to pay for basic living expenses. Obviously, this strategy does nothing to help renters. Meanwhile, it burdens older homeowners with many of the same risks of other consumer debt.

Working Longer

The last big idea for boosting senior citizens' incomes is to push them to work longer.[79] Some proposals would do that by delaying the earliest age for claiming Social Security old-age benefits or raising the full retirement age. Other proposals would relax Social Security's earnings test and its penalties for employment to prod more Social Security recipients to remain employed.[80]

These proposals are deaf to the fact that older people *already* are working longer. In 2022, 65 percent of people ages fifty-five to sixty-four and 27 percent of those ages sixty-five to seventy-five were still working. That was up nine to ten percentage points for those two age groups compared to thirty years ago.[81]

The most likely reasons for this trend are the switch from DB plans to DC plans and prior Social Security reforms.[82] Most DB plans contain strong incentives to retire by a specific age because the pension benefits decline if the beneficiary stays on the job past that age. In contrast, DC plans lack incentives to retire at any particular age, and DC account balances usually grow larger the longer that employees work.[83] Those factors, plus the fact that DC plans are less generous than DB plans on average, induce the average worker with a DC plan to delay retirement.[84]

Meanwhile, Congress revised Social Security in three significant ways to encourage workers to stay on the job and delay retirement. First, it increased the full retirement age from sixty-five to sixty-seven in 1983. Once that reform was fully phased in by 2022, it amounted to a 13.3 percent benefit cut.[85] Second, the 1983 legislation sweetened the boost in benefits from 3 to 8 percent for each year people delay claiming Social Security between full retirement age and age seventy. Finally, Congress modified the earnings test in 2000 to allow people to claim Social Security at full retirement age or later with no reduction in benefits for working.[86]

As these developments indicate, the United States has been pressuring older people to work longer for some time. It is questionable whether there is room to squeeze even more work out of senior citizens across the board, as many proposed Social Security reforms contemplate. Even though working lives are longer on the whole today, there are stark differences in retirement patterns depending on income, education, and race. In particular, the trend toward longer working lives is limited to higher-income senior citizens.[87] By comparison, workers in the bottom half by income are *more* likely to retire early than in the past and to claim Social Security before full retirement age.[88] Race similarly is a factor, with Whites more likely than non-Whites to work into their sixties.[89] Finally, more than half of high school dropouts leave the work force by age sixty-two, compared to college graduates, of whom half do not leave until age sixty-seven.[90]

These disparities raise questions about whether adults retire earlier because they have to or they want to. Workers in physically demanding blue-collar jobs are more than half as likely to file for Social Security early as white-collar employees.[91] When we unpack why people retire early, poor health is the "major factor associated with stopping work."[92] That is especially true for lower-paid workers, with their higher rate of major health problems.[93] Numerous people who file for old-age benefits early have such poor health that it limits their ability to work.[94] In fact, at least half of men and single women who file early are so sick that they actually would qualify for Social Security disability insurance at age sixty-two.[95] Lower-income individuals also are more likely to die prematurely, which may make early filing rational.[96]

Early old-age benefits thus provide a crucial safety net for lower-income workers as their physical ability to work declines with age. Their work capacity is so limited, in fact, that by age sixty-five, people in the bottom 40 percent by income earn almost no wages.[97] It is neither realistic nor humane under those circumstances to tinker with Social Security's work incentives to pressure lower-income older adults to work longer.

WHY RISK SHARING IS CRUCIAL
TO PAYING FOR RETIREMENT

By now, it is obvious that the great American experiment with self-funding retirement has failed for everyone except the affluent. This highlights a larger truth, which is that some people win and some people lose in the economic lottery of life. At birth, none of us knows what life will hold, and our lives may not unfold as expected. Will we end up in well-paying positions or poorly paid jobs? Will our occupations flourish, or will they vanish due to technological obsolescence? Will unemployment strike due to a recession, pandemic, or war? Will artificial intelligence replace our jobs? Will our work be outsourced overseas? Will family caregiving responsibilities preclude us from taking paid work? Will we be well enough to even hold a job, and assuming we are, how long will our health last? Social Security protects us against these uncertainties regarding labor market risks that we all face at birth, many of which are beyond our control.[98]

Social Security's approach to risk sharing is especially well designed to protect workers who end up earning little money. For the average lower-income worker, reality looks like this: retiring early due to health problems, taking Social Security at age sixty-two, and subsisting mostly on those reduced Social Security benefits. For that average worker, Social Security is what stands between a modest existence and penury.

Even though Social Security in its current form will not assure these senior citizens of a life free from want, it does protect most from outright poverty and shields them from most risks presented by DC plans.[99] Social Security can accomplish this because it takes the risk of outliving one's assets and spreads it across the entire population, most of whom have not yet reached retirement. By pooling workers' contributions through mandatory payroll tax deductions, Social Security drafts younger generations to finance the retirements of older generations, with the expectation that their descendants will do the same for them when it comes time for them to retire. Social Security and its overseas equivalents have such a long pedigree that the United States and other major industrialized nations have been using risk-sharing models to finance retirement for over a hundred years.

By sharing risk, Social Security eliminates or substantially reduces an impressive number of financial risks to the aging.[100] For instance, Social Security hedges cumulation risk (the risk of not saving enough) by mandating payroll contributions during working years while providing a threshold living stipend for the poorest retired workers. Social Security also protects against market risk (i.e., market fluctuations) by paying out benefits as a monthly annuity.[101] Those payments are fixed in amount, so Social Security recipients can have confidence that their benefits will not dip from month to month. This same annuity feature protects against two more risks. It fends off security risk (theft) because scamsters lack access to a large lump sum that could wipe out a retiree's life savings if stolen. And the annuity feature guards against the risk of outliving one's money (longevity risk) by guaranteeing monthly old-age benefits until death.[102] Social Security's cost-of-living adjustment meanwhile provides a valuable hedge against inflation.[103] Finally, Social Security is portable from job to job and so does not pose mobility risk.

True, Social Security does pose some solvency risk (as debates over Social Security reform make clear), but the magnitude of that risk is significantly less than the solvency risk of private or state and local DB plans due to the federal government's sovereign immunity and its ability to tax and borrow. At the end of the day, most people expect Congress to take last-minute action and shore up the Social Security system.

In all of these respects, Social Security is the best mechanism by far for improving the retirement security of lower-income adults. Consequently, strengthening Social Security benefits for lower-paid workers should be the top priority in ensuring retirement security. Right now, Social Security benefits are too low for senior citizens on marginal incomes to afford the bare essentials.[104] They are forced to make hard choices between health and daily necessities such as food or utilities. Many fall into unmanageable levels of debt. Raising their Social Security benefits would protect them from economic privation in their last years.

The challenge is how to do that within the difficult, larger task of restoring Social Security to solvency. As it turns out, it is possible, as the next section explains. Economic well-being for lower-income retirees does *not* have to come at the price of stabilizing Social Security.

PROTECTING VULNERABLE SENIOR CITIZENS IN SOCIAL SECURITY REFORM

Any effort to bolster old-age benefits for rank-and-file workers must play out against the backdrop of Social Security reform. When the Trust Fund runs dry, the Social Security Administration will no longer have the authority to pay the full benefits promised.[105] Consequently, the federal government will have to cut old-age benefits by an estimated 21 percent starting in 2035 unless Congress enacts Social Security reforms.[106] Such large benefits cuts would plunge an estimated 29 percent of Social Security recipients into poverty.[107]

Fixing Social Security will require reducing costs (by slowing benefits growth), increasing revenues (by raising tax collections), or probably some combination of both.[108] If Social Security reduced monthly benefits across the board, the "biggest impact" would be "on the lowest-paid."[109] Those retirees cannot withstand any reduction in benefits because their budgets have no fat to cut.[110] Further, they already get less than their fair share of lifetime Social Security benefits because they die earlier on average. Consequently, Social Security reforms must be accomplished in a way that protects financially vulnerable retirees.

Fortunately, these goals are not incompatible. It is possible to shore up Social Security benefits for retirees of modest means while restoring the system to sound footing.[111] There are numerous proposals for returning Social Security to solvency, so this chapter will not reinvent the wheel.[112] Instead, I will focus on targeted revisions to Social Security to enable lower-income older adults to retire with adequate basic income. These proposals already are part of a mainstream discussion over larger plans to restore Social Security to health by slowing the growth in future benefits and raising additional revenue. All of the reforms discussed here would be phased in, often over two decades, to enable today's workers to plan ahead and to soften any sting to wealthier employees.

In instituting reforms, it is crucial to avoid changes that would further undermine the financial security of cash-strapped retirees. Chief among them are proposals to delay the earliest eligibility age past age sixty-two. Doing so would inflict hardship on lower-income workers who are too sick by their early sixties to keep on working. It would further exacerbate the gap in lifetime Social Security benefits that benefits the rich at the expense of the poor.[113]

It is not even clear that delaying the earliest eligibility age would achieve cost savings. For one thing, recipients who were forced to claim at a later age would collect the same total benefits because their monthly benefits would rise for each year of delay.[114] Further, at least half of men and single women who file early would qualify for Social Security disability benefits at sixty-two, which would negate any savings from denying them old-age benefits at that age.[115] Those disability claims would *worsen* the cost pressures on Social Security, because the federal government pays substantially more for disability benefits at age sixty-two than for old-age benefits at that age.[116] Meanwhile, other impaired workers who did not go on disability might cling to their jobs past the point of productivity.[117]

For similar reasons, Congress should not extend the full retirement age again.[118] Currently there are proposals to raise it as high as seventy, based on growing life expectancies.[119] But delaying that age would amount to an across-the-board benefits cut that financially pressed senior citizens cannot afford.[120] Prolonging the full retirement age also would widen the gap in lifetime benefits between the haves and have-nots.[121] Both proposals— the first to make people wait longer for old-age benefits and the other to reduce the amounts—are too blunt because they would affect everyone, regardless of whether life dealt them a bad hand in terms of income or health.[122] As the economist Paul Krugman observed: "Anyone invoking rising life expectancy as a reason to delay Social Security benefits is, in effect, saying that aging janitors must keep working (or be cast into extreme poverty) because bankers are living longer."[123]

Consequently, in enacting reforms, Congress must not lose sight of Social Security's role in providing economic security to workers, especially modestly paid workers, at retirement.[124] This will require Congress to ensure that Social Security provides a financial lifeline to workers while restoring the system to the black.

Congress needs to address two separate problems to repair that financial lifeline. First, old-age benefits are too low currently for some retirees to even meet basic living expenses. And second, the growing gap in lifetime benefits needs to be reversed. Accomplishing both goals will require increasing revenue or scaling back future benefits elsewhere in the Social Security program. But there are ways to preserve Social Security's objective of preventing poverty while reining in the cost.

With respect to the first reform: Social Security's current benefit structure results in stingy retirement benefits for workers with low lifetime earnings. Some of those people worked full-time for decades but were poorly paid; others could only secure part-time work or were in and out of the labor force due to illness or caregiving responsibilities. These people are at heightened risk of economic want in retirement due to low benefits levels.

Over the years, Congress has twice sought to address this problem by granting low-paid workers a small guaranteed benefit. Unfortunately, the latest iteration (the so-called special minimum benefit) became obsolete some years back once regular Social Security benefits exceeded that minimum amount due to adjustments for inflation.[125] Meanwhile, the lowest levels of regular Social Security benefits are not enough to live on.

Consequently, Congress should approve a special minimum benefit that is large enough to allow low-income retirees to avoid financial hardship. This minimum benefit would be targeted by income and payable if it exceeded someone's regular Social Security benefit. Ideally, the new minimum benefit would bring retirees up to 200 percent of the FPL, but even pegging it at 125 percent of FPL would boost benefits meaningfully.[126] This would help struggling retirees cover their living expenses.

The second set of reforms would address the overall increase in life expectancy and its fallout for Social Security's solvency. Right now, Social

Security is indexed for inflation, but not for longevity.[127] This increases the cost pressure on Social Security because as "life expectancy increases, benefits just get paid for more years."[128] Soon this financial pressure will be unsustainable. Meanwhile, the gap in lifetime benefits between rich and poor continues to widen.

Tackling the problem of longevity could address both problems. Adjusting payroll taxes and benefits for projected increases in longevity would go a long way toward restoring Social Security to solvency.[129] Essentially, this would right-size people's benefits and payroll taxes according to expected lifespans. One proposal by Diamond and Orszag would do this by splitting the cost of adjusting for longevity between future retirees (by slowing the growth in benefits) and future workers (by adjusting payroll taxes for longevity).[130]

Congress could raise additional revenue by charging Social Security payroll taxes on a larger income base. Recall that Social Security only taxes each person's first X dollars in income every year (which happened to be $168,600 in 2024). Anyone earning more than that a year does not owe payroll taxes on the excess. As income inequality surged over the past forty years, the amount of income free from Social Security taxes almost doubled, from 10 percent of earnings in 1983 to 18 percent in 2022.[131] Most high earners who escape payroll taxes on income over the ceiling have higher longevity and higher expected old-age benefits as well. They draw more in Social Security benefits than anyone else, yet they shoulder less responsibility for paying for Social Security than rank-and-file workers. To fix this problem, Congress should increase the amount of earned income that is subject to payroll taxes.

Further savings could be located by changing the formula for Social Security benefits to pay fewer cents on the dollar for the highest levels of earnings. The result would be to slow benefits growth for workers with high lifetime earnings.[132]

As I explain in greater detail in the final chapter, these proposals can restore Social Security to fiscal soundness while alleviating hardships on retirees in financial straits. The deadline for reforming Social Security is rapidly approaching. When it comes, Congress will have to decide, will it deepen the financial plight of lower-income retirees? Or will it use Social Security reform as a springboard to improve their economic well-being?

11 What It Will Take

America celebrates itself as the land of opportunity, where people can pursue dreams of education, homeownership, and more. It aspires to be free from hunger, cold, and want. It takes pride in its world-class health care and a well-earned retirement for workers.

But for families in the bottom half, those hopes are increasingly hollow. Too often, economic well-being is reserved for the wealthy. Meanwhile, households in the bottom half are staggering under onerous financial risks that government and employers foisted on them. Those risks have left them in serious financial straits on multiple fronts. They do not earn a living wage and have barely any savings. They must make trade-offs between one necessity of life and another. Half of renters cannot afford their rent without scrimping on other essentials.[1] At least half of US adults cannot pay their medical bills, forcing many to skip needed medical care or paying other bills.[2] Half of student borrowers beyond their grace periods are behind on their college loans. Too many workers face a hand-to-mouth retirement because their employers do not offer them workplace pension plans. And the list goes on. With more than half of US households barely hanging on financially, the nation has reached a tipping point.

How are people supposed to survive and achieve major life goals with such unstable finances? The official answer has two parts. First, the United States increasingly expects families to save large amounts of cash to pay for those goals. But it is ludicrous to expect families who cannot make ends meet to save tens or hundreds of thousands of dollars for retirement or college.

Second, if people cannot pony up the cash to pay for major financial goals, then the United States stands by while they go into debt, or worse, plies them with loans. Every family should be able to make ends meet, buy a home if they choose, receive quality health care, send their children to college, and look forward to a secure retirement. Current policies make this dubious for the bottom half of households, however, because reaching all five milestones requires unrealistic sums of savings or dangerous levels of debt.

It is time to be honest about what economic well-being will take for ordinary households. If the nation continues to require households to amass large savings and go into debt when their wages are depressed, then the bottom half will continue to experience financial hardship. But if the nation draws on its long experience in sharing and managing risk, it can provide those families with economic well-being. A surprising number of programs more than pay for themselves through future tax revenues and other benefits, which is further reason to adopt a risk-sharing approach.

THE CENTRAL ROLE OF RISK SHARING

Throughout this book, I have advocated spreading risk to safeguard ordinary families from financial hardship. There is nothing revolutionary about this approach. The nation has used risk sharing for years to shield households from unmanageable hazards. Social Security, for instance, protects against poverty in retirement. Unemployment insurance alleviates lost income from joblessness. Health insurance covers medical bills. And Pell Grants help pay for college for students from lower-income backgrounds. These time-honored mechanisms are well-established, but they need serious modernization to achieve economic well-being for all.

Usually, it is more efficient to protect people from major risks through risk sharing. If individuals had to bear large losses alone, they would confront a hard choice: either save large amounts of money for disasters that may never transpire or be wiped out financially if catastrophe strikes. But by pooling funds and covering losses collectively, people can cover everyone's risk at a lower total cost because most people will escape that risk in a given year. Sharing risk is a win-win proposition because it protects more people from risk at reduced total cost.[3]

Risk sharing also enables society to reap positive spillover effects from the activities of private individuals. In the college context, for instance, society will benefit if more high school graduates invest in undergraduate training and increase their contributions to the nation's tax base and economic growth.

In other instances, risk sharing is less common, but other risk-allocation or risk-management techniques are available. For example, the fact that home purchases usually are financed with mortgages makes strong risk management critical in preventing defaults. Similarly, living wage legislation is not the same as sharing risk. But those laws serve a comparable purpose by allocating risk. They do so by requiring employers and their shareholders to pay the full price of their labor costs before drawing profits, instead of shifting the risk of subpar pay onto individual workers and society.

In chapter 1, I defined economic well-being as *"having access to sufficient financial resources* to pay current bills in full, withstand financial shocks, have financial freedom, and achieve long-term financial goals." Risk sharing and risk-allocation mechanisms such as living wage laws provide the added financial resources needed when a family's income and wealth fall short. In the process, risk sharing and risk allocation allow families to make ends meet, enjoy good health, attend college, and retire comfortably, while stabilizing family finances in anticipation of owning a home.

Ultimately, risk sharing and similar mechanisms are what it will take to enable everyone, especially families in the bottom half, to attain economic well-being. What it will take also is a question of money. Risk sharing raises questions about costs, particularly when it involves social insurance or other government benefits. In the remainder of this chapter, I explore those fiscal implications and, in many cases, how investment today could reap handsome financial returns in years to come.

COVERING BASIC LIVING EXPENSES

At its most basic, economic well-being requires the ability to pay for basic living expenses as they come due, without incurring debt. If households lack the funds to cover the necessities of life, they will experience hardship and have nothing to fall back on if disaster strikes. Other important milestones, such as college education for their children or owning a home, will be beyond reach. For these reasons, a living income is of top importance and the linchpin for all other aspects of economic well-being.

Working Families

The first step toward stabilizing the finances of low-wage workers is enacting a federal minimum wage keyed to the living wage for a single, childless worker. On top of that, expanding the EITC and the CTC for less well-off families would give them the financial boost they require to cover the necessities of life.

A LIVING MINIMUM WAGE

For working families, a living wage for a single, childless full-time worker is step one to financial survival. Market forces have not produced a widespread living wage because pay scales can drop whenever labor conditions deteriorate. Accordingly, the United States needs to mandate a basic floor by raising the federal minimum wage to a living wage. To remain up to date, this national living wage should be adjusted automatically for local cost conditions as well as for inflation. In addition, the updated federal law should close the loopholes that exclude certain groups of workers from minimum wage protection.

Recent studies have split over the fiscal effect of raising the minimum wage. In 2023 the Congressional Budget Office (CBO) concluded that raising the federal minimum wage to $17 an hour would increase the federal deficit.[4] CBO reasoned that a higher minimum wage would prompt employers to shed positions, requiring higher federal expenditures on Medicaid and unemployment insurance. However, CBO's assumption ran counter to the overwhelming body of research showing that raising the minimum wage does not boost unemployment.[5] Based on that research, a different study of an earlier proposal for a $15 minimum hourly wage predicted that increasing the minimum wage would shrink the federal deficit by $65.4 billion a year.[6] Those savings would result from higher payroll and income taxes paid by the benefited workers plus lower spending on public assistance and Social Security benefits.[7] Thus, if data continue to show that a higher minimum wage does not raise unemployment, a living minimum wage could benefit low-wage workers while actually *reducing* the federal deficit.

TAX CREDITS FOR DEPENDENTS

As chapter 6 discussed, minimum wage reforms are necessary but not sufficient to achieve a living income for everyone. Low-wage employees with dependents often need additional support. The same is true for workers who want full-time work but cannot find it due to work schedules that only offer irregular hours.

The good news is that the United States already has a well-established risk-sharing arrangement to build on in the form of the EITC and the CTC. Right now, these programs fall short of raising the worst-paid families to a living income. But both programs could get there with incremental changes.

The top priority is to increase the tax credits for the poorest families. For the CTC, this would entail four changes: granting those families the same full tax credit as higher-income families, raising the tax credit to $3,000 for every child age six to seventeen and to $3,600 for children under six years old, making the CTC fully refundable, and scaling back the phase-out thresholds for the wealthiest families in order to save money. Those are some of the same reforms that Congress temporarily approved in the American Rescue Plan Act in 2021. Meanwhile, Congress should increase the EITC for the worst-paid workers to the same dollar amount that middle-income workers receive. Those changes would alleviate hardship for the poorest working families.

In addition, Congress should grant the CTC to every minor child of a stay-at-home parent or grandparent. Congress similarly should extend the EITC to other stay-at-home relatives who provide care without pay. These reforms would provide long overdue recognition for the crucial and selfless support that these caregivers give to society. Spouses who stay at home to care for relatives support the formal economy by making it possible for breadwinners to hold full-time jobs. Caregivers also relieve the state of the cost of caring for disabled or elderly individuals. Society heavily depends on unpaid caregivers for their work, and the EITC and the CTC should assure them of a living income.

Strikingly, the EITC and CTC are two of the most cost-effective investments taxpayers can make in future generations. A recent major study of the EITC concluded that the program can deliver $73 billion a year to lower-income families for only $12 billion annually because the program increases employment and tax revenues, while reducing spending on public assistance. When researchers further adjusted this $12 billion net cost to reflect the value of the EITC's positive spillover effects to society (in the form of improved health; reduced crime; and better education, employment, and earnings of recipients' children), they found that "each $1 of EITC spending generates over $3 in social value." In other words, the EITC "'pays for itself.'"[8]

The same is true for the CTC. Economists at Columbia University recently concluded that making the CTC "expansion permanent would cost $97 billion per year and generate social benefits with net present value of $982 billion per year," producing "very high net returns for the U.S. population."[9] They projected that the social benefits to children of an expanded CTC include higher lifetime earnings, higher tax payments, better health in adulthood, and longer lives. In sum, they estimated, "the present discounted value of the long-term benefits to society for a one-child, single-parent, low-income family [would be] more than five times as large as the initial transfer."[10] These large benefits from shoring up struggling families make an expanded CTC "a bargain."[11]

Retirees

Like numerous younger workers, many elderly adults are in financial distress. Changes to the federal minimum wage plus the EITC and CTC usually will not help these retirees, however, when they no longer participate in the workforce. Instead, another historic risk-sharing scheme—Social

Security—provides the best avenue for lifting poor and near-poor retirees to a living income.

Social Security is ideal for reaching this goal because it spreads a risk that everyone faces—low lifetime earnings—over the entire working population. Social Security also is preferable because other retirement income arrangements do not work for low-wage employees. Many lower-income adults are not healthy enough by their early sixties to work longer. Few have DB pensions. And DC plans have failed this group in multiple respects. Most of them lack access to 401(k) plans at work. For those who do have DC savings plans, their average balances are too small to fund retirement. Further, DC plans present risks that retirees on subsistence budgets cannot afford. Social Security benefits avoid these problems because they are available to virtually every worker and provide reliable, fixed monthly payments that continue until death.

Consequently, a modest top-off in Social Security old-age benefits for lower-income adults age sixty-two and up is the best way to assure them of a living income without increasing their financial risks. Congress could accomplish this by enacting a special minimum benefit that assured a living income. Part of the cost would be offset by reduced outlays for cash public assistance, SNAP food benefits, rental subsidies, and Medicaid. These offsets are so large that CBO estimated in 2015 that a special minimum benefit paying 125 percent of the FPL would increase the deficit only by 0.2 percentage points.[12] In the greater scheme of things, that is a "negligible amount."[13] Increasing the special minimum benefit to 200 percent of the FPL would cost more, but would substantially improve the lives of retirees who are near-poor.

Meanwhile, there are additional ways to offset these costs while restoring Social Security to fiscal balance. Chief among them is assessing payroll taxes on a larger income base. Eliminating the taxable maximum altogether would shrink Social Security's deficit by 53 percent.[14] Under that proposal, the best-paid employees would pay more in taxes, but their future Social Security benefits would rise.[15] A second proposal, which would assess payroll taxes on all earnings without increasing benefits, would cut the Trust Fund's deficit by 73 percent.[16] This last option would improve Social Security's solvency the most, without widening the gap in lifetime benefits.

More savings could result from adjusting future Social Security benefits and taxes for projected increases in life expectancy.[17] Diamond and Orszag estimated that indexing payroll taxes and benefits for longevity together would cut the Social Security deficit by about a third.[18]

Finally, further savings could be found by adjusting the Social Security benefits formula downward for higher earners.[19] Accomplishing this by gradually decreasing the rate paid on top earnings from fifteen to five cents on the dollar would reduce the deficit by around 11 percent.[20]

By 2033, Congress will have to confront Social Security's finances, which will open a political window to effect these changes. It is eminently possible to restore Social Security to solvency while modestly boosting benefits for retirees most in need. With those changes, careful expansion of the well-accepted Social Security model would go far to put the nation's most vulnerable retirees on firmer financial footing while restoring Social Security to the black.

PROTECTION FROM NEGATIVE ECONOMIC SHOCKS

So far, this chapter has discussed the importance of a living income. By itself, however, a living income is not enough to absorb the negative economic shocks that most households experience from time to time. Some of those shocks are hits to income, especially from involuntary unemployment and reductions in hours and pay. Other negative shocks come from unexpected costs, with high health-care costs leading the list.

Income Shocks

As discussed earlier, the starting point for stabilizing family incomes is through changes to the EITC, the CTC, and the federal minimum wage. These solutions assume that breadwinners are working, however, and do not contemplate a catastrophic drop in income from layoffs, firings, or involuntary reductions in hours or pay. Instead, the United States has used a different, time-honored risk-sharing scheme—unemployment insurance—to provide workers with a safety net in case of unemployment.

The problem is that in the ninety years since Congress created the UI system in the Social Security Act of 1935, UI has not kept up with the dramatic changes in labor market conditions. Those changes left jobless workers with mounting difficulty satisfying UI's outdated eligibility standards. The fact that almost three-quarters of unemployed workers could not qualify for UI in 2019 epitomizes UI's obsolescence. Tragically, UI's safety net unraveled as US workers were experiencing increasing job insecurity after collective bargaining's decline.

If working families are to have economic stability, modernizing UI will be crucial. Above all, Congress needs to put the federal government in charge of minimum UI eligibility, benefits, and duration standards plus assessments on employers. A nationwide system would stop the race to the bottom in UI benefits that the states are waging currently. Next, UI needs a new eligibility test that does not exclude low-wage workers *because* they are low-paid. Scrapping the old, punitive monetary test for an hours-worked test would restore UI benefits to substantially more workers who get pink slips. In addition, Congress should expand UI to cover workers who quit for "good cause." This would extend jobless benefits to workers who experience involuntary cuts in pay or hours, are assigned erratic work schedules, lose pay due to labor disputes, or have to leave for compelling family reasons. A number of states have adopted these sorts of good cause grounds, and the nation should follow their lead. Finally, UI should be revamped to redefine more workers as "employees" instead of "independent contractors," to maintain eligibility for part-time workers who are seeking part-time work, and to increase benefits for workers with the lowest wage bases.

How about the fiscal effects of UI reform? Unemployment insurance has a large multiplier effect because it supplies jobless workers with funds that they spend almost immediately, injecting cash into the economy and creating jobs.[21] This multiplier effect is up to 2.0 for basic UI and extended UI alike, depending on the time period.[22] Given the multiplier effect's large size, CBO reported that enhanced aid to the unemployed during the Great Recession in 2009 had the biggest bang for the buck of any emergency economic aid, expanding gross domestic product by up to $1.90 for every dollar of benefits and producing up to fifteen new jobs for every million dollars in benefits.[23] In this way, by stimulating the economy, UI more than pays for itself.

Unanticipated Expenses

Unexpected costs can also rock family finances. These costs come in all types, from car repairs to rent increases. But the biggest unexpected costs are typically medical expenses. Expensive medical bills are the most high-stakes because they affect patients' health and lives, not just their finances. High medical costs force large numbers of patients to make painful choices among medical treatment, shelter, heat, and food, which are all essential to physical survival. Many of them skip treatment against doctors' orders, while others sacrifice food or other necessities to get medical care. Others drain their savings or take on debt in an effort to pay high medical bills, and disproportionate numbers end up in bankruptcy. Meanwhile, other important financial milestones become unattainable under the onslaught of health costs.

The United States already has a strong risk-sharing platform to build on, in the form of Medicare, Medicaid, Marketplace coverage (Obamacare), and workplace health plans. With the passage of the Affordable Care Act, this system expanded to provide guaranteed access to health insurance for most residents. But Congress left unfinished business when it passed the ACA. Now it needs to take the system to the next level by making health coverage accessible *and* affordable.

The first task is to extend health coverage to more people who are uninsured. The easiest way to do this is to extend Marketplace-subsidized premiums to people who currently do not qualify for them. To do that, Congress should authorize premium-free Marketplace plans for everyone caught in the Medicaid gap, subsidize premiums for lower-income workers in opt-out states even if they qualify for employer-based coverage, and make the enhanced premium tax credits permanent.

These three measures would increase the federal deficit slightly but substantially reduce the number of uninsured. In 2023, for instance, closing the Medicaid gap in opt-out states and subsidizing Marketplace premiums for low-wage workers in those states would have extended coverage to 1.9 million uninsured people at a fiscal outlay of $27 billion.[24] That would have amounted to 1.5 percent of net federal subsidies for health insurance that year, while generating an estimated $11.1 billion in savings to states, employers, and households.[25] Meanwhile, making enhanced premium subsidies permanent for Marketplace policies would cost the federal government $26.6 billion in 2026 while extending health coverage to 3.4 million more people by 2034.[26]

The other task is to get out-of-pocket health costs under control. Lower costs would encourage even more uninsured people to sign up, while enabling those with health insurance to afford the health care they need. To rein in out-of-pocket costs, Congress first needs to address the price of premiums. This will require expanding Marketplace premium subsidies in the ways I just described, while making Medicare premiums affordable. In the latter regard, the Marketplace calibrates premiums to income to make sure that less well-off patients can cover their necessities of life and medical bills alike. Medicare reforms should do the same.

Recent proposals for pegging Medicare Part B and Part D premiums to income vary widely and could cost as much as $42.3 billion a year.[27] One plan propounded by Brookings, however, is designed to pay for itself. Under that proposal, higher Medicare premiums paid by middle- and higher-income beneficiaries would offset all but $5.4 billion of the cost of cutting premiums for seniors with incomes under 400 percent of the FPL. The authors would cover that $5.4 billion difference by raising the net investment income tax rate on interest, dividends, capital gains, and rental income of wealthy taxpayers. Meanwhile, the states would realize cost savings of an estimated $6 billion.[28]

On top of costly premiums, Congress needs to tackle high deductibles, coinsurance, and copays. For Marketplace plans, Congress should extend cost-sharing reductions to up to 400 percent of the FPL and make them more generous. This would reduce patients' cost-sharing expenditures on a sliding scale by income. In 2023, these reforms would have cost $12.2 billion in federal outlays, most of which would have been offset by $9.3 billion in savings to households and employers. Meanwhile, these enhanced CSRs would have cut the uninsured population by 1.5 million, second only to the 2 million who would newly gain coverage by closing the Medicaid gap.[29]

On the Medicare front, there are similar proposals for shaving out-of-pocket charges for retirees who cannot afford them. Those reforms include limiting Medicare to one annual deductible for all medical care, mandating a total annual cap on out-of-pocket expenditures under Original Medicare, and then pegging the deductible and annual cap to beneficiaries' incomes. On the low end, some proposals estimate annual federal cost savings of $12.5 billion to $90 billion from these reforms; on the high end, other analysts predict that similar reforms would be revenue-neutral or require additional federal outlays of up to $8.8 billion.[30] This wide range of cost estimates suggests that shielding lower-income senior citizens from high Medicare out-of-pocket costs could be compatible with federal cost savings, depending on the design of the proposal.

These cost estimates have several takeaways. First, health reforms do not inevitably raise the federal deficit. Some reforms are revenue neutral or could even generate savings. For instance, savings could result by bundling cost-sharing reforms with provisions to discourage overconsumption of medical care (especially under Medigap policies).[31] Meanwhile, reforms that would increase federal spending usually have a substantial payoff, either by reducing the number of uninsured; generating billions of dollars in savings to the states, businesses, and families; or both. Often that payoff comes at a relatively modest cost, moreover. When Congress expanded the Marketplace premium subsidies temporarily, it was projected to cost only slightly more than 1 percent of net federal subsidies for health insurance in 2024 but to cut the uninsured in 2025 by four million people, an impressive 14 percent reduction.[32] Most of the other proposals have a similarly modest price tag.

As this part has stressed, health-care expenses are usually the largest surprise costs that people encounter. But they are not the only surprise costs. A short-term savings account could stabilize family budgets by covering other unanticipated expenses, as I now discuss.

BUILDING ASSETS

Throughout this book, I have argued that the nation's savings policies for the bottom 50 percent are upside-down. In the lower half, the typical family does not have enough income to subsist on, let alone save. The proposals in this book are designed to provide those families with a living income. But even with enough to live on, they will not have much cash to save for long-term, big-ticket-item goals such as college and retirement. Today's policies, which expect poorly paid families to foot much of the bill for college and retirement through large personal savings, are unrealistic to the point of being punitive.

Instead, asset-building policies for lower-income households should focus on strategies that actually work and are of the greatest importance to those households. As it happens, there *are* effective ways to help lower-income households save and build wealth. Well-designed pilot programs have seen success in helping families build short-term savings accounts. These accounts are small but mighty because they provide reserves to cover surprise bills, which are a top worry of cash-strapped families. Meanwhile, homeownership provides some lower-income families with a powerful way to build wealth due to the forced savings feature of residential mortgage loans.

A Universal Savings Plan

As chapter 4 stressed, the government has no meaningful national program to encourage short-term, unrestricted savings. When it comes to lower-income families, this is particularly misguided because they are so exposed to negative shocks and in serious need of emergency reserves. This policy gap exacerbates the wealth gap as well, because lower earners rarely benefit from federal tax incentives for retirement or college savings, which overwhelmingly subsidize upper-income people instead.

The way to bring short-term savings for everyone up to scale is for Congress to create the universal savings plan proposed in chapter 6. Under this plan, every worker would be enrolled automatically in a no-cost, interest-bearing savings account covered by federal deposit insurance. Funding would come from small, regular payroll contributions by workers to their individual accounts, plus a government match for middle-income workers on down, with the largest matches going to the lowest paid. Workers could increase or decrease their contributions or opt out of participation if they chose. Meanwhile, they could tap their account balances for any purpose, whenever they wanted.

Past research indicates that three features of this universal savings plan could have a powerful effect on boosting the number of lower-income families participating. The first is auto-enrollment, the second is automatic payroll deductions, and the third is the government match. These features would be part of an overall federal savings infrastructure (similar to the ones that wealthier employees enjoy) that would help give people greater success in saving.

A universal savings plan would offer numerous dividends. It would assist struggling families to cover unexpected costs that life throws their way. It also would help families avoid going into debt and missing housing and utility payments, while reducing their need for public assistance.[33] In fact, if the experience with the EITC and CTC is any guide, the government match would entice more people to join the labor force in order to receive the match.[34]

That match is patterned after the Saver's Match for retirement savings by lower-income earners, which Congress enacted in 2022.[35] According to the Joint Committee on Taxation, the Saver's Match will cost $2.1 billion when it takes effect in fiscal year 2028 and somewhat less in subsequent years.[36] This forecast provides a useful ballpark estimate for my new federal match on universal savings accounts because it would be targeted at many of the same earners.

This modest cost could be offset fully by repealing or scaling back another tax-preferred savings program that mostly advantages the affluent. Health savings accounts are natural candidates, because they mostly are used by the richest 10 percent of taxpayers and thus mainly subsidize the wealthy. Repealing the tax advantages for HSAs would save the federal budget $19.5 billion in fiscal year 2028 and larger sums in later years.[37] Those savings would more than pay for the new match on universal savings accounts, while enabling lower-income families to save for emergencies.

To summarize, if the nation makes it a priority, it *is* possible for many financially pressed families to build modest amounts of savings. The key is to provide a universal savings infrastructure that makes it easy for them to save. While those savings could be used for any purpose, in all likelihood they would be used for short-term needs. Longer-term savings of any size are usually out of reach for lower-income households unless they have access to and enroll in workplace 401(k) plans. But there is still one vehicle that offers ordinary working families the potential to build long-term wealth, which is homeownership.

Homeownership

As I have stressed, official expectations that people pay for college and retirement with large amounts of savings are jarringly at odds with reality for the bottom half of workers, particularly those who lack retirement plans at work. This does not mean that accumulating wealth is futile for lower-paid workers. On the contrary, homeownership is a common way for ordinary workers to amass wealth. Forced savings make homeownership accessible in a way that other investments are not because it takes a necessary expenditure—housing—and turns it into an investment. Home appreciation and leverage add to the wealth-building potential of owning a home.

Homeownership is the one exception to financial advisers' advice to avoid going into debt. When investing in a home pays off, the homeowner reaps the benefits, which can make a home mortgage advisable under the right circumstances. But it is important to go into homebuying with open eyes, because mortgage debt makes homeownership financially risky, especially for borrowers on limited incomes. When homeownership is successful, it can provide a crucial source of wealth. But when it fails, it can decimate families' finances and leave them worse off.

In view of these risks, housing policy needs to tread carefully. Homeownership's path to wealth for working families is the single biggest reason for lending it official support. That support needs to be designed more intelligently, however, to ensure that homeownership improves economic well-being rather than undermining it.

In chapter 7, I espoused three sets of policies to reduce the risks of homeownership while integrating it with other personal goals. The first set aims to lower the cost of homes and home mortgage loans. That is a tall order, especially when housing prices and interest rates are stuck on high. But it is not insurmountable, judging from the fact that most people become homeowners by late in life, with almost 80 percent of people age sixty-five and up owning homes.[38] New buying opportunities present themselves whenever interest rates or housing prices fall. So, if first-time homebuyers are willing to play the long game, their chances of eventually owning a home will rise.

Meanwhile, zoning reforms, tax incentives, and more construction of modestly priced units would increase the supply of homes and push down prices. A government-operated home mortgage marketplace would increase comparison shopping and keep mortgage prices in check. More down payment assistance plus subsidized rates would give lower-income renters the boost they need to buy homes.

The second set of policies focuses on stabilizing homeownership by making mortgages sustainable. Chapter 7 discussed measures to help homeowners retain their homes, including emphasizing fixed-rate mortgages, assuring borrowers' ability to repay, and foreclosure prevention policies. But most important of all are chapter 6's recommendations for a living income and a universal savings plan.

An adequate, stable income is essential for lower-income homeowners to make the regular mortgage payments that are key to keeping their homes. A universal savings plan would further help homeowners in avoiding default by helping them build cash reserves to cover mortgage payments during emergencies. Currently, the lack of national support for short-term, unrestricted savings often leaves lower-income homeowners house-poor because they have poured their scant savings into down payments.[39] If job loss, poor health, or surprise costs later strike, they will have few reserves to tap for monthly mortgage payments. A universal savings policy is therefore crucial for homeownership to serve as an engine of financial security for ordinary families.

The last group of policies seeks to harmonize homeownership with the other financial milestones. Here, sustainable mortgage payments become doubly important, to ensure that foreclosure does not sabotage other personal financial goals. Other policies center on how to select and use mortgages to free up cash for other purposes, including through comparison shopping, fixed-rate loans, and refinancing to lower rates. Homeowners who pay off their mortgages by retirement, moreover, can significantly cut their expenses.

Homeownership, of all five milestones, is unique in two regards. It is attainable for many workers, even those with limited incomes, because it takes money that would go for rent and uses it to buy a home. Homeownership, moreover, is the only long-term milestone whose payoff may justify debt financing, at least under the right conditions. In contrast, paying for college with loans is not worth the cost for many children of ordinary workers. Unless we reinstate full scholarships for less well-off college students, increasingly the children of the bottom half will be shut out of this crucial avenue to social and economic advancement.

COLLEGE EDUCATION

For as long as most of us can remember, a bachelor's degree has been key to America's technological superiority and a rite of passage into the middle class. But to attain that degree, today's students face a difficult choice. They are told either to save up for college (which, for their parents, may be impossible), work their way through school (detracting from their studies and their grades), incur student loans in the tens of thousands of dollars (with all the attendant risks), or skip college. Most students from lower-income backgrounds who do go to college leave with large amounts of debt that they struggle to pay off. The rest never attend college at all.

For disadvantaged students who do opt for college, student loans often harm their economic well-being. Many student borrowers from financially distressed families do not have enough money to live on every month after making their student loan payments. Over half of student debtors report difficulty building emergency savings. Student borrowers are more likely to skip needed medical care than adults who went to college without student debt. Student loans also cause adults to delay buying homes, often for years. Student debt further may hamper saving for retirement. More generally, college-educated adults who took out student loans only have a third as much wealth on average as their classmates who left college with no student debt. For those borrowers, student loans sap their ability to build a nest egg.

But the pernicious effects of student loans go beyond stalled progress to outright harm. In 2019, right before the federal government suspended student loan payments due to COVID-19, a staggering number of student borrowers—almost half of those past their grace periods—were behind in repaying their loans. Lower-income student borrowers and Black and Hispanic borrowers were the most likely to have trouble. Ruined credit, wage garnishment, depleted savings, and rocky finances face those who end up in default. Meanwhile, their student debt keeps hanging over their heads due to difficulty discharging those loans in bankruptcy.

These problems with student loans give the lie to the myth of America as the land of opportunity. The student loan system thrusts heavy, new financial risks on underprivileged college students that many will be unable to bear. Those risks have reached an unconscionable level. Meanwhile, the nation cannot afford to lose the valuable contributions to society made by talented but cash-strapped students who invest in higher education.

Two sets of reforms—one retroactive and one prospective—are necessary to reverse this situation. The first is student debt cancellation for

Pell Grant recipients. These recipients need debt relief the most, because they come from lower-income backgrounds and are at greater risk of default than affluent borrowers. Economists estimate that forgiving Pell Grant recipients' student debt for up to $20,000 apiece would cost $162 to $250 billion.[40] That is substantially less than the $400 billion cost of the original Biden plan and would make better use of taxpayer dollars by limiting debt relief to borrowers most in need.[41]

Going forward, the United States also should replace student debt with expanded grant support as the main financing tool for college students from lower-income backgrounds. One such plan appeared in the fiscal year 2025 budget, in which President Biden proposed increasing the maximum Pell Grant by expanding its coverage and doubling its size over a ten-year period. According to the Biden administration, that increase would cost $5.1 billion in total over ten years, while expanding Pell Grant aid to 1.1 million more students than received it in 2022.[42]

When the positive spillover effects of expanded student grants are considered, these fiscal costs are likely to be recouped in full. A leading study concluded, for instance, that increased Pell Grant aid to first-time-in-college students increased their college completion rate, earnings, and tax payments so significantly that it "likely [paid] for itself several times over."[43] Other studies have found that government grants to college students often generate such large positive externalities that they more than repay taxpayers' initial outlay.[44] Consequently, student grants benefit society and students alike due to their high return on investment.

In short, economic well-being could be within everyone's reach with three important changes. The first is guaranteeing a living income to workers and retirees. The second is improving risk sharing and management to better protect families from negative economic shocks. And the third is providing full scholarships to underprivileged students, instead of forcing them to go into debt to pay for college.

In the current polarized political environment, the prospects for these measures may seem dim. The 2024 reelection of Donald Trump as president as this book went to press put many of these initiatives on hold and raised further concerns about deep benefits reductions. In fact, immediately after the 2024 election, commentators flagged Medicaid, SNAP, and expanded premium subsidies for Marketplace plans as possible targets for budget cuts by the Trump administration.[45] Compounding those concerns, once the Republicans regained control of both houses of Congress in 2024, they had the votes to make social safety net rollbacks politically feasible.

Such cuts could come at politicians' peril, however. President Trump won reelection partly because so many voters were enraged about "feeling broke."[46] Curtailing Medicaid, food stamps, and Marketplace health insurance subsidies could alienate this key bloc of voters by jeopardizing benefits for at least seventy million low-income Americans, according to the *Washington Post*.[47] Consequently, politicians have reason to tread carefully, because revoking that economic support for tens of millions of constituents could threaten their chances of reelection.

It is no coincidence that citizens voted out the Biden administration for downplaying their economic concerns. Now that fully half of US households lack a living income, they have the voting might to decide elections. This is apparent not only from the 2024 electoral results, but from successful ballot measures by voters in a number of conservative states to opt-in to Medicaid expansion, over the resistance of their home state legislatures.[48]

This electoral tipping point is what will provide the path to stronger social safety net protections in the future. Already, the general public is heavily invested in most of the risk-sharing programs that this book seeks to improve. Those programs have broad popular support, and some have even gained the status of a political third rail. Politicians know that they can boost their chances of reelection by expanding those programs.

In part for these reasons, Congress *has* managed to make important improvements to major safety net programs in recent years. The most notable examples are health insurance and the CTC. Nor is this a Democratic Party phenomenon. Congress has also expanded social safety net supports under Republican administrations. President Gerald Ford, for example, signed the original version of the EITC into law.[49] Homeownership assistance has also enjoyed strong bipartisan support. More recently, the first Trump administration oversaw major expansions to unemployment insurance, health benefits, the EITC, and the CTC during the COVID-19 pandemic. Those measures, while temporary, provided templates for future reforms. Meanwhile, the CTC remains so popular that the 2024 Republican party platform, touted by the Trump campaign, called for expanding that tax credit even further.[50]

This suggests that political and economic stars align from time to time, and when they do, added improvements will enjoy electoral support, as the Affordable Care Act and the pandemic-era reforms both did. Social Security's impending insolvency will likely be another of those moments and will provide a vital opportunity to shore up old-age benefits for retirees. Changing the narrative could further bolster support for expanding safety nets to the bottom half. It bears emphasizing, for example, that affluent taxpayers have their own, tax-subsidized programs that enrich those taxpayers handsomely but are off-limits as a practical matter to the bottom 50 percent. Workplace retirement plans, medical savings plans, and deep subsidies for homeownership are high on that list. Proposals to extend benefits into the middle class by targeting everyone *except* the well-off would provide a needed counterweight to today's programs that favor the rich.

Finally, as part of that narrative, it is important to stress that most of us will be hit by one or more adverse economic events sometime during our lifetimes. Two-thirds of us will experience unemployment by age sixty; over half of us will fall into poverty at some point. Serious illness is an even greater bet before we die. None of us knows exactly who will be hit or when, but the chance of experiencing at least one of these setbacks is greater than 50 percent. Given those odds, we would be better off by joining together and spreading those risks more effectively across families.

Today, we are trapped in a cycle in which the rich are getting richer while the bottom half is barely hanging on. If we can agree that our strength is in numbers, coming together to share risk would pave the way to economic well-being for all.

Notes

PREFACE

1. See, for example, Baker and Bignell (2024) and Smialek (2024).

CHAPTER 1. THE CASH-STRAPPED AMERICAN WORKER

1. Bhaskaran et al. (2024, 30–31, tab. 13).
2. In 2019, the top 10 percent controlled thirty-five times as much wealth as the entire bottom half. Meanwhile, the top 1 percent by income earned more than the bottom half of all wage earners combined. Bricker et al. (2020).
3. See chapter 2.
4. Bricker et al. (2020).
5. National Center for Education Statistics (n.d., tab. 330.10).
6. Sabelhaus and Volz (2019).
7. Buchmueller, DiNardo, and Valletta (1999) and US Bureau of Labor Statistics (2019b).
8. Schmitt, Gould, and Bivens (2018).
9. "How Welfare Has Changed since 1996" (2018).
10. See, for example, Broaddus and Park (2016); Quillian et al. (2017); Sabelhaus and Volz (2019); and Steil et al. (2018).
11. Pew Charitable Trusts (2019).

12. Vega (2014).

13. Sabelhaus and Volz (2019).

14. Bivens and Shierholz (2018).

15. Charles, Hurst, and Schwarz (2018) and Federal Reserve Bank of St. Louis (2018).

16. "How Welfare Has Changed since 1996" (2018).

17. Aladangady et al. (2023).

18. Bricker et al. (2020).

19. Atkinson (2019).

20. *See* Consumer Financial Protection Bureau (2015a). For a literature review, see OECD (2019, 57–60). In the United States, the terms *economic well-being* and *financial well-being* are both used to describe the financial health of individual households. Compare Consumer Financial Protection Bureau (2015a) with Board of Governors of the Federal Reserve System (2021). A separate literature uses "economic well-being" to refer to financial health of countries at the macroeconomic level. OECD (2013, ch. 2, 30–31). In contrast, I define *economic well-being* in terms of the financial health of households.

21. See MacKinnon and Derickson (2012).

22. One of the few, important exceptions is Collins and Lorenze (2020).

23. See Mudrazija and Butrica (2021, 3).

24. See Collins and Lorenze (2020).

25. Board of Governors of the Federal Reserve System (n.d.) and Shrider (2023), data from tab. A-1 (computation by author).

26. Chetty et al. (2019).

27. CollegeBoard (2023, 4, 44).

28. Radpour, Papadopoulos, and Ghilarducci (2021, 6); see chapter 2.

29. Board of Governors of the Federal Reserve System (n.d.). As a rule of thumb, for instance, Fidelity recommends saving ten times annual income for people planning to retire at sixty-seven. Under that rule, someone making $11,167 a year would need to save $111,670 by age sixty-seven to retire comfortably. Fidelity (2024).

CHAPTER 2. COUNTING THE WAYS

1. Lowe (2021).

2. US Bureau of Labor Statistics (2020).

3. US Bureau of Labor Statistics (2020) and US Census Bureau (2020).

4. See US Census Bureau (n.d.-d) for a description. For 2019, the supplemental poverty threshold for a two-adult, two-child household was $29,234 for homeowners with mortgages, $24,980 for homeowners without mortgages, and $28,881 for renters. In contrast, the official federal poverty line was $25,465 for a two-adult, two-child family. Fox (2020), app. tab. 3.

5. Fox (2020, 4, fig. 2).

6. US Census Bureau (2020).

7. Board of Governors of the Federal Reserve System (2020a).

8. US Census Bureau (2020).

9. Moser (2022).

10. Nadeau (2020).

11. Rothbaum (2020).

12. University of Wisconsin Population Health Institute (2022, 5).

13. Glasmeier (2023) and Board of Governors of the Federal Reserve System (n.d.).

14. Glasmeier (2023).

15. Moser (2022) and Semega and Kollar (2022).

16. See Fox (2020); Healthcare.gov (n.d.-d); and US Census Bureau (n.d.-d).

17. See, for example, Tolbert, Singh, and Drake (2024).

18. Senator Elizabeth Warren and Amelia Warren Tyagi eloquently documented the financial insecurity affecting the middle class in their landmark book *The Two-Income Trap* (2016).

19. See US Census Bureau (n.d.-d) (computation by author). Another eighty-five million people that year were poor or near-poor.

20. Federal Reserve Bank of St. Louis (2024c) (computation by author).

21. Board of Governors of the Federal Reserve System (n.d.). These numbers were only slightly better in 2022.

22. Bhutta, Chang, et al. (2020, tab. 3).

23. Board of Governors of the Federal Reserve System (2020a).

24. Board of Governors of the Federal Reserve System (2021) (this included 44% of Blacks, 50% of Hispanics, and 62% of people without a high school degree or GED).

25. Board of Governors of the Federal Reserve System (2020a).

26. Keisler-Starkey and Bunch (2020) and Board of Governors of the Federal Reserve System (2020a).

27. Stropoli (2021).

28. Federal Reserve Bank of New York (2023, 3) and Levey (2022). Another study found that in 2018, nearly three out of every ten households reported having used a payday loan, auto title loan, tax refund advance, pawn shop, rent-to-own store, or other costly lender in the past five years. FINRA Investor Education Foundation (2019).

29. Levey (2022) and Hanson (2023b).

30. *See* Mudrazija and Butrica (2021, 3–5).

31. Board of Governors of the Federal Reserve System (2020a).

32. FINRA Investor Education Foundation (2019).

33. Bhutta, Bricker, et al. (2020).

34. Bhutta, Bricker, et al. (2020).

35. Board of Governors of the Federal Reserve System (2020a).

36. US Bureau of Labor Statistics (n.d.-a).

37. Board of Governors of the Federal Reserve System (2020a, 2020b).

38. Rank, Eppard, and Bullock (2021).

39. Rank, Eppard, and Bullock (2021).

40. Rank, Eppard, and Bullock (2021).

41. Torpey (2021).

42. CollegeBoard (2020); Lake (2020); and Hanson (2023b).

43. See, for example, Aspen Institute Financial Security Program (2020) and Dannenberg and Mugglestone (2018).

44. See chapter 9.

45. Consumer Financial Protection Bureau (2020b); National Association of Realtors (2020); and Peter (2020).

46. The median home value for first-time homebuyers was $215,000 in 2019. National Association of Realtors (2020).

47. National Association of Realtors (2020).

48. Joint Center for Housing Studies of Harvard University (2024b, 1–2).

49. US Census Bureau (2021).

50. Choi et al. (2019).

51. US Census Bureau (n.d.-a).

52. Clingman, Burkhalter, and Chaplain (2020).

53. Copeland (2019).

54. US Bureau of Labor Statistics (n.d.-d, 2023b, tab. 1). These numbers are conservative, with estimates varying depending on the study. Radpour, Papadopoulos, and Ghilarducci (2021, 6–7).

55. Dushi and Trenkamp (2021, tab. 5).

56. National Council on Aging (2023a).

CHAPTER 3. POWER PLAY

1. Hacker (2019) and Rank, Eppard, and Bullock (2021, 38).

2. Gould (2014).

3. Economic Policy Institute (2022).

4. Clausing (2017).

5. Researchers disagree on the reasons for declining pay. The competitive market model holds that labor markets are competitive but that low-paid workers failed to invest in technological skills that employers increasingly demanded. In contrast, the contested market model asserts that labor markets conferred monopsony power on employers, who exercised that power to hold down wages. A final school, the social-institutional approach, builds on the contested market model to emphasize the role of social institutions in depressing wages. See, for example, Howell and Kalleberg (2019, 2, 23–43).

6. Boehm, Flaaen, and Pandalai-Nayar (2019).

7. US Bureau of Labor Statistics (n.d.-c).

8. US Bureau of Labor Statistics (n.d.-b, tab. 2.1, n.d.-c).

9. Nunn, O'Donnell, and Shambaugh (2019).

10. US Bureau of Labor Statistics (2021b).

11. Bronfenbrenner (1996) and Nunn, O'Donnell, and Shambaugh (2019).

12. Buchmueller, DiNardo, and Valletta (1999) and Stansbury and Summers (2020); see also US Bureau of Labor Statistics (2019b).

13. Stansbury and Summers (2020, 8).

14. US Department of the Treasury (2022c).

15. US Bureau of Labor Statistics (n.d.-b).

16. Dynan, Elmendorf, and Sichel (2012, 20–22).

17. US Bureau of Labor Statistics (2011, 2019a) (computation by author).

18. US Department of Labor (n.d.-b).

19. Schneider and Harknett (2019).

20. Board of Governors of the Federal Reserve System (2020a).

21. Morduch and Schneider (2017).

22. FINRA Investor Education Foundation (2019, 22).

23. Farber (2017).

24. Freeman (2013).

25. Badger and Ingraham (2015) and Rank, Eppard, and Bullock (2021).

26. Bivens et al. (2021, 9, 26).

27. Bivens et al. (2021, 18).

28. Bivens et al. (2021, 16–17).

29. Bivens et al. (2021, 13, 23).

30. Bivens et al. (2021, 16).

31. Bivens et al. (2021, 49).

32. Bivens et al. (2021, 91).

33. Bivens et al. (2021, 7, 13, 16–17).

34. Bivens et al. (2021, 91).

35. Mastri et al. (2016, 8–9, tab. I-1).

36. Bivens et al. (2021, 6, 14, 17).

37. Mastri et al. (2016, 6–9, tab. I-1).

38. Bivens et al. (2021, 91).

39. Center on Budget and Policy Priorities (2021).

40. Bivens et al. (2021, 9–10).

41. Bivens et al. (2021, 2–3, 17–18, 32–33).

42. Bivens et al. (2021, 23).

43. Bivens et al. (2021, 5, 13, 21–22, 27).

44. Nadasen (2016).

45. Nadasen (2016).

46. Nadasen (2016).

47. US Department of Health and Human Services (2020, tab. 2) and US Census Bureau (2019).

48. Fox (2020, app. tab. 1).

49. Congressional Research Service (2021a).

50. *See* McCoy (2015, 558–69) and Munnell, Haverstick, and Soto (2007).

51. Revenue Act of 1978.

52. Congressional Research Service (2021a) and Munnell, Haverstick, and Soto (2007).

53. Frolik (2014, 382–87).

54. Forman and Sabin (2015, 764).

55. Maher (2016) and Moore (2004).

56. Board of Governors of the Federal Reserve System (n.d.). See, for example, Broadbent, Palumbo, and Woodman (2006, 30).

57. VanDerhei (2009).

58. Computations by author.

59. National Association of State Retirement Administrators (n.d.).

60. Wooten (2005, 3–5).

61. Pension Benefit Guaranty Corporation (n.d.).

62. See, for example, Munnell, Haverstick, and Soto (2007).

63. Butrica et al. (2009).

64. DB pensions remain strikingly prevalent in the public sector. In March 2021, 86 percent of state and local workers had access to a DB plan, and 87 percent of those with access participated in a plan. US Bureau of Labor Statistics (2021a, tab. 2).

65. Congressional Research Service (2021a).

66. Congressional Research Service (2021a).

67. See chapter 2 and Dushi and Trenkamp (2021, tab. 5).

68. Social Security Administration (2024d, 3). Average Social Security benefits were less than $15,000 a year for low-wage workers who turned sixty-five in 2021 and retired at full retirement age. Social Security Administration (2021, 156). Cf. Center on Budget and Policy Priorities (2024, 7).

69. Torpey (2021).

70. Baum (2015).

71. Baum (2015) and Pew Charitable Trusts (2019).

72. Baum (2015).

73. Mitchell, Leachman, and Saenz (2019).

74. Mitchell (2019). This included tuition and fees and room and board.

75. Mitchell, Leachman, and Saenz (2019).

76. National Center for Education Statistics (n.d., tab. 331.95) (in constant 2022–2023 dollars).

77. CollegeBoard (2022, 40) and Hansen and Shaw (2020).

78. See, for example, Martinchek and Gonzalez (2024).

79. Federal Reserve Bank of St. Louis (2024a) and Kuhn, Schularick, and Steins (2017).

80. Federal Reserve Bank of St. Louis (2024b) and Kuhn, Schularick, and Steins (2017).

81. Federal Reserve Bank of St. Louis (2024b).

82. Ahn, Batty, and Meisenzahl (2018).

CHAPTER 4. THE BROKEN SAVINGS DISCOURSE

1. Karlan, Ratan, and Zinman (2014) and Lusardi, Schneider, and Tufano (2011, 85–86).

2. See Burman and Kravitz (2004, 875 tab.).

3. Brüggen et al. (2017) and Bhutta and Dettling (2018).

4. Board of Governors of the Federal Reserve System (2024, 33–34).

5. Bhutta and Dettling (2018).

6. Board of Governors of the Federal Reserve System (2024, 33, tab. 17).

7. Bhutta and Dettling (2018).

8. Board of Governors of the Federal Reserve System (n.d.).

9. Karlan, Ratan, and Zinman (2014, 37).

10. See, for example, Sherraden and Boshara (2008).

11. 26 U.S.C. 1.

12. 26 U.S.C. 1, 219, 401, 402.

13. Internal Revenue Service (2023e).

14. 26 U.S.C. 219, 408. Roth IRAs, in contrast, do not allow contributions to be deducted from income, but exempt later distributions (including all gains) from income taxation (26 U.S.C. 408A).

15. 26 U.S.C. 219 and Internal Revenue Service (2023e).

16. See Internal Revenue Service (n.d.-d). In the SECURE 2.0 Act of 2022, Congress replaced the saver's credit with a new program called the "saver's match," which provides a 50 percent federal match for contributions by lower-income taxpayers of up to $2,000 to retirement plans (§ 103).

17. The Brookings Institution found that the saver's credit "provides no incentives to tens of millions of low-income filers who qualify on paper for the 50% credit rate, but who do not have any income tax liability against which to apply the credit." Gale, Iwry, and Orszag (2004).

18. Internal Revenue Service (2023b).

19. 26 U.S.C. 529. There are additional tax incentives for education, including Coverdell accounts, the American Opportunity Tax Credit, the lifetime learning tax credit, the tuition and fee deductions, and the student loan interest deduction. Most of these are phased out for higher earners. Internal Revenue Service (n.d.-e).

20. Alternatively, taxpayers who itemize can deduct qualifying medical expenses exceeding 7.5 percent of adjusted gross income from their income on their federal tax returns. See Internal Revenue Service (n.d.-f).

21. Internal Revenue Service (n.d.-c).

22. 26 U.S.C. 223 and Internal Revenue Service (2023c).

23. 26 U.S.C. 223.

24. 26 U.S.C. 125 and Internal Revenue Service (2023d).

25. Internal Revenue Service (2002).

26. *See* Board of Governors of the Federal Reserve System (n.d.).

27. 26 U.S.C. 163(h)(3), 164.

28. 26 U.S.C. 121.

29. Lusardi, Schneider, and Tufano (2011, 85).

30. See chapter 6.

31. SECURE 2.0 Act of 2022, Div. T, § 127.

32. SECURE 2.0 Act of 2022, Div. T, § 115.

33. See, for example, Dynarski (2005, 9) and Helmchen et al. (2015).

34. Sherraden and Boshara (2008).

35. Statista (n.d.).

36. See generally Brown (2021). The one possible exception is the exclusion of gain on sale.

37. Board of Governors of the Federal Reserve System (n.d.) (only 42% of families in the bottom fifth by income owned their homes in 2022, compared to 90% in the top 10%).

38. See Tax Policy Center (n.d.).

39. In 2019, for example, only 1.2 percent of federal taxpayers in the bottom 20 percent by income itemized deductions, compared to well over 50 percent of taxpayers in the top 10 percent. Eastman (2019); see generally Herbert and Belsky (2008, 7–8, 11–13, 34–37).

40. Sherraden and Boshara (2008); see also Doran (2022).

41. Consumer Financial Protection Bureau (2020a).

42. Hanson, Brannon, and Hawley (2022); Reeves and Joo (2017); and Reinhardt (2016).

43. Pub. L. No. 93-406.

44. US Bureau of Labor Statistics (2023b, tab. 1).

45. US Bureau of Labor Statistics (2023b, tab. 1).

46. Internal Revenue Service (n.d.-c).

47. US Bureau of Labor Statistics (2021a, tab. 42) (computation by author).

48. US Bureau of Labor Statistics (2021a, tab. 42).

49. Hannon et al. (2016).

50. Congressional Research Service (2020, 16–17).

51. Federal Deposit Insurance Corporation (2022, 14 tab. 3.1).

52. Federal Deposit Insurance Corporation (2022, 18–19); see also Consumer Financial Protection Bureau (2020a).

53. Karlan, Ratan, and Zinman (2014, 37) and Morduch and Schneider (2017, 98).

54. Sherraden and Boshara (2008).

55. FINRA Investor Education Foundation (2019).

56. These figures exclude home equity. When home equity is included, households that did not receive cash benefits had median net worth of $181,800, compared to $5,797 for households on public assistance. Hays (2021); see also Rank, Eppard, and Bullock (2021, 31).

57. Pew Charitable Trusts (2016).

58. Prosperity Now (2014, 1-2) and Congressional Research Service (2022c); see also Center on Budget and Policy Priorities (2023).

59. Pew Charitable Trusts (2016, 3-4, fig. 1).

60. See Urban Institute (n.d., tab. I.C.1) (search by author).

61. Pew Charitable Trusts (2016, 8) and Prosperity Now (2014, 2-3).

62. Pew Charitable Trusts (2016, 6-8). See also Pew Charitable Trusts (2017).

63. Pew Charitable Trusts (2016, 5).

64. Pew Charitable Trusts (2016, 3).

65. Pew Charitable Trusts (2016, 8). Cf. Mills et al. (2014) (examining the incidence of churn in SNAP).

66. Ratcliffe et al. (2016, 1, 3-4).

67. Ratcliffe et al. (2016, 2, 4). See generally Pew Charitable Trusts (2017, 5-6) (summarizing studies reporting mixed results).

68. Bertrand, Mullainathan, and Shafir (2006, 8) and Sherraden and Boshara (2008).

69. SECURE 2.0 Act of 2022, Div. T, § 101.

70. See Choi et al. (2001, 10, 46 tab. 3); see also Choi et al. (2002) and Madrian and Shea (2001).

71. See Choi et al. (2001, 11).

72. Consumer Financial Protection Bureau (2020a, 27-28, 42).

73. Miller (2022).

74. Miller (2022).

75. Choi et al. (2001, 23); see generally Consumer Financial Protection Bureau (2020a, 41-42).

76. Consumer Financial Protection Bureau (2020a, 27) and Thaler and Benartzi (2004).

77. Barr, Mullainathan and Shafir (2009).

78. Bertrand, Mullainathan and Shafir (2006, 8).

79. Karlan, Ratan, and Zinman (2014, 39).

80. Brobeck (2020).

81. Consumer Financial Protection Bureau (2020a, 20-21).

82. Sherraden and Boshara (2008) and Birkenmeier, Kim, and Maynard (2022).

83. Pew Charitable Trusts (2018).

84. Briscese, Levere, and Pollack (2024, 3–5).
85. Karlan, Ratan, and Zinman (2014); see generally Fernandes, Lynch, and Netemeyer (2014). The one exception is for financial education offered through work, usually in connection with retirement savings plans. Gale, Harris, and Levine (2012, 41–43).

CHAPTER 5. THE IMPORTANCE OF SHARING RISK

1. Baker and Simon (2002).
2. Throughout, I refer to risk pooling and risk spreading together as *risk sharing*.
3. Moss (2002, 22).
4. Miller-Wilson (2022).
5. Knight ([1921] 1971).
6. Kwak (2015, 127, 129); Moss (2002, 28-31); and Varian (1980, 53).
7. See, for example, Abraham (1986, 11–12).
8. See, for example, Abraham (1986, 11–12)
9. Barr (1992, 743).
10. Barr (1992, 753).
11. Atkinson (1991, 118).
12. Moss (2002, 32).
13. Moss (2002, 31) and Barr (1992, 753).
14. Chetty and Finkelstein (2013, 141) and Moss (2002, 46–47); cf. Varian (1980, 50).
15. Baker (2003).
16. Arrow (1963, 959–64); Baker (1996, 239); and Moss (2002, 37).
17. Abraham (1986, 15).
18. Moss (2002, 37).
19. Baker (2003).
20. Akerlof (1970) and Rothschild and Stiglitz (1976).
21. Barr (1992, 750–52); Chetty and Finkelstein (2013, 115–27); and Siegelman (2004, 1235–40).
22. Marmor (1970, 17).
23. Marmor (1970, 18, 33) and US Department of Health, Education and Welfare (1964, 15).
24. Doty et al. (2009, 2–3); see also Claxton et al. (2016) and Chetty and Finkelstein (2013, 132–34).
25. Moss (2002, 11–12).
26. Baker and Siegelman (2010).
27. *See* Moss (2002, 45).
28. Kwak (2015, 130).

29. See, for example, Skinner (2022).

30. Arrow (1963, 947).

31. See, for example, Hornstein (2016); Wriggins (2012–2013, 289–91).

32. See Baker and Simon (2002).

33. See Atkinson (1991, 118).

34. Kwak (2015, 140).

35. Kwak (2015, 133, 135, 144).

36. Blackman and Mukhi (2010, 48–49).

37. Moss (2002, 47–48).

38. The ACA, as originally passed, required people who could afford minimum essential health insurance either to obtain it, qualify for an exemption, or pay a tax penalty. 26 U.S.C. 5000A. The Supreme Court upheld the mandate as constitutional in *National Federation of Independent Business v. Sebelius* in 2012. In 2017, however, Congress neutered the mandate by cutting the penalty for not having health insurance to $0. 26 U.S.C. 5000A(c)(2)(b)(iii).

39. Kwak (2015, 131, 144–45).

40. Kwak (2015, 144, 153) and Arrow (1963, 963–64).

41. Kwak (2015, 132–33).

42. Atkinson (1991, 117).

43. Kwak (2015, 132).

44. Day (2015, 134, 137–39, 143–44).

45. 42 U.S.C. 300gg; see Day (2015, 138–39).

46. The savings subsidies discussed in chapter 4, the Child Tax Credit discussed in chapter 6, and the gaps in lifetime Social Security old-age benefits discussed in chapter 10 are prominent examples.

47. See, for example, Social Security Administration (2024b).

48. If a risk already has materialized or is virtually sure to occur, carriers will not insure it because customers will not be willing to pay premiums for other people's already-realized losses. Barr (1992, 753–54) and Chetty and Finkelstein (2013, 141).

49. Kwak (2015, 129).

50. Kwak (2015, 139).

51. See Kwak (2015, 128, 138, 142–43; 144) ("As our time horizon expands, . . . we have less information about who will suffer losses, and these programs perform more of a risk-spreading role and less of a redistributive role"); and Moss (2002, 47).

52. Kwak (2015, 129).

53. Kwak (2015, 130).

54. Kwak (2015, 152) and Varian (1980, 50–51).

55. Varian (1980) (quoting Stanford D. Ross in *Family Weekly*, June 24, 1979). See also Benartzi (2020) (60% of US households had experienced a significant loss of income or a major expense in the previous twelve months).

56. Auten and Gee (2009, 315 tab. 7); see also Dynan, Elmendorf, and Sichel (2012, 4–6, fig. 3) and Larrimore, Mortenson, and Splinter (2015, 499–501).

57. Hacker and Jacobs (2008, 2, 5–8); see also Dynan, Elmendorf, and Sichel (2012, 2, 3–4, fig. 3; 10–22 [literature review]); Gottschalk and Moffitt (2009, 11, 16–17); and Jäntti and Jenkins (2015, 107–13).

58. Guvenen (2017, 6); see also Guvenen (2016); Hacker and Jacobs (2008, 2); and Dynan, Elmendorf, and Sichel (2012, 2). Income risk is a newer field, with two researchers calling measures of income risk "[r]elatively underdeveloped" as of 2015. Jäntti and Jenkins (2015, 189; see also 63, 70–79).

59. Hacker and Jacobs (2008, 7–9, 13–14); Dynan, Elmendorf, and Sichel (2012, 4–5, fig. 3); and Gottschalk and Moffitt (2009, 13).

60. Fisher et al. (2016, 46, 55) (only 39% of people in the top 20% by income remained in that bracket between 1999 and 2013); see also Fisher et al. (2016, 53–54); Auten, Gee, and Turner (2013, 169); Splinter, Diamond, and Bryant (2009, 1; 2–3); and Larrimore, Mortenson, and Splinter (2015, 500–501).

61. Guvenen (2017, 5). Dynan, Elmendorf, and Sichel (2012, 2) reported a similar result, saying that the run-up in income volatility through 2008 "stemmed primarily from an increasing frequency of very large income changes. " They went on to say that "the increase in income volatility occurred partly because small income shifts were replaced by medium shifts and because large income shifts were replaced by very large shifts" (5; 4, 6, fig. 3). See also Auten and Gee (2009, 315 tab. 7); Larrimore, Mortenson, and Splinter (2022, 2–5); and Gottschalk and Moffitt (2009, 12).

62. Guvenen (2017, 6).

63. Hacker and Jacobs (2008, 3). See also Dynan, Elmendorf, and Sichel (2012, 4–6) (during the run-up to the 2008 financial crisis, 10% of households experienced an income drop of 50% or more and 20% saw their income slump at least 25%).

64. Dynan, Elmendorf, and Sichel (2012, 7–8, 23) draw this distinction, as do Gottschalk and Moffitt (2009, 4).

65. Dynan, Elmendorf, and Sichel (2012, 3–6); see also Gottschalk and Moffitt (2009, 20) and Guvenen (2016, 2017, 6).

66. Dynan, Elmendorf, and Sichel (2012, 8–9, fig. 4, 23).

67. Guvenen (2017, 1); see also Auten and Gee (2009, 316, 318 tab. 9); Auten, Gee, and Turner (2013, 171–72, fig. 2); and Larrimore, Mortenson, and Splinter (2015, 504 tab. 8).

68. Larrimore, Mortenson, and Splinter (2015, 505 tab. 8).

69. Rank, Eppard, and Bullock (2021); see also Larrimore, Mortenson, and Splinter (2020, 3, 28–29); Guvenen (2017, 6); and Semega et al. (2021, 20).

70. Gottschalk and Moffitt (2009, 4).

71. Semega et al. (2021, 20).

72. Larrimore, Mortenson, and Splinter (2020, 26).

73. See, for example, Guvenen (2017, 4) and Splinter (2021, 2, 7–8); see also Berman (2022); Fisher et al. (2016, 55); and Larrimore, Mortenson, and Splinter (2015, 500–501).

74. *See* Klerman and Haider (2004, 866).

75. Fisher et al. (2016, 55).

76. Fullerton and Rao (2019, 382 tab. 4) (computation by author).

77. Fullerton and Rao (2019, 392).

78. Kwak (2015, 149).

79. Social Security Administration (n.d.-a).

80. Atkinson (1991, 120).

81. Moss (2002, 158–59).

82. All states adopted workers' compensation by 1948. Social Security Administration (n.d.-a).

83. See, for example, Kwak (2015, 146).

84. Moss (2002, 162–69) and Social Security Administration (n.d.-a).

85. Pub. L. No. 74-271.

86. Berkowitz (2000) and Social Security Administration (n.d.-a).

87. Social Security Administration (n.d.-a). Separately, Congress instituted the Food Stamp program in 1964 to alleviate hunger among needy families.

88. Berkowitz (2005–2006, 15) and National Archives (n.d.).

89. Social Security Administration (n.d.-a).

90. Tax Reduction Act of 1975 and Congressional Research Service (2022b).

91. Congressional Research Service (2022b, 2–3) and Hungerford and Thiess (2013, 1).

92. Congressional Research Service (2022b, 1, 10).

93. Taxpayer Relief Act of 1997 and Hungerford and Thiess (2013, 3).

94. White House (n.d.).

95. Day (2015, 133–35).

CHAPTER 6. MAKING ENDS MEET

1. Center for Hunger-Free Communities (2021, 5).

2. Maslow (1943).

3. See chapter 2; Moser (2022); and Semega and Kollar (2022, 2).

4. See chapter 3.

5. See chapter 2.

6. Center for Hunger-Free Communities (2021, 4).

7. Jacobs, Perry, and MacGillvary (2021, 3–5, tab. 2).

8. Jacobs, Perry, and MacGillvary (2021, 4). Only 1 percent of those families received cash welfare through TANF (5).

9. US Government Accountability Office (2020, 9–10).

10. US Government Accountability Office (2020, 13–14).

11. US Government Accountability Office (2020, appendices II and III).

12. Jacob, Perry, and MacGillvary (2021, 4, 9).

13. Fair Labor Standards Act of 1938, § 6.

14. 29 U.S.C. 206(a).

15. KFF (n.d.-b).

16. Card and Krueger (2016, 5).

17. Congressional Research Service (2022a, 4–5).

18. See Manning (2021, 3).

19. See Manning (2021, 3–4).

20. Card and Krueger (1994); see also Card and Krueger (1998, 30; 2016, xvi–xvii, chs. 2–4, 12).

21. Card and Krueger (2016, xvi–xx).

22. Manning (2021, 10).

23. See Card and Krueger (2016, xii–xv).

24. Glasmeier (2023); see also Center for Hunger-Free Communities (2021, 1) (estimating a living wage at "between $20 and $26 or more per hour depending on the state").

25. Congressional Research Service (2022a, 11–13).

26. Cooper (2019).

27. Cooper (2019) and Congressional Research Service (2022a, 3, fig. 1).

28. 29 U.S.C. 203(m)(2)(A), 206(g), 213(a)(1), 214(c).

29. Moser (2022).

30. Alston (2019, 381–83); Hoynes and Rothstein (2019, 5); Ortiz et al. (2018, § 1.2); and Van Parijs (1992, 3).

31. See, for example, Ortiz et al. (2018).

32. Alston (2019, 389).

33. Ortiz et al. (2018, § 3).

34. Ortiz et al. (2018, §§ 3.1, 3.2, fig. 5, annex II).

35. Alston (2019, 397); Fleischer and Hemel (2020, 696–702); and Hoynes and Rothstein (2019, 6).

36. See Ortiz et al. (2018, § 3.2).

37. See, for example, Fleischer and Hemel (2020, 697) and Ortiz et al. (2018, § 4).

38. OECD (2017, 14); see Ortiz et al. (2018, §§ 1.1, 1.2, box 1, 4–5).

39. Ortiz et al. (2018, § 3.2 box 2).

40. Greenstein (2022b).

41. Washington (2023).

42. Josephson (2023).

43. Grossberg (2019, 69–70).

44. Greenstein (2022a, 1); see Tax Reform Act of 1986; Congressional Research Service (2022b, 1–9, 10 fig. 2, 12–15); Omnibus Budget Reconciliation Act of 1990; and Omnibus Budget Reconciliation Act of 1993.

45. Republican Party (n.d., 9).

46. See chapter 8.

47. See chapter 8 and KFF (2023c).

48. American Rescue Plan Act of 2021 and Inflation Reduction Act of 2022.

49. Greenstein (2022b, 1-2, 9-18) and Skocpol (1991, 420-28).

50. See, for example, Skocpol (1991, 419).

51. Skocpol (1991, 419); Calnitsky (2016, 34); and Grossberg (2019, 69-70).

52. Internal Revenue Service (n.d.-b).

53. See, for example, Ortiz et al. (2018, § 5).

54. See Hungerford and Thiess (2013, 2).

55. Congressional Research Service (2023, 12).

56. Maag, Congdon, and Yau (2021, 4).

57. Congressional Research Service (2022b, 1, 10 fig. 2).

58. Congressional Research Service (2022b, 1, 10 fig. 2) and US Department of Health and Human Services (2020).

59. Hoynes (2019, 191).

60. Hoynes (2019, 190-91).

61. Internal Revenue Service (n.d.-b).

62. See generally Grossberg (2019, 70, 75) and Hoynes (2019).

63. See Internal Revenue Service (n.d.-a).

64. 26 U.S.C. 32.

65. Dube (2021, 8).

66. Atkinson (1996, 68-69). Some states define *work* to include enrollment in school, job training, and volunteer community service for purposes of other income-targeted programs. See Grossberg (2019, 28-29, 69).

67. Skocpol (1991, 429).

68. Taxpayer Relief Act of 1997 and Hungerford and Thiess (2013, 3).

69. 26 U.S.C. 24.

70. 26 U.S.C. 24 and Center on Budget and Policy Priorities (2022, 3).

71. See Center on Budget and Policy Priorities (2022, 3).

72. Greenstein (2022a, 3, 7).

73. Hoynes (2019, 184).

74. See 26 U.S.C. 24(h)(5).

75. Greenstein (2022a, 2).

76. Greenstein (2022a, 2).

77. US Department of the Treasury (2022b) (based on pre-2021 data).

78. See Greenstein (2022a, 2).

79. Pub. L. No. 117-2.

80. The White House (n.d.).

81. Greenstein (2022a, 1).

82. The White House (n.d.)

83. See Greenstein (2022a, 2).

84. The White House (n.d.). ARPA extended the CTC to children age seventeen, who had not been eligible for it before. Both that change and the increased amount of the CTC expired starting in 2022.

85. Parolin, Collyer, and Curran (2022).

86. Pilkauskas et al. (2022, 3).

87. Greenstein (2022a, 5); see Pilkauskas et al. (2022, 4–5) (summarizing studies).

88. McKernan et al. (2016, 3–5).

89. Hacker (2019, 173–74).

90. See Boshara (2012, 11–12).

91. Alston (2019, 381).

92. *Cf.* Balakrishnan, Lewis, and Nuñez (2020, 7, 12–13).

93. Board of Governors of the Federal Reserve System (2020a, 2020b).

94. Balakrishnan, Lewis, and Nuñez (2020, 22).

95. See, for example, McKay (2017, 2).

96. Other situations, such as illnesses that fall short of a disability, divorce, or a need to stop work to care for a parent or a child, produce negative income shocks as well. My proposals for an expanded EITC and CTC would address the latter two problems (combined with more generous paid family leave for caregivers). Meanwhile, mandatory paid medical leave and short-term, commercial disability policies would help defray income loss from illness.

97. Bivens et al. (2021, 49) and U.S. Bureau of Labor Statistics (2019a, tbl. 1).

98. See chapter 3.

99. See, for example, Bivens et al. (2021, 28). Under this approach, federal standards would establish a floor and the states could adopt more generous standards.

100. See Dube (2021, 6, 10).

101. Bivens et al. (2021, 52).

102. National Employment Law Project (2023).

103. Pub. L. No. 116-136, § 2102.

104. See Bivens et al. (2021, 55) and Dube (2021, 6).

105. Bivens et al. (2021, 65–66) and West et al. (2016, 37, 45).

106. See, for example, Bivens et al. (2021, 55).

107. Pub. L. No. 111-5 and Mastri et al. (2016, 7).

108. Mastri et al. (2016, 8–9, tab. I-1).

109. See Furman (2020, 5–6, 14).

110. Mastri et al. (2016, 6–7, 8–9, tab. I-1).

111. See, for example, Bivens et al. (2021, 58–59).

112. Bivens et al. (2021, 74–75). The Extended Benefits program also needs substantial reform in order to kick in earlier during recessions and serve more effectively as an economic stabilizer. See, for example, Bivens et al. (2021, 76–85) and Dube (2021, 11–12).

113. Bivens et al. (2021, 91–93, tab. 5.1); Dube (2021, 7–8, 12); and Furman (2020, 10–11).

114. Bivens et al. (2021, 96–97) and Mastri et al. (2016, 7–8). In ARRA, Congress approved incentive payments to states that permanently adopted a dependents' allowance of $15 per week per dependent. Relatively few states adopted this allowance, however. Mastri et al. (2016, 7–9, tab. I-1).

CHAPTER 7. OWNING A HOME

1. US Department of Housing and Urban Development (1995).
2. Becker, Stolberg, and Labaton (2008) and Milbank (2002).
3. The American Presidency Project (2002).
4. Pub. L. No. 108-186.
5. Becker, Stolberg, and Labaton (2008).
6. Becker, Stolberg, and Labaton (2008).
7. Engel and McCoy (2011, chs. 2–3, 7–11).
8. Spader and Herbert (2017, 277).
9. See, for example, Biswas et al. (2019, 1).
10. Goodman, Zhu, and Pendall (2017) and Federal Reserve Bank of St. Louis (2023a, 2023b).
11. Compare Federal Reserve Bank of St. Louis (2023a, 2023b, 2023c).
12. See, for example, Asante-Muhammad, Buell, and Devine (2021, 4–8) and Kermani and Wong (2021, 4–5).
13. See, for example, Manturuk, Lindblad, and Quercia (2017).
14. See Bhutta, Bricker, et al. (2020, 16 tab. 3); Goodman and Mayer (2018); Herbert, McCue, and Sanchez-Moyano (2016); Killewald and Bryan (2016, 117–19); and Poterba, Venti, and Wise (2011).
15. See, for example, Goodman and Mayer (2018).
16. See, for example, Goodman and Mayer (2018).
17. Goodman and Mayer (2018, 50–51).
18. Today, most residential mortgages are fully amortizing loans due to the Qualified Mortgage Rule. 15 U.S.C. 1639(b) and 12 C.F.R. 1026.43; see Bureau of Consumer Financial Protection (2019, 61, 64, 71, 116, 120–21, 127–29). But borrowers who obtain less than fully amortizing nonqualified mortgages face the added risk of rising payments.
19. See, for example, Herbert and Belsky (2008, 14, 49–50).
20. See, for example, Herbert and Belsky (2008, 14, 49–50).
21. Board of Governors of the Federal Reserve System (2018, 21–23).
22. See, for example, Elul et al. (2010, 2) and Foster and Van Order (1984).
23. Goodman and Mayer (2018, 53).
24. Federal Reserve Bank of St. Louis (2023d).

25. See Herbert, McCue, and Sanchez-Moyano (2016, 2).

26. See Dreier et al. (2014, 6). Depressed appraisals further reduce home values for Black and Hispanic homeowners. Interagency Task Force on Property Appraisal and Valuation Equity (2022, 3–4) and Brown (2021).

27. *See* Dickerson (2014).

28. Quercia and Riley (2017, 321, 335 tab. 2) and McCoy and Wachter (2020).

29. Goodman and Mayer (2018, 48).

30. See generally Levitin and Wachter (2020, ch. 2).

31. See, for example, Herbert and Belsky (2008, 39–41) (reviewing literature).

32. Reverse mortgage borrowers do not have loan payments but they still have to pay for homeowners' insurance and property taxes. Nonpayment of such insurance and/or property taxes is a leading cause of defaults on FHA-insured reverse mortgages. See US Department of Housing and Urban Development (2015).

33. See Dickerson (2014).

34. See Consumer Financial Protection Bureau (2015c).

35. Pub. L. No. 111-203.

36. 12 C.F.R. pt. 1026, subpts. C and E.

37. Here, I use *plain vanilla* to describe a mortgage loan with no negative amortization, prepayment penalty, interest-only payment, balloon payment, demand feature, shared equity, or shared appreciation. See 12 C.F.R. 1026.36(e).

38. 15 U.S.C. 1639b(c) and 12 C.F.R. 1026.36(e)(1).

39. 15 U.S.C. 1602(bb), 1639 and 12 C.F.R. 1026.35.

40. 12 C.F.R. 1026.34(a)(5) (high-cost mortgages), 1026.36(k) (negative amortization mortgages).

41. Alexandrov and Saunders (2023).

42. See chapter 9.

43. See, for example, Ambrose, Conklin, and Lopez (2021); Bartlett et al. (2022); and Zhang and Willen (2020, 1–6).

44. 15 U.S.C. 1691–1691f and 42 U.S.C. 3605.

45. See, for example, Akinwumi et al. (2021); Bartlett et al. (2022); and Kumar, Hines, and Dickerson (2022).

46. Consumer Financial Protection Bureau (2022a).

47. See, for example, Moulton and Quercia (2013) and MHP (n.d.).

48. Alexandrov and Saunders (2023, n2).

49. See, for example, Ambrose, LaCour-Little, and Huszar (2005); Bhutta, Dokko, and Shan (2017); Campbell and Cocco (2015); Elul et al. (2010); Haurin and Rosenthal (2005); Pennington-Cross and Ho (2010); Quercia, Stegman, and Davis (2007); and Sherlund (2008).

50. 15 U.S.C. 1639c(a).

51. 12 C.F.R. 1026.43.

52. 12 C.F.R. 1026.43. Qualified mortgages are fixed-rate or adjustable-rate fully amortizing mortgages, and come with other safeguards.

53. See, for example, Farrell, Bhagat, and Zhao (2018, 3–7).

54. Low (2021, 6–7).

55. Hsu, Matsa, and Melzer (2018, 51).

56. See McCoy and Wachter (2020).

57. See, for example, Farrell, Bhagat, and Zhao (2018, 8–13) and Rendon and Bazer (2021, 7, 9, 12).

58. Some researchers have found that receiving downpayment assistance does not increase default risk. See Stegman, Riley, and Quercia (2019, 11–12).

59. See McCoy (2014).

60. 12 C.F.R. 1024.41(f)(1).

61. 12 C.F.R. 1024.41(f)(1).

62. McCoy (2014).

63. 12 C.F.R. 1024.39(a).

64. See McCoy (2014, 419–21).

65. The Mortgage Servicing Collaborative (n.d.-a, n.d.-b).

66. See Housing Finance Policy Center (2024).

67. Fannie Mae (n.d.); Freddie Mac (n.d.); US Department of Housing and Urban Development (n.d.); and US Department of Veterans Affairs (2024).

68. During the COVID-19 pandemic, for instance, some mortgage servicers struggled to process the surge in applications for relief by homeowners who were hit by unemployment, illness, or increased caregiving responsibilities. CFPB examiners reported occasional violations of the servicing rules by mortgage servicers during that period. Consumer Financial Protection Bureau (2021a, 2021b, 2021c, 2022c, 2023b). These servicing violations mirrored servicing problems that long predated COVID-19. McCoy (2014).

69. 12 C.F.R. 1024.38(b)(2), 1024.40, 1024.41(c)(1).

70. 12 C.F.R. 1024.41(f)(1), (g).

71. ATTOM (2023); Consumer Financial Protection Bureau (2023b); and Wolfson (2022).

72. Alley et al. (2011, 2294–95) and Pollack and Lynch (2009).

73. Tergesen (2023).

74. Federal Student Aid (n.d.-a).

75. Joint Center for Housing Studies of Harvard University (2022, 6–7, fig. 5).

76. Pollack, Griffin, and Lynch (2010, 518, 521nn5–7, 15).

77. Alley et al. (2011, 2294–95) and Pollack and Lynch (2009).

CHAPTER 8. AFFORDING HEALTH CARE

1. Pub. L. No. 111-148.

2. CAP Action (2023).

3. Rampell (2022) and Schneider et al. (2021).

4. *See* Schneider et al. (2021, exhs. 3–4).

5. Levey (2022).

6. Jost (2007, 42, 50–53, 56–61). Jost points to other motivations for the expansion of employer-based health coverage during the Second World War (59–61).

7. See chapter 5. The individual market offers health insurance directly to consumers instead of through the workplace.

8. Buchmueller, DiNardo, and Valletta (1999); cf. Jost (2007, 3–4, 62–63, 118).

9. Claxton et al. (2016).

10. 26 U.S.C. 5000A. Congress rolled back the ACA's original tax penalty for not having coverage to $0 in 2017, but the individual mandate remains on the books.

11. 42 U.S.C. 18022(a)–(b). There is an exception for catastrophic coverage plans for young adults. 42 U.S.C. 18022(e). In the 2024 open enrollment period, only 1 percent of Marketplace participants enrolled in catastrophic coverage. CMS.gov (2024a, tab. 5).

12. 26 U.S.C. 5000A. Employers who offer insurance lacking essential health benefits must pay penalties. 26 U.S.C. 4980H and 42 U.S.C. 18022(a)–(b).

13. See, for example, Glickman and Weiner (2020, 6–8).

14. US Department of Health and Human Services (n.d.).

15. Biniek et al. (2023). Original Medicare offers a different (and often broader) group of providers, but excludes dental care, eyeglasses, and hearing aids. Many Medicare patients flock to Medicare Advantage because virtually all Advantage policies offer some of these supplemental services, while capping out-of-pocket expenditures (unlike Original Medicare). Freed et al. (2022).

16. Medicaid.gov (n.d.-a).

17. Healthcare.gov (n.d.-b).

18. KFF (2024a).

19. Healthcare.gov (n.d.-a, n.d.-h).

20. See, for example, 42 U.S.C. 18031(b)(1).

21. In 2022, for instance, 20 percent of people surveyed were either uninsured or were insured but had experienced a coverage gap in the preceding year. Collins, Haynes, and Masitha (2022).

22. See Jost (2007, 3–4).

23. Medicaid.gov (n.d.-b).

24. Assistant Secretary for Planning and Evaluation (2023, 3).

25. Emergency Medical Treatment and Labor Act. See Jost (2007, 7).

26. Internal Revenue Code § 501(r)(4); see Internal Revenue Service (1969).

27. Mathews, McGinty, and Evans (2022).

28. Branham et al. (2022, 7); Consumer Financial Protection Bureau (2022b, 2); Mathews, McGinty, and Evans (2022); and Kliff and Silver-Greenberg (2023).

29. Tolbert, Singh, and Drake (2024).

30. CMS.gov (2024b).

31. Hanson et al. (2023, 743 exh. 1).

32. KFF (2022, § 2).

33. Internal Revenue Code §§ 105(b), 106(a).

34. 26 U.S.C. 4980H(a) and KFF (2022, § 2, 2024a). *Full-time workers* are those who work thirty hours a week or more on average. 26 C.F.R. 54.4980H-3 and Joint Committee on Taxation (2016, 13).

35. KFF (2022, § 2).

36. KFF (2022, §§ 2–3).

37. KFF (2022, § 3).

38. See chapter 3. In 2022, for instance, only about two-thirds of employees at companies with a large share of lower-wage workers qualified for workplace health insurance, compared to 80 percent at companies with predominantly well-paid workers. KFF (2022, § 3).

39. KFF (2020) and US Department of Labor (n.d.-a).

40. KFF (2020). Congress provided temporary subsidies for COBRA coverage during the Great Recession starting in 2009 and briefly during the COVID-19 pandemic in 2021. US Department of Labor (2021) and US Department of the Treasury (n.d., 2).

41. See, for example, KFF (2020) (reporting that in 2017, more than 11.5 million nonelderly adults were unemployed, but only 130,000 were enrolled in COBRA coverage).

42. In addition, veterans, armed services members, and their immediate families may qualify for federal coverage through VA health benefits or TRICARE. See TRICARE (n.d.) and US Department of Veterans Affairs (n.d.).

43. See Center on Budget and Policy Priorities (2020, 4–5).

44. 42 U.S.C. 1396a(a)(10)(A)(i)(VIII).

45. National Federation of Independent Business v. Sebelius.

46. See Center on Budget and Policy Priorities (2020, 4).

47. KFF (2024c).

48. Assistant Secretary for Planning and Evaluation (2023, 2, 6).

49. See Center on Budget and Policy Priorities (2020, 2). In 2023, children in opt-out states could qualify for Medicaid with household incomes of between 146 and 216 percent of the FPL. Children in those same states could qualify for CHIP coverage with even higher household incomes, ranging from 214 to 317 percent of the FPL. KFF (n.d.-c). For pregnant women in those states, the income caps ranged from 146 to 306 percent of the FPL. KFF (n.d.-b).

50. See Center on Budget and Policy Priorities (2020, 2).

51. See Center on Budget and Policy Priorities (2020, 2–3). In 2023, in opt-out states, the income cap for parents ranged from 18 percent of the FPL to 100 percent, depending on the state. KFF (n.d.-c). That year, 18 percent of the FPL amounted to $4,474.80 *a year* for a family of three.

52. Healthcare.gov (n.d.-e).

53. See Healthcare.gov (n.d.-c).

54. LaCarte, Greenberg, and Capps (2021, 1). As I discuss later, however, some of these households may qualify for subsidies to enroll in Marketplace plans. See KFF (2024b).

55. See Center on Budget and Policy Priorities (2020, 3).

56. Rudowitz et al. (2023).

57. The Medicaid gap was an inadvertent result of Congress's assumption when it passed the ACA in 2010 that all states would participate in Medicaid expansion. The ACA provides Marketplace subsidies to people in opt-out states making 100 percent of the FPL or more, while all adults making 138 percent of the FPL or less also have access to Medicaid in expansion states. As a result of the 2012 *Sebelius* decision, some adults in opt-out states who made less than the FPL became ineligible for Medicaid, even though they did not make enough to qualify for Marketplace subsidies. 26 U.S.C. 36B(a), (b)(3)(A)(i), (c)(1) and Rudowitz et al. (2023).

58. Rudowitz et al. (2023).

59. Healthcare.gov (n.d.-h).

60. 42 U.S.C. 300gg-1, 300gg-3, 300gg-4, 18001.

61. 42 U.S.C. 300gg-2.

62. 42 U.S.C. 300gg-11.

63. Weiner and Glickman (2018, 3, 5).

64. Montero et al. (2022).

65. Montero et al. (2022).

66. Levey (2022).

67. See, for example, Carroll (2019) (summarizing studies) and Chandra, Flack, and Obermeyer (2023, 1–6) (same).

68. See Institute of Medicine of the National Academies (2008, ch. 2).

69. US Census Bureau (n.d.-b, tab. P-8).

70. US Census Bureau (n.d.-b, tab. titled "Annual Estimates of the Resident Population for Selected Age Groups by Sex for the United States: April 1, 2020 to July 1, 2023").

71. For general discussion, see KFF (2019).

72. Meanwhile, Part C is the name for Medicare Advantage. Its enrollees receive their Part A and Part B coverage, and often their Part D drug coverage, through their Medicare Advantage plans.

73. Cubanski et al. (2019).

74. Centers for Medicare & Medicaid Services (2024). Monthly premiums can go much higher depending on someone's income, Social Security earnings and tax record, Part D prescription drug coverage, Medigap coverage (for Original Medicare), and sometimes, the decision to go with a Medicare Advantage plan. Medicare.gov (n.d.-a); CMS.gov (2022, 8–9); Freed et al. (2022); and Social Security Administration (n.d.-b).

75. Medicare.gov (n.d.-a). In 2022 Congress *did* enact a $2,000 annual cap on out-of-pocket spending for prescription drugs by Part D participants, effective in 2025. Inflation Reduction Act of 2022, § 11201(a)(3).

76. Centers for Medicare & Medicaid Services (2024).

77. Medicare.gov (n.d.-a).

78. See Washington State Office of the Insurance Commissioner (n.d.).

79. See Primus and Bingham (2024) and Social Security Administration (2024b).

80. Primus and Bingham (2024).

81. Koma, Cubanski, and Neuman (2021).

82. Freed et al. (2022).

83. CMS.gov (2023).

84. National Council on Aging (2023b).

85. Ochieng and Biniek (2022, 13).

86. Branham et al. (2022, 7).

87. 42 U.S.C. 18022(d).

88. See 42 U.S.C. 18022(d) and Branham et al. (2022, 2).

89. 42 U.S.C. 300gg(a)(1).

90. 42 U.S.C. 300gg(a)(1).

91. See Ortaliza et al. (2024, tab. 1).

92. KFF (2023, slides titled "Cost-Sharing for Plans Offered in the Federal Marketplace, 2024") and Ortaliza and Cox (2024). Smaller caps applied in many cases to participants with incomes at or under 250 percent of the FPL. See KFF (2023).

93. Internal Revenue Code § 36B.

94. Internal Revenue Code § 36B; KFF (2024b). Enrollees can choose to apply the credit monthly to their premiums, claim the subsidy as a refundable tax credit on their tax returns, or a combination of both. See KFF (2024b).

95. Congress originally instituted those expanded premium tax credits in the American Rescue Plan Act of 2021 and extended them through 2025 in the Inflation Reduction Act of 2022. Assistant Secretary for Planning and Evaluation (2023, 5).

96. Aron-Dine (2019, 6).

97. This bottom threshold of 138 percent applies in Medicaid expansion states. Congress set the bottom threshold even lower, at 100 percent of the FPL, in opt-out states. Special rules apply to certain indigent immigrants who are lawfully present. KFF (2024b). A "benchmark" Silver plan is the second-cheapest Silver plan available to a given individual in the Marketplace. KFF (2024b). The lowest cost Silver plan also qualifies for this level of subsidy. Internal Revenue Code § 36B and Branham et al. (2022).

98. Cox et al. (2022) and KFF (2024b).

99. KFF (2024b).

100. Full premium subsidies are also available to documented immigrants with incomes under the FPL who meet certain other requirements, with no waiting period. This allows some lawfully present, indigent immigrants who have not finished their five-year waiting period for Medicaid to obtain premium-free coverage immediately through Obamacare instead. See KFF (2024b).

101. CMS.gov (2024a).

102. CMS.gov (2024a).

103. Cf. Weiner and Glickman (2018, 2–3) (analyzing similar cost levels).

104. An estimated 400,000 consumers owe a small premium—generally, only a few dollars—to buy a Marketplace plan. Someone can end up paying a few dollars for the premium if the customer is a smoker or wants a plan that covers some nonessential health benefits such as vision, dental, or abortion services that the premium tax credits do not cover. Over half of this group is near-poor, with incomes at or below 150 percent of the FPL. While the cost of premiums to these customers is low, customers charged $0 in health insurance premiums are more likely to have health coverage than those who must pay a little more. Fiedler (2022) and KFF (2024b); see also Dague, Burns, and Friedsam (2022, 303–5, 311).

105. In addition, people who are eligible for Medicaid do not qualify for Marketplace subsidies. See Healthcare.gov (n.d.-f). Medicaid is financially more attractive because it can provide this group with free or no-cost coverage, unlike Marketplace plans. See Rudowitz et al. (2023, 6).

106. See KFF (n.d.-a).

107. KFF (2024b).

108. KFF (2024b).

109. See CMS.gov (2024a, tab. 5).

110. KFF (2024b).

111. See Healthcare.gov (n.d.-g).

112. KFF (2024b).

113. KFF (2023) and Ortaliza et al. (2024, tab. 1).

114. See Weiner and Glickman (2018, 2–3); cf. Weiner and Glickman (2018, 6) (following passage of the ACA, large numbers of low-income families "still spen[t] more than 19.5% of family income on healthcare").

115. Collins, Haynes, and Masitha (2022); see generally Montero et al. (2022).

116. Dague, Burns, and Friedsam (2022, 303–5, 311) and Montero et al. (2022).

117. Hughes, Gee, and Rapfogel (2022).

118. Hughes, Gee, and Rapfogel (2022).

119. Weiner and Glickman (2018, 4).

120. Employers have also resorted to self-insurance and narrowed the provider networks that they offer. Hughes, Gee, and Rapfogel (2022).

121. US Department of the Treasury (2022a, 61,987); see also Weiner and Glickman (2018, 3–4).

122. Glickman and Weiner (2019, 2–3, 5).

123. In the PPO model, patients have a choice of going inside or outside the PPO's provider network, but those who go outside pay higher out-of-pocket costs. Hughes, Gee, and Rapfogel (2022).

124. Hughes, Gee, and Rapfogel (2022); see also Weiner and Glickman (2018, 4).

125. Hughes, Gee, and Rapfogel (2022); see also Weiner and Glickman (2018, 3).

126. In limited circumstances, federal subsidies are available for premiums for workplace coverage. For example, self-employed individuals can deduct part of their premiums from their income, subject to limits. Internal Revenue Code § 162(*l*). Similarly, a majority of states pay for workplace coverage for workers who are eligible for Medicaid or CHIP. US Department of Labor (n.d.-c).

127. Hughes, Gee, and Rapfogel (2022). Troublingly given this pattern, Black workers are 70 percent more likely than non-Black workers to work for employers who contribute nothing toward their health insurance premiums. Perry et al. (2021).

128. KFF (2022, fig. 3.3).

129. Hughes, Gee, and Rapfogel (2022).

130. Collins, Haynes, and Masitha (2022).

131. KFF (2024b). For family plans in 2024, the caps for workplace plans were $18,400, compared to $6,100 for Marketplace participants at the FPL.

132. 26 U.S.C. 36B(c)(2).

133. US Department of the Treasury (2022a).

134. Internal Revenue Service (2023a).

135. The maximum nominal deductible, for example, is $2.65. Copays and coinsurance for outpatient services are capped between $4 for those with incomes under the FPL and 20 percent of state cost for those with incomes above 150 percent of the FPL. For inpatient services, the caps are between $75 per stay and 20 percent of state cost. Artiga, Ubri, and Zur (2017, 2–3) and Medicaid.gov (n.d.-a).

136. Artiga, Ubri, and Zur (2017, 2–3).

137. KFF (n.d.-d) and Brooks et al. (2020); see also Wray, Khare, and Kayhani (2021, 8).

138. Allen et al. (2021, 1, 6–7, 9); Blavin et al. (2018, 303); Blavin, Karpman, and Amos (2020, 2); and Hill (2015, 344–45, 347).

139. Artiga, Ubri, and Zur (2017, 4–5).

140. Levey (2022).

141. Consumer Financial Protection Bureau (2022b, 24–32) (adding that blemished credit can make it difficult to secure a loan, find a rental home, or land a job). Minor reforms have alleviated these consequences somewhat. Starting in 2023, the three largest credit reporting agencies agreed to remove all paid medical debts, all medical debts less than a year old, and all medical collections under $500 from individuals' credit reports. Consumer Financial Protection Bureau (2023a) and The White House (2022b). In June 2024 the Consumer Financial Protection Bureau went further and started a rulemaking to remove medical bills from most credit reports, prevent debt collectors from using the credit reporting system to coerce people to pay those bills, stop credit reporting companies from sharing medical debts with lenders, and prohibit lenders from making lending decisions based on medical information. Consumer Financial Protection Bureau (2024).

142. Consumer Financial Protection Bureau (2022b, 25).

143. See, for example, Bologna (2021) and Levey (2022).

144. Consumer Financial Protection Bureau (2022b, 29–30); Himmelstein et al. (2019); and Sullivan, Warren, and Westbrook (2020, ch. 5).

145. Levey (2022); see also Artiga, Ubri, and Zur (2017, 4–5); Collins, Haynes, and Masitha (2022); Hughes, Gee, and Rapfogel (2022); and Montero et al. (2022).

146. Montero et al. (2022); see also Collins, Haynes, and Masitha (2022); Koma et al. (2023, 473–74) (Medicare recipients); and Ochieng and Biniek (2022, 13) (same).

147. Consumer Financial Protection Bureau (2022b, 32-33) and Montero et al. (2022).

148. Kliff and Silver-Greenberg (2023) and Levey (2022).

149. Montero et al. (2022); see also Freed et al. (2022).

150. See, for example, Freed et al. (2022).

151. Tolbert, Singh, and Drake (2024).

152. For comparison of outcomes in Medicaid expansion and opt-out states, see Blumenthal, Collins, and Fowler (2020, 967–68); Courtemanche et al. (2018, 2, 6–8); and Rudowitz et al. (2023, 7–8). For comparison of outcomes involving Marketplace coverage, see Courtemanche et al. (2020, 846, 848; 2018, 2, 6–8); but see Baten and Wehby (2023).

153. Carroll (2022) and Chandra, Flack, and Obermeyer (2023, 1–6).

154. See Consumer Financial Protection Bureau (2022b, 34) and Mudrazija and Butrica (2021, 2).

155. Parker (2021) and Perry et al. (2021).

156. Parker (2021) and Perry et al. (2021).

157. Schneider et al. (2021).

158. McDermott and Cox (2021).

159. Assistant Secretary for Planning and Evaluation (2024, 1).

160. Assistant Secretary for Planning and Evaluation (2024, 3, fig. 1) and Hanson et al. (2023, 750).

161. Tolbert, Singh, and Drake (2024).

162. Tolbert, Singh, and Drake (2024).

163. Holahan and Simpson (2022).

164. Holahan and Simpson (2022, 3).

165. Sanger-Katz (2023).

166. This can happen to younger adults who no longer meet the definition of "disabled."

167. Holahan and Simpson (2022) and Tolbert, Singh, and Drake (2024). See also Aron-Dine and Broaddus (2019, 4–6) (states that expanded health insurance subsidies to near-poor households who were just above the poverty line convinced more of them to enroll in health insurance).

168. Montero et al. (2022) and Levey (2022).

169. In order for the Marketplace to be a true alternative to expensive workplace policies, high deductible health plans offered through work also should be banned. See Weiner and Glickman (2018, 4).

170. Premium costs do not appear to be a major deterrent to Part A or Part B enrollment. By age seventy-five, most Medicare recipients enroll in both Parts A and B (Centers for Medicare & Medicaid Services, n.d.-a), often because Social Security deducts their Part B premiums from their Social Security checks. Medicare.gov (n.d.-b).

171. Centers for Medicare & Medicaid Services (n.d.-b) (computation by author).

172. See Koma, Cubanski, and Neuman (2021) (computation by author).

173. Gangopadhyaya et al. (2023) and Primus and Bingham (2024).

174. Holahan and Simpson (2022, 2 tab. 1, 4).

175. Primus and Bingham (2024).

176. For similar proposals, see, for example, Cubanski, Neuman, and Jacobson (2016); Gruber (2013); and Moment of Truth Project (2013, 12, 21–23).

CHAPTER 9. PAYING FOR COLLEGE

1. Sullivan et al. (2019, 1).

2. National Center for Education Statistics (n.d., tab. 104.10).

3. Board of Governors of the Federal Reserve System (2023, 55); see also Emmons, Kent, and Ricketts (2019, 299 fig. 1).

4. National Center for Education Statistics (n.d., tabs. 302.20, 306.10).

5. See, for example, Dynarski, Page, and Scott-Clayton (2022, 1) and Dettling, Goodman, and Reber (2022, 4n3).

6. Federal Student Aid (n.d.-c, "Federal Student Aid Portfolio Summary") and Board of Governors of the Federal Reserve System (2021, 63).

7. CollegeBoard (2024, 44).

8. See Dynarski, Page, and Scott-Clayton (2022, 2).

9. Baum (2015).

10. See Baum (2015) and Dynarski, Page, and Scott-Clayton (2022, 4 tab. 1). State and local governments started increasing their per-student funding again in 2011–2012 (CollegeBoard 2022, 20 fig. CP-11B), but a large gap remains.

11. Mitchell, Leachman, and Saenz (2019, 10–11, fig. 6).

12. Bleemer et al. (2021, 1–2); CollegeBoard (2021); and Mitchell, Leachman, and Saenz (2019).

13. Hanson (2022).

14. CollegeBoard (2021) and Mitchell, Leachman, and Saenz (2019).

15. CollegeBoard (2022, 13 tab. CP-2). In 2022–2023, that total declined to $10,940. See generally Dynarski, Page, and Scott-Clayton (2022, 5 fig. 2).

16. Bleemer et al. (2021, 3).

17. Federal Reserve Bank of New York (2023, 3).

18. Board of Governors of the Federal Reserve System (2023, 60 n53); see also CollegeBoard (2022, 31); Beamer and Nilaj (2022, 8 fig. 1.1); and Dettling, Goodman, and Reber (2022, 6).

19. Despard et al. (2016, 1); Haughwout et al. (2019b, 1); and Scott-Clayton (2018, 4).

20. Dynarski, Page, and Scott-Clayton (2022, 4 tab. 1).

21. US Department of Education (n.d.-b).

22. Federal Student Aid (2024).

23. Hanson (2023a).

24. College Board (2024, 47). This count was for the 2023–2024 school year.

25. US Department of Education (2019, tab. 1.1).

26. US Department of Education (n.d.-c, tab. 3) (data for 2017–2018; computation by author).

27. US Department of Education (n.d.-c, tab. 10A) (data for 2017–2018).

28. CollegeBoard (2022, 4). The decline in Pell Grant recipients was steeper than the decline in undergraduates during that period (44).

29. National Association of Student Financial Aid Administrators (2022, 3).

30. Federal Student Aid (2022) and CollegeBoard (2022, 3).

31. CollegeBoard (2022, 18).

32. National Center for Education Statistics (n.d., tabs. 331.35, 331.60, 331.70).

33. Dettling, Goodman, and Reber (2022, 7, 38 fig. 2).

34. Hanson (2023b).

35. Black et al. (2023, 7).

36. Federal Student Aid (n.d.-c, "Federal Student Aid Portfolio Summary") (computation by author).

37. Federal Student Aid (n.d.-b).

38. Federal Student Aid (n.d.-e).

39. Dependents account for the majority of undergraduate student debt. Black et al. (2023, 3, n4).

40. Federal Student Aid (n.d.-e).

41. Federal Student Aid (n.d.-f).

42. See Dettling, Goodman, and Reber (2022, 6).

43. Looney and Yannelis (2022, 774).

44. Fully amortized payments are higher than under schedules that defer principal repayment, because each monthly payment pays down principal plus interest.

45. Over the years, the department has rolled out four different versions of IDR plans, with the most recent being Saving-on-a-Valuable Education (SAVE). See Herbst (2023, 4) and The White House (2023). As of this writing, conservative state attorneys general were challenging IDR plans in court. Douglas-Gabriel (2024).

46. Baum and Delisle (2022, 11) and CollegeBoard (2022, 42).

47. See Dettling, Goodman, and Reber (2022, 7).

48. Herbst (2023, 5).

49. 11 U.S.C. 523(a)(8).

50. See, for example, Black et al. (2023); Council of Economic Advisers (2016, 10); Dettling, Goodman, and Reber (2022); Dynarski, Page, and Scott-Clayton (2022, 1); and McMahon (2021, 418 tab. 1, 420).

51. CollegeBoard (2020, 23); Hanson (2023b); and Lake (2020). See also National Center for Education Statistics (n.d., tab. 331.35).

52. Board of Governors of the Federal Reserve System (2023, 60–61, fig. 31) and Chakrabarti, Nober, and van der Klaauw (2020, 2–3).

53. See National Center for Education Statistics (n.d., tab. 331.60).

54. Council of Economic Advisers (2016, 10–11).

55. Black et al. (2023, 23–24, 30).

56. New York City Department of Consumer and Worker Protection (2020, 10).

57. Black et al. (2023, 31, appendix tab. C.27).

58. Looney and Yannelis (2022, 774).

59. Looney and Yannelis (2022, 772).

60. See Dettling, Goodman, and Reber (2022, 2).

61. See Gicheva and Thompson (2015, 310–11).

62. Council of Economic Advisers (2016, 16–17, 19).

63. Ambrose, Cordell, and Ma (2015); Biswas (2022, 6–7); Krishnan and Wang (2019); and Rothstein and Rouse (2011); see also Council of Economic Advisers (2016, 56).

64. See Biswas (2022, 6n10); Gicheva (2016); Mezza et al. (2020, 219); and Nau, Dwyer, and Hodson (2015).

65. Herbst (2023, 8 tab. 1); see also Mezza et al. (2020, 227 tab. 1).

66. See Mezza et al. (2020, 250).

67. JPMorgan Chase & Co. (2022).

68. Board of Governors of the Federal Reserve System (2021, 68, tab. 21).

69. Emmons, Kent, and Ricketts (2019, 297–98, tab. 1) and Gicheva and Thompson (2015, 307–10, tab. 9.6).

70. Prudential (2019, 6).

71. Kuperberg, Williams, and Mazelis (2023, 7–8).

72. Despard et al. (2016, 11–14).

73. Anong and Henager (2021, 5, 7–8, tab. 2); Babula and Ersoy-Babula (2022, 1948); and Despard et al. (2016, 14).

74. Beamer and Nilaj (2022, 25–26, tab. 3.3); Biswas (2022, 7–8); Cooper and Wang (2014); Gicheva and Thompson (2015, 304, 307–9); Houle and Berger (2015); Larrimore, Schuetz, and Dodini (2016, 3, 12, 17–18); and Mezza et al. (2020, 218); see also Council of Economic Advisers (2016, 51–53).

75. Bleemer et al. (2021, 3) and Mezza et al. (2020, 218, 235, 238–39 tab. 4); see also Herbst (2023, 18–19) and Prudential (2019, 6).

76. Mezza et al. (2020, 227–29, fig. 1C); see also Bleemer et al. (2021, 3).

77. Mezza et al. (2020, 253–55).

78. Mezza et al. (2020, 248–53); see also Prudential (2019, 7).

79. Mezza et al. (2020, 220) and Gicheva and Thompson (2015, 310).

80. Rutledge, Sanzenbacher, and Vitagliano (2018, 2–3). See also Elliott, Grinstein-Weiss, and Nam (2013, 13–17) and Prudential (2019, 6).

81. Dettling, Goodman, and Reber (2022, 25, 43 figs. 6i–6j).

82. Emmons, Kent, and Ricketts (2019, 316; see also 299, 301, 311–15).

83. Cf. Emmons, Kent, and Ricketts (2019, 317) (discussing the effect of the "explosion in consumer debt").

84. See Bhutta, Bricker et al. (2020, 7 tab. 1, 11 tab. 2, 27–28, tab. A) (computation by author).

85. See Dettling, Goodman, and Reber (2022, 24–26, 42 figs. 6b and 6c, 44 fig. 6n). Although the authors maintain that this gap disappears by late-career ages, they do not account for the fact that the older cohorts were less reliant on student debt to finance their educations than younger age groups (23–25, 30).

86. See Dettling, Goodman, and Reber (2022, 26, 45 fig. 6q).

87. See Dettling, Goodman, and Reber (2022, 28, 44 fig. 6m, 45 fig. 6r, 46 fig. 7c); Mezza et al. (2020, 218, 235, 238–39 tab. 4); and Rutledge, Sanzenbacher, and Vitagliano (2018, 2–3).

88. See, for example, Board of Governors of the Federal Reserve System (2023, 61–62, tab. 33); Chakrabarti, Nober, and van der Klaauw (2020, 3–4); Emmons, Kent, and Ricketts (2019, 317); Miller (2017, 4, tab. 1); Scott-Clayton (2018, 8–11); The Aspen Financial Security Program (2020); and The Institute for College Access and Success (2019, 7).

89. Dettling, Goodman, and Reber (2022, 17–18, 37 fig. 1).

90. For instance, higher student loan balances do not improve Black borrowers' chances of receiving their bachelor's degrees, unlike for Hispanics or Whites. See Black et al. (2023, tab. 11; 27–28, 31); see also Scott-Clayton (2018, 4). But see also Gicheva and Thompson (2015, 301–4, 307–9); and Mezza et al. (2020, 250–53).

91. Black et al. (2023, 27–29).

92. See Black et al. (2023, tab. 11).

93. Federal Reserve Bank of New York (2023, 12–14) and Looney and Yannelis (2022, 771–72).

94. Federal Student Aid (n.d.-c, "Portfolio by Loan Status" and "Portfolio by Delinquency Status") (computations by author). At year-end 2019, fully 18 percent of all federal student loan borrowers were more than 360 days delinquent.

95. Mangrum, Scally, and Wang (2022, 2); see generally Federal Student Aid (n.d.-a); Goss, Mangrum, and Scally (2022, 3–4); and Herbst (2023, 17).

96. Gunn, Haltom, and Neelakantan (2021, 3 fig. 2) and New York City Department of Consumer and Worker Protection (2020, 13–14).

97. Haughwout et al. (2019b, 3); see also Congressional Budget Office (2020, 14–15).

98. Board of Governors of the Federal Reserve System (2023, 61–62, tab. 33); Council of Economic Advisers (2016, 44–46); and The Institute for College Access and Success (2019).

99. The Institute for College Access and Success (2019, 7); see also Miller (2017, 4, tab. 1).

100. See, for example, Avery and Turner (2012, 186).

101. Bricker and Thompson (2016, 664 tab. 1) and Kopparam and Clemens (2020, fig. 1); see also Emmons, Kent, and Ricketts (2019, 317).

102. Beamer and Nilaj (2022, 17–18, fig. 2.5); Haughwout et al. (2019a, 2; 2019b, 4–5); and Kopparam and Clemens (2020, fig. 2).

103. Beamer and Nilaj (2022, 18–19, figs. 2.5–2.6).

104. Scott-Clayton (2018, 8–11); see also Chakrabarti, Nober, and van der Klaauw (2020, 3–4) and The Aspen Financial Security Program (2020).

105. See, for example, Chakrabarti, Nober, and van der Klaauw (2020, 2–3) and Scott-Clayton (2018, 12–13); see also Beamer and Nilaj (2022, 16 fig. 2.4).

106. Sullivan et al. (2019, 3–4, fig. 1).

107. Scott-Clayton (2018, 12–13); see also Beamer and Nilaj (2022, 15 fig. 2.3); Emmons, Kent, and Ricketts (2019, 304); Haughwout et al. (2019a, 2–3); and New York City Department of Consumer and Worker Protection (2020, 10–12).

108. Haughwout et al. (2019a, 2).

109. Sullivan et al. (2019, 7–8).

110. National Center for Education Statistics (n.d., tabs. 326.10, 326.40) and New York City Department of Consumer and Worker Protection (2020, 9–10).

111. Scott-Clayton (2018, 12–13).

112. Hansen and Shaw (2020, 7) and Haughwout et al. (2019a, 4).

113. See Council of Economic Advisers (2016, 16, 44) and Looney and Yannelis (2022).

114. Scott-Clayton (2018, 8–11); see also Dettling, Goodman, and Reber (2022, 10–12); Looney, Wessel, and Yilla (2020); Looney and Yannelis (2015, 2); and Mezza and Sommer (2015).

115. Council of Economic Advisers (2016, 41).

116. Scott-Clayton (2018, 6, tab. 2); see also Mezza and Sommer (2015).

117. Miller (2017, 1, 3–4, tab. 1).

118. Scott-Clayton (2018, 11).

119. Avery and Turner (2012, 180, fig. 5).

120. National Center for Education Statistics (n.d., tabs. 326.10, 326.40) and New York City Department of Consumer and Worker Protection (2020, 9–10). See also Schanzenbach, Bauer, and Breitwieser (2017, 4).

121. Board of Governors of the Federal Reserve System (2023, 61–62, tab. 33); The Aspen Financial Security Program (2020); and The Institute for College Access and Success (2019).

122. Dynarski, Page, and Scott-Clayton (2022, 1).

123. Emmons, Kent, and Ricketts (2019, 299; see also 308–10).

124. Hout and DiPrete (2006); see also Chetty et al. (2016, 15–16, 18) and Schultz (2019, 174).

125. Baum, Ma, and Payea (2013, 5); Black et al. (2023, 37); McMahon (2021, 418 tab. 1, 421); and Rothwell (2015, tab. 2).

126. Baum, Ma, and Payea (2013, 3).

127. Baum, Ma, and Payea (2013, 2); Council of Economic Advisers (2016, 13); and McMahon (2021, 418 tab. 1).

128. Council of Economic Advisers (2016, 13, 50).

129. Aghion et al. (2009) and Council of Economic Advisers (2016, 13). College education produces even more positive externalities from reduced crime and prison costs, greater civil involvement, and vigorous democratic institutions. Council of Economic Advisers (2016, 13); McMahon (2021, 418 tab. 1, 421); and Baum, Ma, and Payea (2013, 2–3).

130. Boatman, Evans, and Soliz (2017).

131. See, for example, Elengold et al. (2021).

132. US Government Accountability Office (2022a); see Morduch and Schneider (2017, 117).

133. See National Center for Education Statistics (n.d., tab. 401.30).

134. See Dynarski, Page, and Scott-Clayton (2022, 4 tab. 1).

135. The Department of Education tackled this issue piecemeal by securing debt forgiveness for over two hundred thousand borrowers through lawsuits alleging that their schools defrauded them. Cowley (2023). In 2023 the department also adopted new rules, effective July 1, 2024, that allowed it to demand financial protections from institutions that have high student default rates, depend too heavily on federal aid for their financing, or devote too much federal aid to academic programs that do not result in gainful employment. US Department of Education (n.d.-a, 2023).

136. In summer 2022, President Biden proposed across-the-board student debt cancellation, which the Supreme Court later struck down. The proposal would have granted $10,000 in relief to all borrowers making up to $125,000 annually (or $250,000 for married couples), plus another $10,000 in relief for every borrower who received a Pell Grant. The White House (2022a).

137. Biden v. Nebraska (2023).

138. Federal Student Aid (n.d.-d).

139. See Herbst (2023, 2). Approximately 15 percent of IDR borrowers who started repaying their loans in 2012 defaulted by 2017. Congressional Budget Office (2020, 17 fig. 2-6); see also Dynarski, Page, and Scott-Clayton (2022, 10).

140. Herbst (2023, 4, 13–14). In 2019 Congress passed the Fostering Undergraduate Talent by Unlocking Resources for Education Act (FUTURE Act), which amended Section 6103 of the Internal Revenue Code to streamline the IDR recertification process. As of 2024, the act was still being implemented.

141. Herbst (2023, 21).

142. Congressional Budget Office (2020, 16).

143. Di Maggio, Kalda, and Yao (2020).

144. See Dynarski, Page, and Scott-Clayton (2022, 22).

145. See, for example, Moment of Truth Project (2013, 30–31).

146. Greenspan (2004).

CHAPTER 10. A FINANCIALLY SECURE RETIREMENT

1. Ding and White (2022).

2. See Bond and Porell (2020) and Center on Budget and Policy Priorities (2024).

3. Bond and Porell (2020, 1).

4. Social Security Administration (2021). Of older people who never receive Social Security, 86 percent are late-arriving immigrants or infrequent workers.

5. Social Security Administration (2024a).

6. Congressional Budget Office (2019, 3) and Social Security Administration (n.d.-e, 2–3).

Disability benefits can continue until full retirement age, when disabled workers are transferred to the old-age benefits program.

7. Social Security Administration (2023b, 3).

8. Social Security does not pay benefits for certain types of work, such as railroad work. AARP (2021).

9. Social Security Administration (2023b, 6).

10. The so-called AIME adjusts a person's highest earnings for up to thirty-five years to account for wage inflation and then computes a monthly average. The 90-cent, 32-cent, and 15-cent rates are paid on that monthly average. Social Security Administration (2024d, 124, 241). The $1,174 and $7,078 figures are called "bend points" and were the numbers that applied to newly eligible retirees in 2024. The Social Security Administration updates the bend points every year according to the Average Wage Index for newly eligible recipients. Diamond (2023, 123, n18).

11. See Congressional Research Service (2021c, 17–18).

12. See Institute for Social Research (2023, 30) and Social Security Administration (2023b, 8).

13. Center on Budget and Policy Priorities (2024, 3) and Diamond and Orszag (2004, 16).

14. Congressional Budget Office (2015, 1) and Diamond and Orszag (2004, 25).

15. Social Security Administration (2024d, 3).

16. Social Security Administration (2024d, 26–27).

17. Burkhalter and Chaplain (2023, 4 tab. B); see also Dettling, Goodman, and Reber (2022, 8n10) (40%).

18. Bond and Porell (2020, 4) and Vanguard Research (2023, 5).

19. Vanguard Research (2023, 5, 8).

20. Congressional Budget Office (2019, 18).

21. See Biggs, Sarney, and Tamborini (2009) and Center on Budget and Policy Priorities (2024, 2).

22. Shmerling (2022). The slump was driven largely by excess deaths from COVID-19 and opioid use. See generally Case and Deaton (2020) (discussing effect of suicides and opioid use on death rates of younger and middle-aged whites) and Shmerling (2022).

23. Chetty et al. (2016, fig. 2).

24. Waldron (2007, 21).

25. Congressional Research Service (2021b, 11, see also 13–14) and Chetty et al. (2016).

26. Chetty et al. (2016, fig. 3); Goldman and Orszag (2014); and Waldron (2007).

27. Steuerle, Cosic, and Quakenbush (2019, 2).

28. See Goldman and Orszag (2014, 6 tab. 2).

29. Goldman and Orszag (2014, 6 tab. 2); see Chetty et al. (2016); National Academies of Sciences, Engineering, and Medicine (2015, 39, 42–53); Reznick et al. (2021, 20–21, 24, 26 tab. 3); and Congressional Research Service (2021c, 19–24).

30. Dushi and Trenkamp (2021, tab. 5); see also Bond and Porell (2020, 4 fig. 1, 6 tab. 1, 15–16, tab. 7).

31. Bond and Porell (2020, 1, 4 fig. 1, 6 tab. 1).

32. Bond and Porell (2020, 1, 4 fig. 1, 6 tab. 1).

33. Bond and Porell (2020, 15 tab. 7); see also Leonesio et al. (2012, 70–71 chart 6).

34. Dushi, Iams, and Trenkamp (2017, 3); Federal Interagency Forum on Aging-Related Statistics (2016, 14, 177); and Leonesio et al. (2012, 70 chart 6, 73). Likewise, personal assets and savings are "a minor source of income" for everyone except older people with incomes in the top 20 percent. Dushi, Iams, and Trenkamp (2017, 3).

35. VanDerhei (2019).

36. Vanguard Research (2023, 4, 10).

37. Social Security Administration (n.d.-d).

38. National Council on Aging (2023a); see also Bond and Porell (2020, 15 tab. 7); and Federal Interagency Forum on Aging-Related Statistics (2020, 13).

39. National Council on Aging (2023a); see also Center on Budget and Policy Priorities (2024, 8–9).

40. Giefer and King (2021); see Bond and Porell (2020, 16–17 & tab. 8).

41. Mutchler, Su, and Roldan (2023, 2).

42. Mutchler, Su, and Roldan (2023, 2, tab. 1).

43. Mutchler, Su, and Roldan (2023, 4, 6); see also Yin, Chen, and Munnell (2023, 1, 4, tab. 3).

44. Joint Center on Housing Studies of Harvard University (2023, 2-3, 14-15) and Molinsky (2020); see also Bond and Porell (2020, 16, tab. 8) and Johnson (2015).

45. See US Government Accountability Office (2021, 79-80) and Institute for Social Research (2023, 53).

46. National Council on Aging (2023a); see also Bond and Porell (2020, 16, tab. 8).

47. Bond and Porell (2020, 16-17, tab. 8).

48. See Employee Benefit Research Institute (2023, 6, 24 fig. 14).

49. US Government Accountability Office (2021, 10, 13-15).

50. US Government Accountability Office (2021, 18, 27-29, 47) (adjusted for inflation).

51. US Government Accountability Office (2021, 75-76, 126 fig. 32; see generally 12-13).

52. Miller (2023) and Zuss (2022). For instance, between 2019 and 2023, private-sector DB plans shed another 1.6 million (13%) of their active participants. Compare US Bureau of Labor Statistics (2023a) (Excel sheet, second tab) with Congressional Research Service (2021a).

53. State and local governments are the one sector in which DB plans remain prevalent. See US Bureau of Labor Statistics (2023a) (Excel sheet, second tab). But many are struggling to fund their pension liabilities and avoid insolvency. See Beerman (2013) and Shnitser (2015, 667-73).

54. See Leonesio et al. (2012, 70 chart 6).

55. Semega and Kollar (2022, 2).

56. Vanguard Research (2023, 10) (the bottom fourth of earners realistically can generate only 2% of their sustainable retirement spending from savings; the next fourth up can generate only 4%).

57. Board of Governors of the Federal Reserve System (n.d.) and Leonesio et al. (2012, 70 chart 6, 73).

58. Argento, Bryant, and Sabelhaus (2015, 14). See also Fidelity Investments (2023, 20).

59. Argento, Bryant, and Sabelhaus (2015, 15). See also Board of Governors of the Federal Reserve System (2023, 69).

60. Blakely-Gray (2024). These state plans resemble the Obama administration's short-lived myRA program, which allowed workers who lacked access to a retirement plan at work to save for retirement through automatic payroll deductions. The first Trump administration discontinued the myRA program in 2017 after a low take-up rate. See Johnson (2017).

61. See, for example, CalSavers Retirement Savings Program (n.d.) and E. Reed (2023).

62. T. Reed (2023).

63. Center for Retirement Initiatives (n.d.) (data as of June 2024); see also Chalmers et al. (2021, 4–5).

64. Computation by author based on data as of June 2024, supplied by the Center for Retirement Initiatives (n.d.); see also Chalmers et al. (2021).

65. Chalmers et al. (2021, 4–7) (computation by author).

66. See Chalmers et al. (2021, 7).

67. See Vanguard Research (2023, 10).

68. Chalmers et al. (2021, 5).

69. Callis (2023).

70. Consumer Financial Protection Bureau (2015b, 5).

71. US Department of Housing and Urban Development (n.d.).

72. Federal Housing Administration (2024, 59).

73. Consumer Financial Protection Bureau (2017, 10–11).

74. See Consumer Financial Protection Bureau (2017, 2–4).

75. See Consumer Financial Protection Bureau (2017, 2–4).

76. Consumer Financial Protection Bureau (2017, 4, 11–14).

77. Consumer Financial Protection Bureau (2017, 10–11).

78. See Consumer Financial Protection Bureau (2015b, 3, 13).

79. See, for example, Bellaby (2006, 1); Coile, Milligan, and Wise (2017); and Laitner (2018).

80. Under the "retirement earnings test," recipients who claim benefits before full retirement age have their benefits reduced one dollar for every two dollars they earn above an annual dollar limit. See Social Security Administration (2023b, 8–9). In a little known fact, Social Security increases their benefits after full retirement age in return, however. Gelber et al. (2021).

81. Dubina (2023); see also Coile (2018, 2–3 & figs. 1–2).

82. See, for example, Coile (2018, 13–18; 2015, 837–42); Coile and Stewart (2021); Coile, Milligan, and Wise (2019, 12–31); Cosic and Steuerle (2021); Friedberg and Webb (2009, 2–3); and MacInnis (2009, 13–14).

83. Most US workers have no mandatory retirement age, because Congress amended the Age Discrimination in Employment Act in 1986 to eliminate age limits for most employment. Age Discrimination in Employment Act Amendments of 1986, § 2.

84. Coile (2018, 11–12, 18) and Friedberg and Webb (2003, 4); see also Coile (2015, 836–37, 839–40).

85. See Coile (2018, 13); MacInnis (2009, 3); and Leonesio et al. (2012, 60, 65, 74).

86. See Leonesio et al. (2012, 60, 65, 74).

87. Dushi, Iams, and Trenkamp (2017, 2).

88. Dushi, Iams, and Trenkamp (2017, 2); Dubina (2023); and Hall and Petrosky-Nadeau (2016, 4, fig. 3.B). See also Coile and Stewart (2021, 406–7, tab. 4); Aaron and Callan (2011); and Bound and Waidmann (2010, 3, tabs. 1, 3–4).

89. Aaron and Callan (2011) and Coile (2018, 3–5, figs. 5–8).

90. Coile (2015, 833–34, 835 fig. 4); see also Aaron and Callan (2011).

91. Glickman and Hermes (2015, 25, 28–29, exhs. 3–4).

92. Institute for Social Research (2023, 22; see also 26–27, 29, 27 fig. 1.5); see also Aaron and Callan (2011); Coile and Stewart (2021, 406–7, tab. 4); Employee Benefit Research Institute (2019, 8); Hurd, Smith, and Zissimopoulos (2004, 768); McClellan (1998, 331–35, 342–43); van den Berg, Elder, and Burdorf (2010, 578); and Wheaton and Crimmins (2012, 30–31).

93. McClellan (1998, 322).

94. See Aaron and Callan (2011) and Bound and Waidmann (2010, 1).

95. Bound and Waidmann (2010, 6–8, tab. 5); see also Montgomery (2022).

96. Chetty et al. (2016, fig. 2) and Glickman and Hermes (2015, 30).

97. See Leonesio et al. (2012, 68–71, chart 6) (for senior citizens in the bottom two income quintiles, earned income only made up 3% and 7%, respectively, of their incomes) and Glickman and Hermes (2015, 32 exh. 8).

98. Diamond and Orszag (2004, 17, 39–40).

99. Romig (2024).

100. For full description of these risks, see chapter 3.

101. Diamond and Orszag (2004, 40–41).

102. Diamond and Orszag (2004, 16).

103. Diamond and Orszag (2004, 16).

104. Diamond and Orszag (2004, 45).

105. Congressional Budget Office (2015, 2) and Moore (2012, 43–51).

106. Social Security Administration (2024d, 26).

107. Congressional Budget Office (2019, 11, exh. 1).

108. Diamond and Orszag (2004, 45) and Moore (2008, 1078–82).

109. Vanguard Research (2023, 4, 17).

110. See, for example, Diamond and Orszag (2004, 99–100).

111. For example, see recent proposals by Congressman John Larson and Senator Bernie Sanders. Goss (2023a, 2023b).

112. See, for example, Congressional Budget Office (2015); Diamond (2023, 123); Diamond and Orszag (2004); National Academies of Sciences, Engineering, and Medicine (2015); and Social Security Administration (n.d.-c).

113. Bound and Waidmann (2010, 7); Congressional Research Service (2021c, 27); Diamond and Orszag (2004, 84); and Glickman and Hermes (2015, 37).

114. See Diamond (2023, 124) ("If the adjustments for early benefits were [actuarially] neutral for the affected population, delayed starts by themselves would have no aggregate financial effect.") and National Academies of Sciences, Engineering, and Medicine (2015, 111) ("this policy change, if enacted on its own, would not generate any savings for the Social Security system, because the projections suggest that benefits would in fact increase slightly").

115. Bound and Waidmann (2010, 6–8, tab. 5) and Pilipiec, Groot, and Pavlova (2021, 296); see also Montgomery (2022).

116. Bound and Waidmann (2010, 7).

117. Bound and Waidmann (2010, 7).

118. Diamond and Orszag (2004, 84).

119. See, for example, Congressional Research Service (2021c, 26) and Romig (2016).

120. Diamond (2023, 124).

121. Congressional Research Service (2021c, 28–30).

122. See Bound and Waidmann (2010, 1).

123. Krugman (2023).

124. Diamond and Orszag (2004, 39).

125. Congressional Research Service (2021b); Diamond and Orszag (2004, 100–102); and Goss (2010, 8).

126. See Congressional Research Service (2021b, 11–12, 17–18).

127. Congressional Research Service (2021c, 19).

128. Diamond and Orszag (2004, 81).

129. Diamond and Orszag (2004, 80–84); see also Congressional Research Service (2021c, 29–30).

130. Diamond and Orszag (2004, 84).

131. Diamond and Orszag (2004, 84) and Social Security Administration (2023a, 149).

132. See, for example, Diamond and Orszag (2004, 86–88).

CHAPTER 11. WHAT IT WILL TAKE

1. Joint Center for Housing Studies of Harvard University (2024a, 2–3).

2. Levey (2022).

3. Barr (1992, 743).

4. Congressional Budget Office (2023, 1).

5. See chapter 6 (discussion of Card and Krueger's findings); Rao and Risch (2024, 1–6); and Wiltshire et al. (2024, 2–4).

6. Reich (2021, 3–4); see also Zipperer, Cooper, and Bivens (2021, 1–3).

7. The theory is that raising the minimum wage induces people nearing retirement age to work longer and delay claiming Social Security benefits. Borgschulte and Cho (2020).

8. Bastian and Jones (2021, 2–4). See also Hendren and Sprung-Keyser (2020, 1257). Expanding the EITC for adults without children also likely would have a low net cost by boosting employment and tax revenues while reducing spending on disability insurance and Supplemental Security Income. See Bastian and Jones (2021, 3, 18).

9. Garfinkel et al. (2022, abstract).

10. Garfinkel et al. (2022, 24).

11. Berlin and Gale (2022).

12. Congressional Budget Office (2015, 66–67, 97 tab. 2). See also Social Security Administration (2024c, 10) (paying a special minimum benefit of up to 133% of the Census monthly poverty level would have zero negative effect on the Social Security deficit).

13. Goss (2023a, 2, 8); cf. Goss (2010, 8).

14. Bernard (2024) and Social Security Administration (2024c, 23).

15. Bernard (2024) and Social Security Administration (2024c, 23).

16. Bernard (2024) and Social Security Administration (2024c, 23).

17. Diamond and Orszag (2004, 80–84).

18. Diamond and Orszag (2004, 84). See also Social Security Administration (2024c, 6) (indexing benefits for longevity alone would reduce Social Security's deficit by 16%, which is about half of the amount Diamond and Orszag estimated for indexing benefits and payroll taxes for longevity together).

19. Diamond and Orszag (2004, 86–88).

20. Social Security Administration (2024c, 7). See also Diamond and Orszag (2004, 87–88, 97 tab. 5-2) (9%) and Congressional Budget Office (2015, 45–46, 94 tab. 2).

21. A multiplier measures the effect of government spending on national income or output. For instance, when the outcome of interest is output, a multiplier of 2 means that $1 in government expenditures produces $2 in additional output. See, for example, Furman (2020, 7–8).

22. Blinder and Zandi (2015); Di Maggio and Kermani (2016, 5); Vroman (2010, iv); and Marinescu (2020); see also Congressional Budget Office (2010, 3, 11–13) (0.4 to 2.1).

23. Congressional Budget Office (2010, 3, 11–13) (estimates for 2010 to 2015) and US Government Accountability Office (2022b, 47–51).

24. Holahan and Simpson (2022, 5–8, tab. 2, 18–19).

25. See Congressional Budget Office (2024) (computation by author) and Holahan and Simpson (2022, 8).

26. Swagel (2024, 3–5, 9 tab. 2).

27. Gangopadhyaya et al. (2023) and Primus and Bingham (2024).

28. Primus and Bingham (2024).

29. Holahan and Simpson (2022, 13–15, tab. 6, 18–19).

30. See, for example, Cubanski, Neuman, and Jacobson (2016, ii); Gruber (2013, 4); and Moment of Truth Project (2013, 12, 21–23). The estimates vary by year and are not adjusted for inflation.

31. See, for example, Cubanski, Neuman, and Jacobson (2016, ii); Gruber (2013, 4); and Moment of Truth Project (2013, 12, 21–23).

32. See Congressional Budget Office (2024); Gustafsson and Collins (2022) (computation by author); and Banthin et al. (2024, 2, 4–5, fig. 1).

33. McKernan et al. (2016).

34. See Greenstein (2022a, 5) and Hoynes (2019, 190–91).

35. The saver's match is no substitute for a universal savings plan, however, because it is restricted to lower-income taxpayers who participate in retirement plans. As we have seen, many lower-income taxpayers lack access to DC retirement plans. In any case, retirement plan savings do not serve the same purpose as emergency savings funds.

36. Joint Committee on Taxation (2022, 1).

37. McBride et al. (2024, 13–14, tab. 2).

38. Callis (2023).

39. See, for example, Herbert and Belsky (2008, 39–40, n24).

40. Looney (2022).

41. Swagel (2022) (in present value terms) and Looney (2022).

42. Office of Management and Budget (2024a, 40). Compare Office of Management and Budget (2024b, 33) with CollegeBoard (2022, 4).

43. Denning, Marx, and Turner (2019, 221).

44. See Hendren and Sprung-Keyser (2020, 1212, 1239 tab. 2, 1249–53, 1258, 1271).

45. Cox (2024).

46. Medina (2024).

47. Bogage, Stein, and Diamond (2024).

48. KFF (2024c).

49. Hungerford and Thiess (2013).

50. Republican Party (n.d., 9).

References

Aaron, Henry J., and Jean Marie Callan. 2011. *Who Retires Early?* Chestnut Hill, MA: Center for Retirement Research. https://crr.bc.edu/wp-content/uploads/2011/05/wp_2011-10-508.pdf.

AARP. 2021. "Are Some Kinds of Employees Not Covered by Social Security?" May 26. https://www.aarp.org/retirement/social-security/questions-answers/kinds-of-employees-not-covered-by-social-security.html.

Abraham, Kenneth S. 1986. *Distributing Risk: Insurance, Legal Theory, and Public Policy.* New Haven, CT: Yale University Press.

Aghion, P., L. Boustan, C. Hoxby, and J. Vandenbussche. 2009. "The Causal Impact of Education on Economic Growth: Evidence from U.S." Working paper, Harvard University, Cambridge, MA, March. https://scholar.harvard.edu/files/aghion/files/causal_impact_of_education.pdf.

Ahn, Michael, Mike Batty, and Ralf R. Meisenzahl. 2018. "Household Debt-to-Income Ratios in the Enhanced Financial Accounts." FEDS Notes, Board of Governors of the Federal Reserve System, Washington, DC, January 11. https://www.federalreserve.gov/econres/notes/feds-notes/household-debt-to-income-ratios-in-the-enhanced-financial-accounts-20180109.htm.

Akerlof, George A. 1970. "The Market for 'Lemons': Quality Uncertainty and the Market Mechanism." *Quarterly Journal of Economics* 84 (3): 488–500.

Akinwumi, Michael, John Merrill, Lisa Rice, Kareem Saleh, and Maureen Yap. 2021. *An AI Fair Lending Policy Agenda for the Federal Financial Regulators.* Economic Studies at Brookings. Washington, DC: Brookings.

https://www.brookings.edu/wp-content/uploads/2021/12/Akinwumi
_Merrill_Rice_Saleh_Yap_12-01-2021-1.pdf.

Aladangady, Aditya, Jesse Bricker, Andrew C. Chang, Sarena Goodman, Jacob
Krimmel, Kevin B. Moore, Sarah Reber, Alice Henriques Volz, and Richard A. Windle. 2023. *Changes in U.S. Family Finances from 2019 to 2022: Evidence from the Survey of Consumer Finances.* Washington, DC, Board of Governors of the Federal Reserve System. https://www.federalreserve.gov
/publications/files/scf23.pdf.

Alexandrov, Alexei, and Elizabeth Saunders. 2023. "Mortgage Data Shows
That Borrowers Could Save $100 a Month (or More) by Choosing Cheaper Lenders." Consumer Financial Protection Bureau Blog, May 24. https://www
.consumerfinance.gov/about-us/blog/mortgage-data-shows-borrowers-could
-save-100-month-choosing-cheaper-lenders/.

Allen, Heidi, Sarah H. Gordon, Dennis Lee, Aditi Bhanja, and Benjamin D.
Sommers. 2021. "Comparison of Utilization, Costs, and Quality of Medicaid vs Subsidized Private Health Insurance for Low-Income Adults." *JAMA Network Open* 4 (1): 1–13.

Alley, Dawn E., Jennifer Lloyd, José A. Pagán, Craig E. Pollack, Michelle
Shardell, and Carolyn Cannuscio. 2011. "Mortgage Delinquency and Changes in Access to Health Resources and Depressive Symptoms in a Nationally Representative Cohort of Americans Older Than 50 Years." *American Journal of Public Health* 101 (12): 2293–98.

Alston, Philip. 2019. "Universal Basic Income as a Social Rights-Based Antidote
to Growing Economic Insecurity." In *The Future of Economic and Social Rights*, edited by Katharine G. Young, 377–403. Cambridge: Cambridge University Press.

Ambrose, Brent, Michael LaCour-Little, and Zsuzsa R. Huszar. 2005. "A Note
on Hybrid Mortgages." *Real Estate Economics* 33 (4): 765–82.

Ambrose, Brent W., James N. Conklin, and Luis A. Lopez. 2021. "Does Borrower
and Broker Race Affect the Cost of Mortgage Credit?" *Review of Financial Studies* 34 (2): 790–826.

Ambrose, Brent W., Larry Cordell, and Shuwei Ma. 2015. "The Impact of Student
Loan Debt on Small Business Formation." Working Paper 15-26, Federal Reserve Bank of Philadelphia, Philadelphia, July. https://www.philadelphiafed
.org/the-economy/the-impact-of-student-loan-debt-on-small-business
-formation.

American Presidency Project, The. 2002. "George W. Bush: Remarks at St. Paul
AME Church in Atlanta, Georgia." June 17. https://www.presidency.ucsb.edu
/documents/remarks-st-paul-ame-church-atlanta-georgia.

Anong, Sophia, and Robin Henager. 2021. "Student Loans and Health-
related Financial Hardship." *Journal of Student Financial Aid* 50 (2): article 3.

Argento, Robert, Victoria L. Bryant, and John Sabelhaus. 2015. "Early With-drawals from Retirement Accounts during the Great Recession." *Contemporary Economic Policy* 33 (1): 1–16.

Aron-Dine, Aviva. 2019. *Making Health Insurance More Affordable for Middle-Income Individual Market Consumers.* Washington, DC: Center on Budget and Policy Priorities. https://www.cbpp.org/sites/default/files/atoms/files/3-21-19health.pdf.

Aron-Dine, Aviva, and Matt Broaddus. 2019. *Improving ACA Subsidies for Low- and Moderate-Income Consumers Is Key to Increasing Coverage.* Washington, DC: Center on Budget and Policy Priorities. https://www.cbpp.org/sites/default/files/atoms/files/3-21-19health2.pdf.

Arrow, Kenneth J. 1963. "Uncertainty and the Welfare Economics of Medical Care." *American Economic Review* 53 (5): 941–73.

Artiga, Samantha, Petry Ubri, and Julia Zur. 2017. "The Effects of Premiums and Cost Sharing on Low-Income Populations: Updated Review of Research Findings." Issue Brief, Kaiser Family Foundation, June. https://www.kff.org/medicaid/issue-brief/the-effects-of-premiums-and-cost-sharing-on-low-income-populations-updated-review-of-research-findings/.

Asante-Muhammad, Dedrick, Jamie Buell, and Joshua Devine. 2021. *60% Black Homeownership: A Radical Goal for Black Wealth Development.* Washington, DC: National Community Reinvestment Coalition. https://ncrc.org/wp-content/uploads/dlm_uploads/2021/02/60-Black-Homeownership-FINALb.pdf.

Aspen Institute Financial Security Program, The. 2020. *Making the Case: Solving the Student Debt Crisis.* https://www.aspeninstitute.org/wp-content/uploads/2020/03/SolvingStudentDebtCrisis.pdf.

Assistant Secretary for Planning and Evaluation, Office of Health Policy. 2023. *National Uninsured Rate Reaches an All-Time Low in Early 2023 after the Close of the ACA Open Enrollment Period.* Data Point. HP-2023-20. Washington, DC: US Department of Health and Human Services. https://aspe.hhs.gov/sites/default/files/documents/e06a66dfc6f62afc8bb809038dfaebe4/Uninsured-Record-Low-Q12023.pdf.

———. 2024. *National Uninsured Rate at 8.2 Percent in the First Quarter of 2024.* Data Point. HP-2024-17. Washington, DC: US Department of Health and Human Services. https://aspe.hhs.gov/sites/default/files/documents/ee0475e44e27daef00155e95a24fd023/nhis-q1-2024-datapoint.pdf.

Atkinson, Abbye. 2019. "Rethinking Credit as Social Provision." *Stanford Law Review* 71 (5): 1093–1162.

Atkinson, Anthony B. 1991. "Social Insurance: The Fifteenth Annual Lecture of the Geneva Association." *Geneva Papers on Risk and Insurance Theory* 16 (2): 113–31.

———. 1996. "The Case for a Participation Income." *Political Quarterly* 67 (1): 67–70.

ATTOM. 2023. "U.S. Foreclosure Activity Doubles Annually But Still Below Pre-Pandemic Levels." Press release, January 12. https://www.attomdata.com /news/market-trends/foreclosures/attom-year-end-2022-u-s-foreclosure -market-report/.

Auten, Gerald, and Geoffrey Gee. 2009. "Income Mobility in the United States: New Evidence from Income Tax Data." *National Tax Journal* 62 (2): 301–28.

Auten, Gerald, Geoffrey Gee, and Nicholas Turner. 2013. "Income Inequality, Mobility, and Turnover at the Top in the US, 1987-2010." *American Economic Review: Papers & Proceedings* 103 (3): 168–72.

Avery, Christopher, and Sarah Turner. 2012. "Student Loans: Do College Students Borrow Too Much—Or Not Enough?" *Journal of Economic Perspectives* 26 (1): 165–92.

Babula, Michael, and Alp Idil Ersoy-Babula. 2022. "Falling Behind: The Role of Student Loans on Forgoing Healthcare." *Health and Social Care in the Community* 30 (5): 1944–50.

Badger, Emily, and Christopher Ingraham. 2015. "The Remarkably High Odds You'll Be Poor at Some Point in Your Life." *Washington Post*, July 24, 2015. https://www.washingtonpost.com/news/wonk/wp/2015/07/24/the -remarkably-high-odds-youll-be-poor-at-some-point-in-your-life/.

Baker, Dean, and Wesley Bignell. 2024. "Do People Think the Economy Is Bad Because the Media Failed, or Because the Economy Is Actually Bad?" *Nation*, July 19. https://www.thenation.com/article/economy/debate-economy-bad -media/.

Baker, Tom. 1996. "On the Genealogy of Moral Hazard." *Texas Law Review* 75 (2): 237–92.

———. 2003. "Containing the Promise of Insurance: Adverse Selection and Risk Classification." *Connecticut Insurance Law Journal* 9 (2): 371–96.

Baker, Tom, and Peter Siegelman. 2010. "Tontines for the Invincibles: Enticing Low Risks into the Health-Insurance Pool with an Idea from Insurance History and Behavioral Economics." *Wisconsin Law Review* 2010 (1): 79–120.

Baker, Tom, and Jonathan Simon. 2002. *Embracing Risk: The Changing Culture of Insurance and Responsibility*. Chicago: University of Chicago Press.

Balakrishnan, Sidhya, Michael Lewis, and Stephen Nuñez. 2020. *Reweaving the Safety Net: The Best Fit for Guaranteed Income*. New York: The Jain Family Institute. https://jainfamilyinstitute.org/wp-content/uploads/pdf/reweaving -the-safety-net-12.15.20.pdf.

Banthin, Jessica, Matthew Buettgens, Michael Simpson, and Jason Levits. 2024. *Who Benefits from Enhanced Premium Tax Credits in the Marketplace?* Washington, DC: Urban Institute. https://www.urban.org/sites/default/files /2024-06/Who_Benefits_from_Enhanced_Premium_Tax_Credits_in_the _Marketplace.pdf.

Barr, Michael S., Sendhil Mullainathan, and Eldar Shafir. 2009. "The Case for Behaviorally Informed Regulation." In *New Perspectives on Regulation*, edited by David Moss and John Cisternino, 25–61. Cambridge, MA: The Tobin Project.

Barr, Nicholas. 1992. "Economic Theory and the Welfare State: A Survey and Interpretation." *Journal of Economic Literature* 30 (2): 741–803.

Bartlett, Robert, Adair Morse, Richard Stanton, and Nancy Wallace. 2022. "Consumer-Lending Discrimination in the FinTech Era." *Journal of Financial Economics* 143 (1): 30–56.

Bastian, Jacob E., and Maggie R. Jones. 2021. "Do EITC Expansions Pay for Themselves? Effects on Tax Revenue and Government Transfers." *Journal of Public Economics* 196 (1): 1–21.

Baten, Redwan Bin Abdul, and George L. Wehby. 2023. "Effects of the Affordable Care Act Insurance Expansions on Health Care Coverage, Access, and Health Status of 50–64-Year-Old Adults: Evidence from the First Six Years." *Journal of Applied Gerontology* 42 (8): 1717–26.

Baum, Sandy. 2015. "Declining State Expenditures on Public Universities Are in Fact Driving Tuition Increases." *Urban Wire*, April 5, 2015. https://www.urban.org/urban-wire/declining-state-expenditures-public-universities-are-fact-driving-tuition-increases.

Baum, Sandy, and Jason Delisle. 2022. *Income-Driven Repayment of Student Loans*. Washington, DC: Urban Institute. https://www.urban.org/sites/default/files/2022-04/Income-Driven%20Repayment%20of%20Student%20Loans.pdf.

Baum, Sandy, Jennifer Ma, and Kathleen Payea. 2013. *Education Pays 2013: The Benefits of Higher Education for Individuals and Society*. New York: CollegeBoard. https://research.collegeboard.org/media/pdf/education-pays-2013-full-report.pdf.

Beamer, Laura, and Eduard Nilaj. 2022. *Student Debt and Young America in 2022*. New York: Jain Family Institute. https://jainfamilyinstitute.org/wp-content/uploads/pdf/msd-annual-report-2022-student-debt-and-young-america.pdf.

Becker, Jo, Sheryl Gay Stolberg, and Stephen Labaton. 2008. "White House Philosophy Stoked Mortgage Bonfire." *New York Times*, December 20, 2008. https://www.nytimes.com/2008/12/21/business/21admin.html.

Beermann, Jack J. 2013. "The Public Pension Crisis." *Washington & Lee Law Review* 70 (1): 3–94.

Bellaby, Paul. 2006. "Can They Carry on Working? Later Retirement, Health, and Social Inequality in an Aging Population." *International Journal of Health Services* 36 (1): 1–23.

Benartzi, Shlomo. 2020. "People Don't Save Enough for Emergencies, but There Are Ways to Fix That." *Wall Street Journal*, February 17, 2020. https://www

.wsj.com/articles/people-dont-save-enough-for-emergencies-but-there-are
-ways-to-fix-that-11581951601.

Berkowitz, Edward. 2005–2006. "Medicare and Medicaid: The Past as Prologue."
Healthcare Financing Review 27 (2): 11–23.

Berkowitz, Edward D. 2000. "Statement before the Subcommittee on Social
Security of the Committee on Ways and Means." July 13. Social Security,
Legislative History. https://www.ssa.gov/history/edberkdib.html.

Berlin, Ian, and William G. Gale. 2022. "Let the Child Tax Credit Work." *Up
Front* (blog), Brookings Institution, July 7. https://www.brookings.edu/blog
/up-front/2022/07/07/let-the-child-tax-credit-work/.

Berman, Yonatan. 2022. "Absolute Intragenerational Mobility in the United
States, 1962–2014." *Journal of Economic Inequality* 20 (3): 587–609.

Bernard, Tara Siegel. 2024. "What Will Happen to Social Security after Trump
Takes Office?" *New York Times*, November 14, 2024. https://www.nytimes
.com/2024/11/14/business/trump-social-security-benefits.html.

Bertrand, Marianne, Sendhil Mullainathan, and Eldar Shafir. 2006. "Behavioral
Economics and Marketing in Aid of Decision Making among the Poor."
Journal of Public Policy & Marketing 25 (1): 8–23.

Bhaskaran, Suparna, Fatimah Al-Khaldi, Ofronama Biu, Elaine Chang, Chiderea
Ihejirika, Ana Patricia Muñoz, and Darrick Hamilton. 2024. *Color of Wealth
in Chicago*. New York, The Institute on Race, Power and Political Economy at
The New School. https://racepowerpolicy.org/wp-content/uploads/2024/06
/Color-of-Wealth-in-Chicago-061824.pdf.

Bhutta, Neil, Jesse Bricker, Andrew C. Chang, Lisa J. Dettling, Sarena Goodman, Joanne W. Hsu, Kevin B. Moore, Sarah Reber, Alice Henriques Volz,
and Richard A. Windle. 2020. "Changes in U.S. Family Finances from 2016
to 2019: Evidence from the Survey of Consumer Finances." *Federal Reserve
Bulletin* 106 (5): 1–42.

Bhutta, Neil, Andrew C. Chang, Lisa J. Dettling, and Joanne W. Hsu. 2020.
"Disparities in Wealth by Race and Ethnicity in the 2019 Survey of Consumer
Finances." *FEDS Notes*, Board of Governors of the Federal Reserve System,
September 28. https://www.federalreserve.gov/econres/notes/feds-notes
/disparities-in-wealth-by-race-and-ethnicity-in-the-2019-survey-of
-consumer-finances-20200928.htm.

Bhutta, Neil, and Lisa Dettling. 2018. "Money in the Bank? Assessing Families'
Liquid Savings using the Survey of Consumer Finances." *FEDS Notes*, Board
of Governors of the Federal Reserve System, November 19. https://doi.org/10
.17016/2380-7172.2275.

Bhutta, Neil, Jane Dokko, and Hui Shan. 2017. "Consumer Ruthlessness and
Mortgage Default During the 2007 to 2009 Housing Bust." *Journal of
Finance* 72 (6): 2433–66.

Biggs, Andrew G., Mark Sarney, and Christopher R. Tamborini. 2009. "A
Progressivity Index for Social Security." Issue Paper no. 2009-01, Social

Security Administration, Washington, DC, January. https://www.ssa.gov /policy/docs/issuepapers/ip2009-01.html.

Biniek, Jeannie Fuglesten, Meredith Freed, Anthony Damico, and Tricia Neuman. 2023. "Half of All Eligible Medicare Beneficiaries Are Now Enrolled in Private Medicare Advantage Plans." KFF, May 1. https://www.kff.org /policy-watch/half-of-all-eligible-medicare-beneficiaries-are-now-enrolled -in-private-medicare-advantage-plans/#.

Birkenmeier, Julie, Youngmi Kim, and Brandy Maynard. 2022. "Financial Outcomes of Interventions Designed to Improve Financial Capability through Individual Development Accounts: A Systematic Review." *Journal of Evidence-Based Social Work* 19 (4): 408–39.

Biswas, Arnab, Chris Cunningham, Kristopher Gerardi, and Daniel Sexton. 2019. "Foreclosure Externalities and Vacant Property Registration Ordinances." Working Paper 2019-20, Federal Reserve Bank of Atlanta, Atlanta, GA, November. https://realestateresearch.frbatlanta.org/-/media/documents /research/publications/wp/2019/11/19/foreclosure-externalities-and-vacant -property-registration-ordinances.pdf.

Biswas, Siddhartha. 2022. *The Life-Cycle Impacts of Federal Student Loans: A Brief Literature Review.* Supervisory Research Forum. Philadelphia: Federal Reserve Bank of Philadelphia. https://www.philadelphiafed.org/ -/media/frbp/assets/institutional/banking/surf/spotlights/2022/surf_2022 _q2-spotlight.pdf.

Bivens, Josh, Melissa Boteach, Rachel Deutsch, Francisco Díez, Rebecca Dixon, Brian Galle, Alix Gould-Werth, Nicole Marquez, Lily Roberts, Heidi Shierholz, William Spriggs, and Andrew Stettner. 2021. *Reforming Unemployment Insurance.* Washington, DC: Center for American Progress et al. https://files.epi.org/uploads/Reforming-Unemployment -Insurance.pdf.

Bivens, Josh, and Heidi Shierholz. 2018. *What Labor Market Changes Have Generated Inequality and Wage Suppression?* Washington, DC: Economic Policy Institute. https://files.epi.org/pdf/148880.pdf.

Black, Sandra E., Jeffrey T. Denning, Lisa J. Dettling, Serena Goodman, and Lesley J. Turner. 2023. "Taking It to the Limit: Effects of Increased Student Loan Availability on Attainment, Earnings, and Financial Well-being." NBER Working Paper 27658, National Bureau of Economic Research, Cambridge, MA, February.

Blackman, Jonathan I., and Rahul Mukhi. 2010. "The Evolution of Modern Sovereign Debt Litigation: Vultures, Alter Egos, and Other Legal Fauna." *Law and Contemporary Problems* 73 (4): 47–61.

Blakely-Gray, Rachel. 2024. "State-Mandated Retirement Plans: Don't Get Tripped Up." Patriot Software, November 27. https://www.patriotsoftware .com/blog/payroll/state-mandated-retirement-plans/#:~:text=Massachusetts ,with%2020%20employees%20or%20fewer.

Blavin, Fredric, Michael Karpman, and Diane Amos. 2020. *With New Market-places Created by the Affordable Care Act, Is It Still Less Expensive to Service Low-Income People in Medicaid Than in Private Coverage?* New York: Robert Wood Johnson Foundation. https://www.urban.org/sites/default/files /publication/101998/with-new-marketplaces-created-by-the-affordable-care -act.pdf.

Blavin, Fredric, Michael Karpman, Genevieve M. Kenney, and Benjamin D. Sommers. 2018. "Medicaid Versus Marketplace Coverage for Near-Poor Adults: Effects on Out-of-Pocket Spending and Coverage." *Health Affairs* 37 (2): 299–307.

Bleemer, Zachary, Meta Brown, Donghoon Lee, Katherine Strair, and Wilbert van der Klaauw. 2021. "Echoes of Rising Tuition in Students' Borrowing, Education Attainment, and Homeownership in Post-recession America." *Journal of Urban Economics* 122 (March): 1–24.

Blinder, Alan S., and Mark Zandi. 2015. *The Financial Crisis: Lessons for the Next One.* Washington, DC: Center on Budget and Policy Priorities. https://www.cbpp.org/sites/default/files/atoms/files/10-15-15pf.pdf.

Blumenthal, David, Sara R. Collins, and Elizabeth J. Fowler. 2020. "The Affordable Care Act at 10 Years—Its Coverage and Access Provisions." *New England Journal of Medicine* 382 (10): 963–69.

Board of Governors of the Federal Reserve System. n.d. "Survey of Consumer Finances: 1989–2022, Interactive Chartbook." Accessed November 16, 2023. https://www.federalreserve.gov/econres/scf/dataviz/scf/chart/.

———. 2018. *Report on the Economic Well-Being of U.S. Households in 2017.* https://www.federalreserve.gov/publications/files/2017-report-economic -well-being-us-households-201805.pdf.

———. 2020a. *Report on the Economic Well-Being of U.S. Households in 2019, Featuring Supplemental Data from April 2020.* https://www.federalreserve .gov/publications/files/2019-report-economic-well-being-us-households -202005.pdf.

———. 2020b. *Update on the Economic Well-Being of U.S. Households: July 2020 Results.* https://www.federalreserve.gov/publications/files/2019-report -economic-well-being-us-households-update-202009.pdf.

———. 2021. *Report on the Economic Well-Being of U.S. Households in 2020.* https://www.federalreserve.gov/publications/files/2020-report-economic -well-being-us-households-202105.pdf.

———. 2023. *Economic Well-Being of U.S. Households in 2022.* https://www .federalreserve.gov/publications/files/2022-report-economic-well-being-us -households-202305.pdf.

———. 2024. *Economic Well-Being of U.S. Households in 2023.* https://www .federalreserve.gov/publications/files/2023-report-economic-well-being-us -households-202405.pdf.

Boatman, Angela, Brent J. Evans, and Adela Soliz. 2017. "Understanding Loan Aversion in Education: Evidence from High School Seniors, Community College Students, and Adults." *AERA Open* 3 (1): 1–16.

Boehm, Christoph, Aaron Flaaen, and Nitya Pandalai-Nayar. 2019. "A New Assessment of the Role of Offshoring in the Decline of US Manufacturing Employment." *VoxEU*, August 15. https://voxeu.org/article/offshoring-and-decline-us-manufacturing-employment.

Bogage, Jacob, Jeff Stein, and Dan Diamond. 2024. "Trump Allies Eye Overhauling Medicaid, Food Stamps in Tax Legislation." *Washington Post*, November 18, 2024. https://www.washingtonpost.com/business/2024/11/18/gop-targets-medicaid-food-stamps/.

Bologna, Giacomo. 2021. "Painful Price of Health Care: St. Dominic Knew Patients Couldn't Afford Care: It Sued Anyway." *Clarion Ledger*, August 22, 2021. https://www.clarionledger.com/story/news/local/2021/08/23/st-dominic-hospital-jackson-ms-sues-patients-medical-debt-uses-debt-collectors/5526477001/.

Bond, Tyler, and Frank Porell. 2020. *Examining the Nest Egg: The Sources of Retirement Income for Older Americans*. Washington, DC: National Institute on Retirement Security. https://www.nirsonline.org/wp-content/uploads/2020/01/Examining-the-Nest-Egg-Final-1.pdf.

Borgschulte, Mark, and Heepyung Cho. 2020. "Minimum Wages and Retirement." *ILR Review* 73 (1): 153–77.

Boshara, Ray. 2012. "From Asset Building to Balance Sheets." CSD Perspective no. 12-24, Center for Social Development, Washington University, St. Louis, MO, June. https://openscholarship.wustl.edu/cgi/viewcontent.cgi?article=1227&context=csd_research.

Bound, John, and Timothy A. Waidmann. 2010. "The Social Security Early Retirement Benefit as Safety Net." Working Paper WP 2010-240, University of Michigan Retirement Research Center, Ann Arbor, MI, October. https://deepblue.lib.umich.edu/bitstream/handle/2027.42/78357/wp240.pdf?sequence=1&isAllowed=y.

Branham, D. Keith, Christie Peters, Nandy De Lew, and Benjamin D. Sommers. 2022. *Health Insurance Deductibles among HealthCare.gov Enrollees, 2017–2021*. Issue Brief HP-2022-02. Washington, DC: Assistant Secretary for Planning and Evaluation, Office of Health Policy, US Department of Health and Human Services. https://aspe.hhs.gov/sites/default/files/documents/748153d5bd3291edef1fb5c6aa1edc3a/aspe-marketplace-deductibles.pdf.

Bricker, Jesse, Sarena Goodman, Kevin B. More, and Alice Henriques Volz. 2020. "Wealth and Income Concentration in the SCF: 1989–2019." *FEDS Notes*, Board of Governors of the Federal Reserve System, September 28. https://www.federalreserve.gov/econres/notes/feds-notes/wealth-and-income-concentration-in-the-scf-20200928.html.

Bricker, Jesse, and Jeffrey Thompson. 2016. "Does Education Loan Debt Influence Household Financial Distress? An Assessment Using the 2007–2009 Survey of Consumer Finances Panel." *Contemporary Economic Policy* 34 (4): 660–77.

Briscese, Guglielmo, Michael Levere, and Harold Pollack. 2024. *Improving Security for People with Disabilities: The Promise of ABLE Accounts.* Madison: Center for Financial Security, University of Wisconsin Madison. https://rdrc.wisc.edu/files/working-papers/WI23-10_Working-Paper_Pollack -et-al_4.24.pdf.

Broadbent, John, Michael Palumbo, and Elizabeth Woodman. 2006. "The Shift from Defined Benefit to Defined Contribution Pension Plans—Implications for Asset Association and Risk Management." Working paper, Bank for International Settlements, Basel, Switzerland. https://www.bis.org/publ /wgpapers/cgfs27broadbent3.pdf.

Broaddus, Matt, and Edwin Park. 2016. *Affordable Care Act Has Produced Historic Gains in Health Coverage.* Washington, DC: Center on Budget and Policy Priorities. https://www.cbpp.org/sites/default/files/atoms/files/12-15 -16health.pdf.

Brobeck, Stephen. 2020. *Do Big Banks Provide Affordable Access to Lower Income Savers?* Washington, DC: Consumer Federation of America. https://consumerfed.org/wp-content/uploads/2020/03/Affordable-Banking -Access-for-Low-Income-Consumers-Report.pdf.

Bronfenbrenner, Kate. 1996. *Final Report : The Effects of Plant Closing or Threat of Plant Closing on the Right of Workers to Organize.* Ithaca, NY: Cornell University. https://ecommons.cornell.edu/bitstream/handle/1813 /87617/finalreporttheeffectsofplant.pdf?sequence=1&isAllowed=y.

Brooks, Tricia, Lauren Roygardner, Samantha Artiga, Olivia Pham, and Rachel Dolan. 2020. *Medicaid and CHIP Eligibility, Enrollment, and Cost Sharing Policies as of January 2020: Findings from a 50-State Survey.* San Francisco: KFF. https://files.kff.org/attachment/Report-Medicaid-and-CHIP -Eligibility,-Enrollment-and-Cost-Sharing-Policies-as-of-January-2020.pdf.

Brown, Dorothy A. 2021. *The Whiteness of Wealth: How the Tax System Impoverishes Black Americans—And How We Can Fix It.* New York: Crown.

Brüggen, Elisabeth C., Jens Hogreve, Maria Holmlund, Sertan Kabadayi, and Martin Löfgren. 2017. "Financial Well-Being: A Conceptualization and Research Agenda." *Journal of Business Research* 79: 228–37.

Buchmueller, Thomas C., John DiNardo, and Robert G. Valletta. 1999. "Union Effects on Health Insurance Provision and Coverage in the United States." Working paper, Federal Reserve Bank of San Francisco, San Francisco, CA. https://www.frbsf.org/economic-research/files/wp00-04.pdf.

Bureau of Consumer Financial Protection. 2019. *Ability-to-Repay and Qualified Mortgage Rule Assessment Report.* https://s3.amazonaws.com/files.consumer

finance.gov/f/documents/cfpb_ability-to-repay-qualified-mortgage
_assessment-report.pdf.

Burkhalter, Kyle, and Chris Chaplain. 2023. *Replacement Rates for Hypothetical Retired Workers.* Actuarial Note no. 2023.9. Baltimore, MD: Social Security Administration. https://www.ssa.gov/OACT/NOTES/ran9/an2023-9.pdf.

Burman, Leonard E., and Troy Kravitz. 2004. "Lower-Income Households Spend Largest Share of Income." *Tax Notes* 105 (7): 875.

Butrica, Barbara A., Howard M. Iams, Karen E. Smith, and Eric J. Toder. 2009. "The Disappearing Defined Benefit Pension and Its Potential Impact on the Retirement Incomes of Baby Boomers." *Social Security Bulletin* 69 (3): 1–27.

Callis, Robert R. 2023. "Rate of Homeownership Higher Than Before Pandemic in All Regions." *America Counts: Stories.* U.S. Census Bureau, July 25. https://www.census.gov/library/stories/2023/07/younger-householders
-drove-rebound-in-homeownership.html.

Calnitsky, David. 2016. "'More Normal Than Welfare': The Mincome Experiment, Stigma, and Community Experience." *Canadian Review of Sociology* 53 (1): 26–71.

CalSavers Retirement Savings Program. n.d. "Welcome to CalSavers." Accessed November 17, 2023. https://employer.calsavers.com/?language=en#.

Campbell, John Y., and João F. Cocco. 2015. "A Model of Mortgage Default." *Journal of Finance* 70 (4): 1495–1554.

CAP Action. 2023. "13 Years Later: The Affordable Care Act's Enduring Legacy." Center for American Progress Action, March 20. https://www.american
progressaction.org/article/13-years-later-the-affordable-care-acts-enduring
-legacy/.

Card, David, and Alan B. Krueger. 1994. "Minimum Wages and Employment: A Case Study of the Fast-Food Industry in New Jersey and Pennsylvania." *American Economic Review* 84 (4): 772–93.

———. 1998. "A Reanalysis of the Effect of the New Jersey Minimum Wage Increase on the Fast-Food Industry with Representative Payroll Data." NBER Working Paper 6386, National Bureau of Economic Research, Cambridge, MA, January.

———. 2016. *Myth and Measurement: The New Economics of the Minimum Wage.* 20th anniv. ed. Princeton, NJ: Princeton University Press.

Carroll, Aaron E. 2019. "Even a Modest Co-Payment Can Cause People to Skip Drug Doses." *New York Times,* November 11, 2019. https://www.nytimes.com
/2019/11/11/upshot/drugs-cost-diabetes.html.

———. 2022. "What's Wrong with Health Insurance? Deductibles Are Ridiculous, for Starters." *New York Times,* July 7, 2022. https://www.nytimes.com
/2022/07/07/opinion/medical-debt-health-care-cost.html.

Case, Anne, and Angus Deaton. 2020. *Deaths of Despair and the Future of Capitalism.* Princeton, NJ: Princeton University Press.

Center for Hunger-Free Communities. 2021. *Minimum Wage Is Not Enough: A True Living Wage Is Necessary to Reduce Poverty and Improve Health. Policy Brief.* Philadelphia: Drexel University. https://drexel.edu/~/media /Files/hunger-free-center/research-briefs/wage-brief-2021.ashx.

Center for Retirement Initiatives. n.d. "State Program Performance Data." Georgetown University. Accessed July 16, 2024. https://cri.georgetown.edu /states/state-data/current-year/#.

Center on Budget and Policy Priorities. 2020. *Policy Basics: Introduction to Medicaid.* https://www.cbpp.org/sites/default/files/atoms/files/policybasics -medicaid_0.pdf.

———. 2021. *Policy Basics: Unemployment Insurance.* https://www.cbpp.org /sites/default/files/atoms/files/policybasic_introtoui.pdf.

———. 2022. *Year-End Tax Policy Priority: Expand the Child Tax Credit for the 19 Million Children Who Receive Less Than the Full Credit.* https://www.cbpp .org/sites/default/files/11-15-22tax.pdf.

———. 2023. *A Quick Guide to SNAP Eligibility and Benefits.* https://www.cbpp .org/sites/default/files/11-18-08fa.pdf.

———. 2024. *Top Ten Facts about Social Security.* https://www.cbpp.org/sites /default/files/atoms/files/8-8-16socsec.pdf.

Centers for Medicare & Medicaid Services. n.d.-a. "CMS Program Statistics— Medicare Total Enrollment." Accessed August 29, 2023. https://data.cms.gov /summary-statistics-on-beneficiary-enrollment/medicare-and-medicaid -reports/cms-program-statistics-medicare-total-enrollment.

———. n.d.-b. "CMS Program Statistics—Medicare Part D Enrollment." Accessed August 29, 2023. https://data.cms.gov/summary-statistics-on-beneficiary -enrollment/medicare-and-medicaid-reports/cms-program-statistics -medicare-part-d-enrollment.

———. 2024. "2025 Medicare Parts A&B Premiums and Deductibles." November 8. https://www.cms.gov/newsroom/fact-sheets/2025-medicare-parts-b -premiums-and-deductibles.

Chakrabarti, Rajashri, William Nober, and Wilbert van der Klaauw. 2020. "Measuring Racial Disparities in Higher Education and Student Debt Outcomes." *Liberty Street Economics* (blog), Federal Reserve Bank of New York, July 8. https://libertystreeteconomics.newyorkfed.org/2020/07/measuring -racial-disparities-in-higher-education-and-student-debt-outcomes/.

Chalmers, John, Olivia S. Mitchell, Jonathan Reuter, and Mingli Zhong. 2021. "Auto-Enrollment Retirement Plans for the People: Choices and Outcomes in OregonSaves." NBER Working Paper 28469, National Bureau of Economic Research, Cambridge, MA, February.

Chandra, Amitabh, Evan Flack, and Ziad Obermeyer. 2023. "The Health Costs of Cost Sharing." NBER Working Paper 28439, National Bureau of Economic Research, Cambridge, MA, April.

Charles, Kerwin Kofi, Erik Hurst, and Mariel Schwartz. 2018. "The Transformation of Manufacturing and the Decline in U.S. Employment." NBER Working Paper 24468, National Bureau of Economic Research, Cambridge, MA, March.

Chetty, Raj, and Amy Finkelstein. 2013. "Social Insurance: Connecting Theory to Data." In *Handbook of Public Economics,* edited by Alan Auerbach, Raj Chetty, Martin Feldstein, and Emmanuel Saez, 5:111–93. Amsterdam: Elsevier B.V.

Chetty, Raj, Nathaniel Hendren, Maggie R. Jones, and Sonya R. Porter. 2019. "Race and Economic Opportunity in the United States: An Intergenerational Perspective." *Quarterly Journal of Economics* 135 (2): 711–83.

Chetty, Raj, Michael Stepner, Sarah Abraham, Shelby Lin, Benjamin Scuderi, Nicholas Turner, Augustin Bergeron, and David Cutler. 2016. "The Association Between Income and Life Expectancy in the United States, 2001–2014." *JAMA* 315 (16): 1750–66.

Choi, James, David Laibson, Brigitte Madrian, and Andrew Metrick. 2001. "Defined Contribution Pensions: Plan Rules, Participant Decisions, and the Path of Least Resistance." NBER Working Paper 8655, National Bureau of Economic Research, Cambridge, MA.

———. 2002. "For Better or for Worse: Default Effects and 401(k) Savings Behavior." PRC WP 2002-2, Pension Research Council, Philadelphia, PA.

Choi, Jung Hyan, Alanna McCargo, Michael Neal, Laurie Goodman, and Caitlin Young. 2019. *Explaining the Black-White Homeownership Gap.* Washington, DC: Urban Institute. https://www.urban.org/sites/default/files/publication /101160/explaining_the_black-white_homeownership_gap_2.pdf.

Clausing, Kimberly. 2017. "Labor and Capital in the Global Economy." *Democracy,* no. 43. https://democracyjournal.org/magazine/43/labor-and-capital -in-the-global-economy/.

Claxton, Gary, Cynthia Cox, Anthony Damico, Larry Levitt, and Karen Pollitz. 2016. *Pre-existing Conditions and Medical Underwriting in the Individual Insurance Market Prior to the ACA.* San Francisco: Kaiser Family Foundation. https://www.kff.org/health-reform/issue-brief/pre-existing-conditions-and -medical-underwriting-in-the-individual-insurance-market-prior-to-the-aca/.

Clingman, Michael, Kyle Burkhalter, and Chris Chaplain. 2020. *Replacement Rates for Hypothetical Retired Workers.* Actuarial Note no. 2020.9. Baltimore, MD: Social Security Administration. https://www.ssa.gov/oact/NOTES/ran9 /an2020-9.pdf.

CMS.gov. 2022. *Health Coverage Options for Immigrants.* https://marketplace.cms .gov/technical-assistance-resources/health-coverage-options-immigrants.pdf.

———. 2023. "K & L Out-of-Pocket Limits Announcements." October. https:// www.cms.gov/medicare/health-drug-plans/medigap/k-l-out-of-pocket -limits-announcements.

————. 2024a. *Health Insurance Marketplaces 2024 Open Enrollment Report.* https://www.cms.gov/files/document/health-insurance-exchanges-2024 -open-enrollment-report-final.pdf.

————. 2024b. "Incarcerated Medicare Beneficiaries." February 8. https://www .cms.gov/outreach-education/incarcerated-medicare-beneficiaries#:~:text= Individuals%20who%20are%20incarcerated%20when,benefits%20while %20they're%20incarcerated.

Coile, Courtney. 2015. "Economic Determinants of Workers' Retirement Decisions." *Journal of Economic Surveys* 29 (4): 830–53.

————. 2018. "Working Longer in the U.S.: Trends and Explanations." NBER Working Paper 24576, National Bureau of Economic Research, Cambridge, MA.

Coile, Courtney, Kevin Milligan, and David A. Wise. 2017. "Health Capacity to Work at Older Ages: Evidence from the United States." In *Social Security Programs and Retirement around the World: the Capacity to Work at Older Ages,* edited by David A. Wise, 359–94. Chicago: University of Chicago Press.

————. 2019. Introduction to *Social Security Programs and Retirement around the World: Working Longer,* edited by Courtney Coile, Kevin Milligan, and David A. Wise, 1–32. Chicago: University of Chicago Press.

Coile, Courtney, and Susan Stewart. 2021. "Retirement Incentives and Behavior of Private and Public Sector Workers." *Journal of Pension Economics and Finance* 20 (3): 393–409.

CollegeBoard. 2020. *Trends in Student Aid 2019.* https://research.collegeboard .org/pdf/trends-student-aid-2019-full-report.pdf.

————. 2021. *Trends in College Pricing and Student Aid 2021.* https://research .collegeboard.org/media/pdf/trends-college-pricing-student-aid-2021.pdf.

————. 2022. *Trends in College Pricing and Student Aid 2022.* https://research .collegeboard.org/media/pdf/trends-in-college-pricing-student-aid-2022.pdf.

————. 2024. *Trends in College Pricing and Student Aid 2024.* https://research .collegeboard.org/media/pdf/Trends-in-College-Pricing-and-Student-Aid -2024-ADA.pdf.

Collins, J. Michael, and Katie Lorenze. 2020. "Achieving Financial Resilience in the Face of Financial Setbacks." Working paper, Asset Funders Network, Chicago, IL.

Collins, Sara R., Lauren A. Haynes, and Relebohile Masitha. 2022. *The State of U.S. Health Insurance in 2022.* New York: The Commonwealth Fund. https:// www.commonwealthfund.org/sites/default/files/2022-09/Collins_state_of _coverage_biennial_survey_2022_db.pdf.

Congressional Budget Office. 2010. *Policies for Increasing Economic Growth and Employment in the Short Term.* https://www.cbo.gov/publication/25031.

————. 2015. *Social Security Policy Options, 2015.* https://www.cbo.gov /publication/51011#:~:text=The%20program%20has%20two%20parts ,workers%20reach%20the%20age%20at.

————. 2019. "Social Security Replacement Rates and Other Benefit Measures: An In-Depth Analysis." Publication no. 55038. April. https://www.cbo.gov/system/files/2019-04/55038-SSReplacementRates.pdf.

————. 2020. *Income-Driven Repayment Plans for Student Loans: Budgetary Costs and Policy Options*. Publication no. 55968. February. https://www.cbo.gov/system/files/2020-02/55968-CBO-IDRP.pdf.

————. 2023. *The Budgetary and Economic Effects of S. 2488, the Raise the Wage Act of 2023*. https://www.cbo.gov/system/files/2023-12/The_Budgetary_and_Economic_Effects_of_S.%202488_the_Raise_the_Wage_Act_of_2023_1.pdf.

————. 2024. *Health Insurance and Its Federal Subsidies: CBO and JCT's June 2024 Baseline Projections*. https://www.cbo.gov/system/files/2024-06/51298-2024-06-healthinsurance.pdf.

Congressional Research Service. 2020. *Individual Retirement Account (IRA) Ownership Status: Data and Policy Issues*. CRS Report, R46635. December 9. https://sgp.fas.org/crs/misc/R46635.pdf.

————. 2021a. "A Visual Depiction of the Shift from Defined Benefit (DB) to Defined Contribution (DC) Pension Plans in the Private Sector." *In Focus*, December 27. https://crsreports.congress.gov/product/pdf/IF/IF12007.

————. 2021b. *Social Security: Minimum Benefits*. CRS Report, R43615. June 15. https://crsreports.congress.gov/product/pdf/R/R43615/35.

————. 2021c. *The Growing Gap in Life Expectancy by Income: Recent Evidence and Implications for the Social Security Retirement Age*. CRS Report, R44846. July 6. https://sgp.fas.org/crs/misc/R44846.pdf.

————. 2022a. *State Minimum Wages: An Overview*. CRS Report, R43792. September 2. https://sgp.fas.org/crs/misc/R43792.pdf.

————. 2022b. *The Earned Income Tax Credit (EITC): Legislative History*. CRS Report, R44825. April 28. https://sgp.fas.org/crs/misc/R44825.pdf.

————. 2022c. *The Supplemental Nutrition Assistance Program (SNAP): Categorical Eligibility*. CRS Report, R42054. February 25. https://sgp.fas.org/crs/misc/R42054.pdf.

————. 2023. *The Earned Income Tax Credit (EITC): How It Works and Who Receives It*. CRS Report, R43805. November 14. https://crsreports.congress.gov/product/pdf/R/R43805.

Consumer Financial Protection Bureau. 2015a. *Financial Well-Being: The Goal of Financial Education*. https://files.consumerfinance.gov/f/201501_cfpb_report_financial-well-being.pdf.

————. 2015b. *Snapshot of Reverse Mortgage Complaints: December 2011–December 2014*. https://files.consumerfinance.gov/f/201502_cfpb_report_snapshot-reverse-mortgage-complaints-december-2011-2014.pdf.

————. 2015c. *Your Home Loan Toolkit*. https://files.consumerfinance.gov/f/201503_cfpb_your-home-loan-toolkit-web.pdf.

————. 2017. *Issue Brief: The Costs and Risks of Using a Reverse Mortgage to Delay Collecting Social Security*. https://files.consumerfinance.gov/f

/documents/201708_cfpb_costs-and-risks-of-using-reverse-mortgage-to
-delay-collecting-ss.pdf.
———. 2020a. *Evidence-Based Strategies to Build Emergency Savings.*
https://files.consumerfinance.gov/f/documents/cfpb_evidence-based
-strategies-build-emergency-savings_report_2020-07.pdf.
———. 2020b. *Market Snapshot: First Time Homebuyers.* https://files.consumer
finance.gov/f/documents/cfpb_market-snapshot-first-time-homebuyers
_report.pdf.
———. 2021a. *Supervisory Highlights: COVID-19 Prioritized Assessments
Special Edition*, no. 23.
———. 2021b. *Supervisory Highlights*, no. 24.
———. 2021c. *Supervisory Highlights*, no. 25.
———. 2022a. "CFPB Acts to Protect the Public from Black-Box Credit Models
Using Complex Algorithms." Press release, May 26. https://www
.consumerfinance.gov/about-us/newsroom/cfpb-acts-to-protect-the-public
-from-black-box-credit-models-using-complex-algorithms/.
———. 2022b. *Medical Debt Burden in the United States.* https://files.consumer
finance.gov/f/documents/cfpb_medical-debt-burden-in-the-united-states
_report_2022-03.pdf.
———. 2022c. *Supervisory Highlights*, no. 28.
———. 2023a. "Have Medical Debt? Anything Already Paid or under $500
Should No Longer Be on Your Credit Report." Blog, May 8. https://www
.consumerfinance.gov/about-us/blog/medical-debt-anything-already-paid
-or-under-500-should-no-longer-be-on-your-credit-report/.
———. 2023b. *Supervisory Highlights: Junk Fees Special Edition*, no. 29.
———. 2024. "Prohibition on Creditors and Consumer Reporting Agencies
Concerning Medical Information." *Federal Register* 89 (118): 51682–736.
Cooper, Daniel, and J. Christina Wang. 2014. *Student Loan Debt and Economic
Outcomes.* Current Policy Perspectives no. 14-7. Boston: Federal Reserve
Bank of Boston. https://www.bostonfed.org/publications/current-policy
-perspectives/2014/student-loan-debt-and-economic-outcomes.aspx.
Cooper, David. 2019. "Congress Has Never Let the Federal Minimum Wage
Erode for This Long." *Economic Snapshot.* Economic Policy Institute,
June 17. https://www.epi.org/publication/congress-has-never-let-the-federal
-minimum-wage-erode-for-this-long/.
Copeland, Craig. 2019. "Current Population Survey: Checking In on the Retire-
ment Plan Participant and Retiree Income Estimates." EBRI Issue Brief
no. 483. Employee Benefit Research Institute, May 30. https://www.ebri.org
/docs/default-source/ebri-issue-brief/ebri_ib_483_retplans-30may19.pdf
?sfvrsn=6fb03f2f_16.
Cosic, Damir, and C. Eugene Steuerle. 2021. *The Effect of Early Claiming Benefit
Reduction on Retirement Rates.* CRR WP 2021-1. Chestnut Hill, MA: Center

for Retirement Research. https://crr.bc.edu/wp-content/uploads/2021/01/wp
_2021-1.pdf.

Council of Economic Advisers. 2016. *Investing in Higher Education: Benefits, Challenges, and the State of Student Debt.* https://obamawhitehouse.archives
.gov/sites/default/files/page/files/20160718_cea_student_debt.pdf.

Courtemanche, Charles, James Marton, Benjamin Ukert, Aaron Yelowitz, and Daniela Zapata. 2018. "Effects of the Affordable Care Act on Health Care Access and Self-Assessed Health After 3 Years." *Journal of Health Care Organization, Provision, and Financing* 55 (1): 1–10.

———. 2020. "The Impact of the Affordable Care Act on Health Care Access and Self-Assessed Health in the Trump Era (2017–2018)." *Health Services Research* 55, supp. 2: 841–50.

Cowley, Stacy. 2023. "How Millions of Borrowers Got $127 Billion in Student Loans Canceled." *New York Times*, November 11, 2023. https://www.nytimes
.com/2023/11/11/business/student-loans-debt-cancellation.html.

Cox, Cynthia. 2024. "What Trump's 2024 Victory Means for the Affordable Care Act." KFF, November 6. https://www.kff.org/quick-take/what-trumps-2024
-victory-means-for-the-affordable-care-act/.

Cox, Cynthia, Karen Pollitz, Krutika Amin, and Jared Ortaliza. 2022. "Nine Changes to Watch in ACA Open Enrollment 2023." KFF, October 27. https://
www.kff.org/policy-watch/nine-changes-to-watch-in-open-enrollment-2023/.

Cubanski, Juliette, Wyatt Koma, Anthony Damico, and Tricia Neuman. 2019. "How Much Do Medicare Beneficiaries Spend Out of Pocket on Health Care?" Issue Brief, KFF, November 4. https://www.kff.org/medicare/issue-brief/how
-much-do-medicare-beneficiaries-spend-out-of-pocket-on-health-care/.

Cubanski, Juliette, Tricia Neuman, and Gretchen Jacobson. 2016. "Modifying Medicare's Benefit Design: What's the Impact on Beneficiaries and Spending?" KFF, June 29. https://www.kff.org/medicare/report/modifying
-medicares-benefit-design-whats-the-impact-on-beneficiaries-and-spending
/view/print/#:~:text=Proposals%20to%20modify%20Medicare's%20benefit
,by%20employers%20who%20provide%20supplemental.

Dague, Laura, Marguerite Burns, and Donna Friedsam. 2022. "The Line between Medicaid and Marketplace: Coverage Effects from Wisconsin's Partial Expansion." *Journal of Health Politics, Policy and Law* 47 (3): 293–318.

Dannenberg, Michael, and Konrad Mugglestone. 2018. *No Commencement in the Commonwealth: How Massachusetts' Higher Education System Undermines Mobility for Latinos and Others & What We Can Do About It.* Washington, DC: Education Reform Now. https://edreformnow.org/wp
-content/uploads/2018/05/ERN-No-Commencement-in-the-Commonwealth
-WEB.pdf.

Day, John G. 2015. "The Patient Protection and Affordable Care Act: What Does It Really Do?" *Connecticut Insurance Law Journal* 22 (1): 121–69.

Denning, Jeffrey T., Benjamin M. Marx, and Lesley J. Turner. 2019. "ProPelled: The Effects of Grants on Graduation, Earnings, and Welfare." *American Economic Journal: Applied Economics* 11 (3): 193–224.

Despard, Mathieu R., Dana Perantie, Samuel Taylor, Michel Grinstein-Weiss, Terri Friedline, and Ramesh Raghavan. 2016. "Student Debt and Hardship: Evidence from a Large Sample of Low- and Moderate-Income Households." *Children and Youth Services Review* 70: 8–18.

Dettling, Lisa, Sarena Goodman, and Sarah Reber. 2022. *Saving and Wealth Accumulation among Student Loan Borrowers: Implications for Retirement Preparedness.* Finance and Economics Discussion Series 2022-019. Washington, DC: Board of Governors of the Federal Reserve System. https://www.federalreserve.gov/econres/feds/files/2022019pap.pdf.

Di Maggio, Marco, Ankit Kalda, and Vincent Yao. 2020. "Second Chance: Life without Student Debt." NBER Working Paper 25810, National Bureau of Economic Research, Cambridge, MA.

Di Maggio, Marco, and Amit Kermani. 2016. "The Importance of Unemployment Insurance as an Automatic Stabilizer." Harvard Business School Working Paper 17-009, Harvard Business School, Boston, MA.

Diamond, Peter. 2023. "Fixing Social Security: The Politics of Reform in a Polarized Age." *Business Economics* 58 (2): 121–24.

Diamond, Peter A., and Peter R. Orszag. 2004. *Saving Social Security: A Balanced Approach.* Washington, DC: Brookings Institution Press.

Dickerson, Mechele. 2014. *Homeownership and America's Financial Underclass: Flawed Premises, Broken Promises, New Prescriptions.* Cambridge: Cambridge University Press.

Ding, Jaimie, and Ronald D. White. 2022. "Retirement Is a Lot Harder Now: Here's How People Are Making It Work." *Los Angeles Times*, September 29, 2022. https://www.latimes.com/business/story/2022-09-29/people-share -their-retirement-401k-social-security-stories.

Doran, Michael. 2022. "The Great American Retirement Fraud." *Elder Law Journal* 30 (2): 265–347.

Doty, Michelle M., Sara R. Collins, Jennifer L. Nicholson, and Sheila D. Rustgi. 2009. *Failure to Protect: Why the Individual Insurance Market Is Not a Viable Option for Most U.S. Families.* Issue Brief 62. The Commonwealth Fund no. 1300. https://www.commonwealthfund.org/sites/default/files /documents/___media_files_publications_issue_brief_2009_jul_failure _to_protect_1300_doty_failure_to_protect_individual_ins_market_ib _v2.pdf.

Douglas-Gabriel, Danielle. 2024. "The Uncertain Future of Biden's Student Loan Repayment Plan, Explained." *Washington Post*, August 28, 2024. https://www.washingtonpost.com/nation/2024/06/25/save-plan-biden -student-loan-repayment-explained/.

Dreier, Peter, Saqib Bhatti, Rob Call, Alex Schwartz, and Gregory Squires. 2014. *Underwater America: How the So-Called Housing "Recovery" Is Bypassing Many American Communities.* Berkeley, CA: Haas Institute for a Fair and Inclusive Society. https://haasinstitute.berkeley.edu/sites/default/files/haasinsitute_underwateramerica_publish_0.pdf.

Dube, Arindrajit. 2021. *A Plan to Reform the Unemployment Insurance System in the United States.* Policy Proposal 2021-03. Washington, DC: The Hamilton Project, Brookings. https://www.brookings.edu/wp-content/uploads/2021/04/Unemplyment-InsurancePP-v4.2-1.pdf.

Dubina, Kevin S. 2023. "Labor Force and Macroeconomic Projections Overview and Highlights, 2022-32." *Monthly Labor Review* (September). https://www.bls.gov/opub/mlr/2023/article/labor-force-and-macroeconomic-projections.htm#:~:text=Decreasing%20rates%20of%20labor%20oforce,percent%20over%20the%20same%20period.

Dushi, Irena, Howard M. Iams, and Brad Trenkamp. 2017. "The Importance of Social Security Benefits to the Income of the Aged Population." *Social Security Bulletin* 77 (2): 1–24.

Dushi, Irena, and Brad Trenkamp. 2021. "Improving the Measurement of Retirement Income of the Aged Population." ORES Working Paper Series no. 116, Social Security Administration, Washington, DC.

Dynan, Karen, Douglas Elmendorf, and Daniel Sichel. 2012. "The Evolution of Household Income Volatility." *B.E. Journal of Economic Analysis & Policy* 12 (2): article 3.

Dynarski, Susan. 2005. *High-Income Families Benefit Most from New Education Savings Incentives.* Tax Policy Issues and Options Brief no. 9. Urban-Brookings Tax Policy Center. https://www.urban.org/sites/default/files/publication/51791/411147-High-Income-Families-Benefit-Most-from-New-Education-Savings-Incentives.PDF.

Dynarski, Susan, Lindsay C. Page, and Judith Scott-Clayton. 2022. "College Costs, Financial Aid, and Student Decisions." NBER Working Paper 30275, National Bureau of Economic Research, Cambridge, MA.

Eastman, Scott. 2019. "How Many Taxpayers Itemize Under Current Law?" The Tax Foundation blog, September 12. https://taxfoundation.org/standard-deduction-itemized-deductions-current-law-2019/.

Economic Policy Institute. 2022. "The Productivity-Pay Gap." October. https://www.epi.org/productivity-pay-gap/.

Elengold, Kate Sablonsky, Jess Dorrance, Amanda Martinez, Patricia Foxen, and Paul Mihas. 2021. *Dreams Interrupted: A Mixed-Methods Research Project Exploring Latino College Completion.* Chapel Hill: University of North Carolina at Chapel Hill and UNIDOS US. https://unidosus.org/wp-content/uploads/2021/09/unidosus_unc_dreaminterrupted.pdf.

Elliott, William, Michal Grinstein-Weiss, and Ilsung Nam. 2013. "Student Debt and Declining Retirement Savings." CSD Working Paper no. 13-34, Center for Social Development, Washington University, St. Louis, MO.

Elul, Ronel, Nicholas S. Souleles, Souphala Chomsisengphet, Dennis Glennon, and Robert Hunt. 2010. "What 'Triggers' Mortgage Default?" Working Paper no. 10-13, Research Department, Federal Reserve Bank of Philadelphia, Philadelphia, PA, April.

Emmons, William R., Ana H. Kent, and Lowell R. Ricketts. 2019. "Is College Still Worth It? The New Calculus of Falling Returns." *Federal Reserve Bank of St. Louis Review* 101 (4): 297–329.

Employee Benefit Research Institute. 2019. *2019 Retirement Confidence Survey Summary Report.* https://www.ebri.org/docs/default-source/rcs/2019-rcs /2019-rcs-short-report.pdf.

———. 2023. *2023 Retirement Confidence Survey.* https://www.ebri.org/docs /default-source/rcs/2023-rcs/2023-rcs-short-report.pdf.

Engel, Kathleen C., and Patricia A. McCoy. 2011. *The Subprime Virus: Reckless Credit, Regulatory Failure, and Next Steps.* New York: Oxford University Press.

Fannie Mae. n.d. "Retention Options." Accessed May 20, 2023. https://single family.fanniemae.com/servicing/retention-options.

Farber, Henry S. 2017. "Employment, Hours, and Earnings Consequences of Job Loss: US Evidence from the Displaced Workers Survey." *Journal of Labor Economics* 35 (S1): S235–72.

Farrell, Diana, Kanav Bhagat, and Chen Zhao. 2018. *Falling Behind: Bank Data on the Role of Income and Savings in Mortgage Default.* New York: JPMorgan Chase & Co. Institute. https://www.jpmorganchase.com/content /dam/jpmc/jpmorgan-chase-and-co/institute/pdf/insight-income-shocks -mortgage-default.pdf.

Federal Deposit Insurance Corporation. 2022. *2021: FDIC National Survey of Unbanked and Underbanked Households.* https://www.fdic.gov/analysis /household-survey/2021report.pdf.

Federal Housing Administration. 2024. *Fiscal Year 2024 Annual Report to Congress Regarding the Financial Status of the Federal Housing Administration Mutual Mortgage Insurance Fund.* https://www.hud.gov/sites/dfiles /Housing/documents/2024FHAAnnualReportMMIFund.pdf.

Federal Interagency Forum on Aging-Related Statistics. 2016. *Older Americans 2016: Key Indicators of Well-Being.* https://agingstats.gov/docs/LatestReport /Older-Americans-2016-Key-Indicators-of-WellBeing.pdf.

———. 2020. *Older Americans 2020: Key Indicators of Well-Being.* https://aging stats.gov/docs/LatestReport/OA20_508_10142020.pdf.

Federal Reserve Bank of New York. 2023. *Quarterly Report on Household Debt and Credit, 2023: Q3.* https://www.newyorkfed.org/medialibrary/interactives /householdcredit/data/pdf/HHDC_2023Q3.

Federal Reserve Bank of St. Louis. 2018. "The Rise of the Service Economy." FRED. https://fredblog.stlouisfed.org/2018/08/the-rise-of-the-service-economy/.

——. 2023a. "Homeownership Rates by Race and Ethnicity: Black Alone in the United States." FRED. https://fred.stlouisfed.org/series/BOAAAHORUS Q156N.

——. 2023b. "Homeownership Rates by Race and Ethnicity: Hispanic (of Any Race) in the United States." FRED. https://fred.stlouisfed.org/series /HOLHORUSQ156N.

——. 2023c. "Homeownership Rates by Race and Ethnicity: Non-Hispanic White Alone in the United States." FRED. https://fred.stlouisfed.org/series /NHWAHORUSQ156N.

——. 2023d. "S&P/Case-Shiller U.S. National Home Price Index." FRED. https://fred.stlouisfed.org/series/CSUSHPINSA.

——. 2024a. "Financial Soundness Indicator, Households; Debt as a Percent of Gross Domestic Product, Level." FRED. https://fred.stlouisfed.org/series /BOGZ1FL010000336Q.

——. 2024b. "Financial Soundness Indicator, Households; Debt Service and Principal Payments as a Percent of Income, Level." FRED.https://fred.stlouis fed.org/series/BOGZ1FL010000346Q.

——. 2024c. "Total Households." FRED. https://fred.stlouisfed.org/series /TTLHH.

Federal Student Aid. n.d.-a. "COVID-19 Emergency Relief and Federal Student Aid." Accessed October 3, 2023. https://studentaid.gov/announcements -events/covid-19.

——. n.d.-b. "Direct Subsidized and Direct Unsubsidized Loans." Accessed June 25, 2024. https://studentaid.gov/understand-aid/types/loans /subsidized-unsubsidized#interest-rates.

——. n.d.-c. "Federal Student Loan Portfolio." Accessed July 12, 2024. https:// studentaid.gov/data-center/student/portfolio.

——. n.d.-d. "If Your Federal Student Loan Payments Are High Compared to Your Income, You May Want to Repay Your Loans under an Income-Driven Repayment Plan." Accessed October 11, 2023. https://studentaid.gov/manage -loans/repayment/plans/income-driven.

——. n.d.-e. "The U.S. Department of Education Offers Low-Interest Loans to Eligible Students to Help Cover the Cost of College or Career School." Accessed September 14, 2023. https://studentaid.gov/understand-aid/types /loans/subsidized-unsubsidized.

——. n.d.-f. "What Schools Are Eligible for Federal Student Aid?" Accessed September 14, 2023. https://studentaid.gov/help-center/answers/article /schools-eligible-federal-student-aid.

——. 2022. "(GEN-22-04) REVISED 2022–2023 Federal Pell Grant Payment and Disbursement Schedules." Dear Colleague Letter GEN-22-04. March 24.

https://fsapartners.ed.gov/knowledge-center/library/dear-colleague-letters
/2022-03-24/revised-2022-2023-federal-pell-grant-payment-and
-disbursement-schedules#:~:text=117%2D103).,increase%20from%205
%2C846%20to%206%2C206.

———. 2024. "(GEN-24-01) 2024–2025 Federal Pell Grant Maximum and
Minimum Award Amounts." Dear Colleague Letter GEN-24-01. April 5.
https://fsapartners.ed.gov/knowledge-center/library/dear-colleague-letters
/2024-01-31/2024-2025-federal-pell-grant-maximum-and-minimum-award
-amounts-updated-april-5-2024.

Fernandes, Daniel, John G. Lynch Jr., and Richard G. Netemeyer. 2014. "Financial Literacy, Financial Education, and Downstream Financial Behaviors."
Management Science 60 (8): 1861–83.

Fidelity. 2024. "How Much Do I Need to Retire?" February 15. https://www
.fidelity.com/viewpoints/retirement/how-much-do-i-need-to-retire.

Fidelity Investments. 2023. *Building Financial Futures, Q3 2023.* https://www
.fidelityworkplace.com/s/page-resource?cId=Q3_2023_building_financial
_futures_report.

Fiedler, Matthew. 2022. "Eliminating Small Marketplace Premiums Could
Meaningfully Increase Insurance Coverage." USC Schaeffer and Brookings,
June 29. https://www.brookings.edu/articles/eliminating-small-marketplace
-premiums-could-meaningfully-increase-insurance-coverage/.

FINRA Investor Education Foundation. 2019. *The State of U.S. Financial
Capability: The 2018 National Financial Capability Study.* https://finra
foundation.org/sites/finrafoundation/files/NFCS-2018-Report-Natl
-Findings.pdf.

Fisher, Jonathan, David Johnson, Jonathan P. Latner, Timothy Smeeding, and
Jeffrey Thompson. 2016. "Inequality and Mobility Using Income, Consumption, and Wealth for the Same Individuals." *RSF: The Russell Sage Foundation Journal of the Social Sciences* 2 (6): 44–58.

Fleischer, Miranda Perry, and Daniel Hemel. 2020. "The Architecture of a Basic
Income." *University of Chicago Law Review* 87 (3): 625–710.

Forman, Jonathan Barry, and Michael J. Sabin. 2015. "Tontine Pensions." *University of Pennsylvania Law Review* 163 (3): 755–831.

Foster, Chester, and Robert Van Order. 1984. "An Option-Based Model of Mortgage Default." *Housing Finance Review* 3 (4): 351–72.

Fox, Liana. 2020. *The Supplemental Poverty Measure: 2019.* Current Population Reports no. P60-272. Washington, DC: US Census Bureau. https://
www.census.gov/content/dam/Census/library/publications/2020/demo/p60
-272.pdf.

Freddie Mac. n.d. "Flex Modification." Accessed May 20, 2023. https://sf
.freddiemac.com/working-with-us/servicing/products-programs/freddie
-mac-flex-modification.

Freed, Meredith, Jeannie Fuglesten Biniek, Anthony Damico, and Tricia Neuman. 2022. "Medicare Advantage in 2022: Premiums, Out-of-Pocket Limits, Cost Sharing, Supplemental Benefits, Prior Authorization, and Star Ratings." KFF, August 25. https://www.kff.org/medicare/issue-brief /medicare-advantage-in-2022-premiums-out-of-pocket-limits-cost-sharing -supplemental-benefits-prior-authorization-and-star-ratings/.

Freeman, Richard B. 2013. "Failing the Test? The Flexible U.S. Job Market in the Great Recession." *Annals of the American Academy of Political and Social Science* 650 (1): 78–97.

Friedberg, Leora, and Anthony Webb. 2003. "Retirement and the Evolution of Pension Structures." NBER Working Paper 9999, National Bureau of Economic Research, Cambridge, MA, September.

———. 2009. "New Evidence on the Labor Supply Effects of the Social Security Earnings Test." *Tax Policy and the Economy* 23 (1): 1–36.

Frolik, Lawrence A. 2014. "Rethinking ERISA's Promise of Income Security in a World of 401(k) Plans." *Connecticut Insurance Law Journal* 20 (2): 371–403.

Fullerton, Don, and Nirupama Rao. 2019. "The Life Cycle of the 47 Percent." *National Tax Journal* 72 (2): 359–96.

Furman, Jason. 2020. *US Unemployment Insurance in the Pandemic and Beyond.* Policy Brief 20-10. Peterson Institute for International Economics, July. https://www.piie.com/publications/policy-briefs/us-unemployment -insurance-pandemic-and-beyond.

Gale, William G., Benjamin H. Harris, and Ruth Levine. 2012. "Raising Household Saving: Does Financial Education Work?" *Social Security Bulletin* 72 (2): 39–48.

Gale, William G., J. Mark Iwry, and Peter R. Orszag. 2004. "The Saver's Credit: Issues and Options." *Tax Notes* 103 (5): 597–612.

Gangopadhyaya, Ajun, John Holahan, Bowen Garrett, and Adele Shartzer. 2023. *Applying a Premium Cap in Medicare Part B and Part D.* Washington, DC: Urban Institute. https://www.urban.org/research/publication/applying -premium-cap-medicare-part-b-and-part-d.

Garfinkel, Irwin, Laurel Sariscsany, Elizabeth Ananat, Sophie M. Collyer, Robert Paul Hartley, Buyi Wang, and Christopher Wimer. 2022. "The Benefits and Costs of a U.S. Child Allowance." NBER Working Paper 29854, National Bureau of Economic Research, Cambridge, MA.

Gelber, Alexander M., Damon Jones, Ithai Lurie, and Daniel W. Sacks. 2021. "Misperceptions of the Social Security Earnings Test and the Actuarial Adjustment: Implications for Labor Force Participation and Earnings." Retirement and Disability Research Center Paper NB20-09, National Bureau of Economic Research, Cambridge, MA.

Gicheva, Dora. 2016. "Student Loans or Marriage? A Look at the Highly Educated." *Economics of Education Review* 53: 207–16.

Gicheva, Dora, and Jeffrey Thompson. 2015. "The Effects of Student Loans on Long-Term Household Financial Stability." In *Student Loans and the Dynamics of Debt*, edited by Brad Hershbein and Kevin M. Hollenbeck, 287–316. Kalamazoo, MI: W. E. Upjohn Institute for Employment Research.

Giefer, Katherine G., and Michael D. King. 2021. "One in Six Older Americans Received Needs-Based Assistance Even Before Pandemic." *America Counts: Stories*. US Census Bureau, October 28. https://www.census.gov/library /stories/2021/10/what-happens-when-older-adults-struggle-to-make-ends -meet.html#:~:text=Prior%20to%20the%20COVID%2D19,and%20Program %20Participation%20(SIPP).

Glasmeier, Amy K. 2023. "2023 Living Wage Calculator." Massachusetts Institute of Technology, February 1. https://livingwage.mit.edu/articles/103 -new-data-posted-2023-living-wage-calculator.

Glickman, Aaron, and Janet Weiner. 2019. "The Burden of Health Care Costs for Working Families: A State-Level Analysis." Issue Brief. Penn LDI and United States of Care, April. https://ldi.upenn.edu/wp-content/uploads /archive/pdf/Penn%20LDI%20and%20US%20of%20Care%20Cost %20Burden%20Brief_Final.pdf.

———. 2020. "Health Care Cost Drivers and Options for Cost Control." Issue Brief. Penn LDI and United States of Care, April. https://ldi.upenn.edu/wp -content/uploads/2021/06/LDI-Issue-Brief-2020-Vol.-23-No.-4_12.pdf?_ga =2.141773302.53677133.1692475692-873447774.1692475692.

Glickman, Mark M., and Sharon Hermes. 2015. "Why Retirees Claim Social Security at 62 and How It Affects Their Retirement Income: Evidence from the Health and Retirement Study." *Journal of Retirement* 2 (3): 25–39.

Goldman, Dana P., and Peter R. Orszag. 2014. "The Growing Gap in Life Expectancy: Using the Future Elderly Model to Estimate Implications for Social Security and Medicare." *American Economic Review* 104 (5): 230–33.

Goodman, Laurie, Jun Zhu, and Rolf Pendall. 2017. "Are Gains in Black Home-ownership History?" *Urban Wire*. Urban Institute, February 15. https://www .urban.org/urban-wire/are-gains-black-homeownership-history.

Goodman, Laurie S., and Christopher Mayer. 2018. "Homeownership and the American Dream." *Journal of Economic Perspectives* 32 (1): 31–58.

Goss, Jacob, Daniel Mangrum, and Joelle Scally. 2022. "Student Loan Repay-ment during the Pandemic Forbearance." *Liberty Street Economics* (blog), Federal Reserve Bank of New York, March 22. https://libertystreeteconomics .newyorkfed.org/2022/03/student-loan-repayment-during-the-pandemic -forbearance/.

Goss, Stephen C. 2010. Letter to Erskine Bowles and Alan Simpson, Decem-ber 1. https://www.ssa.gov/oact/solvency/FiscalCommission_20101201.pdf.

———. 2023a. Letter to John Larson, July 12. https://www.ssa.gov/OACT /solvency/JLarson_20230712.pdf.

———. 2023b. Letter to Bernie Sanders, February 13. https://www.ssa.gov/OACT /solvency/BSanders_20230213.pdf.

Gottschalk, Peter, and Robert Moffitt. 2009. "The Rising Instability of U.S. Earnings." *Journal of Economic Perspectives* 23 (4): 3–24.

Gould, Elise. 2014. *Why America's Workers Need Faster Wage Growth—And What We Can Do About It.* Briefing Paper no. 382. Washington, DC: Economic Policy Institute. https://files.epi.org/2014/why-americas-workers-need-faster-wage -growth-final.pdf.

Greenspan, Alan. 2004. "Remarks at the Conference on Bank Structure and Competition." Federal Reserve Bank of Chicago, IL, May 6.

Greenstein, Robert. 2022a. *Next Steps on the Child Tax Credit.* Washington, DC: The Hamilton Project, Brookings. https://www.brookings.edu/wp-content /uploads/2022/11/20221129_THP_GreensteinCTC_EA.pdf.

———. 2022b. *Targeting vs. Universalism, and Other Factors That Affect Social Programs' Political Strength and Durability.* Washington, DC: The Hamilton Project, Brookings. https://www.brookings.edu/articles/targeting -universalism-and-other-factors-affecting-social-programs-political -strength/.

Grossberg, Jonathan D. 2019. "Something for Nothing: Universal Basic Income and the Value of Work Beyond Incentives." *Washington and Lee Journal of Civil Rights and Social Justice* 26 (1): 1–84.

Gruber, Jonathan. 2013. *Proposal 3: Restructuring Cost Sharing and Supplemental Insurance for Medicare.* Washington, DC: The Hamilton Project, Brookings. https://www.hamiltonproject.org/assets/legacy/files/downloads _and_links/THP_15WaysFedBudget_Prop3.pdf.

Gunn, Sarah, Nicholas Haltom, and Urvi Neelakantan. 2021. "Should More Student Loan Borrowers Use Income-Driven Repayment Plans?" Economic Brief no. 21-20. Federal Reserve Bank of Richmond, June. https://www .richmondfed.org/publications/research/economic_brief/2021/eb_21-20 #footnote1.

Gustafsson, Lovisa, and Sara R. Collins. 2022. "The Inflation Reduction Act is a Milestone Achievement in Lowering Americans' Health Care Costs." The Commonwealth Fund blog, August 15. https://www.commonwealthfund.org /blog/2022/inflation-reduction-act-milestone-achievement-lowering -americans-health-care-costs.

Guvenen, Fatih. 2016. "Income Risk over the Life Cycle and the Business Cycle: New Insights from Large Datasets." *NBER Reporter*, no. 4: 16–19. https:// www.nber.org/reporter/2016number4/income-risk-over-life-cycle-and -business-cycle-new-insights-large-datasets.

———. 2017. "Understanding Income Risk: New Insights from Big Data." Federal Reserve Bank of Minneapolis, June 26. https://www.minneapolisfed.org /article/2017/understanding-income-risk-new-insights-from-big-data.

Hacker, Jacob S. 2019. *The Great Risk Shift: The New Economic Insecurity and the Decline of the American Dream*. 2nd ed. New York: Oxford University Press.

Hacker, Jacob S., and Elisabeth Jacobs. 2008. *The Rising Instability of American Family Incomes, 1969–2004*. EPI Briefing Paper no. 213. Washington, DC: Economic Policy Institute. https://files.epi.org/page/-/old/briefingpapers/213/bp213.pdf.

Hall, Robert, and Nicolas Petrosky-Nadeau. 2016. *Changes in Labor Participation and Household Income*. FRBSF Economic Letter 2016-02, Federal Reserve Bank of San Francisco, 1–5. https://www.frbsf.org/wp-content/uploads/el2016-02.pdf.

Hannon, Simona, Kevin Moore, Max Schmeiser, and Irina Stefanescu. 2016. "Saving for College and Section 529 Plans." *FEDS Notes*, Board of Governors of the Federal Reserve System, Washington, DC, February 3. https://www.federalreserve.gov/econresdata/notes/feds-notes/2016/saving-for-college-and-section-529-plans-20160203.html.

Hansen, Kiese, and Tim Shaw. 2020. *Solving the Student Debt Crisis*. Washington, DC: The Aspen Institute. https://files.eric.ed.gov/fulltext/ED606386.pdf.

Hanson, Andrew, Ike Brannon, and Zackary Hawley. 2022. "Rethinking Tax Benefits for Homeowners." *National Affairs* (Summer). https://www.nationalaffairs.com/publications/detail/rethinking-tax-benefits-for-home-owners.

Hanson, Caroline, Claire Hou, Allison Percy, Emily Vreeland, and Alexandra Minicozzi. 2023. "Health Insurance for People Younger Than Age 65: Expiration of Temporary Policies Projected to Reshuffle Coverage, 2023–33." *Health Affairs* 42 (6): 742–52.

Hanson, Melanie. 2022. "Average Cost of College by Year." Education Data Initiative, January 9. https://educationdata.org/average-cost-of-college-by-year.

———. 2023a. "Pell Grant Statistics." Education Data Initiative, June 5. https://educationdata.org/pell-grant-statistics.

———. 2023b. "Student Loan Debt Statistics." Education Data Initiative, August 20. https://educationdata.org/student-loan-debt-statistics.

Haughwout, Andrew F., Donghoon Lee, Joelle Scally, and Wilbert van der Klaaw. 2019a. "Just Released: Racial Disparities in Student Loan Outcomes." *Liberty Street Economics* (blog), Federal Reserve Bank of New York, November 13. https://libertystreeteconomics.newyorkfed.org/2019/11/just-released-racial-disparities-in-student-loan-outcomes/#:~:text=When%20owe%20disaggregate%20student%20loan,in%20white%2Dmajority%20zip%20codes.

———. 2019b. "Who Borrows for College—And Who Repays?" *Liberty Street Economics* (blog), Federal Reserve Bank of New York, October 9. https://libertystreeteconomics.newyorkfed.org/2019/10/who-borrows-for-collegeand-who-repays/.

Haurin, Donald R., and Stuart S. Rosenthal. 2005. "The Growth Earnings of Low-Income Households and the Sensitivity of Their Homeownership Choices to Economic and Socio-Demographic Shocks." Working paper, Abt Associates Inc., Cambridge, MA, April. http://www.huduser.org/Publications /pdf/EarningsOfLow-IncomeHouseholds.pdf.

Hays, Donald. 2021. "Government Aid Recipients Have around 97% Less Wealth Than Those Not Receiving Assistance But Same Level of Unsecured Debt." *America Counts: Stories*. US Census Bureau, May 25. https://www.census.gov /library/stories/2021/05/what-is-financial-condition-of-households-getting -government-benefits.html.

Healthcare.gov. n.d.-a. "Canceling a Marketplace Plan When You get Medicaid or CHIP." Accessed June 22, 2023. https://www.healthcare.gov/medicaid -chip/cancelling-marketplace-plan/.

———. n.d.-b. "The Children's Health Insurance Program." Accessed June 22, 2023. https://www.healthcare.gov/medicaid-chip/childrens-health -insurance-program/.

———. n.d.-c. "Coverage for Lawfully Present Immigrants." Accessed July 10, 2023. https://www.healthcare.gov/immigrants/lawfully-present-immigrants/.

———. n.d.-d. "Federal Poverty Line." Accessed January 26, 2024. https://www .healthcare.gov/glossary/federal-poverty-level-fpl/.

———. n.d.-e. "Health Coverage for Incarcerated People." Accessed July 12, 2023. https://www.healthcare.gov/incarcerated-people/.

———. n.d.-f. "Medicaid and CHIP Coverage." Accessed July 12, 2023. https:// www.healthcare.gov/medicaid-chip/.

———. n.d.-g. "Saving Money on Health Insurance: Cost-Sharing Reductions." Accessed August 30, 2023. https://www.healthcare.gov/lower-costs/save-on -out-of-pocket-costs/.

———. n.d.-h. "A Quick Guide to the Health Insurance Marketplace®." Accessed June 22, 2023. https://www.healthcare.gov/quick-guide/eligibility/.

Helmchen, Lorens A., David W. Brown, Ithai Z. Lurie, and Anthony T. Lo Sasso. 2015. "Health Savings Accounts: Growth Concentrated among High-Income Households and Large Employers." *Health Affairs* 34 (9): 1594–98.

Hendren, Nathaniel, and Ben Sprung-Keyser. 2020. "A Unified Welfare Analysis of Government Policies." *Quarterly Journal of Economics* 135 (3): 1209–1318.

Herbert, Christopher E., and Eric S. Belsky. 2008. "The Homeownership Experience of Low-Income and Minority Households: A Review and Synthesis of the Literature." *Cityscape* 10 (2): 5–60.

Herbert, Christopher E., Daniel T. McCue, and Rocio Sanchez-Moyano. 2016. "Update on Homeownership Wealth Trajectories through the Housing Boom and Bust." Working Paper, Joint Center for Housing Studies, Harvard University, Cambridge, MA, February. http://www.jchs.harvard.edu/sites /jchs.harvard.edu/files/2013_wealth_update_mccue_02-18-16.pdf.

Herbst, Daniel. 2023. "The Impact of Income-Driven Repayment on Student Borrower Outcomes." *American Economic Journal: Applied Economics 2023* 15 (1): 1–25.

Hill, Steven C. 2015. "Medicaid Expansion in Opt-Out States Would Produce Consumer Savings and Less Financial Burden Than Exchange Coverage." *Health Affairs* 34 (2): 340–49.

Himmelstein, David U., Steffie Woolhandler, Robert M. Lawless, Deborah Thorne, and Pamela Foohey. 2019. "Medical Bankruptcy: Still Common Despite the Affordable Care Act." *American Journal of Public Health* 109 (3): 431–33.

Holahan, John, and Michael Simpson. 2022. *Next Steps in Expanding Coverage and Affordability after the Inflation Reduction Act: Research Report.* New York: The Commonwealth Fund. https://www.urban.org/sites/default/files /2022-09/Next%20Steps%20in%20Expanding%20Coverage%20and %20Affordability%20after%20the%20Inflation%20Reduction%20Act.pdf.

Hornstein, Donald T. 2016. "Lessons from U.S. Coastal Wind Pools about Climate Finance and Politics." *Boston College Environmental Affairs Law Review* 43 (2): 345–86.

Houle, Jason N., and Lawrence Berger. 2015. "Is Student Loan Debt Discouraging Homeownership among Young Adults?" *Social Science Review* 89 (4): 589–621.

Housing Finance Policy Center. 2024. *Housing Finance at a Glance: A Monthly Chartbook.* May. Washington, DC: Urban Institute. https://www.urban.org /sites/default/files/2024-05/Housing-Finance-At-A-Glance-Monthly -Chartbook-May-2024.pdf.

Hout, Michael, and Thomas A. DiPrete. 2006. "What We Have Learned: RC28's Contribution to Knowledge about Social Stratification." *Research in Social Stratification and Mobility* 24 (1): 1–20.

"How Welfare Has Changed since 1996, in Three Charts." 2018. Marketplace, July 23. https://www.marketplace.org/2018/07/23/how-welfare-has-changed -1996-three-charts/.

Howell, David R., and Arne L. Kalleberg. 2019. "Declining Job Quality in the United States: Explanations and Evidence." *RSF: The Russell Sage Foundation Journal of the Social Sciences* 5 (4): 1–53.

Hoynes, Hilary. 2019. "The Earned Income Tax Credit." *Annals of the American Academy of Political and Social Science* 686 (1): 180–203.

Hoynes, Hilary W., and Jesse Rothstein. 2019. "Universal Basic Income in the US and Advanced Countries." NBER Working Paper 25538, National Bureau of Economic Research, Cambridge, MA, February. https://www.nber.org /papers/w25538.

Hsu, Joanne W., David A. Matsa, and Brian T. Melzer. 2018. "Unemployment Insurance as a Housing Market Stabilizer." *American Economic Review* 108 (1): 49–81.

Hughes, Sam, Emily Gee, and Nicole Rapfogel. 2022. *Health Insurance Costs Are Squeezing Workers and Employers*. Washington, DC: Center for American Progress. https://www.americanprogress.org/article/health-insurance-costs-are-squeezing-workers-and-employers/.

Hungerford, Thomas L., and Rebecca Thiess. 2013. *The Earned Income Tax Credit and the Child Tax Credit*. Issue Brief no. 370. Washington, DC: Economic Policy Institute. https://files.epi.org/2013/The-Earned-Income-Tax-Credit.pdf.

Hurd, Michael D., James P. Smith, and Julie M. Zissimopoulos. 2004. "The Effects of Subjective Survival on Retirement and Social Security Claiming." *Journal of Applied Econometrics* 19 (6): 761–75.

Institute for College Access and Success, The. 2019. *Casualties of College Debt: What Data Show and Experts Say about Who Defaults and Why*. https://ticas.org/wp-content/uploads/2019/09/casualities-of-college-debt.pdf.

Institute for Social Research. 2023. *The Health and Retirement Study: Aging in the 21st Century—Challenges and Opportunities for Americans*. Ann Arbor: University of Michigan. https://hrsonline.isr.umich.edu/sitedocs/databook/inc/pdf/HRS-Aging-in-the-21St-Century.pdf.

Institute of Medicine of the National Academies. 2008. *Retooling for an Aging America: Building the Health Care Workforce*. Washington, DC: National Academies Press.

Interagency Task Force on Property Appraisal and Valuation Equity. 2022. *Action Plan to Advance Property Appraisal and Valuation Equity*. https://pave.hud.gov/sites/pave.hud.gov/files/documents/PAVEActionPlan.pdf.

Internal Revenue Service. n.d.-a. "Earned Income and Earned Income Tax Credit (EITC) Tables." Accessed July 4, 2024. https://www.irs.gov/credits-deductions/individuals/earned-income-tax-credit/earned-income-and-earned-income-tax-credit-eitc-tables#EITC%20Tables.

———. n.d.-b. "EITC Fast Facts." Accessed January 2, 2023. https://www.eitc.irs.gov/partner-toolkit/basic-marketing-communication-materials/eitc-fast-facts/eitc-fast-facts.

———. n.d.-c. "Health Savings Accounts and Other Tax-Favored Health Plans." Accessed June 21, 2022. https://www.irs.gov/pub/irs-pdf/p969.pdf.

———. n.d.-d. "Retirement Savings Contributions Credit (Saver's Credit)." Accessed June 21, 2022. https://www.irs.gov/retirement-plans/plan-participant-employee/retirement-savings-contributions-savers-credit.

———. n.d.-e. "Tax Benefits for Education." Accessed June 21, 2022. https://www.irs.gov/pub/irs-pdf/p970.pdf.

———. n.d.-f. "Topic Number 502 Medical and Dental Expenses." Accessed June 21, 2022. https://www.irs.gov/taxtopics/tc502.

———. 1969. "Revenue Ruling 69-545."

———. 2002. "Health Reimbursement Arrangements." Notice 2002-45. https://www.irs.gov/pub/irs-drop/n-02-45.pdf.

———. 2023a. "Internal Revenue Bulletin: 2023-37." September 11. https://www
.irs.gov/pub/irs-irbs/irb23-37.pdf.

———. 2023b. "Internal Revenue Bulletin: 2023-48." November 27. https://www
.irs.gov/irb/2023-48_IRB#REV-PROC-2023-34.

———. 2023c. "Rev. Proc. 2023-23." https://www.irs.gov/pub/irs-drop/rp-23
-23.pdf.

———. 2023d. "2024 Flexible Spending Arrangement Contribution Limit Rises
by $150." Press release IR-2023-234, December 8. https://www.irs.gov
/newsroom/irs-2024-flexible-spending-arrangement-contribution-limit
-rises-by-150-dollars#:~:text=An%20employee%20who%20chooses%20to
,Security%20tax%20or%20Medicare%20tax.

———. 2023e. "2024 Limitations Adjusted as Provided in Section 415(d), etc."
Notice 2023-75. https://www.irs.gov/pub/irs-drop/n-23-75.pdf.

Jacobs, Ken, Ian Eve Perry, and Jenifer MacGillvary. 2021. *The Public Cost of a
Low Federal Minimum Wage.* Research Brief. Berkeley: UC Berkeley Center
for Labor Research and Education. https://laborcenter.berkeley.edu/wp
-content/uploads/2021/01/The-Public-Cost-of-a-Low-Federal-Minimum
-Wage.pdf.

Jäntti, Markus, and Stephen P. Jenkins. 2015. "Income Mobility." In *Handbook
of Income Distribution*, edited by A. B. Atkinson and F. Bourguignon,
2A:807–935. Amsterdam: North-Holland Elsevier.

Johnson, Richard W. 2015. "Low-Income Older Adults Face High Housing Costs
and Financial Challenges." *Cascade*, no. 91. https://www.philadelphiafed.org
/community-development/low-income-older-adults-face-high-housing-costs
-and-financial-challenges.

———. 2017. "The Demise of myRA Raises the Stakes for State Retirement
Initiatives." *Urban Wire.* Urban Institute, August 8. https://www.urban.org
/urban-wire/demise-myra-raises-stakes-state-retirement-initiatives.

Joint Center for Housing Studies of Harvard University. 2022. *The State of the
Nation's Housing 2022.* https://www.jchs.harvard.edu/sites/default/files
/reports/files/Harvard_JCHS_State_Nations_Housing_2022.pdf.

———. 2023. *Housing America's Older Adults 2023.* https://www.jchs.harvard
.edu/sites/default/files/reports/files/Harvard_JCHS_Housing_Americas
_Older_Adults_2023_Revised_040424.pdf.

———. 2024a. *America's Rental Housing 2024.* https://www.jchs.harvard.edu
/sites/default/files/reports/files/Harvard_JCHS_Americas_Rental_Housing
_2024.pdf.

———. 2024b. *The State of the Nation's Housing 2024.* https://www.jchs.harvard
.edu/sites/default/files/reports/files/Harvard_JCHS_The_State_of_the
_Nations_Housing_2024.pdf.

Joint Committee on Taxation. 2016. "Exclusion for Employer-Provided Health
Benefits and Other Health-Related Provisions of the Internal Revenue Code:

Present Law and Selected Estimates." JCX-25-16, April 12. https://www.jct
.gov/CMSPages/GetFile.aspx?guid=bob9d55b-2a24-41b5-9434-2e05417
6b5bd.

———. 2022. "Estimated Revenue Effects of H.R. 2617, The 'Consolidated
Appropriations Act,' as Passed by the Senate." JCX-21-22, December 22.
https://www.jct.gov/publications/2022/jcx-21-22/.

Josephson, Amelia. 2023. "2023–2024 Child Tax Credit: What Will You
Receive?" Smart Asset, December 15. https://smartasset.com/taxes/all-about
-child-tax-credits.

Jost, Timothy Stolzfus. 2007. *Health Care at Risk: A Critique of the Consumer-
Driven Movement*. Durham, NC: Duke University Press.

JPMorgan Chase & Co. 2022. "Income Driven Repayment: Who Needs
Student Loan Payment Relief?" June. https://www.jpmorganchase.com
/institute/research/household-debt/student-loan-income-driven-repayment
#finding-2.

Karlan, Dean, Aishwarya Lakshmi Ratan, and Jonathan Zinman. 2014.
"Savings by and for the Poor: A Research Review and Agenda." *Review of
Income & Wealth* 60 (1): 36–78.

Keisler-Starkey, Katherine, and Lisa N. Bunch. 2020. *Health Insurance
Coverage in the United States: 2019*. Report no. P60-271. Washington, DC:
U.S. Census Bureau. https://www.census.gov/content/dam/Census/library
/publications/2020/demo/p60-271.pdf.

Kermani, Amir, and Francis Wong. 2021. "Racial Disparities in Housing
Returns." NBER Working Paper 29306, National Bureau of Economic
Research, Cambridge, MA, September.

KFF. n.d.-a. "Characteristics of Poor Uninsured Nonelderly Adults in the ACA
Coverage Gap." Accessed July 12, 2023. https://www.kff.org/health-reform
/state-indicator/characteristics-of-poor-uninsured-nonelderly-adults-in-the
-aca-coverage-gap/?dataView=1&currentTimeframe=0&sortModel=%7B
%22colId%22:%22Ineligible%20for%20Financial%20Assistance%20due
%20to%20Citizenship%22,%22sort%22:%22desc%22%7D.

———. n.d.-b. "Medicaid and CHIP Income Eligibility Limits for Pregnant
Women as a Percent of the Federal Poverty Level." Accessed July 11, 2023.
https://www.kff.org/health-reform/state-indicator/medicaid-and-chip
-income-eligibility-limits-for-pregnant-women-as-a-percent-of-the-federal
-poverty-level/?currentTimeframe=0&sortModel=%7B%22colId%22:
%22Location%22,%22sort%22:%22asc%22%7D.

———. n.d.-c. "Medicaid Income Eligibility Limits for Adults as a Percent of the
Federal Poverty Level." Accessed July 11, 2023. https://www.kff.org/health
-reform/state-indicator/medicaid-income-eligibility-limits-for-adults-as-a
-percent-of-the-federal-poverty-level/?currentTimeframe=0&sortModel=
%7B%22colId%22:%22Location%22,%22sort%22:%22asc%22%7D.

———. n.d.-d. "Premium and Cost-Sharing Requirements for Selected Services for Medicaid Adults, as of January 1, 2020." Accessed August 5, 2023. https://www.kff.org/health-reform/state-indicator/premium-and-cost-sharing-requirements-for-selected-services-for-medicaid-expansion-adults/?currentTimeframe=0&sortModel=%7B%22colId%22:%22Location%22,%22sort%22:%22asc%22%7D.

———. 2019. "An Overview of Medicare." Issue Brief, February. https://www.kff.org/medicare/issue-brief/an-overview-of-medicare/#:~:text=Medicare%20provides%20protection%20against%20othe,under%20Parts%20A%20and%20B.

———. 2020. "Key Issues Related to COBRA Subsidies." May 28. https://www.kff.org/private-insurance/issue-brief/key-issues-related-to-cobra-subsidies/.

———. 2022. *2022 Employer Health Benefits Survey.* https://files.kff.org/attachment/Report-Employer-Health-Benefits-2022-Annual-Survey.pdf.

———. 2023. "Deductibles in ACA Marketplace Plans, 2014-2024." December 22. https://www.kff.org/affordable-care-act/issue-brief/deductibles-in-aca-marketplace-plans/.

———. 2024a. "Employer Responsibility under the Affordable Care Act." February 29. https://www.kff.org/infographic/employer-responsibility-under-the-affordable-care-act/.

———. 2024b. "Explaining Health Care Reform: Questions about Health Insurance Subsidies." October 25. https://www.kff.org/health-reform/issue-brief/explaining-health-care-reform-questions-about-health-insurance-subsidies/.

———. 2024c. "Status of State Medicaid Expansion Decisions." November 12. https://www.kff.org/status-of-state-medicaid-expansion-decisions/.

Killewald, Alexandra, and Brielle Bryan. 2016. "Does Your Home Make You Wealthy?" *RSF: The Russell Sage Foundation Journal of the Social Sciences* 2 (6): 110–28.

Klerman, Jacob Alex, and Steven J. Haider. 2004. "A Stock-Flow Analysis of the Welfare Caseload." *Journal of Human Resources* 39 (4): 865–86.

Kliff, Sarah, and Jessica Silver-Greenberg. 2023. "This Nonprofit Health System Cuts Off Patients with Medical Debt." *New York Times*, June 1, 2023. https://www.nytimes.com/2023/06/01/business/allina-health-hospital-debt.html.

Knight, Frank H. (1921) 1971. *Risk, Uncertainty, and Profit.* Boston: Houghton Mifflin; Chicago: University of Chicago Press.

Koma, J. Wyatt, Jean Fuglesten Biniek, Juliette Cubanski, and Tricia Neuman. 2023. "Access Problems and Cost Concerns of Younger Medicare Beneficiaries Exceeded Those of Older Beneficiaries in 2019." *Health Affairs* 42 (4): 470–78.

Koma, Wyatt, Juliette Cubanski, and Tricia Neuman. 2021. "A Snapshot of Sources of Coverage Among Medicare Beneficiaries in 2018." KFF, March 23. https://www.kff.org/medicare/issue-brief/a-snapshot-of-sources-of-coverage

-among-medicare-beneficiaries-in-2018/#:~:text=Under%20traditional
%20Medicare%2C%20beneficiaries%20without,most%20physician%20and
%20other%20outpatient.

Kopparam, Raksha, and Austin Clemens. 2020. *The Rising Number of U.S.
Households with Burdensome Student Debt Calls for a Federal Response.*
Issue Brief. Washington, DC: Washington Center for Equitable Growth.
https://equitablegrowth.org/the-rising-number-of-u-s-households-with
-burdensome-student-debt-calls-for-a-federal-response/.

Krishnan, Karthik, and Pinshuo Wang. 2019. "The Cost of Financing Education:
Can Student Debt Hinder Entrepreneurship?" *Management Science* 65 (10):
4522–54.

Krugman, Paul. 2023. "Nikki Haley Is Coming for Your Retirement." *New York
Times,* November 27, 2023. https://www.nytimes.com/2023/11/27/opinion
/nikki-haley-social-security.html.

Kuhn, Moritz, Moritz Schularick, and Ulrike I. Steins. 2017. "The Great American
Debt Boom, 1949–2013." Working paper, University of Bonn, Bonn, Germany,
September. https://www.stlouisfed.org/~/media/files/pdfs/hfs/assets/2017
/moritz_schularick_the_great_american_debt_boom.pdf?la=en.

Kumar, I. Elizabeth, Keegan E. Hines, and John P. Dickerson. 2022. "Equaliz-
ing Credit Opportunity in Algorithms: Aligning Algorithmic Fairness
Research and U.S. Fair Lending Regulation." In *Proceedings of the 2022
AAAI/ACM Conference on AI, Ethics, and Society (AIES '22), August 1–3, 2022,
Oxford, United Kingdom,* 357–68. https://doi.org/10.1145/3514094.3534154.

Kuperberg, Arielle, Kenneshia Williams, and Joan Maya Mazelis. 2023.
"Student Loans, Physical and Mental Health, and Health Care Use and
Delay in College." *Journal of American College Health* 71 (January 3): 1–11.
https://pubmed.ncbi.nlm.nih.gov/36595565/.

Kwak, James. 2015. "'Social Insurance', Risk Spreading, and Redistribution." In
Research Handbook on the Economics of Insurance Law, edited by Daniel
Schwarcz and Peter Siegelman, 127–59. Northampton, MA: Edward Elgar
Publishing.

LaCarte, Valerie, Mark Greenberg, and Randy Capps. 2021. *Medicaid Access
and Participation: A Data Profile of Eligible and Ineligible Immigrant
Adults.* Issue Brief. Washington, DC: Migration Policy Institute. https://
www.migrationpolicy.org/sites/default/files/publications/mpi-hsi_medicaid
-brief_final.pdf.

Laitner, John. 2018. "Addressing Social Security's Solvency While Promoting
High Labor Force Participation." WP 2018-386, Michigan Retirement
Research Center, Ann Arbor, MI.

Lake, Rebecca. 2020. "Student Loan Debt Crisis Breakdown." *The Balance,*
July 3. https://www.thebalance.com/student-loan-debt-crisis-breakdown
-4171739.

Larrimore, Jeff, Jacob Mortenson, and David Splinter. 2015. *Income and Earnings Mobility in U.S. Tax Data.* Finance and Economics Discussion Series 2015-061. Washington, DC: Board of Governors of the Federal Reserve System. https://www.federalreserve.gov/econresdata/feds/2015/files /2015061pap.pdf.

———. 2020. "Presence and Persistence of Poverty in U.S. Tax Data." NBER Working Paper 26966, National Bureau of Economic Research, Cambridge, MA.

———. 2022. "Earnings Shocks and Stabilization during Covid-19." *Journal of Public Economics* 206: article 104597.

Larrimore, Jeff, Jenny Schuetz, and Samuel Dodini. 2016. *What Are the Perceived Barriers to Homeownership for Young Adults?* Finance and Economics Discussion Series 2016-021. Washington, DC: Board of Governors of the Federal Reserve System. https://www.federalreserve.gov/econresdata /feds/2016/files/2016021pap.pdf.

Leonesio, Michael V., Benjamin Bridges, Robert Gesumaria, and Linda Del Bene. 2012. "The Increasing Labor Force Participation of Older Workers and Its Effect on the Income of the Aged." *Social Security Bulletin* 72 (1): 59–77.

Levey, Noam N. 2022. "100 Million People in America Are Saddled With Health Care Debt." *KFF Health News*, June 16. https://kffhealthnews.org /news/article/diagnosis-debt-investigation-100-million-americans-hidden -medical-debt/.

Levitin, Adam J., and Susan M. Wachter. 2020. *The Great American Housing Bubble.* Cambridge, MA: Harvard University Press.

Looney, Adam. 2022. "Does Biden's Student Debt Forgiveness Achieve His Stated Goals?" Brookings, Commentary, September 26. https://www .brookings.edu/articles/does-bidens-student-debt-forgiveness-achieve-his -stated-goals/.

Looney, Adam, David Wessel, and Kadija Yilla. 2020. "Who Owes All That Student Debt? And Who'd Benefit If It Were Forgiven?" Brookings, Commentary, January 28. https://www.brookings.edu/articles/who-owes-all-that -student-debt-and-whod-benefit-if-it-were-forgiven/.

Looney, Adam, and Constantine Yannelis. 2015. "A Crisis in Student Loans? How Changes in the Characteristics of Borrowers and in the Institutions They Attended Contributed to Rising Loan Defaults." *Brookings Papers on Economic Activity* (Fall): 1–68.

———. 2022. "The Consequences of Student Loan Credit Expansions: Evidence from Three Decades of Default Cycles." *Journal of Financial Economics* 143 (2): 771–93.

Low, David. 2021. "What Triggers Mortgage Default? New Evidence from Linked Administrative and Survey Data." Working Paper, Consumer Financial Protection Bureau, December. https://www.aeaweb.org/conference /2022/preliminary/paper/BAsrTiHD.

Lowe, Jaime. 2021. "What We Spent in a Month." *New York Times*, May 18, 2021.
   https://www.nytimes.com/interactive/2021/05/18/magazine/money-diaries
   .html?searchResultPosition=2.

Lusardi, Annamaria, Daniel Schneider, and Peter Tufano. 2011. "Financially
   Fragile Households: Evidence and Implications." *Brookings Papers on
   Economic Activity* (Spring): 83–134.

Maag, Elaine, William J. Congdon, and Eunice Yau. 2021. *The Earned Income
   Tax Credit: Program Outcomes, Payment Timing, and Next Steps for
   Research*. OPRE Report no. 2021-34. Washington, DC: Office of Planning,
   Research, and Evaluation, US Department of Health and Human Services.
   https://www.acf.hhs.gov/sites/default/files/documents/opre/earned-income
   -tax-credit-timing-of-payments-and-program-outcomes%20feb%202021.pdf.

MacInnis, Bo. 2009. *Social Security and the Joint Trends in Labor Supply and
   Benefits Receipt among Older Men*. CRR WP 2009-22. Chestnut Hill, MA:
   Center for Retirement Research. https://crr.bc.edu/wp-content/uploads
   /2009/10/wp_2009-22-508.pdf.

MacKinnon, Danny, and Kate Driscoll Derickson. 2012. "From Resilience to
   Resourcefulness: A Critique of Resilience Policy and Activism." *Progress in
   Human Geography* 37 (2): 253–70.

Madrian, Brigitte C., and Dennis F. Shea. 2001. "The Power of Suggestion:
   Inertia in 401(k) Participation and Savings Behavior." *Quarterly Journal of
   Economics* 116 (4): 1149–87.

Maher, Brendan S. 2016. "Regulating Employment-Based Anything." *Minnesota
   Law Review* 100 (4): 1257–1322.

Mangrum, Daniel, Joelle Scally, and Crystal Wang. 2022. "Three Key Facts from
   the Center on Microeconomic Data's 2022 Student Loan Update." *Liberty
   Street Economics* (blog), Federal Reserve Bank of New York, August 9.
   https://libertystreeteconomics.newyorkfed.org/2022/08/three-key-facts-from
   -the-center-for-microeconomic-datas-2022-student-loan-update/.

Manning, Alan. 2021. "The Elusive Employer Effect of the Minimum Wage."
   Journal of Economic Perspectives 35 (1): 3–26.

Manturuk, Kim R., Mark R. Lindblad, and Roberto G. Quercia. 2017. *A Place
   Called Home: The Social Dimensions of Homeownership*. New York: Oxford
   University Press.

Marinescu, Ioana. 2020. *Moving from Federal Pandemic Unemployment
   Compensation to a Job Losers' Stimulus Program amid the Coronavirus
   Recession*. Issue Brief. Washington, DC: Washington Center for Equitable
   Growth. https://equitablegrowth.org/moving-from-federal-pandemic
   -unemployment-compensation-to-a-job-losers-stimulus-program-amid-the
   -coronavirus-recession/.

Marmor, Theodore R. 1970. *The Politics of Medicare*. London: Routledge &
   Kegan Paul.

Martinchek, Kassandra, and Dulce Gonzalez. 2024. *How Many Families Take on Debt to Pay for Groceries?* Washington, DC: Urban Institute. https://www.urban.org/sites/default/files/2024-05/How_Many_Families_Take_on_Debt_to_Pay_for_Groceries.pdf.

Maslow, Abraham H. 1943. "A Theory of Human Motivation." *Psychological Review* 50 (4): 370–96.

Mastri, Annalisa, Wayne Vroman, Karen Needels, and Walter Nicholson. 2016. *States' Decisions to Adopt Unemployment Compensation Provisions of the American Recovery and Reinvestment Act.* Princeton, NJ: Mathematica Policy Research. https://www.dol.gov/sites/dolgov/files/OASP/legacy/files/UCP_State_Decisions_to_Adopt.pdf.

Mathews, Anna Wilde, Tom McGinty, and Melanie Evans. 2022. "Big Hospitals Provide Skimpy Charity Care—Despite Billions in Tax Breaks." *Wall Street Journal*, July 25, 2022. https://www.wsj.com/articles/nonprofit-hospitals-vs-for-profit-charity-care-spending-11657936777.

McBride, Will, Huaqun Li, Garrett Watson, and Alex Durante. 2024. *Simplifying Saving and Improving Financial Security through Universal Savings Accounts.* Washington, DC: The Tax Foundation. https://taxfoundation.org/wp-content/uploads/2024/05/Simplifying-Saving-and-Improving-Financial-Security-through-Universal-Savings-Accounts.pdf.

McClellan, Mark. 1998. "Health Events, Health Insurance, and Labor Supply: Evidence from the Health and Retirement Study." In *Frontiers in the Economics of Aging*, edited by David A. Wise, 301–50. Chicago: University of Chicago Press.

McCoy, Patricia A. 2014. "The Home Mortgage Foreclosure Crisis: Lessons Learned." In *Homeownership Built to Last: Balancing Access, Affordability, and Risk after the Housing Crisis*, edited by Eric S. Belsky, Christopher E. Herbert, and Jennifer H. Molinsky, 418–64. Washington, DC: Brookings Institution Press.

———. 2015. "Degrees of Intermediation." *Wake Forest Law Review* 50 (3): 551–79.

McCoy, Patricia A., and Susan M. Wachter. 2020. "Why the Ability-to-Repay Rule Is Vital to Financial Stability." *Georgetown Law Journal* 108 (3): 649–98.

McDermott, Daniel, and Cynthia Cox. 2021. "A Closer Look at the Uninsured Marketplace Eligible Population Following the American Rescue Plan Act." KFF, May 27. https://www.kff.org/private-insurance/issue-brief/a-closer-look-at-the-uninsured-marketplace-eligible-population-following-the-american-rescue-plan-act/.

McKay, Katherine Lucas. 2017. *Reforming Unemployment Insurance to Support Income Stability and Financial Security.* Washington, DC: The Aspen Institute. https://www.aspeninstitute.org/wp-content/uploads/2017/09/ASPEN_EPIC_UNEMPLOYMENT_INSURANCE_02.pdf.

McKernan, Signe-Mary, Caroline Ratcliffe, Brena Braga, and Emma Kalish. 2016. *Thriving Residents, Thriving Cities.* Washington, DC: Urban Institute. https://www.urban.org/sites/default/files/publication/79776/2000747 -thriving-residents-thriving-cities-family-financial-security-matters-for -cities_0.pdf.

McMahon, Walter W. 2021. "The External Social Benefits of Higher Education: Theory, Evidence, and Policy Implications." *Journal of Education Finance* 46 (4): 398–430.

Medicaid.gov. n.d.-a. "Medicaid Eligibility." Accessed June 22, 2023. https://www.medicaid.gov/medicaid/eligibility/index.html.

———. n.d.-b. "August 2024 Medicaid & CHIP Enrollment Data Highlights." Accessed November 29, 2024. https://www.medicaid.gov/medicaid /program-information/medicaid-and-chip-enrollment-data/report -highlights/index.html.

Medicare.gov. n.d.-a. "Costs." Accessed June 16, 2024. https://www.medicare .gov/basics/costs/medicare-costs.

———. n.d.-b. "How to Pay Part A & Part B Premiums." Accessed June 16, 2024. https://www.medicare.gov/basics/costs/pay-premiums.

Medina, Jennifer. 2024. "For Minority Working-Class Voters, Dismay with Democrats Led to Distrust." *New York Times*, November 19, 2024. https:// www.nytimes.com/2024/11/19/us/politics/trump-working-class-voters.html.

Mezza, Alvaro, Daniel Ringo, Shane Sherlund, and Kamila Sommer. 2020. "Student Loans and Homeownership." *Journal of Labor Economics* 38 (1): 215–60.

Mezza, Alvaro, and Kamila Sommer. 2015. "A Trillion Dollar Question: What Predicts Student Loan Delinquency Risk?" *FEDS Notes*, Board of Governors of the Federal Reserve System, Washington, DC, October 16. https://www .federalreserve.gov/econresdata/notes/feds-notes/2015/trillion-dollar -question-what-predicts-student-loan-delinquency-risk-20151016.html#:~: text=A%20borrower's%20credit%20score%20(even,completion%20and %20for%2Dprofit%20attendance.

MHP. n.d. "One+Boston." Accessed April 9, 2023. https://www.mhp.net/one -mortgage/one-plus-boston.

Milbank, Dana. 2002. "Bush Calls for Increasing Minority Homeownership." *Washington Post*, June 17, 2002. https://www.washingtonpost.com/archive /politics/2002/06/18/bush-calls-for-increasing-minority-homeownership /82f701a6-7db6-4ed9-bc38-db83823d820e/.

Miller, Ben. 2017. *Who Are Student Loan Defaulters?* Washington, DC: Center for American Progress. https://www.americanprogress.org/wp-content /uploads/sites/2/2017/12/StudentLoanDefault-brief1.pdf.

Miller, G. E. 2022. "Does your 401K Match Up against the Averages?" 20 Some- thing Finance, January 7. https://20somethingfinance.com/401k-match/.

Miller, Mark. 2023. "Could Defined-Benefit Pension Plans Make a Comeback?" Morningstar, March 22. https://www.morningstar.com/retirement/could -defined-benefit-pension-plans-make-comeback.

Miller-Wilson, Kate. 2022. "What Are the Odds of Dying in a Car Crash? Know the Risk." Love to Know, May 31. https://dying.lovetoknow.com/death -cultures-around-world/odds-dying-car-crash-real-facts.

Mills, Gregory, Tracy Vericker, Heather Koball, Kye Lippold, Laura Wheaton, and Sam Elkin. 2014. *Understanding the Rates, Causes, and Costs of Churning in the Supplemental Nutrition Assistance Program (SNAP): Final Report. Research Report.* Washington, DC: Urban Institute. https://www .urban.org/sites/default/files/publication/33566/413257-Understanding-the -Rates-Causes-and-Costs-of-Churning-in-the-Supplemental-Nutrition -Assistance-Program-SNAP-.PDF.

Mitchell, Michael. 2019. "Rising Costs Making It Hard for Students, Particularly of Color, to Afford College." *Off the Charts* (blog), Center on Budget and Policy Priorities, October 25. https://www.cbpp.org/blog/rising-costs -making-it-hard-for-students-particularly-of-color-to-afford-college.

Mitchell, Michael, Michael Leachman, and Matt Saenz. 2019. *State Higher Education Funding Cuts Have Pushed Costs to Students, Worsened Inequality.* Washington, DC: Center on Budget and Policy Priorities. https://www .cbpp.org/sites/default/files/atoms/files/10-24-19sfp.pdf.

Molinsky, Jennifer. 2020. "Ten Insights about Older Households from the 2020 State of the Nation's Housing Report." *Housing Perspectives* (blog), Joint Center for Housing Studies of Harvard University, December 17. https:// www.jchs.harvard.edu/blog/ten-insights-about-older-households-2020 -state-nations-housing-report.

Moment of Truth Project. 2013. *A Bipartisan Path Forward to Securing America's Future.* Washington, DC: Committee for a Responsible Federal Budget. https://www.crfb.org/sites/default/files/media/documents/Securing %20America%27s%20Future_Full.pdf.

Montero, Alex, Audrey Kearney, Liz Hamel, and Mollyann Brodie. 2022. "Americans' Challenges with Health Care Costs." KFF, July 14. https://www .kff.org/health-costs/issue-brief/americans-challenges-with-health-care -costs/.

Montgomery, David H. 2022. "Who's Not Working in the U.S.? Learn the Basics." Federal Reserve Bank of Minneapolis, September 1. https://www .minneapolisfed.org/article/2022/whos-not-working-in-the-us-learn-the -basics#:~:text=More%20than%2026%20percent%20of,disability %20prevents%20them%20from%20working.

Moore, James H., Jr. 2004. "Measuring Defined Benefit Plan Replacement Rates with PenSync." *Monthly Labor Review* (November): 57–68. http://www .bls.gov/opub/mlr/2004/11/art6full.pdf.

Moore, Kathryn L. 2008. "The Future of Social Security: Principles to Guide Reform." *John Marshall Law Review* 41 (4): 1061–89.

———. 2012. "Social Security in an Era of Retrenchment: What Would Happen If the Social Security Trust Funds Were Exhausted?" *ABA Journal of Labor and Employment Law* 28 (1): 43–57.

Morduch, Jonathan, and Rachel Schneider. 2017. *The Financial Diaries*. Princeton, NJ: Princeton University Press.

Mortgage Servicing Collaborative, The. n.d.-a. "What Is Default Servicing?" Urban Institute. Accessed May 20, 2023. https://www.urban.org/policy -centers/housing-finance-policy-center/projects/mortgage-servicing -collaborative/help-me-understand-mortgage-servicing/what-default -servicing.

———. n.d.-b. "Who Is Involved with Mortgage Servicing?" Urban Institute. Accessed May 20, 2023. https://www.urban.org/policy-centers/housing -finance-policy-center/projects/mortgage-servicing-collaborative/help-me -understand-mortgage-servicing/who-involved-mortgage-servicing.

Moser, Stephanie. 2022. "A Calculation of the Living Wage." Massachusetts Institute of Technology, May 19. https://livingwage.mit.edu/articles/99-a -calculation-of-the-living-wage.

Moss, David A. 2002. *When All Else Fails: Government as the Ultimate Risk Manager*. Cambridge, MA: Harvard University Press.

Moulton, Stephanie, and Roberto G. Quercia. 2013. "Access and Sustainability for First Time Homebuyers: The Evolving Role of State Housing Finance Agencies." Working Paper HBTL-10, Joint Center for Housing Studies, Harvard University, October. https://www.jchs.harvard.edu/sites/default /files/hbtl-10.pdf.

Mudrazija, Stipica, and Barbara A. Butrica. 2021. *How Does Debt Shape Health Outcomes for Older Americans?* CRR WP 2021-17. Chestnut Hill, MA: Center for Retirement Research. https://crr.bc.edu/wp-content/uploads/2021/11/wp _2021-17.pdf.

Munnell, Alicia H., Kelly Haverstick, and Mauricio Soto. 2007. *Why Have Defined Benefit Plans Survived in the Public Sector?* Chestnut Hill, MA: Center for Retirement Research. https://crr.bc.edu/wp-content/uploads /2007/12/slp_2.pdf.

Mutchler, Jan, Yan-Jhu Su, and Nidya Velasco Roldan. 2023. *Living Below the Line: Economic Insecurity and Older Americans, Insecurity in the States, 2022*. Center for Social and Demographic Research on Aging Publication 2-2023. Boston: Gerontology Institute, University of Massachusetts Boston. https://scholarworks.umb.edu/demographyofaging/66/.

Nadasen, Premilla. 2016. "Welfare Reform and the Politics of Race." *Perspectives on History*, August 22. https://www.historians.org/perspectives-article /welfare-reform-and-the-politics-of-race-20-years-later-september-2016/.

Nadeau, Cary Ann. 2020. "New Living Wage Data Available for Now on the Tool." Massachusetts Institute of Technology, May 17. https://livingwage.mit .edu/articles/61-new-living-wage-data-for-now-available-on-the-tool.

National Academies of Sciences, Engineering, and Medicine. 2015. *The Growing Gap in Life Expectancy by Income: Implications for Federal Programs and Policy Responses*. Washington, DC: The National Academies Press.

National Archives. n.d. "Medicare and Medicaid Act (1965)." Accessed November 23, 2024. https://www.archives.gov/milestone-documents/medicare-and -medicaid-act.

National Association of Realtors. 2020. *2019 Profile of Home Buyers and Sellers*. https://www.nysar.com/wp-content/uploads/2020/01/2019-NAR-HBS.pdf.

National Association of State Retirement Administrators. n.d. "Cost of Living Adjustments." Accessed March 15, 2022. https://www.nasra.org/cola.

National Association of Student Financial Aid Administrators. 2022. *Doubling the Maximum Pell Grant*. NASFAA Issue Brief. https://www.nasfaa.org /uploads/documents/Issue_Brief_Double_Pell.pdf.

National Center for Education Statistics. n.d. "Digest of Education Statistics." US Department of Education. Accessed June 25, 2024. https://nces.ed.gov /programs/digest/current_tables.asp.

National Council on Aging. 2023a. "Get the Facts on Economic Security for Seniors." June 8. https://www.ncoa.org/article/get-the-facts-on-economic -security-for-seniors.

———. 2023b. "What You'll Pay in Out-of-Pocket Medicare Costs in 2024." October 13. https://www.ncoa.org/article/what-you-will-pay-in-out-of -pocket-medicare-costs-in-2024.

National Employment Law Project. 2023. *Monetary Eligibility Requirements*. https://www.nelp.org/app/uploads/2023/11/Policy-Advocacy-Brief-Monetary -Eligibility-11-2023.pdf.

Nau, Michael, Rachel E. Dwyer, and Randy Hodson. 2015. "Can't Afford a Baby? Debt and Young Americans." *Research in Social Stratification and Mobility* 42 (December): 114–22.

New York City Department of Consumer and Worker Protection. 2020. *Upwardly Immobile: Low-Income Borrowers and the High Cost of College Education*. https://www.nyc.gov/assets/dca/downloads/pdf/partners/SLD -lowincome_report.pdf.

Nunn, Ryan, Jimmy O'Donnell, and Jay Shambaugh. 2019. *The Shift in Private Sector Union Participation: Explanation and Effects*. Washington, DC: The Hamilton Project, Brookings. https://www.hamiltonproject.org/assets/files /UnionsEA_Web_8.19.pdf.

Ochieng, Nancy, and Jeannie Fuglesten Biniek. 2022. "Beneficiary Experience, Affordability, Utilization, and Quality in Medicare Advantage and Traditional Medicare: A Review of the Literature." KFF, September 16.

https://www.kff.org/medicare/report/beneficiary-experience-affordability
-utilization-and-quality-in-medicare-advantage-and-traditional-medicare-a
-review-of-the-literature/view/footnotes/.

OECD (Organisation for Economic Co-operation and Development). 2013. *OECD Framework for Statistics on the Distribution of Household Income, Consumption and Wealth*. Paris: OECD Publishing. https://www.oecd -ilibrary.org/docserver/9789264194830-en.pdf?expires=1722967070&id=id& accname=guest&checksum=0C533330C5B62A8630AA7A063D4CAC0A.

———. 2017. *Basic Income as a Policy Option: Can It Add Up?* No. 2017/01. Paris: OECD Publishing. https://www.oecd.org/en/publications/basic-income-as-a -policy-option_77d7fe00-en.html.

———. 2019. *Financial Markets Insurance and Pensions: Inclusiveness and Finance*. Paris: OECD Publishing. https://web-archive.oecd.org/2019-04-29 /516644-financial-markets-insurance-and-pensions-2019.htm.

Office of Management and Budget. 2024a. *Analytical Perspectives: Budget of the U.S. Government Fiscal Year 2025*. https://www.whitehouse.gov/wp -content/uploads/2024/03/spec_fy2025.pdf.

———. 2024b. *Budget of the U.S. Government Fiscal Year 2025*. https://www .whitehouse.gov/wp-content/uploads/2024/03/budget_fy2025.pdf.

Ortaliza, Jared, and Cynthia Cox. 2024. "The Affordable Care Act 101." KFF, July 29. https://www.kff.org/health-policy-101-the-affordable-care-act /?entry=table-of-contents-what-did-the-aca-change-about-health-coverage -in-the-u-s.

Ortaliza, Jared, Justin Lo, Matt McGough, and Cynthia Cox. 2024. "How ACA Marketplace Premiums Changed by County in 2024." KFF, June 6. https://www.kff.org/affordable-care-act/issue-brief/how-aca-marketplace -premiums-changed-by-county-in-2024/.

Ortiz, Isabel, Christina Behrendt, Andrés Acuña-Ulate, and Quynh Anh Nguyen. 2018. "Universal Basic Income Proposals in Light of ILO Standards: Key Issues and Global Costing." Extension of Social Security, Working Paper no. 62, International Labour Office, Geneva, Switzerland. https://www.ilo .org/wcmsp5/groups/public/---ed_protect/---soc_sec/documents /publication/wcms_648602.pdf.

Parker, Claire. 2021. "U.S. Health-Care System Ranks Last among 11 High-Income Countries, Researchers Say." *Washington Post*, August 5, 2021. https://www.washingtonpost.com/world/2021/08/05/global-health -rankings/.

Parolin, Zachary, Sophie Collyer, and Megan A. Curran. 2022. *Sixth Child Tax Credit Payment Kept 3.7 Million Children Out of Poverty in December*. Poverty and Social Policy Brief 6, no. 1. New York: Columbia University Center on Poverty and Social Policy. https://www.povertycenter.columbia .edu/publication/montly-poverty-december-2021.

Pennington-Cross, Anthony, and Giang Ho. 2010. "The Termination of Subprime Hybrid and Fixed-Rate Mortgages." *Real Estate Economics* 38 (3): 399–426.

Pension Benefit Guaranty Corporation. n.d. "Who We Are." Accessed March 15, 2022. https://www.pbgc.gov/about/who-we-are.

Perry, Andre M., Joia Crear-Perry, Carl Romer, and Nana Adjeiwaa-Manu. 2021. "The Racial Implications of Medical Debt: How Moving toward Universal Health Care and Other Reforms Can Address Them." Brookings, October 5. https://www.brookings.edu/articles/the-racial-implications-of -medical-debt-how-moving-toward-universal-health-care-and-other -reforms-can-address-them/.

Peter, Bianca. 2020. "What Is the Average Credit Score in America?" Wallet-Hub, May 6. https://wallethub.com/edu/cs/average-credit-scores/25578.

Pew Charitable Trusts. 2016. *Do Limits on Family Assets Affect Participation in, Costs of TANF?* Issue Brief. https://www.pewtrusts.org/-/media/assets/2016/07 /do_limits_on_family_assets_affect_participation_in_costs_of_tanf.pdf.

———. 2017. *Do States Benefit from Restricting Safety-Net Eligibility Based on Wealth?* Issue Brief. https://www.pewtrusts.org/-/media/assets/2017/09 /summary_asset_limits_brief_draft.pdf.

———. 2018. *Can Contests Help Fill Americans' Savings Gap?* Issue Brief. https://www.pewtrusts.org/en/research-and-analysis/issue-briefs/2018/11 /can-contests-help-fill-americans-savings-gap.

———. 2019. *Two Decades of Change in Federal and State Higher Education Funding.* Issue Brief. https://www.pewtrusts.org/-/media/assets/2019/10 /fedstatefundinghigheredu_chartbook_v1.pdf.

Pilipiec, Patrick, Wim Groot, and Milena Pavlova. 2021. "The Effect of an Increase of the Retirement Age on the Health, Well-Being, and Labor Force Participation of Older Workers: A Systematic Literature Review." *Journal of Population Ageing* 14 (2): 271–315.

Pilkauskas, Natasha, Katherine Michelmore, Nicole Kovski, and H. Luke Schaefer. 2022. "The Effects of Income on the Economic Wellbeing of Families with Low Incomes: Evidence from the 2021 Expanded Child Tax Credit." NBER Working Paper 30533, National Bureau of Economic Research, Cambridge, MA.

Pollack, Craig Evan, Beth Ann Griffin, and Julia Lynch. 2010. "Housing Affordability and Health Among Homeowners and Renters." *American Journal of Preventive Medicine* 39 (6): 515–21.

Pollack, Craig Evan, and Julia Lynch. 2009. "Health Status of People Undergoing Foreclosure in the Philadelphia Region." *American Journal of Public Health* 99 (10): 1833–39.

Poterba, James, Steven Venti, and David Wise. 2011. "The Composition and Drawdown of Wealth in Retirement." *Journal of Economic Perspectives* 25 (4): 95–118.

Primus, Wendell, and Paris Rich Bingham. 2024. "Reducing Premiums for
Low-Income Medicare Beneficiaries." Brookings Commentary, February 15.
https://www.brookings.edu/articles/reducing-premiums-for-low-income
-medicare-beneficiaries/.

Prosperity Now. 2014. *Lifting Assets Limits in Public Benefit Programs.*
Resource Guide. https://prosperitynow.org/sites/default/files/resources/rg
_LiftingAssetsLimitsInPublicBenefitPrograms_2014.pdf.

Prudential. 2019. "Student Loan Debt: Implications on Financial and Emotional
Wellness." https://www.prudential.com/wps/wcm/connect/b6a99ee5-5fb8
-4b03-b839-2255566c9a4f/Student_Loan_Debt.pdf?MOD=AJPERES&
CVID=mMoGhAY.

Quercia, Roberto G., and Sarah Riley. 2017. "Expanding the Mortgage Credit
Box: Lessons from the Community Advantage Program." *Boston College
Journal of Law and Social Justice* 37 (2): 315–38.

Quercia, Roberto G., Michael A. Stegman, and Walter Davis. 2007. "The Impact
of Predatory Loan Terms on Subprime Foreclosures: The Special Case of
Prepayment Penalties and Balloon Payments." *Housing Policy Debate* 18 (2):
311–46.

Quillian, Lincoln, Devah Pager, Arnfinn H. Midtbøen, and Ole Hexel. 2017.
"Hiring Discrimination Against Black Americans Hasn't Declined in 25
Years." *Harvard Business Review*, October 11. https://hbr.org/2017/10/hiring
-discrimination-against-black-americans-hasnt-declined-in-25-years.

Radpour, Siavish, Michael Papadopoulos, and Teresa Ghilarducci. 2021. *Trends
in Employer-Sponsored Retirement Plan Access and Participation Rates:
Reconciling Different Data Sources.* Research Note no. 2021-01. New York:
Schwartz Center for Economic Policy Analysis and Department of Economics,
The New School for Social Research. https://www.economicpolicyresearch.org
/images/docs/research/retirement_security/Retirement_Plan_Access_and
Participation-_Feb_2_-_V3.pdf.

Rampell, Catherine. 2022. "The U.S. Is on the Verge of a Major Health-Care
Achievement, and No One Seems to Have Noticed." *Washington Post,*
January 6, 2022. https://www.washingtonpost.com/opinions/2022/01/06/us
-is-verge-major-health-care-achievement-no-one-seems-have-noticed/.

Rank, Mark Robert, Lawrence M. Eppard, and Heather E. Bullock. 2021. *Poorly
Understood: What America Gets Wrong about Poverty.* Oxford: Oxford
University Press.

Rao, Nirupama, and Max Risch. 2024. "Who's Afraid of the Minimum Wage?
Measuring the Impacts on Independent Businesses Using Matched U.S. Tax
Returns." Working paper, Social Science Research Center, Rochester, NY,
March. https://papers.ssrn.com/sol3/papers.cfm?abstract_id=4781658.

Ratcliffe, Caroline, Signe-Mary McKernan, Laura Wheaton, and Emma Kalish.
2016. *The Unintended Consequences of SNAP Asset Limits.* Washington, DC:

Urban Institute. https://www.urban.org/sites/default/files/publication/82886/2000872-The-Unintended-Consequences-of-SNAP-Asset-Limits.pdf.

Reed, Eric. 2023. "State-Mandated Retirement Plans." Smart Asset, February 28. https://www.nasdaq.com/articles/state-mandated-retirement-plans.

Reed, Trenton. 2023. "What Is a State-Sponsored Retirement Plan?" Human Interest, October 4. https://humaninterest.com/learn/articles/what-is-a-state-sponsored-retirement-plan/.

Reeves, Richard V., and Nathan Joo. 2017. "A Tax Break for 'Dream Hoarders': What to Do about 529 College Savings Plans." Brookings, June 29. https://www.brookings.edu/research/a-tax-break-for-dream-hoarders-what-to-do-about-529-college-savings-plans/.

Reich, Michael. 2021. "Effect of a Federal Minimum Wage Increase to $15 by 2025 on the Federal Budget." Working Paper, Center on Wage and Employment Dynamics, University of California, Berkeley, CA, February.

Reinhardt, Uwe E. 2016. "Tax Deductibility as a Regressive Federal Subsidy." *Health Affairs Forefront* (blog), October 3. https://www.healthaffairs.org/content/forefront/tax-deductibility-regressive-federal-subsidy.

Rendon, Silvio, and Kevin Bazer. 2021. "Individual and Local Effects of Unemployment on Mortgage Defaults." Working Paper WP 21-39, Federal Reserve Bank of Philadelphia, Philadelphia, PA, November.

Republican Party. n.d. "2024 GOP Platform: Make America Great Again!" Accessed November 27, 2024. https://rncplatform.donaldjtrump.com/.

Reston, Laura. 2022. "12 Economically Insecure Americans on What Keeps Them Up at Night." *New York Times*, February 11, 2022. https://www.nytimes.com/2022/02/11/opinion/economy-voters.html.

Reznick, Gayle L., Kenneth A. Couch, Christopher R. Tamborini, and Howard M. Iams. 2021. "Changing Longevity, Social Security Retirement Benefits, and Potential Adjustments." *Social Security Bulletin* 81 (3): 19–34.

Romig, Kathleen. 2016. "Raising Social Security's Retirement Age Cuts Benefits for All Retirees." *Off the Charts* (blog), Center on Budget and Policy Priorities, January 20. https://www.cbpp.org/blog/raising-social-securitys-retirement-age-cuts-benefits-for-all-retirees#:~:text=A%20higher%20retirement%20age%20means,would%20be%20nearly%2020%20percent.

———. 2024. *Social Security Lifts More People Above the Poverty Line Than Any Other Program.* Washington, DC: Center on Budget and Policy Priorities. https://www.cbpp.org/sites/default/files/atoms/files/10-25-13ss.pdf.

Rothbaum, Jonathan. 2020. "Census Bureau Still Studying Full Impact of Pandemic on Census Data." *America Counts: Stories.* U.S. Census Bureau, September 15. https://www.census.gov/library/stories/2020/09/was-household-income-the-highest-ever-in-2019.html#:~:text=Census%20Bureau%20Still%20Studying%20Full%20Impact%20of%20Pandemic

%20on%20Income%20Data&text=The%20U.S.%20median%20household %20income,Census%20Bureau%20statistics%20released%20today.

Rothschild, Michael, and Joseph Stiglitz. 1976. "Equilibrium in Competitive Insurance Markets: An Essay on the Economics of Imperfect Information." *Quarterly Journal of Economics* 90 (4): 629–49.

Rothstein, Jesse, and Cecilia Elena Rouse. 2011. "Constrained after College: Student Loans and Early-Career Occupational Choices." *Journal of Public Economics* 95 (1–2): 149–63.

Rothwell, Jonathan. 2015. "What Colleges Do for Local Economies: A Direct Measure Based on Consumption." Brookings, November 17. https://www .brookings.edu/articles/what-colleges-do-for-local-economies-a-direct -measure-based-on-consumption/.

Rudowitz, Robin, Patrick Drake, Jennifer Tolbert, and Anthony Damico. 2023. "How Many Uninsured Are in the Coverage Gap and How Many Could Be Eligible If All States Adopted the Medicaid Expansion?" Issue Brief. KFF, March 31. https://web.archive.org/web/20230331221726/https://www.kff.org /medicaid/issue-brief/how-many-uninsured-are-in-the-coverage-gap-and -how-many-could-be-eligible-if-all-states-adopted-the-medicaid-expansion/.

Rutledge, Matthew S., Geoffrey T. Sanzenbacher, and Francis M. Vitagliano. 2018. *Do Young Adults with Student Debt Save Less for Retirement?* Paper no. 18-13. Chestnut Hill, MA: Center for Retirement Research. https://crr.bc .edu/wp-content/uploads/2018/06/IB_18-13.pdf.

Sabelhaus, John, and Alice Henriques Volz. 2019. "Are Disappearing Employer Pensions Contributing to Rising Wealth Inequality?" *FEDS Notes*, Board of Governors of the Federal Reserve System, Washington, DC, February 1. https://www.federalreserve.gov/econres/notes/feds-notes/are-disappearing -employer-pensions-contributing-to-rising-wealth-inequality-20190201.htm.

Sanger-Katz, Margot. 2023. "Obamacare Sign-Ups Top 16 Million for 2023, Setting Another Record." *New York Times*, January 25, 2023. https://www .nytimes.com/2023/01/25/us/politics/obamacare-enrollment.html.

Schanzenbach, Diane Whitmore, Lauren Bauer, and Audrey Breitwieser. 2017. *Eight Economic Facts on Higher Education*. Washington, DC: The Hamilton Project, Brookings. https://www.brookings.edu/wp-content/uploads/2017/04 /thp_20170426_eight_economic_facts_higher_education.pdf.

Schmitt, John, Elise Gould, and Josh Bivens. 2018. *America's Slow-Motion Wage Crisis*. Washington, DC: Economic Policy Institute. https://files.epi.org/pdf /153535.pdf.

Schneider, Daniel, and Kristen Harknett. 2019. *It's About Time: How Work Schedule Instability Matters for Workers, Families, and Racial Inequality*. SHIFT Research Brief. Berkeley: University of California. https://shift.hks .harvard.edu/files/2019/10/Its-About-Time-How-Work-Schedule-Instability -Matters-for-Workers-Families-and-Racial-Inequality.pdf.

Schneider, Eric C., Arnav Shah, Michelle M. Doty, Roosa Tikkanen, Katharine Fields, and Reginald D. Williams II. 2021. *Mirror, Mirror 2021: Reflecting Poorly*. New York: The Commonwealth Fund. https://www.commonwealth fund.org/sites/default/files/2021-08/Schneider_Mirror_Mirror_2021.pdf.

Schultz, Michael A. 2019. "The Wage Mobility of Low-Wage Workers in a Changing Economy, 1968 to 2014." *RSF: The Russell Sage Foundation Journal of the Social Sciences* 5 (4): 159–89.

Scott-Clayton, Judith. 2018. "The Looming Student Loan Default Crisis Is Worse Than We Thought." *Evidence Speaks Reports* 2 (34). https://www .brookings.edu/wp-content/uploads/2018/01/scott-clayton-report.pdf.

Semega, Jessica, and Melissa Kollar. 2022. *Income in the United States: 2021*. Current Population Reports no. P60-276. Washington, DC: U.S. Census Bureau. https://www.census.gov/content/dam/Census/library/publications /2022/demo/p60-276.pdf.

Semega, Jessica, Melissa Kollar, Emily A. Shrider, and John F. Creamer. 2021. *Income and Poverty in the United States: 2019*. Current Population Reports no. P60-270. Washington, DC: US Census Bureau. https://www.census.gov /content/dam/Census/library/publications/2020/demo/p60-270.pdf.

Sherlund, Shane M. 2008. *The Past, Present, and Future of Subprime Mortgages*. Finance and Economics Discussion Series 2008-63. Washington, DC: Board of Governors of the Federal Reserve System. https://www .federalreserve.gov/pubs/feds/2008/200863/200863pap.pdf.

Sherraden, Michael, and Ray Boshara. 2008. "Learning from Individual Development Accounts." In *Overcoming the Saving Slump*, edited by Annamaria Lusardi, ch. 10. Chicago: University of Chicago Press.

Shmerling, Robert H. 2022. "Why Life Expectancy in the US Is Falling." *Diseases and Conditions* (blog), Harvard Health Publishing, October 20. https://www.health.harvard.edu/blog/why-life-expectancy-in-the-us-is -falling-202210202835#:~:text=A%20dramatic%20fall%20in%20life,just %20over%2076%2C%20in%202021.

Shnitser, Natalya. 2015. "Funding Discipline for U.S. Public Pension Plans: An Empirical Analysis of Institutional Design." *Iowa Law Review* 100 (2): 663–714.

Shrider, Em. 2023. "Poverty Rate for the Black Population Fell Below Pre-Pandemic Levels." *America Counts: Stories*. U.S. Census Bureau, September 12. https://www.census.gov/library/stories/2023/09/black-poverty-rate.html.

Siegelman, Peter. 2004. "Adverse Selection in Insurance Markets: An Exaggerated Threat." *Yale Law Journal* 113 (6): 1223–81.

Skinner, Victor. 2022. "Federal Flood Insurance May Become Unaffordable." *Biz New Orleans*, July 26. https://www.bizneworleans.com/federal-flood -insurance-may-become-unaffordable/.

Skocpol, Theda. 1991. "Targeting within Universalism: Politically Viable Policies to Combat Poverty in the United States." In *The Urban Underclass*, edited by

Christopher Jencks and Paul E. Peterson, 411–36. Washington, DC: The Brookings Institution.

Smialek, Jeanna. 2024. "Why Are People So Down about the Economy? Theories Abound." *New York Times*, May 30, 2024. https://www.nytimes.com/2024/05/30/business/economy/inflation-economy-americans.html.

Social Security Administration. n.d.-a. *Historical Development*. Accessed January 2, 2024. https://www.ssa.gov/history/pdf/histdev.pdf.

———. n.d.-b. "Medicare Information." Accessed July 18, 2023. https://www.ssa.gov/disabilityresearch/wi/medicare.htm.

———. n.d.-c. "Office of the Chief Actuary's Estimates of Proposals to Change the Social Security Program or the SSI Program." Accessed January 2, 2024. https://www.ssa.gov/oact/solvency/index.html.

———. n.d.-d. "Projected Social Security Benefit Distribution in 2024." Accessed June 28, 2024. https://www.ssa.gov/policy/docs/projections/tables/beneficiaries.html.

———. n.d.-e. Survivors Benefits. Accessed November 8, 2023. https://www.ssa.gov/pubs/EN-05-10084.pdf.

———. 2021. "Population Profiles: Never Beneficiaries, Aged 60 or Over, 2020." August. https://www.ssa.gov/policy/docs/population-profiles/never-beneficiaries.html.

———. 2023a. The 2023 Annual Report of the Board of Trustees of the Federal Old-Age and Survivors Insurance and Federal Disability Insurance Trust Funds. https://www.ssa.gov/oact/TR/2023/tr2023.pdf.

———. 2023b. Understanding the Benefits. https://www.ssa.gov/pubs/EN-05-10024.pdf.

———. 2024a. "Monthly Statistical Snapshot, October 2024." https://www.ssa.gov/policy/docs/quickfacts/stat_snapshot/.

———. 2024b. "Program Operations Manual System (POMS), HI 03020.055 Income Limits for Subsidy Eligibility." April 12. https://secure.ssa.gov/poms.nsf/lnx/0603020055.

———. 2024c. "Summary of Provisions that Would Change the Social Security Program." September 25. https://www.ssa.gov/OACT/solvency/provisions/summary.pdf.

———. 2024d. *The 2024 Annual Report of the Board of Trustees of the Federal Old-Age and Survivors Insurance and Federal Disability Insurance Trust Funds*. https://www.ssa.gov/OACT/TR/2024/.

Spader, Jonathan, and Christopher Herbert. 2017. "Waiting for Homeownership: Assessing the Future of Homeownership, 2015–2035." *Boston College Journal of Law and Social Justice* 37 (2): 267–94.

Splinter, David. 2021. "Income Mobility and Inequality: Adult-Level Measures from the U.S. Tax Data Since 1979." *Review of Income and Wealth* 68 (4): 906–21.

Splinter, David, John Diamond, and Victoria Bryant. 2009. "Income Volatility and Mobility: U.S. Income Tax Data, 1999–2007." *Proceedings. Annual*

Conference on Taxation and Minutes of the Annual Meeting of the National Tax Association 102: 1–10.

Stansbury, Anna, and Lawrence H. Summers. 2020. "The Declining Work Power Hypothesis: An Explanation for the Recent Evolution of the American Economy." *Brookings Papers on Economic Activity* (Spring): 1–96. https://www.brookings.edu/wp-content/uploads/2020/12/StansburySummers-Final-web.pdf.

Statista. n.d. "Share of Households in the United States That Paid No Individual Income Tax in 2022, by Income Level." Accessed November 21, 2024. https://www.statista.com/statistics/242138/percentages-of-us-households-that-pay-no-income-tax-by-income-level/.

Stegman, Michael A., Sarah F. Riley, and Robert G. Quercia. 2019. "A Cautionary Tale of How the Presence and Type of Down Payment Assistance Affects the Performance of Affordable Mortgage Loans." Joint Center for Housing Studies of Harvard University Blog, October. https://www.jchs.harvard.edu/blog/how-the-presence-and-type-of-down-payment-assistance-affects-the-performance-of-affordable-mortgage-loans.

Steil, Justin, Len Albright, Jacob Rugh, and Douglas S. Massey. 2018. "The Social Structure of Mortgage Discrimination." *Housing Studies* 77 (5): 759–76.

Steuerle, C. Eugene, Damir Cosic, and Caleb Quakenbush. 2019. *How Do Lifetime Social Security Benefits and Taxes Differ by Earnings?* Washington, DC: Urban Institute. https://www.urban.org/sites/default/files/publication/99795/how_lifetime_ss_benefits_and_taxes_differ_by_earnings_0.pdf.

Stropoli, Rebecca. 2021. "How the 1 Percent's Savings Buried the Middle Class in Debt." *Chicago Booth Review*, May 25.

Sullivan, Laura, Tatjana Meschede, Thomas Shapiro, and Fernanda Escobar. 2019. *Stalling Dreams: How Student Debt Is Disrupting Life Chances and Widening the Racial Wealth Gap.* Waltham: Institute on Assets and Social Policy, Brandeis University.

Sullivan, Teresa A., Elizabeth Warren, and Jay Lawrence Westbrook. 2020. *The Fragile Middle Class: Americans in Debt.* Rev. ed. New Haven, CT: Yale University Press.

Swagel, Phillip L. 2022. Letter to Richard Burr and Virginia Foxx, September 26. Washington, DC: Congressional Budget Office. https://www.cbo.gov/system/files/2022-09/58494-Student-Loans.pdf.

———. 2024. Letter to Jodey Arrington and Jason Smith, June 24. Washington, DC: Congressional Budget Office. https://www.cbo.gov/system/files/2024-06/60437-Arrington-Smith-Letter.pdf.

Tax Policy Center. n.d. "What Are the Tax Benefits of Homeownership?" *Briefing Book.* Accessed June 1, 2024. https://www.taxpolicycenter.org/briefing-book/what-are-tax-benefits-homeownership.

Tergesen, Anne. 2023. "Short on Cash, More Americans Tap 401(k) Savings for Emergencies." *Wall Street Journal*, February 2, 2023. https://www.wsj.com

/articles/short-on-cash-more-americans-tap-401-k-savings-for-emergencies
-11675305976.

Thaler, Richard H., and Shlomo Benartzi. 2004. "Save More Tomorrow™: Using Behavioral Economics to Increase Employee Saving." *Journal of Political Economy* 112 (S1): S164-S187.

Tolbert, Jennifer, Rakesh Singh, and Patrick Drake. 2024. "The Uninsured Population and Health Coverage." KFF, May 28. https://www.kff.org/health -policy-101-the-uninsured-population-and-health-coverage/?entry=table-of -contents-introduction.

Torpey, Elka. 2021. "Education Pays, 2020." US Bureau of Labor Statistics, June. https://www.bls.gov/careeroutlook/2021/data-on-display/education -pays.htm.

TRICARE. n.d. "TRICARE 101." Accessed November 30, 2024. https://www .tricare.mil/Plans/New#:~:text=What%20is%20TRICARE%3F,and%20 certain%20former%20spouses%20worldwide.

University of Wisconsin Population Health Institute. 2022. *2022 County Health Rankings National Findings Report.* https://www.countyhealthrankings.org /reports/2022-county-health-rankings-national-findings-report.

Urban Institute. n.d. "Policy Tables." Welfare Rules Database. Accessed November 21, 2024. https://wrd.urban.org/policy-tables.

US Bureau of Labor Statistics. n.d.-a. "Civilian Unemployment Rate." Accessed August 7, 2024. https://www.bls.gov/charts/employment-situation/civilian -unemployment-rate.htm.

———. n.d.-b. "Employment by Major Industry Sector." Accessed May 10, 2024. https://www.bls.gov/emp/tables/employment-by-major-industry-sector.htm.

———. n.d.-c. "Mass Layoff Statistics." Accessed May 10, 2024. https://www.bls .gov/mls/miltprod.htm.

———. n.d.-d. "Retirement Benefits: Access, Participation, and Take-Up Rates for Defined Benefits and Defined Contribution Plans." Accessed August 7, 2024. https://www.bls.gov/charts/employee-benefits/percent-access -participation-takeup-retirement-benefits.htm.

———. 2011. "Monthly Establishment Data—National." Table B-2. December. https://www.bls.gov/ces/data/employment-and-earnings/2011/home.htm.

———. 2019a. "Characteristics of Unemployment Insurance Applicants and Benefit Recipients." Table 1. https://www.bls.gov/news.release/uisup.toc.htm.

———. 2019b. "Union Workers More Likely Than Nonunion Workers to Have Healthcare Benefits in 2019." *TED: The Economic Daily* (blog), October 28. https://www.bls.gov/opub/ted/2019/union-workers-more-likely-than -nonunion-workers-to-have-healthcare-benefits-in-2019.htm.

———. 2020. "Job Market Remains Tight in 2019, as the Unemployment Rate Falls to Its Lowest Level since 1969." *Monthly Labor Review*, April. https:// www.bls.gov/opub/mlr/2020/article/job-market-remains-tight-in-2019-as -the-unemployment-rate-falls-to-its-lowest-level-since-1969.htm.

———. 2021a. "National Compensation Survey: Employee Benefits in the United States, March 2021." September. https://www.bls.gov/ebs/publications /september-2021-landing-page-employee-benefits-in-the-united-states -march-2021.htm.

———. 2021b. "Union Members—2020." Press release USDL-21-0081, January 22. https://www.bls.gov/news.release/pdf/union2.pdf.

———. 2023a. "Employee Benefits in the United States—March 2023." https://www.bls.gov/ebs/publications/employee-benefits-in-the-united -states-march-2023.htm.

———. 2023b. "Employee Benefits in the United States—March 2023." Press release. https://www.bls.gov/news.release/archives/ebs2_09212023.pdf.

US Census Bureau. n.d.-a. "American Community Survey." Accessed December 1, 2020. https://www.census.gov/programs-surveys/acs.

———. n.d.-b. "Historical Income Tables: People." Accessed June 16, 2024. https://www.census.gov/data/tables/time-series/demo/income-poverty /historical-income-people.html.

———. n.d.-c. "National Population by Characteristics: 2020–2023." Accessed June 16, 2024. https://www.census.gov/data/tables/time-series/demo/popest /2020s-national-detail.html.

———. n.d.-d. "Supplemental Poverty Measure." Accessed June 16, 2024. https:// www.census.gov/topics/income-poverty/supplemental-poverty-measure.html.

———. 2019. "2019 U.S. Population Estimates Continue to Show the Nation's Growth Is Slowing." News release, December 30. https://www.census.gov /newsroom/press-releases/2019/popest-nation.html.

———. 2020. "Income, Poverty and Health Insurance Coverage in the United States: 2019." Press release, September 15. https://www.census.gov/newsroom /press-releases/2020/income-poverty.html.

———. 2021. "Quarterly Residential Vacancies and Homeownership, First Quarter 2021." Press release no. CB21-56.

US Department of Education. n.d.-a. "Fact Sheet: Protecting Students through Final Regulations That Strengthen Department of Education Oversight and Monitoring of Colleges and Universities." Accessed November 13, 2023. https://www2.ed.gov/policy/highered/reg/hearulemaking/2021/non-ge-final -rules-fact-sheet.pdf.

———. n.d.-b. "Federal Pell Grant Program." Accessed September 12, 2023. https://www2.ed.gov/programs/fpg/index.html.

———. n.d.-c. *Federal Pell Grant Program 2017-2018 End of Year Report.* Accessed September 12, 2023. https://www2.ed.gov/finaid/prof/resources /data/2017-2018pelloeyreports.zip.

———. 2019. *Trends in Pell Grant Receipt and the Characteristics of Pell Grant Recipients: Selected Years, 2003-04 to 2015-16.* https://nces.ed.gov/pubs2019 /2019487.pdf.

———. 2023. "Financial Responsibility, Administrative Capability, Certification Procedures, Ability to Benefit (ATB): Final Regulations." *Federal Register* 88 (209): 74568–710. https://www.govinfo.gov/content/pkg/FR-2023-10-31 /pdf/2023-22785.pdf.

US Department of Health and Human Services. n.d. "Who's Eligible for Medicare?" Accessed June 22, 2023. https://www.hhs.gov/answers/medicare -and-medicaid/who-is-eligible-for-medicare/index.html.

———. 2020. *Characteristics and Financial Circumstances of TANF Recipients Fiscal Year (FY) 2019.* https://www.acf.hhs.gov/sites/default/files/documents /ofa/fy19_characteristics_final.pdf.

US Department of Health, Education and Welfare. 1964. "Chart Book of Basic Health Economics Data." Public Health Service Publication no. 947-3. https://babel.hathitrust.org/cgi/pt?id=mdp.39015020619691&view=1up&seq =10&skin=2021.

US Department of Housing and Urban Development. n.d. "How the HECM Program Works." Accessed November 21, 2023. https://www.hud.gov /program_offices/housing/sfh/hecm/hecmabou.

———. 1995. *The National Homeownership Strategy: Partners in the American Dream.* Washington, DC: US Department of Housing and Urban Development.

———. 2015. "Insights on Reverse Mortgage Default." *PD&R Leading Edge.* https://www.huduser.gov/portal/pdredge/pdr_edge_research_092214 .html.

US Department of Labor. n.d.-a. "COBRA Continuation Coverage." Accessed July 7, 2023. https://www.dol.gov/agencies/ebsa/laws-and-regulations/laws /cobra.

———. n.d.-b. "History of Changes to the Minimum Wage Law." Accessed March 22, 2022. https://www.dol.gov/agencies/whd/minimum-wage/history.

———. n.d.-c. "Premium Assistance under Medicaid and the Children's Health Insurance Program (CHIP)." Accessed August 25, 2023. https://www.dol.gov /sites/dolgov/files/ebsa/laws-and-regulations/laws/chipra/model-notice.pdf.

———. 2021. "FAQs about COBRA Premium Assistance under the American Rescue Plan Act of 2021." April 7. https://www.dol.gov/sites/dolgov/files /EBSA/about-ebsa/our-activities/resource-center/faqs/cobra-premium -assistance-under-arp.pdf.

US Department of the Treasury. n.d. *COBRA Insurance Coverage Since the Recovery Act: Results from New Survey Data.* Accessed July 7, 2023. https:// home.treasury.gov/system/files/226/COBRA_Insurance_Coverage_since _the_Recovery_Act_Results_from_New_Survey_Data_MAY2010.pdf.

———. 2022a. "Affordability of Employer Coverage for Family Members of Employees: Final regulations." *Federal Register* 87 (197): 61,979–62,003.

———. 2022b. "Fact Sheet: The Impact of the American Rescue Plan after One Year." Press release, March 9. https://home.treasury.gov/news/press-releases

/jyo645#:~:text=One%20year%20after%20the%20passage%20of%20the
%20ARP%20and%20months,ARP%20continue%20to%20provide%20a.

———. 2022c. *The State of Labor Market Competition.* https://home.treasury.gov
/system/files/136/State-of-Labor-Market-Competition-2022.pdf.

US Department of Veterans Affairs. n.d. "Eligibility for VA Health Care."
Accessed June 23, 2023. https://www.va.gov/health-care/eligibility/.

———. 2024. *VA Servicer Handbook.* https://www.benefits.va.gov/WARMS/docs
/admin26/m26_04/m26-4-chapter5-loss-mitigation.pdf.

US Government Accountability Office. 2020. *Federal Social Safety Net Programs:
Millions of Full Time Workers Rely on Federal Health Care and Food Assistance Programs.* GAO-21-45. 2020. https://www.gao.gov/assets/gao-21-45.pdf.

———. 2021. *Retirement Security: Debt Increased for Older Americans over
Time, but the Implications Vary by Debt Type.* GAO-21-170. 2021. https://
www.gao.gov/assets/720/713816.pdf.

———. 2022a. *Student Loans: Education Has Increased Federal Cost Estimates
of Direct Loans by Billions Due to Programmatic and Other Changes.*
GAO-22-105365. https://www.gao.gov/products/gao-22-105365.

———. 2022b. *Unemployment Insurance: Pandemic Programs and DOL Could
Better Address Customer Service and Emergency Planning.* GAO-22-104251.
https://www.gao.gov/assets/d22104251.pdf.

van den Berg, Tilja I. J., Leo A. M. Elder, and Alex Burdorf. 2010. "Influence of
Health and Work on Early Retirement." *Journal of Occupational and
Environmental Medicine* 52 (6): 576–83.

Van Parijs, Philippe. 1992. "Competing Justification for Unconditional Basic
Income." In *Arguing for Basic Income: Ethical Foundations for a Radical
Reform,* edited by Philippe Van Parijs, 3–29. London: Verso.

VanDerhei, Jack. 2009. "The Impact of the Recent Financial Crisis on 401(k)
Account Balances." *EBRI Issue Brief* 326 (1): 3–21.

———. 2019. "Retirement Savings Shortfalls: Evidence from EBRI's 2019 Retirement Security Projection Model®." *EBRI Issue Brief* 475 (March 7): 4–14.

Vanguard Research. 2023. "The Vanguard Retirement Outlook: A National
Perspective on Retirement Readiness." https://institutional.vanguard.com
/insights-and-research/report/vanguard-retirement-outlook-a-national
-perspective-on-retirement-readiness.html.

Varian, Hal R. 1980. "Redistributive Taxation as Social Insurance." *Journal of
Public Economics* 14 (1): 49–68.

Vega, Lilia. 2014. "The History of UC Tuition since 1868." *Daily Californian,*
December 22, 2014. https://www.dailycal.org/2014/12/22/history-uc-tuition
-since-1868/.

Vroman, Wayne. 2010. *The Role of Unemployment Insurance as an Automatic
Stabilizer during a Recession.* Wellesley: IMPAQ International. https://www
.dol.gov/sites/dolgov/files/ETA/publications/ETAOP2010-10.pdf.

Waldron, Hilary. 2007. "Trends in Mortality Differentials and Life Expectancy for Male Social Security-Covered Workers, by Socioeconomic Status." *Social Security Bulletin* 67 (3): 1–28.

Warren, Elizabeth, and Amelia Warren Tyagi. 2016. *The Two-Income Trap: Why Middle-Class Parents Are (Still) Going Broke.* Rev. ed. New York: Basic Books.

Washington, Katelyn. 2023. "How Much Is the Child Tax Credit for 2024?" Kiplinger, November 14. https://www.kiplinger.com/taxes/how-much-is-the-child-tax-credit-for-2024.

Washington State Office of the Insurance Commissioner. n.d. *July–September 2023 Approved Medicare Supplement (Medigap) Plans.* Accessed August 29, 2023. https://www.insurance.wa.gov/sites/default/files/documents/medicare-supp-plans_64.pdf.

Weiner, Janet, and Aaron Glickman. 2018. "What Is 'Affordable' Health Care?" Issue Brief. Penn LDI and United States of Care, November. https://ldi.upenn.edu/wp-content/uploads/archive/pdf/Penn%20LDI%20and%20USofC%20Affordability%20Issue%20Brief_Final.pdf.

West, Rachel, Indivar Dutta-Gupta, Kali Grant, Melissa Boteach, Claire McKenna, and Judy Conti. 2016. *Strengthening Unemployment Protections in America.* Washington, DC: Center for American Progress et al. https://cdn.americanprogress.org/wp-content/uploads/2016/05/31134245/UI_JSAreport.pdf?_ga=2.37950563.1557479040.1612811783-255215476.1611591129.

Wheaton, Felicia, and Eileen M. Crimmins. 2012. "The Demography of Aging and Retirement." In *The Oxford Handbook of Retirement,* edited by Mo Wang, 22–41. Oxford: Oxford University Press.

White House, The. n.d. "The Child Tax Credit." Accessed January 5, 2023. https://www.whitehouse.gov/child-tax-credit/.

———. 2022a. "Fact Sheet: President Biden Announces Student Loan Relief for Borrowers Who Need It Most." Statement, August 24. https://www.whitehouse.gov/briefing-room/statements-releases/2022/08/24/fact-sheet-president-biden-announces-student-loan-relief-for-borrowers-who-need-it-most/.

———. 2022b. "Fact Sheet: The Biden Administration Announces New Actions to Lessen the Burden of Medical Debt and Increase Consumer Protection." Statement, April 11. https://www.whitehouse.gov/briefing-room/statements-releases/2022/04/11/fact-sheet-the-biden-administration-announces-new-actions-to-lessen-the-burden-of-medical-debt-and-increase-consumer-protection/.

———. 2023. "What They Are Reading in the States: More Than 4 Million Student Loan Borrowers Enrolled in New Biden-Harris Administration SAVE Plan." Statement, September 9. https://www.whitehouse.gov/briefing-room/statements-releases/2023/09/09/what-they-are-reading-in-the-states-more-than-4-million-student-loan-borrowers-enrolled-in-new-biden-harris

-administration-save-plan/#:~:text=The%20Biden%20administration
%20unveiled%20the,a%20certain%20period%20of%20time.

Wiltshire, Justin C., Carl McPherson, Michael Reich, and Denis Sosinskiy. 2024. "Minimum Wage Effects and Monopsony Explanations." Working paper, Institute for Research on Labor and Employment, University of California, Berkeley, CA, February. https://irle.berkeley.edu/publications /working-papers/minimum-wage-effects-and-monopsony-explanations/.

Wolfson, Alisa. 2022. "Foreclosures Are Up 187% from a Year Prior: But It Doesn't Mean What You Might Think." MarketWatch, September 17. https://www.marketwatch.com/picks/foreclosures-are-up-187-from-a-year -prior-but-it-doesnt-mean-what-you-might-think-01663335558.

Wooten, James A. 2005. *The Employee Retirement Income Security Act of 1974: A Political History.* Berkeley: University of California Press.

Wray, Charlie M., Meena Khare, and Salomeh Kayhani. 2021. "Access to Care, Cost of Care, and Satisfaction with Care among Adults with Private and Public Health Insurance in the US." *JAMA Network Open* 4 (6): 1–12.

Wriggins, Jennifer B. 2012–2013. "Mandates, Markets, and Risk: Auto Insurance and the Affordable Care Act." *Connecticut Insurance Law Journal* 19 (2): 275–323.

Yin, Yimeng, Anqi Chen, and Alicia H. Munnell. 2023. *The National Retirement Risk Index with Varying Claiming Ages.* Brief no. 23-23. Chestnut Hill, MA: Center for Retirement Research. https://crr.bc.edu/wp-content/uploads /2023/11/IB_23-23.pdf.

Zhang, Davi Hao, and Paul Willen. 2020. "Do Lenders Still Discriminate? A Robust Approach for Assessing Differences in Menus." Working Paper no. 20-19, Federal Reserve Bank of Boston, Boston, MA, December.

Zipperer, Ben, David Cooper, and Josh Bivens. 2021. *A $15 Minimum Wage Would Have Significant and Direct Effects on the Federal Budget.* Washington, DC: Economic Policy Institute. https://files.epi.org/pdf/219304.pdf.

Zuss, Noah. 2022. "Defined Benefit Plans May Have New Life." Plan Sponsor, August 9. https://www.plansponsor.com/defined-benefit-plans-may-new-life/.

LEGAL SOURCES

Cases

Biden v. Nebraska, 600 U.S. 477 (2023)
National Federation of Independent Business v. Sebelius, 567 U.S. 519 (2012)

Statutes

11 U.S.C. 523
15 U.S.C. 1602, 1639, 1639b, 1639c

26 U.S.C. 1, 24, 32, 36B, 121, 125, 163, 164, 219, 223, 401, 402, 408, 408A, 529, 4980H, 5000A

29 U.S.C. 203, 206, 213, 214

42 U.S.C. 300gg through 300gg-4, 300gg-11, 1396a, 18001, 18022, 18031

Age Discrimination in Employment Act Amendments of 1986, Pub. L. No. 99-592, 100 Stat. 3342

Age Discrimination in Employment Act of 1967, Pub. L. No. 90-202, 81 Stat. 602

American Dream Downpayment Act of 2003, Pub. L. No. 108-186, 117 Stat. 2685

American Recovery and Reinvestment Act of 2009, Pub. L. No. 111-5, 123 Stat. 115

American Rescue Plan Act of 2021, Pub. L. No. 117-2, 135 Stat. 4

Consolidated Omnibus Budget Reconciliation Act of 1985, Pub. L. No. 99-272, 100 Stat. 82

Coronavirus Aid, Relief, and Economic Security Act, Pub. L. No. 116-136, 134 Stat. 281 (2020)

Dodd-Frank Wall Street Reform and Consumer Protection Act, Pub. L. No. 111-203, 124 Stat. 1376 (2010)

Emergency Medical Treatment and Labor Act, Pub. L. No. 99-272, 100 Stat. 164-167 (2016)

Employee Retirement Income Security Act of 1974, Pub. L. No. 93-406, 88 Stat. 829

Equal Credit Opportunity Act, Pub. L. No. 93-495, tit. V, 88 Stat. 1521 (1974)

Fair Housing Act, Pub. L. No. 90-284, tit. VIII, 82 Stat. 81 (1968)

Fair Labor Standards Act of 1938, 52 Stat. 1060 (June 25, 1938)

Fostering Undergraduate Talent by Unlocking Resources for Education Act (FUTURE Act), Pub. L. No. 116-91, 133 Stat. 1189 (2019)

Higher Education Act of 1965, Pub. L. No. 89-329, 79 Stat. 1219

Inflation Reduction Act of 2022, Pub. L. No. 117-169, 136 Stat. 1818

Internal Revenue Code §§ 36B, 105, 106, 162, 501, 6103

Omnibus Budget Reconciliation Act of 1990, Pub. L. No. 101-508, 104 Stat. 143

Omnibus Budget Reconciliation Act of 1993, Pub. L. No. 103-66, 107 Stat. 312

Patient Protection and Affordable Care Act, Pub. L. No. 111-148, 124 Stat. 119 (2010)

Personal Responsibility and Work Opportunity Reconciliation Act of 1996, Pub. L. No. 104-193, 110 Stat. 2015

SECURE 2.0 Act of 2022, Pub. L. No. 117-328, 136 Stat. 4459

Social Security Act of 1935, Pub. L. No. 74-271, 49 Stat. 620

Tax Cuts and Jobs Act of 2017, Pub. L. No. 115-97, 131 Stat. 2054

Tax Reduction Act of 1975, Pub. L. No. 94-12, 89 Stat. 26

Tax Reform Act of 1986, Pub. L. No. 99-514, 100 Stat. 2099

Taxpayer Relief Act of 1997, Pub. L. No. 105-34, 111 Stat. 788

The Revenue Act of 1978, Pub. L. No. 95-600, 92 Stat. 2763

Rules

12 C.F.R. 1024.38 through 1024.41
12 C.F.R. pt. 1026
12 C.F.R. 1026.34 through 1026.36, 1026.43
26 C.F.R. 54.4980H-3

Index

sharing, 77; bipartisan support for, 65, 75–76, 185–86; cost effectiveness of, 172, 224n8; critiques, 38, 77–78; effect on child poverty, 77; effect on labor market participation, 77, 180; effect on public assistance eligibility, 44; eligibility standards, 75, 76; federal savings policy and, 38; history of, 65, 75, 185; low-wage worker participation, 71, 77; overview of, 38–39, 76–79, 78*fig*; proposed reforms to, 71, 76–79, 83, 170–72, 202n96; public support for, 75; temporary expansion during 2021, 185–86. *See also* income-targeted programs

economic well-being: access to financial resources and, 7–8, 169; adequate regular income, 170–74; asset building, 178–82; college education, 182–84; definition, 6–8, 169, 188n20; economic opportunity, current roadblocks to, 18–20, 89–92, 102, 136–45, 159, 183, 211n141; financial freedom and, 6; financial security, 6; how to achieve, 167–70, 184; integrated approach, 8–10; macroeconomic context, 6–7; milestones, 8–10, 69; negative economic shocks, protection from, 174–78; political prospects, 75–76, 184–86; poor state of, 3–6, 14–18; 69–70, 167; risk sharing, role of, 7–8, 10, 56–63, 168–69. *See also* health insurance; higher education; homeownership; making ends meet; retirement education. *See* higher education

EITC. *See* Earned Income Tax Credit (EITC)
Elder Index, The, 154–55
emergency savings. *See* savings; savings, public policy and; savings vehicles
Employee Benefit Research Institute, 154
Employee Retirement Income Security Act (ERISA) (1974), 30, 40
employment: college degree and, 135–36, 143–44; EITC, effect on, 77, 172; employer-based health insurance plans, 109–10, 119–21; employment discrimination laws, 24–25; job insecurity and social safety net, 24–27; labor markets, shifts in, 22–23, 63–64; length of working lives, 159–61, 164; minimum wage laws, effect on, 72, 170–71; risk-sharing systems to blunt lost income, 83–86; stagnant wages and job insecurity, 4–5, 22–24, 32, 70, 143, 170, 190n5; wages, manufacturing *vs.* service sector, 23–24. *See also* health insurance; labor markets, changes in; Social Security; unemployment; unemployment insurance (UI)

Equal Credit Opportunity Act (ECOA) (1974), 96

Fair Housing Act (1968), 19, 89; Title VIII, 96
Fannie Mae, 100–101
Federal Housing Administration (FHA), 100–101
federal poverty level (FPL), 15, 71–72, 118, 188n4; Marketplace (ACA) subsidies tied to, 75, 117–19, 121, 125, 126, 127–28, 177, 208n57, 209n97, 210n104; Medicaid eligibility and, 110–11, 118, 207n49, 209n97; supplemental poverty level, 14–15, 28, 188n4. *See also* health insurance; poverty
financial distress, extent of, 16–18, 19, 35, 113, 136–37, 139–43, 154–56
financial literacy, limits of, 48
financial risk. *See* risk; risk sharing
financial security. *See* economic well-being; risk sharing
food: food security or lack thereof, 9, 14–15, 63, 69, 70, 102, 122–23, 154–55, 163, 176; SNAP and other food assistance, 17–18, 44, 71, 154, 173, 185, 199n87. *See also* making ends meet
Ford, Gerald, 185
for-profit post-secondary schools, 135, 142, 143, 145, 147. *See also* higher education; student loans
401(k) plans. *See* defined-contribution (DC) pensions
Freddie Mac, 100–101

gift tax, 37, 39
gig work: financial instability of, 5, 23–24, 175; unemployment insurance eligibility and, 26, 85, 185. *See also* labor markets, changes in
government, role vis-à-vis private-sector: American tradition of risk pooling and spreading, 63–66; income-targeted programs, risk pooling and spreading, 60–63; social insurance, risk pooling and spreading, 56–60
Great Depression, social insurance programs, 64–65
Greenspan, Alan, 147–48
Greenstein, Robert, 75–76
Guvenen, Fatih, 61

Hacker, Jacob, 82–83
health care: affordability crisis, 103–4, 113–22, 126–28; disparities by race, ethnicity, and

unemployment insurance as, 7, 84, 168; universal savings plan as, 82–83, 179–80, 182; welfare as, 64–65; workers' compensation as, 64
risk shift, 21–33, 34, 48; in generosity of Social Security benefits, 160; in government subsidies for higher education, 32, 130–32; in growing debt burdens, 5–6, 16–18, 32–33, 132–33, 141–42; in growing job insecurity, 4–5, 23–25, 63–64, 165, 175; in health coverage, 22–23, 65–66, 104–5; in pension benefits, 4–5, 19, 21–23, 25, 28–31, 31*fig*, 153–54, 156–61; in unemployment insurance coverage and benefits, 25–27, 84–86; in welfare benefits, 27–28; wage stagnation due to changing labor markets, 4–5, 22–24, 32, 70, 143, 170, 190n5
Ross, Stanford D., 50

savings: as source of retirement income, 9–10, 19, 29, 149; asset caps, effect on, 43–44; bank account balances, size, 15–16; capacity to save, 5, 29, 34–35, 42, 84, 91–92, 156–58; college savings accounts, low participation and balances, 41, 123; disparities by race, ethnicity, and income, 15–17; effect of low savings on economic opportunity, 18–20; emergencies and, 34, 91; emergency savings, 35, 48, 82–83, 91, 99–101, 137, 178–80, 182; financial literacy, effect on, 48; health savings accounts, low participation, 41–42; house-poor homeowners, 91–92; lack of access to tax-sheltered savings plans, 10, 19, 31, 40–41, 48–49, 153, 157, 173, 180, 221n60, 221n61, 226n35; living wage and, 15; medical debt, effect on, 123, 176; mortgage payments as forced savings, 90, 181; motivation to save, 42, 44; relationship to indebtedness, 16–17, 35, 137–39, 146, 168; retirement accounts, low participation and balances, 10, 16, 29, 35, 41–42, 46, 123, 173; risk of theft, 30, 162; role in economic well-being, 9–10, 15, 34, 84; savings innovations for lower-income households, 47–48; student debt, effect on, 137–39, 146; unbanked, extent, 42; unemployment and, 26–27. *See also* bank accounts; defined-contribution (DC) pensions; Individual Retirement Accounts (IRAs); pensions; savings, public policy and; savings vehicles

savings, public policy and: competing savings demands, 34, 99–100, 156–57, 168, 180–81; financial literacy, limits of, 48; impediments to saving, 5, 29, 35, 41–44, 91–92; limitations as policy tool for economic well-being, 10, 34–49; moral expectations, 34–35; personal responsibility narrative, 34–35; policy emphasis on, 34–49; role of institutional support in take-up rates, 35, 41–42, 45–47; tax policy bias against short-term savings, 38–39, 92; tax policy bias toward long-term investments and health savings, 36–39; tax policy bias toward the affluent, 36, 39–40, 45–46. *See also* bank accounts; defined-contribution (DC) pensions; Individual Retirement Accounts (IRAs); pensions; savings; savings vehicles
savings vehicles: ABLE accounts, 47–48; bank accounts, 42, 47; college savings plans, 37, 41, 123, 193n19; flexible savings arrangements (FSAs), 37–38, 41; health reimbursement arrangements (HRAs), 37–38, 41; health savings accounts (HSAs), 37–38, 41–42, 180; health savings plans, 37–38, 41–42; Individual Development Accounts (IDAs), 42, 47–48; Individual Retirement Accounts (IRAs), 36–37, 41–42, 45–47, 193n14; prize-linked savings accounts (PLS), 47–48; retirement savings, 28–31, 31*fig*, 36–37, 41–42, 45–47; short-term savings, 24, 38, 42, 47–48, 179–80, 182; side-car emergency fund accounts, 38; universal savings plan, 82–83, 86–87, 99–101, 178–80, 182. *See also* bank accounts; defined-contribution (DB) plans; Individual Retirement Accounts (IRAs); pension plans; savings; savings, public policy and
SECURE 2.0 Act (2022), 38, 193n16
Skocpol, Theda, 75–76
social insurance: actuarial model, 58–59; adverse selection and, 57–58; as risk pooling and spreading mechanism, 7–8, 56–60, 66; as risk sharing, 55–60, 63, 66; as solution to limits on private insurance, 53–58; distinguished from redistribution, 58–60; government authority to tax and, 56–57; Great Depression programs, 64–65; importance to economic well-being, 7, 10, 56–57; intertemporal contributory model, 59–60, 62, 77; mandates, 57; Marketplace, ACA health insurance plans,

repayment, 18, 142–43; number of student borrowers, 17, 130; rate of college attendees with student debt, 9; reform proposals, 146–48, 183–84, 218n135, 218n136; repayment difficulties, 18, 139–42, 183; repayment experience by race, ethnicity, income, and balances, 32, 139–42, 183; rising debt-to-income ratios, 141; rising nonpayment rates, 140; risks to borrowers, 134, 136–43; senior citizens with student debt, 155; student debt burden by race, ethnicity, and income, 18, 134–35; tradeoffs of, 134–36; tuition increases and reliance on student loans, 32, 130–31; wage premium hypothesis, 18, 134–36, 138–43; wealth, effect on, 138–39, 183. *See also* higher education, student grants
Supplemental Nutrition Assistance Program (SNAP), 43–44, 71, 74, 76, 173, 184, 195n65. *See also* income-targeted programs
Supplemental Security Income (SSI), 9, 47, 64–65, 110–11, 154, 224n8. *See also* income-targeted programs

temporary agency workers, 26, 109
Temporary Assistance to Needy Families (TANF), 28, 43–44, 65, 77, 199n8. *See also* income-targeted programs
Title IV, Higher Education Act (1965), 133
Title VIII, Fair Housing Act, 96
Trump, Donald, 184–86

UI. *See* unemployment insurance (UI)
unemployment: growing long-term unemployment, 24; home mortgage repayment and, 91, 99, 206n68; income volatility and, 61–62; industrialization and, 63–64; job insecurity and, 4–5, 22–25, 175; minimum wage, effect on, 72, 170–71; poverty and, 62; private-sector inability to insure, 53–54; probability of unemployment over lifetime, 24, 186; social safety nets for, 7, 17, 25–27, 83–84, 161, 174–75; unemployment levels, 2019–2020, 14, 17. *See also* employment; labor markets, changes in; making ends meet; risk shift; unemployment insurance (UI)
unemployment insurance (UI): as economic stabilizer, 25; as example of risk sharing, 7, 83–84, 168, 174; as income replacement for joblessness, 25–26, 84–86, 168, 174; contraction in, 21, 27, 85, 175; cost-effectiveness of reforms, 175; disparities

by race, ethnicity, gender, and disability, 26–27; eligibility rate, 17, 25–27, 84, 175; eligibility standards, 25–26, 84–86, 175; employer lobbying to cut back, 27, 85; exclusions, 26, 84–86, 109; expansion during COVID-19, 17, 185; expectation of savings cushion, 26–27; financing through payroll taxes on employers, 27, 84; history of, 27, 64; homeownership, effect in retaining, 99, 101; job search requirement, 26; labor market conditions, changes in, 27, 84, 174–75; low benefit amounts, 26, 85–86; minimum wage legislation, effect on, 170–71; need for uniform national standards, 25–27, 84–86, 175, obsolescence of, 25–27, 50, 84–86, 174–75; overview of, 25–27; public-private nature, 25; reform proposals, 84–86, 175; state determination of eligibility standards, 25–27, 85. *See also* employment; labor markets, changes in; making ends meet; risk shift; unemployment
unionization and its decline, 4–5, 21–25, 27, 70, 104. *See also* labor markets, changes in
universal basic income (UBI), 71, 74–77, 83
University of California (Berkeley), 4
University of Massachusetts Boston, 154–55

Vanguard Research, 152, 154, 156–57
Varian, Hal, 61

wages. *See* income; labor markets, changes in; making ends meet
wealth: asset caps for income-targeted programs, effect on, 43; college degree, effect on, 138–39; debt burdens, effect on, 5, 89–91, 137–39, 148, 183; economic well-being and, 6–8, 142; homeownership, effect on, 18–19, 89–90, 92, 97, 99–100, 179–82; intergenerational transmission, 61; risk aversion and expected wealth, 52; student debt, effect on, 137–39, 148, 183; universal savings plan and, 82–83, 86–87, 99–101, 179–80. *See also* income tax; pensions; wealth gap
wealth gap: disparities by race, ethnicity, income, and student borrower status, 3–4, 6, 8, 19, 33, 38–40, 138–39, 142, 179, 187n2. *See also* income gap
welfare. *See* income-targeted programs
wildfires, risk of, 53–54
workers' compensation, 64, 199n82

Founded in 1893,
UNIVERSITY OF CALIFORNIA PRESS
publishes bold, progressive books and journals
on topics in the arts, humanities, social sciences,
and natural sciences—with a focus on social
justice issues—that inspire thought and action
among readers worldwide.

The UC PRESS FOUNDATION
raises funds to uphold the press's vital role
as an independent, nonprofit publisher, and
receives philanthropic support from a wide
range of individuals and institutions—and from
committed readers like you. To learn more, visit
ucpress.edu/supportus.